SAUCES
&
SHAPES

BY ORETTA ZANINI DE VITA, TRANSLATED BY MAUREEN B. FANT

Encyclopedia of Pasta

Popes, Peasants, and Shepherds: Recipes and Lore from Rome and Lazio

ORETTA ZANINI DE VITA

MAUREEN B. FANT

SAUCES
&
SHAPES

Pasta the Italian Way

Illustrations by **LUCIANA MARINI**

Photography by **GENTL & HYERS/EDGE**

W. W. Norton & Company

New York   London

For information about permission to reproduce selections from this book,
write to Permissions, W. W. Norton & Company, Inc.,
500 Fifth Avenue, New York, NY 10110

For information about special discounts for bulk purchases, please contact
W. W. Norton Special Sales at specialsales@wwnorton.com or 800-233-4830

Manufacturing by Courier Kendallville
Book design by Obek Design
Production manager: Julia Druskin

Library of Congress Cataloging-in-Publication Data

Zanini De Vita, Oretta, 1936–
Sauces & shapes : pasta the Italian way / Oretta Zanini De Vita, Maureen B. Fant ;
illustrations by Luciana Marini ; photography by Gentl & Hyers/Edge. — First edition.
    pages cm
Includes bibliographical references and indexes.
ISBN 978-0-393-08243-2 (hardcover : alkaline paper)
1. Cooking (Pasta) 2. Cooking, Italian. 3. Sauces. 4. Soups.
5. Pasta products. I. Fant, Maureen B. II. Title.
TX809.M17Z36 2013

641.82'2—dc23

                                        2013021921

W. W. Norton & Company, Inc.
500 Fifth Avenue, New York, N.Y. 10110
www.wwnorton.com

W. W. Norton & Company Ltd.
Castle House, 75/76 Wells Street, London W1T 3QT

1 2 3 4 5 6 7 8 9 0

To the memory of my mother-in-law,
Mamma Viola, and her *ferricelli*

—O.Z.D.V.

Sororibus optimis
For my sisters-in-law, Patience, Daniela, and Leda

—M.B.F.

ACKNOWLEDGMENTS

Nobody makes a journey through the world of Italian pasta without plenty of company. Even if there were no one else, we'd have had the generations of resourceful, creative Italians, mostly women, who first formed lumps of dough into strings, balls, hats, spindles, lozenges, disks, and variously shaped and decorated dumplings and gave them witty names. But we have more than ghosts to thank.

If you've reached this page, you already have an idea of our debt to the photographers Andrea Gentl and Marty Hyers and to Michael Pedersen, food stylist, and his assistant Tracy Keshani, a crack team that turned our modest dishes into works of art—and did it in record time with patience, care, intelligence, and *simpatia*. Luciana Marini, in Rome, has our gratitude for her beautiful and accurate drawings and for her friendship and the chickpeas from her garden.

Numerous expert friends generously and enthusiastically provided useful information, material assistance, and wise advice, editorial and otherwise, from the most varied points of view (and answered cries for help with alacrity). In the United States they include Nick Anderer, Charlotte Cox, Fanny Farkas, Susan Friedland, and Arthur Schwartz, always there when needed. Then there were the specialists. Jim Zurer could always come up with a relevant Web link with the speed of light. Craig (Meathead) Goldwyn knows, and tells, *everything* about pork. Nancy Harmon Jenkins and Sara Jenkins consulted on lobster from Maine.

Michael Putnam approved our remarks about Horace. Lisa Sasson assured us that pasta deserves a place in a balanced diet. Hank Shaw, forager, was our rabbit and hare man. Michelle Farkas was our Stateside Italian-wine consultant and is responsible for most of the pairings we suggest in this book (but if anyone disagrees with them, don't blame Michelle!).

Fanny Farkas, Michelle's mother, stepped up and started cooking our recipes in New York, which sometimes involved leaving the comfort of her Upper East Side kitchen to seek exotic seafood in Chinatown. Her perspective and skill were crucial to making many of the recipes suitable for North American kitchens, and her friendship and solidarity crucial, period.

Chris Tucker provided venison advice from Australia. From France came the counsel of a great editor and a great wine writer, Robert Marino and Jacqueline Friedrich.

We also thank Leeann Graham and Marc Kagan for their very helpful suggestions, as well as Judith and David Barrett for their wisdom and encouragement.

In Italy, our friend Amalia Palleschi was always available (often to help Oretta with English). Gaetano Basile, in Palermo, provided authoritative notes on Sicilian cooking. Mario Mozzetti, of the restaurant Alfredo alla Scrofa, graciously provided the original Alfredo recipe. Naina Vohra appeared like magic in Rome in an early stage of the work to knead and measure until the wind changed. Leda Tripodi took such an interest in the project that she dragged her friend Maria Antonietta Castiello over to my house to show me how the women of Basilicata roll the most delicate *fusilli* on a piece of straw. Leda also had a friend's father in Campania make a *ferretto* for me, making me perhaps the only home cook in Rome (I would guess) to own a *ferretto* she did not inherit from a southern mother or grandmother. (Oretta's *ferretto* belonged to her mother-in-law.) Mina Botti shared her skill with the *ferretto* and dough in general.

Iris Carulli, another Manhattanite transplanted to Rome and most precious friend, provided invaluable culinary, editorial, and moral support, as well as that essential experience of two worlds that we share. She is also responsible for most of the Web-shopping guide, with contributions from Jim and Fanny.

But a book is more than words on a page. I owe a debt to the wonderful vendors in the Testaccio quarter of Rome, who have been patiently sharing their experience with me for more than thirty years. Oretta particularly thanks Aldo Palmieri, who cares for her Sabine garden, often invoked in these pages, Renato Adamo, whose great olive oils underlie many of these recipes, and her brilliant butcher, Marco Coppotelli—and as a frequent beneficiary of all, so do I. Francesco Filippi, Franco, my husband, tasted several pastas a week for about a year and a half (somebody's got to do these tough jobs), hosted multipasta dinner parties, and patiently watched me spend all my time between meals writing or talking on the phone to Oretta. He has been an intelligent, enthusiastic, and much-loved guinea pig and companion throughout.

Our wonderful agent, Jennifer Griffin, has provided good advice all along the way, and the best advice of all was to work with Maria Guarnaschelli, a great editor, inspiring to her authors and unsparing also of herself to make a better book. We are extremely proud to be published by Norton and are obliged there also to Julia Druskin, Ingsu Liu, Nancy Palmquist, and Susan Sanfrey, as well as to Melanie Tortoroli, Will Glovinsky, and Mitchell Kohles, Maria's former and current assistants. Laura Starrett's careful proofreading will surely have saved many a dinner.

Grateful thanks to all, while blame for any failings must be ours.

Most of all, Oretta and I thank each other. I am honored to be her voice in English, and she has been my generous friend, teacher, and counselor over these decades of learning to know and love Italy through its food.

INTRODUCTION

THINK OF THE chewy resistance of *al dente penne*, pasta quills, sauced spicily *all'arrabbiata* with tomatoes, garlic, and chile; the voluptuous feel of tender, freshly made *tagliatelle*, flat egg noodles, with hearty Bolognese *ragù*; the black mystery of spaghetti *con nero di seppia*, squid ink; the complex fragrance of *trofiette*, little pasta twists, with potatoes, green beans, and freshly made *pesto alla genovese*; or *orecchiette*, pasta "ears," smothered in peppery, nutritious greens. Think of pillowy handmade ravioli filled with sheep's milk ricotta, coated only with melted butter, fresh sage leaves, and grated parmigiano-reggiano cheese. For that matter, think of parmigiano-reggiano cheese. Think of "priest stranglers," "husband blinders," "strings," "worms," and all the other funny names.

Are you smiling yet? Italian pasta is the ultimate feel-good food. The savage breast calms right down when you put a bowl of *tonnarelli cacio e pepe* in front of it. The ravelled sleave of care? Knit it up with homely spaghetti *al tonno*, tuna fish. A broken heart is no match for a perfect *carbonara*. And temper tantrums quail before *pappardelle*, broad noodles, with rich *ragù di cinghiale*, wild boar.

Pasta can stick its pinky out or put its elbows halfway across the table. Its shapes may be familiar or wild, its sauces piquant or mild. The weak take strength from delicate *pastina in brodo*, while the bold thrill to the challenge of *bucatini all'amatriciana*—to keep it on the fork and off the shirt.

This book is for cooks of all levels of expertise who want to know more about how pasta is traditionally prepared in Italian homes. It's for all the people who write to ask us for the definitive recipe for *ragù bolognese* or *carbonara*, for those who believe that generations of Italian families have got it right. It's for the visitors to Italy who honor us by wanting to cook with Oretta and me, our way, in our own kitchens in Rome. It's *not* for people who think it doesn't matter what you do as long as you enjoy it. Let us give the people who gave the world the *Divine Comedy*, the Sistine Chapel, and the Ferrari car some credit for having devised, over generations, the best way to handle their favorite food.

And that it most certainly is. The Italian love of pasta is visceral. Pasta is synonymous with family, with hearth and home, with grandmother's kitchen and the genuine flavors of days gone by. It's still the centerpiece of the meal and practically synonymous with nourishment. Even working people who want a quick bite will often choose a ready-made pasta at a cafeteria rather than a sandwich.

But it's more than food. The many shapes and names contain history, politics, religion, irony, beauty, inventiveness, and fantasy and embody all the characteristics that make Italians, all Italians, what they are. *Maltagliati*, "badly cut," and *strascinati*, "dragged," suggest that pasta is just a homely, humble thing. *Strozzapreti* (page 344), "priest stranglers," recall a time of papal domination and resistance by sarcasm. *Fusilli* (page 354) take their name from the spindle, symbol of traditional womanhood since ancient times. *Lagane* (page 334) have a name straight from the Latin and recall an ancient Roman precursor of modern pasta. *Cappelletti* are jaunty little hats, *cappellacci* big old ones. *Volarelle* fly, and so do *farfalle. Pizzicotti*, little pinches, recall the less-than-gentlemanly way Italian boys used to demand the attention of foreign girls.

Pasta is a unifier of families. For special family occasions or religious holidays, there are special pastas, and for every day there's the ubiquitous tomato sauce. It takes careful timing to get the pasta *al dente* and properly sauced to the table. Everyone has to be seated and waiting for it at the same time. Stragglers and individualists who don't grace the family table risk eating cold mush later, and no Italian alive would choose that.

What Is in This Book?

THIS BOOK was conceived to continue and complement Oretta's 2009 *Encyclopedia of Pasta*, which I translated. That book told the story of more than 300 shapes of Italian pastas, with full "biographical" information and description, to say nothing of their 1,300-plus variant names. It told how each shape is, or was, made and what sauces or soups it was customarily served with, but stopped short of giving recipes. Professional chefs told us they cooked from the descriptions, even without instructions, but home cooks asked for a proper cookbook.

Thus we began to think about a book that would explain how to make the handmade shapes—not so much *tagliatelle*, already well served by many books in English, but *strozzapreti, strascinati, fusilli, farfalle,* and other shapes that could be fashioned by hand

in modern kitchens and that would make a change from spaghetti, *linguine*, and rigatoni. We omitted such bizarre and difficult forms as the Sardinian *filindeu*, a pasta gauze, or the *pi.fasacc* of Lombardia, which look like tiny swaddled infants, and others best learned from one's great-grandmother.

Our selection of pastas needed sauces and soups to match, but many of the very traditional ones are impractical for the modern kitchen, especially outside their area of origin. They depend on a local fresh cheese or an herb that grows wild on a certain hillside. Thus instead of sticking closely to the pairings of shape and sauce in *Encyclopedia of Pasta*, we decided to give recipes for about a hundred traditional sauces and soups still being made in home kitchens throughout Italy and to suggest matches with both homemade and store-bought pasta shapes. This approach, we felt, would both respect tradition and make life easier for modern home cooks, especially those cooking outside Italy.

Soon we had twice as many sauces and soups as shapes. We added a sort of user's manual for pasta—all the large and small concepts, precepts, habits, rules, laws, and misconceptions that surround the preparation and consumption of the greatest of Italy's many great gifts to humankind. The result is this book.

Here is what you will find:

• Advice for: cooking, serving, and eating pasta; stocking a pantry and choosing ingredients; and generally approaching pasta as much like an Italian as anyone outside Italy can.
• Recipes for sauces and suggestions for what shapes go best with them. These are grouped as "last-minute" sauces (made with the staples you ran out and bought after reading chapter one),

fresh vegetable sauces, fish and seafood sauces, and meat sauces.

• Recipes for traditional soups that contain pasta, again with suggested shapes.

• Recipes for making pasta from scratch. This section begins with the two basic doughs and *la sfoglia*, the pasta sheet from which so many shapes derive. Then come techniques for shaping a number of traditional formats, including some suitable for beginners and others that are trickier. Where the pastas are inseparable from their sauces (for example, the lasagne), the complete recipe is given, while most are meant to be paired with the sauces or soups in their respective sections.

• A bibliography, a glossary of pasta shapes mentioned in the book, and advice for online shopping for ingredients.

Why Us?

ONE OF the ways that this book differs from other pasta books, in English or in Italian, is that the recipes are, at their heart, written by Italians for Italians, but have been adapted, with restraint, for North American kitchens and expectations. Anyone who has ever consulted an Italian cookbook understands that no speaker of English would have the patience to cook from a book of truly Italian recipes, with their refusal to take positions (Q: How long? A: How should I know? It's *your* stove! Q: How much salt? A: Taste the capers!), to say nothing of their assumption that you already know how to cook the dish and just need to be reminded—preferably in the future perfect tense ("which you will have . . ."). And yet there is an elegance to the formal, elliptical Italian recipe style, which

Oretta represents. There is something seductive about cooking without a safety net of numbers, and there is considerable logic to the refusal to give temperatures and timing for somebody else's equipment or for quantities of salt without first tasting the salty ingredients. Are we all cooking in identical laboratories? Certainly not.

The first time I wrote Italian recipes for an American publisher, I was shocked to realize how far over to the Italian side I'd slid in my thirty years in Italy. I didn't own an instant-read thermometer and hadn't touched my measuring spoons in decades. I knew when my garlic was golden by looking at it—no idea how long it took to get there. And yet, when you get right down to it, I still have my U.S. passport, and I still want a recipe to tell me what to do.

Two more different experiences of Italian food than Oretta's and mine would be hard to imagine.

Oretta became an expert pasta maker as a child in convent school in Bologna, and went on to become a distinguished Italian food historian, food writer, teacher, and, not least, pasta authority. Her mentor was the famous Sister Attilia, whom the Communist mayor of Bologna used to borrow for his ceremonial dinners. I'm not even Italian, except by marriage. I started coming to Rome as an archaeology student, but eventually became a fair Roman home cook and discovered a knack for explaining the local food culture to other foreigners. I began translating some of Oretta's work, and, twenty-some years and a few hundred thousand words later, here we are, filtering her scholarship and expertise through my experience of the two worlds.

Sources of the Recipes

NEARLY ALL the recipes are drawn from Oretta's collection of traditional home recipes, compiled over decades of research and travel throughout the Italian peninsula and islands since the 1950s. We have adapted them to include the missing steps that Italian cooks think any idiot knows but that American cooks like to have spelled out as long as they've gone to the trouble of consulting a recipe.

The sources of the recipes are necessarily varied. A few come from our families, friends, and (much more rarely) favorite restaurants. But most come from Oretta's research, seeking out and talking to home cooks and visiting archives throughout Italy. She compared the recipes they recounted with the sacred texts of Italian food in order to distinguish true traditions from the idiosyncrasies of individual cooks or families. Thus the database she created became a true codex of Italian home cooking, numbering some 2,200 recipes in all.

Of the countless written sources she consulted, she selected a handful as reliable controls, principally written by anthropologists of food and other researchers, who often published their work privately. Many of those works can be consulted only in private libraries, and in fact, Oretta's own library tops three thousand works, some of which exist in only a few copies. The most important works, old and new, are given in the bibliography on page 384.

WELCOME TO THE WORLD OF
ITALIAN PASTA

A FEW PRELIMINARIES

THE RECIPES ARE drawn from the home-cooking traditions of all parts of Italy, and some are common throughout the country. In not dividing the recipes by region or (more realistically) locality, we aim to emphasize characteristics of *Italian* home cooking.

Judicious suggestions for substitutions are made, but overall the recipes are quite faithful to their roots. And therein lies a challenge to you, dear reader. If you observe a few basic precepts, the recipes will reward you with dishes you might (almost) find in Italian homes and trattorias. But if you start second-guessing and adding more ingredients or substituting cheap oil for good, oil for pork fat (except where authorized), dried herbs for fresh, all bets are off. Here are the ground rules:

- Use the best ingredients you can find in every category.
- Skip an ingredient sooner than use a poor imitation.
- Look at the pot, not the clock.
- Don't obsess over measurements of ingredients and sizes of cookware.
- Do obsess over quality of ingredients.

The main difference between Italian cooking in Italy and elsewhere is the number of ingredients. That's worth repeating. Outside Italy, cooks like to keep adding things, such as ever more garlic, or garlic where there's already an onion doing a fine job on its own, or hot pepper or cheese that will overpower delicate flavors. Italian palates are used to picking up subtleties and do not appreciate these brash jumbles of aggressive flavors.

Most of these recipes depend on the excellence of the main ingredient. Or rather the second ingredient, because the main ingredient is the pasta. All the sauces and soups in this book, and in Italian cooking in general, depend on the quality of their ingredients. Nowadays a decently stocked Italian pantry is within reach of anyone willing to do a little Web surfing. If imported canned tomatoes, dried pasta, anchovies, capers, olives, and extra virgin olive oil are not available at your local store, there is always the Internet. A shopping guide is provided on page 386.

From this point of view, the pasta recipes are probably the easiest part. Much Italian pasta is already made from North American flour, and fresh eggs aren't hard to come by (but, please, from happy chickens). Perfect fresh pasta takes technique and practice, but, yes, you can learn outside Italian borders, nor will we ever berate you for seeking help from a machine.

But the sauces and soups! A couple of anchovies, a can of tomatoes, a sprinkling of oregano—What is so complicated about that? skeptics may ask. We say the difference between the good Italian versions and everything else is the difference between eating in black-and-white and eating in 3D. Buy decent tomatoes, tuna, extra virgin olive oil listing country of origin, and pasta.

Even though we use the word "sauce," we prefer the Italian word *condimento* as a generic term. Is a handful of cheese tossed on bare spaghetti a sauce? It is certainly a *condimento*. *Condimento* covers just about everything you can add to a bowl of pasta, while "sauce" has connotations of liquidity and advance preparation, which are not always relevant.

WHILE THE REST of the noodle-eating world stayed stuck on, well, noodles, Italian housewives and, later, professional pasta makers invented all those whimsically named and imaginatively fashioned shapes. Outside Italy, even the most unregenerate seekers of the new and bizarre have only ever seen a relative handful of shapes for sale or described in recipe books. But the real story is how the ordinary Italian housewife took inspiration from every possible source—even the tail of the mouse scurrying across her kitchen floor—and took her materials from where she could get them, including the flour swept off the mill floor. She dressed this pasta with a handful of cheese or pork cracklings or, more usually, tossed it in a soup of freshly gathered wild greens. The rich meat sauces we think of today as typical and traditional were for the privileged or at least for special occasions.

Against this background, it is absurd to hammer today's home cooks with rules, pronouncements, and inflexible directives. And indeed, when we get to the recipes, you'll find plenty of room to maneuver. But first we need to get through the handful of basic principles that all Italians agree on. To cook like an Italian,

you have to think like an Italian. Thinking like an Italian means embracing imagination, improvisation, and paradox and not getting hung up on exact amounts or certain brands. When we don't specify a cut of meat or variety of potato, it's because it really doesn't matter. People have always made do with what they had. Trust us, when specificity matters, we'll give it to you. When no compromise is possible, you'll know.

MOST ITALIAN PASTA is made with one of two kinds of wheat, *grano tenero*, soft wheat, and *grano duro*, durum wheat. *Semolino*, which, infuriatingly, becomes semolina in English, is durum wheat flour. The two wheats have different properties and generally come from different areas. *Grano tenero*, favored in the North, is usually combined with eggs to make a delicate egg pasta. It is also used to make most bread. Most Italian *grano duro* is grown mainly in Sicily and Puglia (that is, the South) and, to oversimplify, is traditionally combined with water to make the more rustic handmade shapes. These two broad categories of pasta are called *pasta all'uovo* (egg pasta) and *pasta acqua e farina* (flour-and-water pasta). Factory-made pasta in Italy is, by law, always made with *grano duro*, even when it contains eggs and even when the same shapes would be made at home with *grano tenero*. Some specialty pasta makers in southern Italy grow their own *grano duro*, usually in Puglia.

Pasta can be (a) rolled into a sheet (*sfoglia*) and cut, by either hand or machine; (b) shaped with hands or rudimentary tools; or (c) extruded through dies, usually on an industrial scale, though there are home extruders on the market. Both *pasta all'uovo* and *pasta acqua e farina* can be rolled and cut. Egg dough, the more tender of the two, can be rolled thinner.

To put some names to these types, spaghetti, *bucatini*, rigatoni, *penne*, and everything round in section or tubular or odd-shaped (such as *fusilli* or *gigli*) are made with durum wheat and water and are extruded. Almost everything noodle-like, that is, flat and cut from a thin sheet, contains eggs and, if fresh, soft wheat; *tagliatelle*, *fettuccine*, *pappardelle*, and *tagliolini* all fall into this category. There are, however, some flour-and-water noodles, such as *lagane* (page 334), sometimes simply called *fettuccine* or *tagliatelle*, making it a good idea always to read the ingredients on the package. Many of the lumpier or irregular shapes (such as the whole group that derives from *gnocchetti*, pages 341–49) are made by hand from flour-and-water dough.

Not all pasta is made of wheat flour. Poverty, endemic for centuries, sharpened the women's ingenuity and when they could not afford costly wheat, they used other cereals. Farro, for example, is extremely adaptable to mountain terrains, and during World War II was not rationed and thus easier to find at competitive prices.

Grown on the latifundia, enormous estates, of wealthy owners, wheat was once prohibitively expensive for the rural poor. After the harvest, women known as *spigolatrici*, gleaners, went into the fields to gather what little grain was left behind. When the stubble was burned, they returned to pick up anything they had missed before, only now it too was burned. This *grano arso*, or burned wheat, found its way into all the best-known homemade pastas of the Italian South—*cavatelli*, *orecchiette*, *strascinati*, *fusilli* all contained some *grano arso*, and thus the pasta became more affordable. The only advantage to this burned flour was that it was better than none at all, but the taste acquired in poverty eventu-ally gave rise to the luxurious smokiness of the gourmet version of *grano arso* found in the niche market today.

Meanwhile, throughout the North, poor housewives, in a tour de force of recycling, patiently made a sort of flour from stale bread. In the Alps, bread was baked as seldom as once a month, by the end of which anything left was hard as a rock. They would mix the resurrected flour with a little wheat flour to make the famous local dumplings called *canederli* (page 362).

Ingenious country women also also produced pasta with flours made from legumes or other plants. The mountains and hills of Liguria used to be covered with chestnuts, and breads and pastas made from chestnut flour are still made and eaten there. In the mountains of the North, especially in the Valtellina area of Lombardia, buckwheat is grown for noodles called *pizzoccheri* (page 366).

Eventually corn (maize) came to Italy and came to be used, famously, in polenta, but was also mixed with wheat flour as an economical stretcher in pasta. Inevitably this practice went upmarket, and nowadays fashionable restaurants in the Marche serve *tacconi* (page 368), of mixed corn and wheat flours, with a hearty *ragù* of sausage and tomato (like that on page 216) and sometimes beans. Pasta made of corn flour is widely available as a gluten-free alternative to wheat.

In the South of Italy, in the part of the mountainous Calabrian hinterland known as the Pollino, there used to be a type of pasta made with a mix of wheat, barley, chickpea, and fava flours. It was called *mischiglio*, meaning mix, and looked something like *orecchiette*. Today the tiny local production of this pasta is exported throughout the world, especially North America.

All these stories of poverty and ingenuity not

only serve to illustrate the resilience and imagination of Italians in the kitchen, but also show that it is pointless to worry too much about the exact content of your dough today, whether in Italy or in America. The rural women experimented with what they had and knew by feel when their dough would work. Today, we should accept the guidelines of recipes but in following them pay more attention to what we feel with our fingers than what we read with our eyes.

COOKING PASTA

THE FREEWHEELING, eyeballing casual Italian approach to measurement can be deceptive. When it comes to boiling the pasta, everyone in Italy knows the metric formula: for every 100 grams (3½ ounces) of pasta, 1 liter (1 quart) of rapidly boiling water is needed, and 10 grams (2 teaspoons) of coarse salt are added along with the pasta. Thus a pound (450 grams, but call it half a kilo) takes 5 liters of water and 50 grams (about 3 tablespoons) of kosher salt (or half as much fine table salt). That nobody ever actually measures to get the exact quantities is beside the point.

Do not be stingy with the water, even if you're in a hurry. If you use enough water and stir the pasta occasionally with a wooden spoon, especially at the beginning, it will not stick together, but it does need that room in the pot. Bring the water to a boil, add the salt, add the pasta, stir. Cover the pot briefly to bring the water quickly back to a boil; uncover the pot before it boils over. Stir occasionally; drain when the pasta is *al dente*, a concept we'll address in a minute. In the case of spaghetti or other long forms, press the end that protrudes from the pot until the bottom has collapsed so that the whole length slips down into the pot. Then stir. Do not even think about breaking spaghetti to make it fit the pot. As soon as the spaghetti is submerged, put the lid on the pot so the water will return to the boil quickly.

Kosher salt is generally considered the closest equivalent outside Italy to ordinary Italian coarse salt, called *sale grosso*. (There are no religious implications.) If you use ordinary table salt (*sale fino*), use about half the amount of kosher salt. You can (and should) taste the water to check. It should be pleasantly salty. Some people say it should taste like seawater, but not all seas are equally salty. Just make sure you can taste salt. And speaking of the sea, it doesn't have to be sea salt. Nothing in Italian tradition dictates any particular kind of salt, either in the water or in the sauce, but some salt is essential. You may adjust the suggested quantities to personal taste or diet, but pasta boiled with no salt at all will never taste right. Most pasta doughs do not contain salt, and if they do, it is only a pinch. The pasta will absorb its salt from the water as it boils, and this is essential to the final flavor of the dish. I repeat: you will never get the right flavor adding salt late or too stingily.

Oil is not normally added to the water. The principal exception is that it may be added for the brief cooking of just-made pasta sheets to be assembled for, say, lasagne. While *tagliatelle* and other noodle shapes dry a bit before cooking, lasagne go into the pot practically as they are made. In case two sheets of this very fresh dough have stuck together, the oil in the water will cause them to separate. For normal pasta cooking, use a big enough pot and stir, and that will be enough to prevent sticking. You don't want to lubricate your spaghetti while it boils.

Cooking times will vary, especially for homemade pasta. In general, the more rustic the manufacture, the longer the cooking time. Some thick artisanal sun-dried pastas take as long as

20 minutes to cook. In contrast, pasta made on a huge industrial scale cooks quickly because it has been blast-dried, which is practically like pre-cooking. Nowadays the cooking times written on the packages are reasonably accurate. Set your timer for a minute sooner than the package says and keep a close eye on it, especially if you are using a shape or brand for the first time.

Everybody knows you're supposed to cook the pasta *al dente*, but what does that mean? Literally it means "to the tooth," which is to say, chewy or resistant to the tooth. But it's subjective; not all Italians agree on the exact degree of *al dente*. Generally speaking, the farther south you go, the chewier the pasta. Northerners find southern pasta too raw; southerners find northern pasta too mushy. It is far from the only difference between North and South, but it is an important and persistent one. One thing is certain. The worst comment a cook can hear is "*La pasta è scotta,*" meaning "the pasta is overcooked." The shame is nigh unbearable.

As a general guideline, drain the pasta when it has *just* lost its white center, and you can tell this by feel as you stir it with the wooden spoon. Or else you can cut into a piece with a knife or your fingernail.

Bear in mind that pasta will continue to cook for about 30 seconds after draining and even longer if you finish using the skillet method—that is, tossing the cooked pasta in the pan containing the sauce before transferring all to a serving dish, or serving straight from the pan. An extreme skillet method is used by certain perfectionists in the Basilicata region, in the deep South. They boil homemade *fusilli* (see page 354) until only a bit more than half done (this takes experience) then mix them with the sauce, a hearty lamb *ragù*, in a bowl which they cover and place over hot water until the pasta has fin-

ished cooking. By that time it is *al dente* but has absorbed the fragrant essence of the sauce. But don't try this at home. It is very difficult to regulate the cooking time of the pasta, which remains in the hot sauce and can easily overcook. The peasants of yesteryear were less obsessive over *al dente* pasta than Italians today.

However, some traditional methods of cooking pasta are still used in rural areas. In the Sabine Hills northeast of Rome, *sagne*, the local thin egg *fettuccine*, are cooked with near-surgical precision. The women warn against adding too much pasta at once to the boiling water because the water will take too long to return to the boil and "the *sagne* will get sick." Local physicians are helpless against this malady, so the women are careful.

The term *pastasciutta*, literally "dry pasta," means pasta that is drained of its cooking liquid and served with a sauce, as opposed to pasta served in soup. (It is a common error to think the dryness refers to the freshness of the pasta.) *Pastasciutta* is a phenomenon of modern, wealthy times. As late as the first half of the twentieth century, small towns and rural areas ate their pasta in broth or in vegetable or legume soups. The Roman poet Horace (first century B.C.), self-declared country mouse despite his high patronage in Rome, famously looked forward to a bowl of leeks, chickpeas, and something called *lagana* when he returned from the capital to his farm. His *lagana* were not strictly pasta as we use the term today—they were more like matzos—but their role in the legume soup was exactly the same as the *lagane* (same name, but definitely a pasta) in a traditional chickpea soup still popular in the Puglia region (page 244). As it happens, Horace's modest, yet immortalized, birthplace, Venosa (Venusium), was in what today is Puglia. And in Puglia today *ciceri e tria* is a chickpea soup containing a pasta that is first fried and then added to the soup.

Another curious, and quite rare, way to cook fresh pasta is to fry the pieces and put them in certain soups, where they take on flavor. In L'Aquila, capital of the Abruzzo region, this is done traditionally on Christmas Eve with *zuppa di cardi* (cardoons) *e volarelle*. *Volarelle* (page 338) are a sort of small *maltagliati* (page 336) cooked in this famous cardoon broth, but to make the dish more festive, half the pasta is held back and fried. These pieces are added to the soup at the table.

Back to our boiling pot. Once you have determined that it's time to drain the pasta, every second counts. Everything you're going to need—sauce, cheese, bowl, oil for finishing—should be ready and in place near where you will drain the pasta.

Have your serving bowl or platter warm. This is not optional or a luxury or just for company. If you have absolutely no place in your kitchen to warm it, which is unlikely (a low oven? an electric food warmer? the radiator?), take the chill off it by sloshing a couple of ladles of the pasta water around in it (then discard of course) or just rinsing it with hot water.

There are two approaches to draining, the dumping into a colander in the sink method and the scooping out right into the bowl method. (The ultimate film reference for draining pasta is *The Apartment*, directed by Billy Wilder in 1960; a tennis racquet used as a colander makes great cinema, but do *not* drain spaghetti the way Jack Lemmon does in that otherwise splendid film.)

If you use the colander method, always reserve a cup of the cooking water before you pour out the contents of the pot. You may need it to smooth out your sauce. You can also place the colander right over your serving bowl to let the water heat the bowl. Unless the recipe says to drain very well, don't worry about getting every last drop of water off. The little bit of salty, starchy water that stays with the pasta will not do your sauce any harm, and a good pasta will soon absorb any excess water.

An excellent variation of the colander method is the pot with built-in colander, like a double boiler, which you can simply lift right out of the water. You need to hold it high above the pot for several seconds while the water runs out, then set it back over the pot at an angle to finish dripping.

With the scooping-out method, you avoid having to clear the sink, find potholders, yell "Coming through!" and fog your glasses, so in many ways it is preferable. Ravioli, gnocchi, and other delicate forms should always be scooped out. The disadvantage is you have to work very fast or the last scoops risk being overcooked while they wait their turn to be fished out. The dexterous are able to hoist long formats, such as spaghetti and *bucatini*, out of the pot with two kitchen forks. This is best for such dishes as *cacio e pepe* (page 102), when the pasta should be absolutely dripping wet. Spider strainers are ideal for short or stuffed pasta (if you work fast) and, with a little practice, work for spaghetti too. Because the water passes through more efficiently, they are preferable to slotted spoons.

Adding the Sauce

THERE ARE various methods of combining sauce and pasta, and each recipe in this book makes recommendations according to its own exigencies or tradition. The usual home method is to put the drained pasta in a warm serving dish, toss with cheese (if the recipe so specifies), top with the sauce and toss again, and serve, usually at the speed of light lest the pasta get cold. If you add the cheese first, as Oretta recommends, it sticks better to the pasta and combines with the sauce to make everything creamy.

For some years now the skillet method of saucing pasta has been in vogue, having migrated to home kitchens after taking hold in restaurants. The method is called *spadellare* in Italian, a verb meaning to sauté (the skillet is called *padella*), but more than that—to mix the food by tossing it in the air in the pan without the aid of utensils. This requires a certain courage and wrist technique not everybody is going to want to get into. Oretta has definite opinions about when it is appropriate, and the recipes in this book follow her precepts. If the recipe does not specify finishing the dish in the skillet, the method is not recommended. Even where the skillet is allowed, we still suggest transferring the sauced pasta to a heated serving dish after tossing, to be perfectly proper, but of course you can serve directly from the skillet for casual meals. Do not use the skillet method with liquid or semiliquid sauces, such as those that contain a great deal of tomato, nor those where cheese is preponderant. Finally, even though we usually add the cheese first and then the sauce, in the skillet the order is necessarily reversed.

When serving, I like to set aside the first portion, which always winds up with less sauce, then, after I've dished up a couple of portions, throw it back in and mix it again with the sauce that always collects at the bottom. A large spoon and fork are best for serving all forms of pasta, except baked, which need a spatula.

Matching Sauce and Shape

THE TRICK—if that is the word—of pairing sauces and pasta shapes is both more and less mysterious than non-Italians think. Some pairings can be explained by science, but that is of no interest to the generations of Italian families who devised them. Some are simply traditional because they are based on local products. Many make no difference at all. Choices can be eccentric and highly subjective. Each sauce recipe in this book lists one or more pastas that for one or more reasons will go well with it. Sometimes the pastas are very different from one another. *Sugo ai frutti di mare* (seafood) is paired with pastas as different as *strascinati* (page 348) and *paglia e fieno* (page 331). No amount of badgering is going to get you a straight answer as to why. I've tried. The pairings are combinations that are found at family tables in Italy, and they work. Period.

The truth is that almost any kind of pasta goes reasonably well with almost any kind of sauce, and people who get all serious and talk about the importance of correct sauce pairing are probably overthinking. And yet, just try and pair spaghetti with, say, cauliflower, and everybody will recognize you for the foreigner, or aberrant, that you are. The bits of florets cry out for a shape with a cavity or a tube they can hide in. Oily or liquid sauces like to slip down and coat long strands. Flat noodles are very versatile. The broader surface grabs bits of meat nicely (think of *pappardelle* with hare or wild boar, pages 230 and 235), but they are long and can handle liquids well too. Over generations, the most compatible pairings have been repeated until they have taken root in the national psyche, and once that happens, *almost* nobody does anything else.

Still, pairing choices can be extremely subjective. Oretta tells the story of a young woman who complained, disgusted, that a restaurant had served a short pasta *all'amatriciana* instead of the usual spaghetti or *bucatini*. The horror! Actually, I think I know that restaurant, and their delicious *maccheroni all'amatriciana* don't seem to bother anyone else.

Most people would agree that there is very little difference between spaghetti and *linguine*. *Linguine* are flattish and lens shaped, but the length and amount of surface area is about the same as spaghetti. Both have to be twirled on the fork with an identical technique. Last summer at our favorite seafood restaurant our waiter asked, almost apologetically, whether *linguine* would be all right with our fish sauce. "Huh?" we replied. He said that indeed *linguine* would be normal with seafood, but many people inexplicably refuse to eat them. We accepted the *linguine*.

Pasta with legumes typically takes *cannolicchi*, *ditalini*, or *tubettini*, small tubular shapes, but *maltagliati* are also widely used. They sort of wrap themselves around the beans. Sometimes broken spaghetti and *linguine* are tossed in, a reminder of past poverty, when the bottom of the barrel was scraped for edible remnants.

In *brodo*, broth, tiny *pastina* is de rigueur. But broth is also the only acceptable vehicle for *capelli d'angelo* (angel hair, page 332), which are too thin for sauce. *Tortellini* (page 309) must be served in broth as well. No true Emilian would serve the precious stuffed morsels with sauce, but the rule does not hold for other stuffed shapes. Ravioli and *agnolotti*—and don't try to overparse the names; you will get nowhere—are usually served as *pastasciutta*. Generally speaking, the larger the stuffed format, the more likely it is to be sauced instead of served in broth.

For the large and varied stuffed-pasta family (let us call them all ravioli for short), the rule is that what you put in the filling, you don't put in the sauce. Thus a meat filling should not have a meat sauce. Italian cooks do break this rule sometimes without having to surrender their passports, but I wouldn't try it around Oretta, who roundly reprimanded a young friend of mine when he proudly described to her his latest creation—artichoke-filled ravioli with an artichoke sauce. In contrast, fish-filled ravioli—very popular today—are an exception and do quite well with a sauce that is redolent of the sea.

Tuna and tomato (page 58), a homely, flavorful sauce of no pretensions whatsoever, demands spaghetti for no reason but tradition.

Small handmade formats with an indentation or hole, originally intended to facilitate drying, today (now that we have highly effective industrial drying techniques) are recognized as just the thing to grab and hold sauces, particularly those with bits of meat, fish, or vegetable.

Chefs today are always studying new and creative pairings, and pasta makers launch new shapes on the market, and so the last word on pasta pairings has not yet been written. Tradition remains strong.

Serving and Eating

"LIVE AND LET LIVE" does not apply to the service and consumption of Italian pasta, for which there are approved methods and unapproved methods and not much of a gray area between.

In the normal Italian meal, pasta or soup (or rice or polenta) is a *primo piatto*, first course, but is actually most people's favorite part of the meal and often the most important course. With a substantial meat or fish sauce, it can be treated as a *piatto unico*, or one-dish meal. Don't take that too literally, as there will always be other courses, just not a main. The *primo piatto* is eaten alone. No side dishes, no nothing. If you want just pasta and salad for dinner, you have pasta first and then salad. If you serve pasta and salad together to an Italian guest, you will observe that, when the blood returns to his shocked, pale face, he will politely eat the pasta first and only when he has finished will he turn to the salad.

When *Encyclopedia of Pasta* was published, the American Academy in Rome organized a buffet lunch to follow a morning of presentations about the book. Guests who didn't know any better—which was practically everybody—blithely put salad on their plates alongside the precious handmade *gnocchi ricci* that Oretta had personally driven two hours to Amatrice to procure and two hours back. Quite rightly, she became apoplectic and went from table to table instructing the hapless diners not to touch the salad until they had finished their pasta—and there were four kinds of pasta to taste.

Serve *pastasciutta*—sauced pasta—on a plate, not in a bowl, to be excruciatingly proper. The soup plate, favored by trattorias and other informal eateries, is widely used and very practical, but is considered informal, suitable for family. The soup plate is perfect for thick soups containing pasta, of course, but broths with *pastina* or *tortellini* or the like should be served in a cup or deep bowl, like any clear soup.

The spoon you may see at your place when you sit down in an Italian restaurant or trattoria will be removed after you order *pastasciutta*. It is there only in case you order soup. You do *not* use a spoon to assist with the eating of *pastasciutta*. Ever. To eat spaghetti, hold your fork in your right hand (if right-handed) almost parallel to the table and skim off one or two strands. Pull the spaghetti gently away from the mass

and twirl away from you, resting the tips of the tines in the curve of your plate while you twirl. It will give you just as much support as a spoon and will look more dignified. If the spaghetti is properly *al dente*, there will probably be ends that will never wrap around the fork. Get them into your mouth as best you can, but do not bite them off and absolutely do not inhale. Don't stare at anyone eating spaghetti and they won't stare at you.

But we are not utterly heartless. There is one time when you can use a spoon to eat long pasta—when it's in soup. *Capelli d'angelo* (angel hair), as we've said, are properly served in broth despite the insistence outside Italy on serving them as *pastasciutta*. Obviously they have to be twirled somehow. You take your fork in your left hand, twirl a couple of strands of pasta in the spoon, and deliver it to your mouth on the spoon along with some broth. It sounds harder than it is.

Need I tell anyone never to cut pasta with a knife? Cut spaghetti is impossible to eat (except in soup, with a spoon), but even large formats that need to be reduced into bite-sized pieces, such as lasagne or cannelloni, must be cut with a fork. Nor may you hold the knife in your right hand to push your pasta onto a fork held in the left (as the French insist on doing). You hold the fork in your right hand and rest your empty left hand demurely on the edge of the table (yes, really).

It is not kind to serve hard-to-eat tomatoey or oily spaghetti or, even more difficult, *bucatini* at dinner parties. If you're simply bursting to make *bucatini all'amatriciana* (page 70), at least warn your guests to wear red sweatshirts. They will thank you. In general, it would be good of you to serve a short pasta to guests who have honored you by wearing clean shirts. When needed, you can protect your necktie or new silk blouse by pressing your napkin (daintily) to your breast with your left hand, but don't tuck it into your collar or tie it like a bib except *en famille*. The considerate host or hostess will take the guests' comfort into consideration when planning the menu. If you have lovely clams you want to share with your friends, make *fregula con le arselle* (page 273), not spaghetti *alle vongole* (page 177), unless the occasion is very casual or your guests very expert.

Cheese is not served with many types of sauce. If your host has not put it on the table, either the correct amount of cheese has been applied in the kitchen, and a confident cook will not offer extra, or cheese does not go with that dish. In restaurants you can always ask if cheese is used with what you ordered, but in home settings, watch the host or hostess. Unless you know them to be very forgetful, follow their lead.

The question of scooping up extra sauce with your bread comes up often. The practice is cryptically known as *fare la scarpetta*, "doing the slipper," and it is not considered terrific manners. Nevertheless, it is widely practiced, and cooks always look on it as evidence of success. Some will even worry that if you don't do the *scarpetta*, you didn't like the sauce. Bottom line: do it at home if you wish, and when a guest, watch what your hosts do. According to the Italian etiquette books, bread should be brought to the table only with the *secondo piatto*, that is, after the pasta or soup. But restaurants—and even the most superficially formal don't often consult the books—long ago realized that bread was a good way for patrons to keep body and soul together while waiting for their meals, so they began serving it immediately. And, of course, how are you going to do the *scarpetta* with no bread on the table?

THE LARDER

I T IS A fact of modern life that to eat the poor-folks' foods of yesteryear we have to go to very special sources, often fine restaurants or gourmet shops. The precious porcini mushrooms that once waited to be discovered under a tree we now buy dried in costly cellophane packets. The chestnut flour that used to be a cheaper alternative to wheat is a niche item. And *grano arso* is today a delicately smoky pasta served by gourmet chefs with highly refined seafood sauces.

Even if your larder is half a shelf over a hotplate, if you're going to make pasta sauces, it should contain certain staples of an Italian kitchen that will keep well and be there when you need them.

- Extra virgin olive oil;
- Top-quality factory-made pasta, at least one long format and one short format;
- Anchovies, salt-packed or oil-packed or both;
- Capers, salt-packed;
- Black olives, preferably in brine, and preferably Gaeta or taggiasche;
- Italian canned peeled tomatoes and tomato puree;
- Italian or Spanish tuna;
- Moderately hot dried chile, whole, not flakes;
- Garlic;
- Onions;
- Dried oregano (not essential).

If you can manage a potted plant of parsley and one of basil, you'll always have a fresh supply.

Tomatoes (*Pomodori*)

THE TOMATO came to Europe from Mexico in the 1500s with the returning Conquistadores, probably Hernán Cortès, whose men described a red fruit, called *tomatl*, that the Maya combined with peppers to make a very piquant sauce. But in Italy it was cultivated merely as an ornamental plant and considered a curiosity by botanists. Only in the eighteenth century was the fruit recognized as edible (earlier the leaves had been eaten, but impressed no one, not least because they are poisonous), and the fortunate encounter with pasta took place still later.

And then, in the twentieth century, commercial growers developed strains designed to bounce off a speeding truck with impunity (and that's not even that much of an exaggeration). The trade-off was flavor, and the insipid "fresh" tomato on the supermarket shelf became a symbol of all that was wrong with the North American food supply. Fortunately American palates finally rebelled, and countless varieties of good-tasting heirloom tomatoes are available as seeds for your own gardens and at farmers' markets across the continent. It's well worth experimenting and doing your own research in your own area, and talking to local growers, to find at least two varieties—one to use raw, one to cook—available near you *in season*.

Pasta with a simple tomato sauce (page 90) is the most popular dish of households all over Italy today, not only in the South. Still, we hope that anyone who still thinks most pasta sauces contain some form of tomato will be surprised and enlightened by how many recipes in this book contain none at all.

The recipes in this book call for various kinds of fresh tomatoes, usually by type, such as "salad" or "sauce."

For salads, and raw eating in general, Italians prefer a somewhat unripe tomato with a good bit of green still showing. It should be crisp and acidic, making vinegar unnecessary in the salad. In Italy, recipes for dishes containing raw tomatoes sometimes call for salad tomatoes, by which is meant greenish and firm. Such tomatoes are not intended to survive to full ripeness so they are *not* to be used for sauces when they mature. They will never have the needed full, round flavor of a good sauce tomato.

Those nice big round red tomatoes on the vine you bought at your local farmers' market would never be used in salad in Italy. They would be too mushy. *Those* are the ones to use when the recipe says "sauce tomatoes." Even better for sauce are the long San Marzano type, the elite member of the elongated, or plum, family. Properly speaking, San Marzano tomatoes should be grown in a designated area around San Marzano in the volcanic soil around Mount Vesuvius (near Naples), but the descendants of San Marzano emigrant seeds are widely available. The type can be grown in gardens anywhere, and real Italian San Marzano tomatoes are available canned. Look for DOP on the label (PDO, protected designation of origin, in English, a guarantee of origin and production methods).

Cherry tomatoes, *ciliegini* in Italian, are younger in Italy than in America, but dare we say they are more flavorful? Cherry tomatoes are, of course, eaten raw, but can also be baked or quickly sautéed for pasta. Originally a hybrid

of a native Italian and an Israeli, the best *ciliegini* come from the Pachino area at the southeastern tip of Sicily, a particular microclimate where the tomatoes take on salt from the soil and develop sweetness from the sun. Although not correct, and not to be encouraged, popular usage has made Pachino synonymous with cherry tomatoes. However, the Pachino DOP extends to several different types of tomatoes, of which the *ciliegino* is only the best known. Grape tomatoes, which are often more flavorful than cherry and about the same size, may be used instead. Even though these small tomatoes are used raw, they are not good when green and are always eaten red and ripe.

The small, pointed *piennolo* tomatoes grown on Mount Vesuvius, and included in the Slow Food Association's list of endangered foods, are among the world's most flavorful and can be purchased online in cans or jars.

When a recipe calls for a specific kind of fresh tomato, this will be stated in general terms—such as "sauce," "red, ripe," or "salad"— so that you can choose a tomato of the same general type. Usually good-quality canned or bottled tomatoes can be substituted, and where you need fresh or nothing, we say so. Canned tomatoes are usually peeled (*pelati*), which may give the impression that peeling is desirable. Actually, it isn't. In addition to nutrients, the skins contain a good deal of flavor and are perfectly edible. Even where our recipes call for tomatoes to be seeded, we mean to leave skin on unless otherwise stated.

If you have a garden that produces decent tomatoes, you really should do as Oretta does and put them up in jars or bottles for the winter, a traditional practice lately being rediscovered as even Italians complain about the quality of produce available for sale off season and speculate about the true origin of the contents of familiar cans on the supermarket shelves. Thus what used to be done to save money is now done to ensure quality. Buy hermetically sealable jars, not too large—about a pint (500 milliliters) or smaller if you like. Simply wash small tomatoes or cut larger ones in pieces and fill the jars. You can add a basil leaf and/or a small piece of garlic to some of them. Close the jars and put them in a large pot. Just cover them with cold water, bring the water to a boil, and boil for 30 minutes. Oretta puts a folded kitchen towel on the bottom of the pot and another lining the walls. Let the jars cool in the pot, and that is all. If you open a jar and don't finish it, the rest will keep in the refrigerator for a few days. And they're delicious right out of the jar slathered with extra virgin olive oil for a quick bruschetta.

Tomato puree (*passata di pomodoro*) is called for less often than canned whole tomatoes (*pomodori pelati*, or simply *pelati*), but it's still an essential item in your pantry. You can make it yourself quickly with either fresh tomatoes or *pelati*. For this, an old-fashioned food mill works best. A food processor will simply grind up the skins and incorporate a great deal of air into the puree, resulting in a pink froth. A food mill, which you crank to force the food through a sort of sieve, purees the tomatoes gently and removes the skin and seeds. Drop nice ripe red sauce tomatoes into boiling water for a few minutes, then drain. Set your food mill up over a bowl and put in the drained tomatoes, in batches if they don't all fit at once. Start cranking. The faster you go, the more centrifugal force you create and the better it works. For puree of canned *pelati*, just pour them into the food mill, juice and all.

Some recipes call for a small amount of tomato paste, *concentrato*. It is commonly sold in a tube in Italy, like toothpaste, which suggests how sparingly it is used.

However, some recipes do call for tomato puree, and even where they don't, you may have a delicate stomach or fussy eater at your table. A freshly made tomato puree (*passata di pomodoro*) is the way to go.

Extra Virgin Olive Oil

Fragrant, flavorful, and sensual as it flows from the cold press—nothing says "Italian food" like extra virgin olive oil. And extra virgin is what you want, for all uses. It is a natural product obtained by mechanical means (that is, pressing) without solvents or excessive heat.

Visitors to Italy always ask us what brand of olive oil they should buy, but there is no answer. In Italy people who care about food buy directly from a producer they know and trust or through the mediation of a trusted person who knows one. If we run out, sooner than run to the store for an emergency bottle, we call a friend or relative to ask if they can spare any from their own supply. Still, it might happen that even with the best planning, somebody has to buy a bottle of oil in a store. In that case, we would avoid mass-market brands, especially those that advertise. The best advice we can offer is to read the label and examine the packaging and storage conditions. You don't need to see the color of the oil. That's worth repeating: don't worry about the color. Rather, you need to be sure the oil has been protected from light. Ideally it is in an opaque container. Light and extreme temperatures (and abrupt changes of temperature) are the enemies of olive oil. It is much more important for the oil to be shielded from the light than for you to see the color.

The label should tell you where the olives were grown and where the oil was pressed, and sometimes the type of olives used. There may be quality designations, such as an organic farming certification or a guarantee of origin (IGP or DOP). In general, the narrower the information regarding the provenance of the oil, the better. "Italy" is too general. More specific designations, such as "Toscana" or "Sabina," are legally delimited areas with excellent oils. Some designations are even narrower—the best oil often comes from a single estate within one of the designated areas, but those bottles tend to be quite expensive and thus are usually reserved for finishing or salads.

In order to maintain the flavor and health benefits, as well as the chemical composition required for classification as extra virgin olive oil, the oil needs to be stored away from light and extreme temperatures. The ideal temperature is 59°F (15°C). Don't keep it near the stove, and don't store it in the refrigerator. Use an opaque container or wrap the bottle in foil or cloth. Use a metal or synthetic stopper, not natural cork.

Beware of low prices. Growing olives and making good oil are expensive and labor-intensive. Factors ranging from the age of the trees and altitude of the orchards to the method and time of harvesting affect the quality of the taste and health benefits. Look for bargains in your phone plan, not your extra virgin olive oil.

The only oil called for in these recipes is extra virgin olive oil, and many recipes specify whether the taste should be lightly fruity, medium fruity, or intensely fruity. We express this as a preference so as not to frighten you into thinking you need to fill your larder with bottles of oil. However, most careful Italian cooks and eaters do pay attention to an oil's intensity of flavor and will not use the same oil to drizzle on a white fish as they will slather on a bruschetta or a bowl of beans. Now, some mass-market oils are offered in different intensities, but those are not what we mean. If you are unable to achieve the ideal of keeping two or three different oils, choose one basic good-quality Italian extra virgin olive oil and set your mind at rest. Add to that perhaps a small bottle of boutique oil you'll use uncooked for finishing, and you're all set. It is wishful thinking to imagine our readers have a pantry stocked with several bottles of imported oil from which to choose, and even in Italy it is a modern phenomenon, certainly not something the rural poor who fried in pork fat ever enjoyed.

Olio nuovo, new oil, is the brash first oil of the season. Its bright green color, assertive taste and fragrance, and high polyphenol content (for health) ensure its popularity. There is nothing like it for bruschetta, soups, salads, and other dishes in which the oil is used uncooked and an upfront olive flavor is desirable.

Good olive oil brings out the flavor of other ingredients, much as wine does. An oil with a well-structured flavor accentuates the sweetness of tomatoes with basil. A fruity oil does best on a cold seafood salad. A rustic pasta dressed with garlic, oil, and chile wants a robust flavor for its oil.

Butter

IN MUCH of the north of Italy, butter (*burro*) is far more traditional than olive oil, and even in parts of the South and Center, some recipes call for butter (e.g., *burro e salvia*, page 84). Unsalted butter is always preferred, and the best butter, if you can find it, comes from the cheese makers of northern Italy (page 392).

Pork Products

ALL THIS attention to extra virgin olive oil, a product that has been around for millennia, is relatively new. Once upon a time, except in the major olive-growing areas, the most accessible fat available for cooking was from pork. And in traditional recipes, to approximate the traditional taste, even in our modern kitchens, there is no use pretending that extra virgin olive oil is an acceptable substitute.

Guanciale is salt-cured, not smoked, pork cheek. It can be seen hanging in *salumerie* and presents itself in either a loaf shape or a triangle. It is quite fatty and has a delicate, almost sweet flavor. North American *guanciale* exists, but in our limited experience, most of it is still a pale imitation or else is tarted up with herbs in fear that the pork flavor will be insufficient. Also, lipophobic producers butcher the hogs to maximize the lean meat, which is missing the point. *Guanciale* should be flavored only with black or red pepper and be mostly fat. Trim off the rind and the outside of the skinless side (which has been rubbed with pepper) and cut as directed in the recipes, usually in small strips or dice. Pancetta is similarly cured pork belly. It comes rolled (*arrotolata*) or in slab form (*tesa*). It doesn't matter which you use. Pancetta is easier to find outside Italy than *guanciale* and is an acceptable substitute. Bacon, which is smoked, is not a good substitute for either.

Lardo is not lard but cured back fat. The English word "lard" is *strutto* in Italian. Because of the possible confusion, we have left *lardo* in Italian, but have translated *strutto* as "lard." *Lardo* is used as a cooking fat in some traditional recipes. It can be very delicate, and *lardo di Colonnata*, cured in marble caves near Carrara, in northern Tuscany, is a gourmet item, especially when sliced thin and draped elegantly over a piece of warm focaccia. Lard does not add an extra flavor to dishes, as extra virgin olive oil does, and is sometimes preferred for that reason.

Pork rinds (*cotenna* or *cotiche* in Italian) are used in many traditional sauces, usually in small amounts. They can be purchased fresh from specialty stores and Latin American markets. Before use, scrape them (there may be bristles), cut them into strips, and drop them into a small saucepan of boiling water for 2–3 minutes. Drain and set aside until you need them.

Prosciutto is the generic Italian word for ham. It means "dried out," which alludes to the curing process. The recipes in this book follow normal American usage: "prosciutto" corresponds to Italian *prosciutto crudo*, which is also what is sometimes called Parma ham, whether or not it actually comes from Parma. We use the English word "ham" for the rare occurrences of any other kind, that is, boiled or baked. While prosciutto for eating is usually sliced thin, for cooking it may be purchased in a single piece and then diced. Sometimes just the fat is called for. You can ask for some at the deli counter or cut it off the lean meat yourself, but if need be, you can use pancetta or *lardo*.

Anchovies

A SURPRISING number of people have never thought about how the anchovies (*acciughe* or *alici*) they buy in jars filled with oil were once real fish, swimming in the sea. The small fresh fish are common in Italian markets, where they are sold either whole or filleted. They can be cooked in numerous ways and are delicious on pasta (pages 161 and 163). They can also be marinated (sold as *boquerones*, the Spanish name, and often popularly called "white anchovies"), but those are not used on pasta. Or they can be preserved in salt. This can be done at home, but it is usually done professionally on a larger scale. These salted anchovies (not the fresh fish) can then be cleaned and packed in oil.

Salt-packed anchovies have been decapitated but not gutted or boned. To prepare them for use, slit the belly with a small knife, or even your fingernail, and remove the backbone and guts as you separate the fish into two fillets. The hairlike little bones are edible. Flick off the larger pieces of salt with your knife and rinse the fish in water or vinegar. Blot on paper towels and either use immediately or place in a small glass dish or jar and cover with olive oil for later use. They are delicious on bread or toast. The widely sold oil-packed anchovies are simply this done on an industrial scale. You can improve your store-bought anchovies by draining off the oil in which they are packed and replacing it with your own extra virgin olive oil. Keep them covered with oil and store in a dark cupboard. They keep for a long time. People who claim to hate anchovies have often tasted only poor-quality oil-packed

specimens on top of low-grade pizza; they would do well to try some good ones, such as those from the Cantabrian Sea off northern Spain. No, they are not Italian, but nobody's perfect.

"*Odori*" (Fresh Flavorings)

THE FIRST time I heard an Italian shopper ask a vegetable vendor for some "*odori*," I thought I was hallucinating. The word, which appears over and over in traditional recipes, literally means "smells," but that is so reductive. What the market people give their customers, free of charge, is a carrot, a celery rib, an onion, and a handful of parsley. These are also sold packaged together in the supermarket. Minced and sautéed until tender in olive oil or butter or a combination, or also pancetta, they are the basic ingredients of the *soffritto*, the basis of so many Italian sauces. Sometimes garlic and other herbs are added too.

Different parts of Italy favor different herbs, of course, and the time of year will also affect the choice. Oregano (*origano*) belongs to the South. Dill (*aneto*) is practically unknown outside the North. Marjoram (*maggiorana*), bay leaves (*alloro*), thyme (*timo*), and chives (*erba cipollina*) are found pretty much everywhere. Wherever there are fresh tomatoes, there is fresh basil (*basilico*). It's a must in tomato salads and quick-cooked sauces, but has to be added at the end because it loses its fragrance when cooked.

Sage (*salvia*) and rosemary (*rosmarino*) are ubiquitous partners of garlic with roast meats. Summer savory (*santoreggia*) together with rosemary and sage goes with furred game meat. Marinades for meat or fish usually contain a mix of herbs. In southern Italy, grated lemon or orange zest is often added to the herbs, a delicious idea that has begun to climb northward along the peninsula.

Naturally most herbs should be fresh, but dried oregano can be superb. The flavor of the South, oregano (*origano*) can be either fresh (and more subtly flavored) or dried (and stronger). Southern cooks can be quite opinionated about their oregano, with Puglian, Calabrian, and Sicilian factions. And the differences are there. Connoisseurs have no trouble distinguishing the oregano grown on the rugged Aspromonte of Calabria from that of the Monti Iblei of eastern Sicily. But they would all agree that you should immediately throw away those old jars from the supermarket. The best dried oregano is sold still on the stem. (Well wrapped, oregano like this will keep for quite some time.) Rub the leaves between your hands directly onto the food. The stems can also be used as miniskewers and as brushes for applying oil to food on the grill.

Mint, both spearmint and peppermint, turns up in pasta sauces (where the recipe usually specifies which is wanted), and can often make a refreshing change from basil or oregano with tomatoes. It is always used fresh.

Rosemary (*rosmarino*) bushes grow with great abandon in public and private places throughout Italy, and so the issue of fresh versus dried never comes up. Try to use fresh.

Don't even bother with dried sage or basil. But with a can of tomatoes and some fresh basil, you'll never be without a quick and delicious sauce for spaghetti. Bay leaves, which proliferate even in planters on Italian city streets, are used both fresh and dried.

The only parsley (*prezzemolo*) used in Italy is fresh, flavorful flat-leaf parsley. The curly-leafed kind isn't even on the radar. Try to keep a plant handy so as always to have a supply of perfectly fresh parsley. If you don't have a plant, snip the bottom of the stems and put the bunch of parsley in a glass of water, like cut flowers. It will keep for a few days in a cool place or the refrigerator. Don't underestimate the importance, or the flavor, of good parsley.

Tuna

BLUEFIN TUNA, *tonno rosso* (*Thunnus thynnus*), caught off Sicily or Sardinia by traditional methods, processed by hand, and packed in olive oil is one of the great traditional products of the Mediterranean, but it is hard to find and expensive, and its fishing in many parts of the world is controversial. Most good Italian tuna will be yellowfin (*pinna gialla*, *Thunnus albacares*). Italian tuna cans are color-coded. Red is for the familiar fillet; yellow for the prized tender belly meat called *ventresca* (try it straight from the can alongside boiled beans dressed with red onion, extra virgin olive oil, and red-wine vinegar); and green for the *tarantello*, the very lean, dark meat from near the backbone. For sauces, buy the red can. The depth of flavor of a tuna sauce depends on the quality of the tuna, so don't get any ideas about saving a few calories by using water-packed tuna from the supermarket.

Pepper and Chile

UNTIL A few decades ago, one of the many fissures of Italian society was along the pepper lines. Chile (*peperoncino*), which originated in the New World, used to be found in Italy only in the South, where it was considered the poor folks' substitute for black pepper (*pepe*), originally from Asia and known to the ancient Romans. Today both are used throughout Italy, usually in moderation and rarely together.

Chile is used to add a note of piquancy, but it should not, as in some of the world's other great cuisines, bring tears to the eyes. The fierier varieties of Mexico, Szechuan, and India are likely to be too strong in all but the smallest quantities. Try to find Spanish or Italian varieties. The specific variety is not important. The correct way to use chile is to put a length of pepper (with the seeds to make it hotter, without to make it milder) in the pan with the oil and to discard it when it colors. (The recipes give this instruction when called for.) It should never be allowed anywhere near burning. A piece of chile, dried or fresh, is usually partnered by a crushed garlic clove, which suffers the same fate. Hot red pepper flakes are rarely used in cooking and, because they burn easily and cannot be removed, are never heated directly in oil. Add them only when there is no chance they'll burn, as in uncooked sauces or after a dish is removed

from the heat. They can also be placed on the table in a little bowl from which chile addicts can help themselves. This is customary for *pasta e fagioli* (page 253).

Capers

CAPERS (*CAPPERI*), an essential flavoring in the cuisine of many parts of Italy, are the tightly closed flower buds of a small Mediterranean bush that takes root on cliff sides and even in old walls. The best ones come from the sea-swept, sun-drenched Aeolian Islands off Sicily, but also from Sardinia and other islands. Once picked, they are packed in coarse salt and kept there until use. Rinse salt-packed capers well, then soak in clean water for at least 15 minutes, but preferably 2 hours or more. Drain well and use as directed, either chopped or whole. Note that caper berries, sold in brine and consumed with cocktails, are the fruit, not the bud, and are absolutely *not* interchangeable with capers.

When vinegar-packed capers are called for, simply drain them without rinsing. To make your own vinegar-packed capers, rinse salt-packed capers as directed above and blot dry on paper towels. Then simply put them in a jar with a mild white vinegar. They will keep in the cupboard indefinitely.

Olives

IN MOST recipes calling for black olives, the Gaeta type, packed in brine, is best, or the small Ligurian taggiasche, which are highly prized and may be easier to find in gourmet emporia outside Italy. An expensive Ligurian olive would not be the first choice of a working mother in, say,

Campania, but, outside Italy, it would certainly be preferable to those awful little bullets you get on pizzas. For green olives, Barouni, Cerignola (also available black), and Frantoio are the Italian varieties to choose, but Spanish sevillana and hojiblanca or French Picholine are good too.

Lemons

THE RECIPES always call for organic lemons. Pesticides make the skin inedible and can even get inside the lemon and affect the juice. Grated lemon zest is an essential flavoring in many sauces.

Dried Porcini

DRIED *BOLETUS EDULIS* mushrooms are a kitchen workhorse, adding flavor and substance to a wide variety of sauces. Buy the most beautiful you can find. The smaller pieces are cheaper, but you'll also find a lot more grit in the package and fewer pieces that actually resemble mushrooms. Store the dried mushrooms in the freezer in an airtight container (to protect against bugs). To use them, soak for about 20 minutes in warm water. Rinse the mushrooms thoroughly, remove any tenacious grit with a small knife or your fingers, then squeeze them dry and chop them coarsely. French *cèpes* are interchangeable with porcini because they are the same thing.

Flour

ITALIAN *FARINA 00* (zero-zero) is a finely ground soft-wheat flour and is what is used for making *pasta all'uovo* at home. North American all-purpose flour is generally considered about the same thing. For flour-and-water pastas, use durum flour or, better yet, semolina. Semolina (*semolino* in Italian) is the same as durum flour but ground slightly coarser. The whole-wheat flour (and factory-made pastas), *farina integrale*, widely available on the market today contain fiber, yes, and some bran, but the germ of the wheat has usually been removed for more lucrative uses. Only artisanal (stone-ground) or high-end flours contain the germ. The taste of pasta made with whole-wheat flour will not normally be as good as that of a good durum semolina. Frankly, we'd rather take our penance as Hail Marys and get our fiber from legumes (try *pasta e fagioli*, page 253, or *sagne e lenticchie*, page 249). If you are determined, however, look at the recipe for *bigoli in salsa* (page 54) a traditional dish using whole-wheat pasta. All the pasta pairings we suggest can be replaced by equivalent whole-wheat pastas, but the ones that work best are the heartiest sauces, especially those containing meat.

Cheese

TWO FACTS about the relationship of cheese with pasta still have the power to surprise: (1) not all pasta dishes are finished with cheese, and (2) parmigiano-reggiano may be nine hundred years old and the greatest cheese on earth, but it was not widely used throughout Italy until the second half of the twentieth century.

Let us take the second point first. Parmigiano will enhance any pasta dish that takes cheese, but its strong presence and high quality have had the effect of shoving numerous other excellent local cheeses to the sidelines even though these are more appropriate, or at least more traditional, for local pasta dishes. That is a great pity. In many recipes, we list traditional alternatives to parmigiano. You may encounter these hard-to-find cheeses at high-end cheese emporia near home, online, or on your travels in Italy (vacuum-packed aged cheese can be brought into the United States). But if you accept the parmigiano alternative, have no fear. It is one of the world's greatest cheeses, and the dish will be delicious. By parmigiano we mean, of course, parmigiano-reggiano DOP, aged at least 24 months. Inexplicably the single word "reggiano" has been afoot for some years in America to signify this cheese, but it is not the terminology used in Italy. Parmigiano means parmigiano-reggiano, but note the spelling. Variant numbers of g's and r's are sometimes used to slip an imitation past the unwary ("What do you mean counterfeit? Our cheese has a completely different name, 'parmiggiano'!"). The English term "Parmesan" is ambiguous. Under the jurisdiction of the European Commission, it is the translation of parmigiano-reggiano DOP, but in the United States it is legal for a wide variety of imitators, emulators, and even frauds. Look for the Italian name branded on the rind to be sure.

Now let's look at pecorino. All pecorino cheese is made from sheep's milk (parmigiano is made from cow's milk): *pecora* means sheep. But not all *pecorini* are the same. The best known is pecorino romano DOP, which is made in the regions of Lazio and Sardegna (Sardinia) and the province of Grosseto, in southern Toscana (Tuscany). It is sharper, saltier, and less mellow than parmigiano-reggiano and is used younger—five months for eating (as with sweet raw fava beans in early spring), eight for grating. There is also a *pecorino sardo* DOP, not to be confused with the pecorino romano produced in Sardinia. In fact, the South and islands of Italy produce hundreds of kinds of pecorino, and an extremely interesting and delicious itinerary could be constructed around the tasting of these delicious cheeses. They vary in fat content from almost soft to rather dry and in flavor from quite mild to quite sharp, with subtle differences deriving from the particular grasses the sheep ate. Others are made in the Marche, Emilia-Romagna, and Tuscany. *Pecorino campano*, from Campania, is milder than pecorino romano. More and more are finding their way to gourmet shops outside Italy and are well worth tasting.

Today pecorino romano for the pastas that originated in the Apennines of Lazio and Abruzzo is considered traditional, but an Abruzzese or Calabrian or Sicilian pecorino, less well known and established nationally, would be good too.

Grate with a normal old-style grater, with star-shaped holes, not the kind with little rectangles. Grate cheese as late in your preparations as possible, and stick pretty close to the quantities given in the recipes. Mix the cheese with the pasta *before* adding the sauce. To keep her guests from ruining her carefully calibrated dishes, Oretta adds the cheese in the kitchen and rarely passes more at the table. The cheese should not cover the taste of the other ingredients. It will take over the whole show if you let it.

As should be clear, tradition chooses the cheese, and tradition is not black and white. *Pasta all'amatriciana* has an entire town defending its use of pecorino—no one would dare use parmigiano!—but the orphan *carbonara* has evolved to include some parmigiano with the pecorino. That's how it goes.

Factory-Made Pasta

People often ask us if we make our own pasta, as though expecting us to say we would have nothing to do with store-bought. That, however, is not the right approach. Factory-made pasta, well made from the best durum wheat and cooked *al dente*, is a fragrant, nutty, chewy thing of beauty. The production methods—the machines and dies for extrusion, the controlled drying—are unlikely to be reproducible at home; the shapes too—from *spaghettini* to *ruote*, wagon wheels—are best left to industry. Tender egg noodles, made at home by hand or hand-operated machinery, are a different thing. Fortunately we don't have to choose which we like better.

While some sauces are better with fresh pasta, some are meant to be served with dried—but not just any old supermarket spaghetti, of course. Today, generally all the pastas on the market meet certain minimum standards and are of reasonably good quality. Still, there are differences. Price is the first. The most expensive is not necessarily the best, but the least expensive is probably the worst.

Think of the variables. Read the label on the spaghetti package. If the ingredients include anything besides durum wheat (possibly listed as flour, *farina*, *semolino*, or semolina of durum wheat, or *grano duro*) and water, put down the package and try another. Some pasta makers grow their own wheat in Italy and experiment with traditional, near-extinct varieties. Others carefully select wheat grown elsewhere. Still others buy up the wheat that nobody else wanted. Which do you want for dinner?

The other ingredient, water, may also affect the taste of the pasta. Some manufacturers boast about the quality of their water, which flows from mountain springs straight into their machines, and they are probably right.

Then take production methods. Very little is actually involved in the making of our spaghetti. Flour and water are mixed and extruded through interchangeable dies that give the pasta its shape. The material of the die affects the surface of the pasta. The smoother the die, the smoother the pasta. We don't want smooth spaghetti. The rougher the surface, the better. The roughness indicates that the pasta has a greater surface area. Bronze dies are considered the best and are usually mentioned on the labels of pastas made with them. The nice salted water in which the pasta is boiled passes through our spaghetti for more flavor and more even cooking. The sauce will not only stick to the pasta; it will be absorbed into the strands. Have you ever come to the bottom of a bowl of pasta only to find a watery residue? That was probably due less to insufficient draining than to the cheapness of the pasta.

Finally the pasta must be dried. Big industry uses big drying, hot and fast. It has to or it could never produce the quantities it does, but this has the effect of pre-cooking the pasta. Small, quasi-artisanal producers use a lower temperature and take longer to dry. This means longer cooking times too, and the pasta will taste better. The subtle but very real flavor of the wheat will come out.

The cooking times indicated on the package have improved greatly from the days when they seemed to have been pulled out of a hat. To be on the safe side, set your timer for a minute sooner than the minimum on the package, and check. In any case, it's not a good idea to leave boiling pasta unattended for too long. It needs to be stirred, and as you stir, you will get a feel for how far along it is and when to turn off the heat.

EQUIPMENT

Traditional Italian kitchens, and many state-of-the-art ones, have certain pieces of equipment and utensils worth taking a look at.

Once upon a time, and not so long ago, the few utensils used were made of a neutral wood, such as beech or maple, that is, a wood that does not impart a scent or flavor to the food (as, say, pine might). The rural people knew nothing of chemistry, but they had identified certain woods as best for their spoons, forks, rolling pins, cutting boards, work surfaces, and whatever else they needed. The food-safety experts of Hazard Analysis & Critical Control Points (HACCP) issue guidelines that try to frighten us into replacing wood with some sort of sanitary plastic, but Italian cooks, especially in the countryside, are having none of it.

The board, called *spianatoia*, can be any large, stable surface of neutral wood. Those who do not have a sturdy wooden table or counter can buy a *spianatoia* to use as needed. This is a simple board, at least 16 by 31 inches (40 by 80 centimeters), with a raised border on one side that goes over the edge of a table to keep the board steady during strenuous kneading and rolling. The wood imparts a desirable texture to the dough, and, says Oretta, nothing else will do.

The truly traditional Bolognese rolling pin, *mattarello*, looks like nothing else on earth—perhaps a bat for a long-forgotten form of stickball. It has one tapered end to assist the obsessive Bolognese pasta maker in maintaining a perfect circle. It should be as long as you can manage, and Oretta's is about 39 inches (1 meter). My simple specimen, of which Oretta approves, is a dowel, about 2 inches (5 centimeters) in diameter and only about 26 inches (65 centimeters) long, no handles, no fancy tips, just smoothly rounded at both ends. The important thing is, of course, that the rolling pin has to be longer than the maximum diameter of your circle of dough, which will be the ultimate length of your *tagliatelle*. Naturally, the rolling pin must also be made of a neutral wood. Both board and pin should be wiped with a damp cloth and stored in a cloth bag.

If you have unlimited storage space for kitchen gadgets, you can buy those cute wooden drying racks. Otherwise you don't need them. When the time comes, have a supply of clean kitchen towels or trays ready and a space to lay them out.

For cutting, you'll need at least a straight and a scalloped wheeled pastry cutter (or one double-duty two-wheeler) and, for handmade *tagliatelle*, a large, very sharp, nonserrated knife. Oretta's makes me think of a machete, but I exaggerate.

Oretta has no objection to starting the dough in a food processor as long as you knead it by hand for several minutes on a wooden board after the machine stage. She will allow the use of a rolling and cutting machine, even though, with the metal rollers, you lose that nice roughness you get from the wood. You can add a motor to the machine and save a good deal of time and labor over hand-cranking.

You do not need one of those ravioli trays. All the stuffed pastas in this book are filled by much simpler methods.

For draining pasta, certainly a colander is important, but you also need a skimmer, spider strainer, or large slotted spoon for gnocchi and the ravioli family. Tongs are useful for fishing lasagne and other large sheets of pasta out of boiling water.

My collection of American measuring spoons and cups are a source of hilarity or fascination to Italian visitors to my Roman kitchen, who seem to regard the need for them as a sign of weakness. If you want to take the Italian approach, you will quickly learn to measure your volumes by eye or feel. But you must have a small kitchen scale for measuring flour, cheese, vegetables, *guanciale*, and everything else whose measurable volume can vary with size of piece, fineness of grind, and other factors. The scale is also essential for portioning pasta before cooking. It is very easy to get used to the scale, and more and more Americans are doing so.

You'll need a large wooden fork and spoon for stirring the pasta as it boils and, of course, for stirring sauces and soups.

The sauce recipes in this book are calculated to dress a pound of pasta, and to boil that amount of pasta, you'll need an 8-quart (8-liter) pot, preferably with a lid. If you don't use enough water, the pasta will suffer claustrophobia and probably stick together. The kind of pot with a built-in colander, mentioned above, is very handy.

The recipes sometimes call for a terracotta pot or pan for sauces or soups. These are very common and inexpensive in Italy and come in every conceivable size and shape, from a skillet-like flat pan to something that could pass for a soup tureen. They can be used on a gas flame or on an electric burner with a flame diffuser and have the advantage of cooking slowly and evenly. Imported terracotta cookware, usually from France and Italy, is available at many high-end kitchen shops and online (page 392). Despite the disadvantages (it's heavy; it breaks if you drop it), there is nothing like terracotta for slow, even cooking.

THE RECIPES

IT IS FASHIONABLE to say there is no such thing as Italian cooking—there is only Tuscan, Sicilian, Emilian, and so forth—but that is misguided. For all the unquestionable differences, for all the variations and local specialties, much unites Italian home cooks from the Alps to the islands. Modern communications and travel, to say nothing of the growing serious interest in traditional foods, are making more and more Italians aware of what the rest of the country eats. People buy national brands in chain supermarkets and shops. Television cooking shows are broadcast everywhere, and newsstands are full of glossy food magazines. Logistics has made it possible to supply inland Milan with the finest fish and for seaside Naples to make sauces with hare and boar meat. Thanks to the Slow Food Association, endangered food products from all over Italy have become of national interest. And everywhere in Italy, people are eating pasta, even where there is a stronger tradition of rice or polenta.

The boundaries of the twenty Italian regions are largely political. Italian food scholars no longer speak of regional cuisines but of broad areas that may approximate the political boundaries but are not interchangeable with them. For example, the province of Mantova (Mantua), in eastern Lombardia, Milan's region, enjoys squash-filled ravioli (page 307) and other dishes we think of as typical of Emilia-Romagna, which it borders. Southern Lazio, Rome's region, has more in common with Campania (where Naples is capital) than with its own north, whose *strozzapreti* (page 344) would be at home in Umbria

or Tuscany. For that matter, parts of Tuscany could, gastronomically speaking, be in Liguria.

Perhaps only the island regions, Sicily and Sardinia, can claim a strictly regional cuisine, and even they have internal gastronomic divisions. *Busiata* with *pesto alla trapanese* (page 119) is served in western Sicily, while spaghetti *alla norma* (page 130) is the pride of Catania, in the east. Sardinia has distinct inland and coastal cuisines, of which the land-based is by far more traditional (but don't miss *fregula con le arselle*, page 273). One of the lessons of *Encyclopedia of Pasta* is that the gastro-geographical divisions of Italy can come in all sizes, from, say, the entire south of the country to a single town or valley, and for once, forget the politics.

However we draw the map, age-old dishes are closely guarded and made with the local products (known as an area's "*prodotti tipici*," typical products, a concept much talked about at farmers' markets). Our recipes here come from a wide range of local traditions, and if some of the recipes have spread throughout Italy, that just means generations of Italians have enjoyed eating them.

We have generally not included recipes that really can't be made outside their place of origin. In the interest of authenticity—which we might define as fidelity to the version handed down by tradition as original or best (not always the same)—we have not encouraged substitutions, as are common in American recipes. Nevertheless, we do want people to cook from this book, not just read it, and where it's possible to follow the method using your own local ingredients—shellfish, cheeses, mushrooms, sausages, herbs—give it a try. The dish will undoubtedly be delicious just the same.

REMEMBER THAT these are home recipes. People used what they had. Don't take the quantities given too literally. If you have extra fish or *guanciale*, toss it in. If you're short half a cup of tomatoes, make the recipe anyway. If you have oregano but no basil, in most cases that will be fine. This point bears pounding a bit. This is not a codified cuisine. Italian cooks express themselves freely and change their minds often and do not know the meaning of the word routine. All right, sometimes they do. I was greatly amused when Oretta told of a visit from a young Bolognese cousin. What would he like to eat during his stay in Rome, she asked him. "Anything but *ragù*!" was his plaintive reply. At home, *tagliatelle* sauced with *ragù bolognese*, a rare treat anywhere else, was, for him, the daily dose. We will encounter the Bolognese mania for codifying when we get to *ragù* (page 207) and *tagliatelle* (page 328). But the usual practice is to vary often, measure by eye, improvise with what's in the larder or garden, and simply do without whatever is missing. Ingredients are handled in many ways, one as good as the next. If you want to chop your onion coarsely instead of finely, go ahead. If you'd rather slice, slice. Peel the eggplant or not. It really doesn't matter. And if some of our recipes seem to give less excruciating detail than what you're used to, it's because we have faith that anyone who wants to cook pasta the Italian way will very quickly get the feel of when the garlic has sautéed long enough, when the sauce is thick enough, and what will go with what.

But suppress any thoughts that begin with

"Gee, I could add . . ." One of the unifying characteristics of the recipes is the concentration of a few flavors. Rarely will your guests scratch their heads wondering what's in the dish. If you use good ingredients and not too many of them, people will taste exactly what is there. This also happens to be the main difference between Italian food cooked in Italy and Italian food cooked, even by very good cooks, outside Italy. Americans, generally speaking, seek strong flavors and love to add ingredients. If a little garlic is good, more is better—or so many people think. Italians, on the other hand, appreciate subtle tastes. They want to taste everything and know that too many different tastes, or too much of one overpowering flavor, make that impossible. I confess I had to learn the Italian way, but now I'm convinced. And don't forget: you want to taste the pasta as well as the sauce.

Quantities of salt are usually not given because Italian cooks cannot bring themselves to prescribe something they see as depending on too many variables, from how the tomatoes were packed (or even where they were grown) to your spouse's blood pressure. Be sure to taste and be sure to use enough. You'll know it's enough because the flavors will pop out. You shouldn't be aware of the salty taste per se so much as have a heightened awareness of all the other tastes. Keep in mind that salt gets into your sauce from the pasta itself (which gets it from the salted cooking water), pasta water you add directly to the sauce, anchovies, capers, and most cheeses. Salt added directly to the sauce or, worse, at the table to the individual dish, is the least effective.

MANY SAUCES can be made in the time it takes to boil the water and cook the pasta, or much less. A minority, mainly meat sauces, need an hour or more of cooking; these are usually even more delicious the day after they are made. Other *condimenti* are made quickly, but only after some prepping, which can range from ten minutes or less of chopping *guanciale*, onions, or fresh herbs to the tedious trimming and slicing of artichokes. We have tried to address the logistics, adding make-ahead notes so you'll know which sauces have to be done at the last minute, which you can get a head start on earlier in the day, which you should hold till the next day, and which you can freeze. Once you've added the pasta to a soup, the clock starts ticking. The pasta should be added as close to serving time as possible, preferably at the last minute.

EACH SAUCE recipe, except where noted, is calibrated to dress one standard pound package of store-bought pasta or one recipe of fresh pasta in this book. That package may be 450 grams or a full half kilo, 500 grams, or 1.1 pounds. Those 50 grams make absolutely no difference. The soups are calculated to provide about the same amount of food, usually with half the amount of pasta. A pound of pasta works out to about six portions for a *primo piatto* and four to six for a *piatto unico*, a one-dish meal. The soup recipes give about six generous bowls. Of course, even with a *piatto unico*, you'll probably have an antipasto course and follow the pasta with one or more vegetables or salads, so it really always depends on how much else you're serving.

You may sometimes think that the recipe is insufficient to cover that much pasta, but just mix them thoroughly and, where we suggest it, add a finishing swirl of extra virgin olive oil.

In Italy, the pasta is the main attraction, not an excuse to eat sauce. The *condimento* should never drown the pasta.

WHERE A recipe does not list a cheese, no cheese is to be used with that dish. Not an option. Many cheese suggestions include an ideal cheese (hard or impossible to find) and a realistic one (easy to find in North America), though often the two coincide in the form of parmigiano-reggiano or pecorino romano, excellent cheeses widely used in Italy and obtainable abroad. Suggestions for finding cheeses that are merely difficult, not impossible, are given on page 391.

EACH RECIPE is followed by a wine suggestion, and that needs some explanation. We have not invited a great deal of personal preference in this book because our objective is to relate how most Italians handle these dishes. But when it comes to wine, although there are objective, even scientific criteria for pairing, people like what they like and if you like a wine and like a food, you're likely to like them together.

These dishes are largely traditional and are usually made in homes or locally oriented trattorias and restaurants. For that reason, other things being equal, we have preferred to suggest local or regional wines even though expert analysis of the ingredients might indicate a wine from some distant place. We have also tried to choose wines available in North America, a criterion that excludes some interesting wines. That said, very often with regional cooking in wine-producing countries, the recipes have been created to go with a specific style of wine or particular grape. Where possible, those are the wines we chose. A good example of this would be Aglianico del Vulture rosé with spicy sauces of Calabria or Basilicata.

The old rules used to be that you always paired red wine with heavier foods and red meats and white wines with lighter foods and seafood, but for many of the recipes in this book either color would do fine, especially considering all the experimentation and rule-bending going on in Italian wine making today. And don't turn your nose up at rosé (*rosato*) for fear it will be too fruity or sweet. Some very good rosés are being made in southern Italy, offering the perfect compromise for many of these dishes, especially where a red might be too harsh, but not only.

Sometimes a good pairing is based less on science or tradition than on intuition. Our friend Michelle Farkas, who helped us choose the wines, read the recipe for *Sugo con le cozze* (page 175) and knew she wanted bubbles with it. She cooked the dish, served it with Prosecco, and stands by her choice, which we give here.

The most important criterion to remember is that wine needs to complement, not compete with, a dish. With a particularly rich dish, a wine with some acidity cuts through the fat. With a salty dish, sparkling wine always works. But so would something more middle-of-the-road as regards tannins and fruit. For example, Greco di Tufo, a Campanian white, is proposed with a pasta sauce whose main components are capers, olives, and anchovies (page 64). Spicy dishes work best with aromatic whites and rosés to complement, or tone down, the piquancy. Light dishes generally tend to do better with light, fresh wines, and an example of that would be using Sauvignon Blanc with the zucchini and shrimp sauce (page 183). Earthy dishes need

earthy wines, period. A classic pairing example would be truffles and Nebbiolo, and, as it happens the grapes and truffles both come from the same part of Piedmont. Herbaceous dishes tend to lend themselves better to wines with aromatic qualities, such as those from Liguria and Alto Adige.

Italian wines are one of the great bargains of the universe, and the ones worth knowing do not all begin with B (though we recommend some of them too). Get to know your local wine merchant. When Oretta plans a dinner party, she marches in to her wine shop menu in hand to seek expert advice (that is, even more expert).

IF YOU remember nothing else as you cook these recipes, please remember this. They come from generations of Italian families, not a laboratory, and the Italian way is to be quick to improvise when necessary and never to be literal-minded. Take the recipes as being told to you by Italian friends over coffee, not by someone in a white coat, or even a toque. Each friend has a different opinion on the details, but they agree on what the dish should taste like. What this means for you is that you will eventually make them your own—not by adding ingredients but by honing your technique, whether for something difficult or laborious, such as artichokes or tortellini, or for simply knowing how long the sauce takes on your stove in your favorite pan.

Now, pour yourself a glass of crisp Friulian white (or a sunny Sicilian, for that matter) and decide what to make for dinner. All those generations of Italian women are standing behind you to encourage you. Just don't overcook the pasta.

SAUCES

Last-Minute Sauces

All the sauces in this section can be made with ingredients you probably already have in your kitchen—no extra shopping needed if you've stocked your larder with a few good Italian staples. They're perfect for when you return from a trip or have last-minute guests or even when you just want something tasty all by yourself. As a bonus, most of them can be started after you put the pot on to boil.

FISH AND MEAT

Sugo con la bottarga di tonno o muggine

(Dried tuna or gray-mullet roe)

THE POSSIBILITY of having spaghetti *con la bottarga* every day is an excellent reason to take a vacation in Sardinia. Bottarga is the dried and pressed roe of the tuna (*tonno*) or gray mullet (*muggine*). It is used from Provence to Tunisia, but the best is the *bottarga di muggine* from Sardinia, a luxury artisanal product par excellence. Whole bottarga, a lovely amber color, is roughly tongue-shaped and encased in a thin, papery skin, which needs to be peeled away. It used to be encased in wax, but vacuum packaging has made that unnecessary.

If you have a whole bottarga, slice it very thin and use the slices immediately. It has a sort of soapy consistency. The rest will keep for months wrapped in foil. If it dries out, grate it instead of slicing. Bottarga is also sold already grated, in jars, which is very convenient for use on pasta. The color is a deep gold, and it's a bit drier than freshly grated, but works perfectly well and actually blends better with the oil and pasta. It too will keep for months in the refrigerator. Bottarga used to be served as an hors d'oeuvre marinated in olive oil and lemon juice, but today the favored use is on pasta, though creative cooks are always finding new places to put it, such as salads, especially those containing some seafood.

The flavorful oil and pasta provide a comforting, filling base for the super-sophisticated taste of the bottarga, which is like nothing so much as the sea itself. If you use sliced bottarga instead of grated, you'll also have a contrasting texture to bite.

PASTA SHAPES This *condimento* goes with flour-and-water pasta, either long or short, but if you go to Sardinia, you'll almost always find it served on spaghetti or *spaghettini*. Still, feel free to use *linguine/bavette/trenette*, *bucatini*, *vermicelli*, *sedani*, *penne*, or *ruote*—all factory-made shapes—or, for homemade, *lagane* (page 334), *fregnacce* (page 337), *cavatelli* (page 345), *maltagliati* (page 336), or *strascinati* (page 348).

bottarga

For the *condimento*:

6 tablespoons extra virgin olive oil, preferably medium fruity
1 heaping tablespoon very finely minced fresh flat-leaf parsley
salt

To make the dish:

1 pound (450 grams) pasta (see suggestions above)
freshly ground black pepper
7 ounces (200 grams) whole bottarga, peeled and sliced very thin, or 5 ounces (150 grams) grated bottarga in a jar

Put the oil, parsley, and a pinch of salt in a serving bowl and let the flavors blend in a warm place for about 30 minutes.

Bring 5 quarts (5 liters) of water to a boil in an 8-quart (8-liter) pot over high heat. Add 3 tablespoons kosher salt, then add the pasta and cook, stirring occasionally, until *al dente*.

Warm the serving bowl or platter in a low oven. If the oven is not practical, warm the bowl just before use with hot water, even a ladleful of the pasta cooking water.

Drain the pasta and transfer it to the serving bowl. Grind on a little pepper, and mix well. If using grated bottarga, scatter it over the pasta and mix well. If using thin slices, spread the bottarga on top of the pasta but do not mix. The pasta should make its appearance completely covered. Serve immediately and mix it at the table.

WINE SUGGESTION: Argiolas Costamolino Vermentino DOC, from Sardinia

---

Salsa di acciughe

(Salt-packed anchovies)

THIS QUICK AND EASY sauce is very popular throughout Italy, but especially in Liguria, where it originated and where it is still common to cure anchovies in salt at home. Oretta learned this useful skill from an old woman on the beach in Pegli, near Genoa, who would sit at the water's edge cleaning fresh anchovies, tossing the heads and guts to the seagulls waiting patiently at a discreet distance.

The ideal anchovies to use are the nice fat ones found in the Mediterranean in June and July. Cleaning them and then layering them with coarse salt is really pretty simple, but all over Italy they can be purchased by the piece from large cans as needed. Outside Italy, you can buy cans of different sizes and store them in the refrigerator for months till needed. These can be ordered from many sources on the Internet (see page 389 for some examples). Before use, flick off the salt, fillet the little fish, rinse, and pat dry. Details of this process are given on page 34. Yes, oil-packed anchovies—the ones you buy cleaned and ready to use—will do, but the fresher, more intense flavor of the salted ones is well worth the extra step, especially where, as in this recipe, the anchovies are practically the whole show.

This is one of those blessed sauces you can start making after you've put the water on and whose ingredients you almost always have handy. It's so good that no one need ever know it was a last-minute emergency measure. Yes, there will always be guests who refuse to touch anchovies, but if you can persuade them to take just a bite, they may find that your beautiful salt-packed specimens, carefully rinsed so as not to be excessively salty, remind them more of a dip in the ocean than of cheap pizza. If you've managed to find a really fruity extra virgin olive oil, it will provide a wonderful vehicle for the highly assertive anchovies and the contrast of the parsley.

 PASTA SHAPES The sauce's natural partner is freshly made flour-and-water pasta, such as *gnocchetti* (page 342), *orecchiette* (page 349), *strozzapreti/pici* (page 344), *cordelle sabine* (page 364), *cecamariti* (page 361), or *cavatelli* (page 345), but it's also good on any number of factory-made shapes, such as spaghetti, *linguine/bavette/trenette*, *bucatini*, *paccheri*, *penne*, *sedani*, and *vermicelli*. It's also delicious on *agnolotti con i carciofi* (page 300). Don't make the mistake I once did, however, and use it on *spaghettini* (I had an oversupply I was eager to use up). The long, thin shape had too much surface area—the engineers at the table explained—and absorbed too much sauce.

For the *condimento*:

6 tablespoons extra virgin olive oil, preferably intensely fruity

1 large clove garlic, crushed

1 piece dried chile, as large as you like

4–6 salt-packed anchovies, about 2 ounces (60 grams), cleaned as described on page 34, or about 15 oil-packed anchovy fillets, drained, blotted dry, and coarsely chopped

To make the dish:

1 pound (450 grams) pasta (see suggestions above)

1 heaping tablespoon minced fresh flat-leaf parsley

extra virgin olive oil for finishing

Put 5 quarts (5 liters) of water on to boil in an 8-quart (8-liter) pot over high heat, then start the sauce.

In a large skillet, heat the oil on medium low and add the garlic and chile. When the garlic is golden, about 3 minutes, remove and discard it and the chile (don't worry about stray seeds that stay in the pan). Add the chopped anchovies to the flavored oil. Lower the heat and let the anchovies disintegrate while you help them along by mashing with a fork. Turn off the heat and cover the pan until the pasta is ready.

When the water boils, add 3 tablespoons kosher salt, then the pasta, and cook, stirring occasionally, until *al dente*. Drain the pasta and transfer it to the skillet. Sprinkle with the parsley, take the skillet off the heat, and blend the pasta and sauce with two wooden spoons for at most 30 seconds.

Warm a serving bowl or platter in a low oven. If the oven is not practical, warm the bowl just before use with hot water, even a ladleful of the pasta cooking water. Transfer to the heated serving bowl, add a swirl of oil, and serve.

 WINE SUGGESTION: Vermentino di Gallura DOCG, from Sardinia

Bigoli in salsa

(Whole-wheat spaghetti with anchovies and onions)

SO CLOSELY ARE sauce and shape associated that it would be cruel to attempt to separate them here.

When people think of Venetian food, this pasta may well be the dish that first comes to mind, an economical sauce made only of onions, oil, and salt-cured fish (today anchovies, but at one time sardines were more commonly used). The flavor is salty, but not overly as it is tempered by the considerable sweetness of the onions. Both onions and anchovies dissolve completely to make a smooth sauce, almost the same color as the whole-wheat spaghetti with which it is customarily served.

Bigoli today are essentially whole-wheat spaghetti and factory made, but for purists they are hand extruded through a machine called a *torchio* and sometimes contain eggs, often duck. They are also good with duck sauces, such as that on page 203, or giblets, such as the sauce on page 198.

 PASTA SHAPES The sauce is married for life to Venetian *bigoli*, but factory-made whole-wheat spaghetti are what you'll usually find, even in Venice. *Bigoli* are so closely identified with this sauce that it's almost impossible to suggest any other pasta to go with it, and yet any other robust, long shape, such as *tonnarelli* (page 334) or *spaghettoni* would certainly be suitable.

For the *condimento*:

½ cup (120 milliliters) lightly fruity extra virgin olive oil
6 ounces (150 grams) white onions, finely chopped
10 ounces (300 grams) salt-packed anchovies (or sardines) prepared as directed on page 34
freshly ground black pepper

To make the dish:

1 pound (450 grams) whole-wheat spaghetti (or see suggestions above)

Put the oil in a saucepan over low heat, add the onions, and cover. Cook slowly until the onions have completely disintegrated, about 20 minutes, stirring occasionally. While they are cooking, you can add a few tablespoons of warm water if the pan begins to look dry. The onions should not color at all.

Stir in the anchovies and cook over very low heat, stirring, until everything has completely disintegrated into a delicious mush, 10–15 minutes. Grind on a little pepper and taste for salt. With all those anchovies, it is unlikely you will want to add any.

Bring 5 quarts (5 liters) of water to a boil in an 8-quart (8-liter) pot over high heat. Add 3 tablespoons kosher salt, then add the pasta and cook, stirring occasionally, until *al dente*.

Warm a serving bowl or platter in a low oven. If the oven is not practical, warm the bowl just before use with hot water, even a ladleful of the pasta cooking water.

Drain and transfer the pasta to the heated serving bowl. Add the sauce and mix well. Serve immediately.

 WINE SUGGESTION: One of the many lovable things about Venice is the carafes of Prosecco, the local white, served in trattorias. But a light red, such as a merlot from the Veneto, might be a better match.

Pasta "ammuddicata"

(Anchovies and breadcrumbs)

THE NAME IN proper Italian would be *pasta con la mollica*, pasta with soft breadcrumbs. *Mollica* is the crumb of the loaf, what's left after you cut off the crusts, though like much terminology it tends to be used loosely and not everybody thinks it's necessary to cut off the crust. Also, the same word is used for both the whole crustless loaf and the crumbs made from it. The crumbs are made from day-old bread, not rock-hard (which would make *pan grattato*, or "grated bread," meaning dry breadcrumbs). Still pliable, day-old bread can be crumbled with the hands or in the food processor. *Mollica* turns up in many places throughout the meal. For example, *mollica* can be added to meatballs to make them soft. Our friend Angelica Mallamo, from Calabria, makes the most delicious *involtini*, rolls of beef filled with *mollica* and provolone.

This recipe is used throughout the South—Puglia, Basilicata, Calabria, and Sicily. Although its origins lie in poverty—nothing edible was ever thrown away—it survives because those crunchy little fried crumbs taste so good. This isn't one of those sauces where the anchovies fade discreetly into the background. With only stale bread and black pepper for company, they are right out there, so it's well worth it to take the trouble with the salt-packed version.

 PASTA SHAPES Spaghetti is the traditional pasta choice, but any long flour-and-water pasta, such as *linguine/bavette/trenette*, would do.

For the *condimento*:

¾ cup (180 milliliters) extra virgin olive oil
4 salt-packed anchovies, prepared as directed on
     page 34 and coarsely chopped
About 2 cups (100 grams) crumbs made from
     day-old country-style bread

To make the dish:

1 pound (450 grams) spaghetti
2 heaping tablespoons minced fresh flat-leaf
     parsley, about 16 sprigs
1 level tablespoon ground black pepper

Put 5 quarts (5 liters) of water on to boil in an 8-quart (8-liter) pot over high heat.

Heat the oil in a skillet over medium-low heat for a minute and then add the anchovies. Mash them gently with a fork until they disintegrate, about 2 minutes. Add the breadcrumbs.

Raise the heat to medium high and fry the breadcrumbs, stirring, for about 3 minutes, or until they turn golden brown. Remove from the heat, cover, and keep warm.

When the water boils, add 3 tablespoons kosher salt, then add the pasta and cook, stirring occasionally, until *al dente*.

Warm a serving bowl or platter in a low oven. If the oven is not practical, warm the bowl just before use with hot water, even a ladleful of the pasta cooking water.

Drain the pasta and transfer it to the warm serving bowl. Add the anchovies and breadcrumbs and toss well. Sprinkle with the parsley and the pepper. Serve immediately.

 WINE SUGGESTION: a white blend from Southern Italy with a touch of acidity, such as Planeta La Segreta, from Sicily, or a light red from Sicily

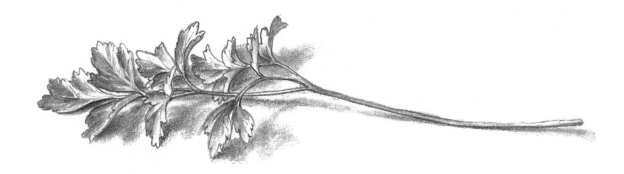

Sugo con il tonno e il pomodoro

(Canned tuna and tomato)

A PASTA WITH this spicy tuna and tomato sauce is Italian comfort food—so nutritious, delicious, and easy to make that you might hesitate to serve it to guests. It's extremely popular in Italian households, to the extent that given the choice between this and truffles, most people would probably prefer the tuna. But, while you can certainly make it with the first cans you find at the supermarket, if you use superior Italian tomatoes, which will be sweet, and imported canned *tonno di tonnara*, tuna caught and processed by traditional methods in the waters off Calabria, Sicily, or Sardinia, the dish acquires depth and interest, and you need apologize to no one. That it can be made in about the time it takes to boil the water and cook the pasta is merely a plus.

Make it as piquant or as mild as you like, but let us hear no talk of (tasteless) water-packed tuna. It's a nice, saucy tomato sauce in which you want that good tuna taste to emerge.

 PASTA SHAPES This sauce is traditionally paired with long, thin industrial pasta shapes, such as spaghetti, *spaghettini*, or *linguine/bavette/trenette*.

For the *condimento*:

6 tablespoons very fruity extra virgin olive oil
1 medium white or yellow onion, finely chopped
1 clove garlic, crushed
2 salt-packed anchovies, cleaned and rinsed (page 34), or 4 oil-packed fillets, drained, blotted dry, and coarsely chopped
1 pound (450 grams) canned Italian peeled tomatoes with their liquid

1 small piece dried chile
2 7-ounce (200-gram) cans best-quality Italian oil-packed tuna, drained

To make the dish:

1 pound (450 grams) pasta (see suggestions above)
extra virgin olive oil for finishing
1 tablespoon minced fresh flat-leaf parsley

Put the oil, chopped onion, and garlic in a skillet and sauté gently over medium-low heat until the onion is transparent, about 5 minutes. Discard the garlic when it begins to color. Add the chopped anchovies and continue cooking for another 2 minutes. Use a fork to help the anchovies disintegrate.

Add the tomatoes and chile. Lower the heat and simmer the sauce for about 20 minutes, or until it is visibly reduced and the oil comes to the surface. Remove the pan from the heat. Discard the chile.

Put 5 quarts (5 liters) of water on to boil in an 8-quart (8-liter) pot over high heat. When the water boils, add 3 tablespoons kosher salt, then add the pasta and cook, stirring occasionally, until *al dente*.

Warm a serving bowl or platter in a low oven. If the oven is not practical, warm the bowl just before use with hot water, even a ladleful of the pasta cooking water.

While the pasta is cooking, finish the sauce. Break the tuna up with a fork and add it to the pan. Taste for salt and add sparingly if needed (between the anchovies and the tuna, you may not need any at all). Simmer the sauce over medium heat for 5–6 minutes.

Drain the pasta and transfer to a heated serving bowl. Add the sauce and a swirl of oil and mix well. Sprinkle with the chopped parsley and serve immediately.

 WINE SUGGESTION: a young Sangiovese or other light, fruity red

---

canned tuna and fresh tomato

Sugo con tonno alla liparese

(Canned tuna with olives and capers)

THE AEOLIAN, or Lipari, Islands are an archipelago off northeastern Sicily known for containing an active and a dormant volcano (Stromboli and Vulcano). In early September, the sea around the little islands is an emerald sheet. A single glance takes in small vineyards among the rocks and caper bushes, both gripping cliff sides and in plantations on the islands' limited flat land. The capers, which are the flower buds, are picked and stored, mixed with coarse salt, in enormous clay jars. There the capers' flavor develops until they are ready to be shipped to gourmet emporia through-

out Italy and, increasingly, the world, while on the islands they're used nearly fresh and full of fragrance.

This dish is the pride of the islands' cuisine because it uses their two principal products, tuna and capers. It's also the quintessential last-minute sauce and will amaze your guests with its decisive flavors—tuna, capers, and olives, with a background of fragrant oil, garlic, and pepper. With no tomatoes, it's the oil that serves as sauce and vehicle for distributing the solids, so an assertively fruity oil is the best choice.

 PASTA SHAPES Use it on *pasta lunga:* spaghetti, *linguine/bavette/trenette, tonnarelli* (page 334), *bucatini,* or *busiata* (page 356).

For the *condimento:*

4 tablespoons (60 grams) salt-packed capers, rinsed free of all salt (page 36)
½ cup (120 grams) pitted black olives in brine, preferably Gaeta or taggiasche
2 cloves garlic
½ cup (100 milliliters) extra virgin olive oil, preferably intensely fruity

1 7-ounce (200-gram) can top-quality imported oil-packed tuna, drained well
freshly ground black pepper

To make the dish:

1 pound (450 grams) pasta (see suggestions above)
2 heaping tablespoons minced fresh flat-leaf parsley

Chop the capers, olives, and garlic together (in the food processor if desired). Combine with the oil in a skillet large enough to hold the pasta later and sauté for 3–4 minutes. Crumble the tuna into the pan and mix well. Grind on plenty of pepper. Cook for 5 another minutes, then remove from the heat and keep warm.

Bring 5 quarts (5 liters) of water to a boil in an 8-quart (8-liter) pot over high heat. Add 3 tablespoons kosher salt, then add the pasta and cook, stirring occasionally, until *al dente*.

Stir 3–4 tablespoons of the pasta water into the contents of the skillet. Drain the pasta and add to the skillet. Mix well, sprinkle on the parsley, and serve immediately directly from the skillet.

 WINE SUGGESTION: a sparkling white—Franciacorta or Prosecco—or else Insolia, from Sicily

---

Sugo con tonno, uova e capperi

(Canned tuna, eggs, and capers)

THIS TANGY, TOMATOLESS sauce, fashionable in the 1960s, will remind you of all the ways you love tuna fish, as long as you use a good-quality tuna packed in olive oil. Think of *vitello tonnato* with pasta instead of veal and you'll get the idea.

 PASTA SHAPES It works well on any shape of long or short dried pasta, especially spaghetti, but also *linguine/bavette/trenette*, *tonnarelli* (page 334), *bucatini*, or *busiata* (page 356).

For the *condimento*:

1 large white onion, finely chopped
6 tablespoons extra virgin olive oil
1 7-ounce (200-gram) can oil-packed tuna, preferably Italian or Spanish, drained
1 cup (200 milliliters) dry white wine
½ fish bouillon cube or ½ cup (100 milliliters) fish broth (page 242)
the juice of 1 organic lemon
4 tablespoons (60 grams) salt-packed capers, rinsed free of all salt (page 36), half of them chopped coarsely, half left whole

To make the dish:

1 pound (450 grams) pasta (see suggestions above)
2 egg yolks
2 tablespoons whole milk or heavy cream
extra virgin olive oil for finishing

In a small skillet, sauté the chopped onion gently in the oil until translucent, about 5 minutes. Add the tuna and let the flavors blend while you break up the tuna with a wooden spoon. After about 4 or 5 minutes, the tuna should be completely flaked and coated with the oil.

Raise the heat and add the wine. Let bubble until the odor of alcohol has disappeared, about 3 minutes.

Crumble the bouillon cube into the pan, or add the fish broth, then add the lemon juice and all the capers. Cook over medium heat for a few more minutes, until the sauce has begun to thicken and the oil has come to the surface. Then set aside.

MAKE-AHEAD NOTE: This much can be prepared before dinner if convenient and kept at room temperature. In that case, reheat the tuna sauce gently while the pasta is cooking.

Bring 5 quarts (5 liters) of water to a boil in an 8-quart (8-liter) pot over high heat. Add 3 tablespoons kosher salt, then add the pasta and cook, stirring occasionally, until *al dente*.

While the pasta is cooking, gently reheat the tuna sauce, if necessary. Combine the egg yolks and milk or cream in a small bowl and beat with a fork until completely blended.

Warm a serving bowl or platter in a low oven. If the oven is not practical, warm the bowl just before use with hot water, even a ladleful of the pasta cooking water.

Drain and transfer the pasta to the heated bowl. Toss first with the tuna sauce, then add the egg mixture and toss again. Finish with a swirl of oil and serve.

 WINE SUGGESTION: a floral Arneis, from Piedmont

Capperi, olive e acciughe

(Capers, olives, and anchovies)

ONCE YOU KNOW what to look for—a sort of fluffy hanging plant rooted in a vertical plane— it's easy to spot caper plants growing all over Italy, even on the Aurelian Walls of Rome and the sides of many palazzi. But the best come from cliff sides and plantations on the islands off Sicily, most famously Pantelleria, but also Favignana, Salina, and Stromboli.

Everybody has anchovies, capers, and olives in the cupboard (or ought to), and this may seem a modest sauce, easily thrown together from handy ingredients while you wait for the water to boil. And yet, in its apparent humility, it proves what we keep saying about ingredients. The best salt-packed anchovies and capers and Gaeta olives on a homemade or artisanal pasta ennoble the dish so that the flavor of each ingredient emerges on its own and together they let us imagine our dinner is taking place on an island in the southern Mediterranean.

 PASTA SHAPES These southern tastes go best with flour-and-water pasta, such as spaghetti, *spaghettini*, *scialatielli*, *paccheri*, *fileja*, or *fusilli* (page 354).

For the *condimento*:

6 tablespoons extra virgin olive oil, preferably intensely fruity

½ cup (100 grams) pitted black olives, preferably Gaeta or taggiasche type

½ cup (100 grams) salt-packed capers, rinsed free of all salt (page 36)

12–15 (about 150 grams) salt-packed anchovies, cleaned as described on page 34

1 clove garlic

1 small piece dried chile

1 teaspoon dried oregano

To make the dish:

1 pound (450 grams) pasta (see suggestions above)

6 tablespoons extra virgin olive oil, preferably intensely fruity

3½ ounces (100 grams) crustless fresh bread ground quite fine in a food processor

2 tablespoons minced fresh flat-leaf parsley

Put 5 quarts (5 liters) of water on to a boil in an 8-quart (8-liter) pot over high heat. When the water boils, add 3 tablespoons kosher salt, then add the pasta and cook, stirring occasionally, until *al dente*.

While you wait for the water to boil, put 6 tablespoons of the oil in a skillet large enough to hold the pasta later.

Put the olives, capers, anchovies, and garlic in the bowl of a food processor and chop fine, but stop well before they turn to a paste. Add the mixture to the skillet, followed by the chile and the oregano. Sauté gently until the anchovies have completely disintegrated, about 5 minutes. Lower the heat to the minimum, just to keep it warm.

Heat the remaining 6 tablespoons of oil over medium-high heat in a small skillet and add the bread-crumbs. Fry, stirring occasionally, until they are crisp and golden brown, about 5 minutes.

Warm a serving bowl or platter in a low oven. If the oven is not practical, warm the bowl just before use with hot water, even a ladleful of the pasta cooking water.

Drain the pasta and transfer to the skillet with the anchovy mixture. Sprinkle on the toasted bread-crumbs. Toss well for not more than 30 seconds. Sprinkle with the parsley, transfer to the heated serving bowl or platter, and serve immediately.

 WINE SUGGESTION: a low-acid white, such as Greco di Tufo

Carrettiera

(Canned tuna, porcini, and meat sauce)

TRUST A LONG-DISTANCE freight hauler to find a tasty, hearty bowl of spaghetti without leaving the road. The osterias (wine shops) and taverns that lined the great roads radiating out from Rome like the spokes of a wheel used to dish this well-endowed pasta out to hurried wagon drivers (*carrettieri*), stopping briefly on their way into town. The ingredients were always in the larder, and the sauce could be made quickly, before the road warriors had to get going. This particular sauce was typical of the osterias of the Castelli Romani, the towns in the volcanic hills southeast of Rome, known for their pleasant white wines and fresh air, a winning combination that still attracts visitors from the capital, especially in fall and spring, when the weather is pleasantly warm.

Until just before World War II, osterias were invariably family run. The wife was in the kitchen, and her well-fed husband greeted the guests and served at table. The food was based on local products and home cooking, such as legumes and wild herbs (some of which were considered medicinal) as well as eggs, snails, and freshwater fish and crayfish from nearby ponds and streams. Salt cod was the only sea fish. A pig, a few sheep, and some chickens and rabbits would end their days spit-roasted or stewed.

Today the sauce seems a little retro. You'll sometimes find it on trattoria menus, and in homes, but never very far up the scale. Make it when you've had it with foams, molecules, and squeeze bottles of balsamic reduction. In short, it's comfort food, but with quite a bit going on, in a straightforward sort of way: robust dark tuna (no water-packed white meat, please), fragrant porcini, a rich and elusive base of tomatoey meat sauce (the kind without visible meat) aided by fat from the *guanciale*, with plenty of assertive pecorino romano over it all.

While the recipe may seem complex, if your pantry is in a permanent state of readiness, you'll be feeding it to your own wagon drivers when they come roaring home hungry and you haven't shopped. The traditional mushrooms to use are fresh porcini, but dried are fine and full of flavor. You can also use a combination of fresh button mushrooms (*champignons*) and dried porcini. But, of course, if you are making a last-minute sauce, you will use dried. Likewise, you will need to have a container of meat sauce in the freezer, a practice we heartily recommend.

❧ **PASTA SHAPES** *Cordelle sabine* (page 364) are classic, but *cecamariti* (page 361), spaghetti, *vermicelli*, and *tacconi* (page 368) work very well too.

For the *condimento*:

2 ounces (60 grams) *guanciale*, in thin strips (about ¼ cup)

2 cloves garlic, crushed

2 tablespoons extra virgin olive oil, preferably intensely fruity

1 ounce (30 grams) dried porcini, reconstituted as on page 37 and coarsely chopped, or 10 ounces (300 grams) fresh porcini, wiped clean with a damp cloth and sliced

1 3½-ounce (100-gram) can Italian or Spanish oil-packed tuna, drained and crumbled

about 2 cups (400 grams) *Ragù di carne* (page 220)

salt

freshly ground black pepper

To make the dish:

1 pound (450 grams) pasta (see suggestions above)

about ¾ cup (80 grams) grated pecorino romano

Put the *guanciale*, garlic, and oil in a 10-inch (25-centimeter) skillet. Sauté gently over medium heat until the *guanciale* just begins to crisp and the garlic is golden, about 3 minutes.

Add the mushrooms to the skillet and stir. Add the crumbled tuna and stir that too. Cook over low heat, covered, for about 8 minutes if using fresh mushrooms and 3 minutes if using dried porcini. Taste for salt (how much you need will depend on your *guanciale*) and add a few grinds of pepper.

 MAKE-AHEAD NOTE: The sauce can be made up to this point earlier in the day.

Warm the meat sauce separately in a saucepan.

Bring 5 quarts (5 liters) of water to a boil in an 8-quart (8-liter) pot over high heat. Add 3 tablespoons kosher salt, then add the pasta and cook, stirring occasionally, until *al dente*.

Warm a serving bowl or platter in a low oven. If the oven is not practical, warm the bowl just before use with hot water, even a ladleful of the pasta cooking water.

Drain and transfer the pasta to the warm bowl. Toss first with the cheese, then mix in the meat sauce, and finally the tuna and mushrooms.

 WINE SUGGESTION: a young, fresh Barbera from Piedmont, or Sangiovese DOCG from Tuscany

---

Puttanesca

(Tomatoes, olives, and anchovies)

SINCE THE NAME literally means "prostitute-style," the story circulates that working girls used to whip up this dish on street corners in the rougher neighborhoods of Naples. But actually the word is used to describe anything squalid or sordid, lower on the scale than simply poor. "Quick and dirty" might be a good translation.

It's certainly quick and spicy, but so much more, with a sophisticated saltiness from the anchovies, and the olives and capers making themselves known through the dense tomato base. When vine-ripened garden-fresh tomatoes exist only in your dreams, use the best imported Italian canned or jarred tomatoes you can find.

 PASTA SHAPES Spaghetti is traditionally the only format used with this sauce. There is no logical reason.

For the *condimento*:

6 oil-packed anchovy fillets, drained and blotted dry
2 cloves garlic
6 tablespoons extra virgin olive oil, preferably intensely fruity
a 1-inch piece dried chile, or to taste
1 tablespoon salt-packed capers, rinsed free of all salt (see page 36) and chopped

1¼ cups (300 grams) canned peeled tomatoes, preferably San Marzano, with their juice, or 6 fresh ripe sauce tomatoes, preferably San Marzano–type, seeded and diced
1 cup (150 grams) coarsely chopped pitted black olives, preferably Gaeta

To make the dish:

1 pound (450 grams) spaghetti
extra virgin olive oil for finishing (optional)
2 heaping tablespoons minced fresh flat-leaf parsley

Chop the anchovies finely together with the garlic. Put the oil in a small saucepan and add the anchovies, garlic, and chile. Heat gently over low heat and mash with a fork until the anchovies have completely disintegrated, about 2 minutes.

Add the capers, tomatoes, and olives to the pan and let the flavors blend over medium heat for about 10 minutes.

MAKE-AHEAD NOTE: This much may be done ahead, but cooking ahead is hardly the point of this dish.

Meanwhile bring 5 quarts (5 liters) of water to a boil in an 8-quart (8-liter) pot over high heat. Add 3 tablespoons kosher salt, then add the spaghetti and cook, stirring occasionally, until *al dente*.

Warm a serving bowl or platter in a low oven. If the oven is not practical, warm the bowl just before use with hot water, even a ladleful of the pasta cooking water.

Drain the pasta and transfer to the heated serving bowl. Toss with the sauce and a swirl or two of oil if desired and sprinkle with the parsley. Serve immediately.

 WINE SUGGESTION: a dry Lambrusco, even though it's from Emilia-Romagna, far from Naples

Amatriciana

(*Guanciale*, tomato, and pecorino romano)

THIS SIMPLE BUT delicious sauce is named for the town of Amatrice, in the mountainous northeastern panhandle of Lazio, near Abruzzo and the Marche. It seems incredible for such an easy, humble sauce, but this is one of the dishes self-appointed purists (read fanatics) will fight over to the death, or at least death by boredom. You have to use spaghetti or *bucatini*, they say—nor is it that simple, since there are spaghetti-only and *bucatini*-only factions. No cheese but pecorino is permitted. And woe betide you if you use pancetta in place of *guanciale*.

There is, however, some room for individual expression. Some cooks use onion and chile, some not. A few swear by a splash of white wine "to cut the fat."

The pecorino should ideally be that made in Amatrice or Abruzzo or Sicily, milder and fattier than pecorino romano, but pecorino romano is certainly what you'll find used in Rome. (Pecorino romano is a kind of cheese from a large designated area that includes the entire Lazio and Sardegna regions and the province of Grosseto in Tuscany, not just Rome; it is widely available in the United States.) Parmigiano is not used in *amatriciana*; it's made with cow's milk, and Rome and its mountainous hinterland is traditionally a land of sheep, after all. The shepherds of yesteryear, who spent months in the hills with their flocks, would make this flavorful dish for themselves. You can imagine that they were not worried about someone calling the food police if they grabbed a piece of pancetta instead of *guanciale* or one kind of sheep cheese instead of another. But they would never have used smoked bacon, which is not part of their tradition.

Like many rustic, simple sauces that have found immortality on trattoria menus throughout Italy (and beyond), this dish is only as good as its ingredients. Take the tomatoes. The rugged mountainous area of northeastern Lazio where Amatrice is located was never great tomato-growing territory, or at least not for most of the year, so it was normal to use canned or jarred tomatoes. But the most delicious *amatriciana* I've ever tasted was made by Oretta (of course) at her house about halfway between Rome and Amatrice with tomatoes from her garden. After her ecstatic guests had practically licked their plates, she announced with an air of regret that this delicious dish was "not really *l'amatriciana*" because she had used fresh tomatoes. She later revised the statement to the more reasonable pronouncement that if you have a basketful of gorgeous San Marzano tomatoes from your garden, *of course* you

should peel and seed them and make the sauce, and handed me a jar of her home-canned tomatoes to use in the winter. Whether you use fresh or canned, the result is a red sauce studded with bits of lightly fried pork, but you don't want it *too* red. The pasta and *guanciale* should be coated with a thin mantle of sauce, not hidden. Don't let the gloppy, oversauced trattoria version be your model. The cheese is sharp and salty, but, again, don't use too much.

See *la gricia* (page 73) for the tomatoless version.

Many people consider onion a deviation from the sacred original, but hardly anyone thinks it doesn't taste good. In fact, it is delicious. If you use it, add a small chopped onion to the *guanciale* fat and sauté until transparent, then add the tomato.

 PASTA SHAPES This sauce is used on flour-and-water shapes—spaghetti or *bucatini*, of course, but rigatoni, *casarecce*, or some of the handmade flour-and-water shapes, such as *strozzapreti/pici* (page 344), do nicely too.

For the *condimento*:

2½ ounces (70 grams) *guanciale* (see page 33), cut into thin strips

2–3 tablespoons extra virgin olive oil

1 small onion (any kind), chopped (optional but recommended)

1 pound (450 grams) red, ripe sauce tomatoes, broken into pieces, or canned Italian peeled tomatoes, drained

1 small piece dried chile

salt

To make the dish:

1 pound (450 grams) pasta (see suggestions above)

7 rounded tablespoons (70 grams) grated pecorino (see headnote)

Put the *guanciale* and oil in a saucepan. Turn the heat to medium and heat gently so the *guanciale* renders some fat and starts to brown. Taste a piece to assess how salty it is. Then, when it just begins to become crisp, add the chopped onion (if using) and sauté gently until transparent. Add the tomatoes and chile, then taste for salt (how much you need will depend on the *guanciale*).

Finish cooking the sauce, covered, over low heat. You'll know it's done when the liquid has thickened somewhat and the fat shows on the surface, about 20 minutes.

 MAKE-AHEAD NOTE: This much can be done earlier in the day, but this sauce is not customarily made in advance or kept, except casually as leftovers for the next day.

Bring 5 quarts (5 liters) of water to a boil in an 8-quart (8-liter) pot over high heat. Add 3 tablespoons kosher salt, then add the pasta and cook, stirring occasionally, until *al dente*.

Warm a serving bowl or platter in a low oven. If the oven is not practical, warm the bowl just before use with hot water, even a ladleful of the pasta cooking water.

Drain the pasta and put it in the warmed serving bowl. Toss it first with the grated cheese, then with the sauce. Serve immediately.

 WINE SUGGESTION: Pecorino rosso d'Abruzzo

Gricia

(*Guanciale* and pecorino romano)

ALSO KNOWN AS "the white *amatriciana*," for the absence of tomatoes, *pasta alla gricia* is one of the simplest yet tastiest of traditional pastas of Rome and its region. For purists, spaghetti or *bucatini* is the only acceptable pasta format, though others are found even in the restaurants and trattorias of the ultra-Roman Testaccio quarter (Checchino dal 1887 uses *bucatini*; Felice *mezze maniche*). The format is unimportant, but the quality of the *guanciale* and pecorino romano is crucial. This is one of the many cases where if you can't find good ingredients, you should make something else.

Any *condimento* that consists entirely of pork fat and cheese is bound to be hearty and full-bodied, but the flavor is also surprisingly interesting. The cheese is salty and tangy, while good *guanciale*, milder than bacon or pancetta, adds richness, depth, and a lovely pork taste. The sauce is merely the creamy combination of the fat, cheese, and water from the pasta and comes into existence directly on the pasta.

 PASTA SHAPES This *condimento* is usually used on factory-made flour-and-water pastas: spaghetti, *bucatini*, *penne*, rigatoni, or *mezze maniche*.

For the *condimento*:

3 tablespoons extra virgin olive oil
4¼ ounces (120 grams) *guanciale*, in thin strips
7 rounded tablespoons (70 grams) grated pecorino romano

To make the dish:

1 pound (450 grams) pasta (see suggestions above)

Put the oil and *guanciale* in a large skillet and sauté gently for about 3 or 4 minutes, or until the *guanciale* is shiny and becoming crisp. It shouldn't be too crisp.

Bring 5 quarts (5 liters) of water to a boil in an 8-quart (8-liter) pot over high heat. Add 3 tablespoons kosher salt, then add the pasta and cook, stirring occasionally, until quite *al dente*.

Lift the pasta out of the pot with two forks or a handheld colander or spider strainer (you want to carry some water with it) and transfer to the skillet with the *guanciale* and its fat. Mix well to distribute the fat, sprinkle on the pecorino, and mix again. The water, fat, and cheese should combine to form a creamy coating for the strands of pasta.

Warm a serving bowl or platter in a low oven. If the oven is not practical, warm the bowl just before use with hot water, even a ladleful of the pasta cooking water. Transfer the pasta to the heated bowl and serve immediately in warm dishes.

 WINE SUGGESTION: a soft, aromatic white, such as Frascati DOC, from the Castelli Romani near Rome

---

guanciale

Carbonara

(*Guanciale*, egg, and pecorino romano)

MORE THAN FORTY years ago, I returned from a college semester in Rome to a New York still awash in thick tomato sauce. My Roman discovery, spaghetti *alla carbonara*, was still unknown, and my friends were skeptical of a sauce that wasn't red. Today Americans have adopted *carbonara* with a vengeance and feel free to vary it as they please. But while it is very tempting to add things to the basic *carbonara*, and far be it from us to step on your creativity, don't call it *carbonara* if you add mushrooms or peas or anything else.

The *carbonara* wars are even more heated than the *amatriciana* wars (page 70). Not even Oretta and I agree on every detail. Oretta feels some oil helps the *guanciale* to cook evenly, while I, from a North American bacon culture, find that starting the *guanciale* in a cold pan will render enough fat to obtain the same result without introducing another ingredient and another flavor, especially one that the inventors of the dish did not use. If you start playing with the formula to reduce the cholesterol, however, just skip it and make a broccoli sauce.

The more or less civil disagreements are over minor variations. There is debate over whether to use whole eggs or just yolks (it's unlikely the pastoral creators of the dish were going to whip up a meringue with the unused whites) and whether parmigiano is admissible—yes, it's widely accepted on grounds of deliciousness, but pecorino romano alone is more faithful to the lost original. Experts and aficionados pretty much agree that the meat of choice should be *guanciale*, with pancetta as understudy. Bacon, which is smoked, imparts an undesirable breakfasty taste. No butter, no cream—but a slosh of starchy pasta water can be used to smooth things out if you start to panic.

It is incorrect to speak of "*carbonara* sauce" because the dish belongs to the group of pastas that are inseparable from their condiment. The ingredients are prepped and ready for action, but the "sauce"—a golden cream studded with glistening *guanciale* bits—is created right on the pasta itself. And, careful, "cream" here means something creamy. There is no cream in *carbonara*. The charcoal makers of northern Lazio, Abruzzo, and Umbria used to make it outdoors. Do you think they used butter and cream?

This simple dish requires practice; don't make it for company till you've tried it in private. You will eventually develop your own moves and rhythm and find just the spot in your kitchen where everything will keep warm without cooking. Long ago I became devoted to the Salton Hotray®, an electric food warmer and popular wedding present in the era of my first marriage. I still love it for *carbonara* (and much else).

Use the best, freshest eggs you can find, and don't even think of making this dish with eggs from stressed-out battery chickens. You *can* taste the difference. If you can find real *guanciale*, so much the better. Once the eggs have been added to the pasta, do not let the pan touch the heat directly or you will wind up with scrambled eggs. A low setting on an electric food warmer, like my old Hotray, is safe and effective.

PASTA SHAPES The canonical pasta for *carbonara* is spaghetti, but *bucatini* are close behind. *Penne* and rigatoni are short formats often found *alla carbonara* and easier to handle in quantity.

For the *condimento*:

4 ounces (115 grams) *guanciale*, cut into ¼-inch (½-centimeter) dice
2 generous tablespoons extra virgin olive oil, preferably lightly fruity
3 large eggs, at room temperature
10 rounded tablespoons (100 grams) freshly grated pecorino romano, or half pecorino romano and half parmigiano-reggiano
freshly ground black pepper

To make the dish:

1 pound (450 grams) pasta (see suggestions above)

Put the *guanciale* and oil in a large skillet. Sauté over medium heat until the edges of the *guanciale* pieces are just turning brown, about 2 minutes. Don't let it get too crisp. Set the pan and its contents aside but keep warm.

Bring 5 quarts (5 liters) of water to a boil in an 8-quart (8-liter) pot over high heat. When the water boils, add 3 tablespoons kosher salt, then add the pasta and cook, stirring occasionally, until *al dente*.

While the pasta is cooking, break the eggs into a small bowl and add all the cheese and a generous grinding of pepper. Whisk gently until the mixture is smooth.

Drain the pasta (reserving and keeping warm a cup of its water) and put it in the skillet with the *guanciale* over low heat. Toss quickly to mix well.

Holding the skillet slightly above but not touching the burner, pour the egg and cheese mixture in a stream into the pasta. Now, if you have the skill, toss the pasta with a deft movement of the wrist to blend all the contents of the pan. If you don't, remove the pan from the heat and mix quickly with two wooden spoons. If you have a warm spot, such as a food warmer or even over a pilot light, rest the pan there while you work.

Whatever you do, work fast or the pasta will get cold and the eggs will stay raw and runny. Ideally the heat of the pasta will cook the egg just enough, and the sauce should be creamy. You can mix in a tiny bit of the reserved water to smooth things out, but you probably won't need to.

Transfer to individual heated bowls or plates and serve instantaneously.

WINE SUGGESTION: Frascati would be the choice in a Roman trattoria, but the *carbonara* wars extend also to the wine pairing. Suggestions range from light red Cerasuolo d'Abruzzo, to a delicate rosé Franciacorta, to a sparkling white from Lombardia, to Champagne, to Barolo, a big red from Piedmont.

Sugo finto

(Mock meat sauce)

THE ITALIAN IMAGINATION, and sense of humor, must be heightened by adversity, because there is whole category of humble foods in which some costly missing ingredient is alluded to in the name. The extreme example of this is the "fish" soup flavored with a rock from the seabed and nary a fin. Here ham fat provides the only meat for this otherwise meatless sauce, a native of the Lazio region but used throughout central Italy, which even so manages to achieve something approaching the rich, rounded taste of a true *sugo*.

 PASTA SHAPES Use this sauce on any shape except *capelli d'angelo* and *pastina*.

For the *condimento*:

½ cup (100 milliliters) broth, any kind
3 tablespoons (40 grams) tomato paste
1 rib celery
1 carrot
1 small spring onion, white part and just the
    beginning of the green part
5 or 6 leaves fresh basil
1¾ ounces (50 grams) *lardo* or prosciutto fat,
    diced fine
salt
freshly ground black pepper

To make the dish:

1 pound (450 grams) pasta (see suggestions
    above)
7 rounded tablespoons (70 grams) grated
    pecorino romano
2 heaping tablespoons minced fresh flat-leaf
    parsley

In a small saucepan, heat the broth over medium-high heat and add the tomato paste, stirring until dissolved. Set aside.

Mince finely together the celery, carrot, onion, and basil (the food processor is fine). Put the *lardo* or fat in a saucepan over low heat. When the fat has almost melted, add the celery mixture and let it wilt for 2 or 3 minutes.

Add the broth with the tomato paste and continue cooking for about 15 minutes, or until the sauce has become quite dense. Taste for salt and pepper.

Bring 5 quarts (5 liters) of water to a boil in an 8-quart (8-liter) pot over high heat. Add 3 tablespoons kosher salt, then add the pasta and cook, stirring occasionally, until *al dente*.

Warm a serving bowl or platter in a low oven. If the oven is not practical, warm the bowl just before use with hot water, even a ladleful of the pasta cooking water.

Drain the pasta and transfer to the warm serving bowl. Toss first with the cheese and then with the sauce and the parsley. Serve immediately.

 WINE SUGGESTION: red, but not too aggressive, such as Sangiovese di Romagna

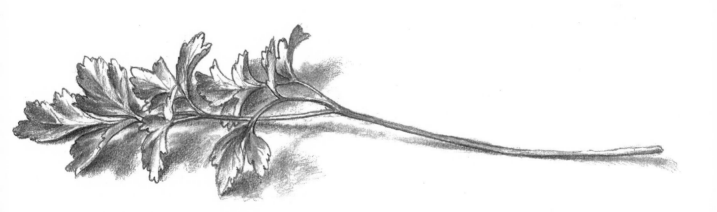

Sugo con il battuto

(*Lardo* and flavorings)

THIS SAUCE IS a real piece of food history, but it still has a role in the kitchens of busy cooks. In olden times, when there were no supermarkets selling ready-made sauces, Italian women invented their own convenience foods, which are still valid today. Peasant families throughout the center and south of Italy would make this handy condiment to keep all winter in lieu of fresh flavorings. The name *battuto* (literally, "beaten") is Roman and comes from the action of chopping *lardo* and *odori*, vegetable flavorings, on a wooden board.

You'll use only a tablespoon of *battuto* in the sauce for a pound of pasta. Put the rest in a glass jar in the fridge, where it will keep for months. Today it's a great resource for last-minute sauces with a homemade taste that evokes a fireplace in the country. The sauce is light red with a touch of piquancy and an underlayer of richness, thanks to the *lardo*.

 PASTA SHAPES It goes very well with all the traditional flour-and-water short shapes used, but not necessarily born, in Rome—notably, *tortiglioni*, *tubetti*, *sedani*, rigatoni, *penne*, *paccheri*, *corzetti* (page 347), *farfalle* (page 336), *fregnacce* (page 337), and *fusilli* (page 354)—but also *garganelli* (page 338), *orecchiette* (page 349), and *pasta strappata* (page 335).

For the *battuto*:

5 ounces (40 grams) top-quality *lardo* (see page 33)
1 white onion
1 small rib celery
6–8 sprigs fresh flat-leaf parsley, including the stems
1 tablespoon salt

For the *condimento*:

2 tablespoons (40 grams) tomato paste
½ cup (100 milliliters) broth, any kind

To make the dish:

1 pound (450 grams) pasta (see suggestions above)
1 small piece dried chile or a pinch of red pepper flakes
7 rounded tablespoons (70 grams) grated pecorino romano

Chop finely together the *lardo* with the onion, celery, and parsley (in the food processor if desired). Add the salt and mix in well.

 MAKE-AHEAD NOTE: This much is the *battuto*, which can be stored for months in a glass jar in the refrigerator. Use it any time to make the sauce.

Dissolve the tomato paste in the broth.

Bring 5 quarts (5 liters) of water to a boil in an 8-quart (8-liter) pot over high heat. Add 3 tablespoons kosher salt, then add the pasta and cook, stirring occasionally, until *al dente*.

While the pasta is cooking, put a heaping tablespoon of *battuto* in a small saucepan over low heat. Stir in the tomato paste and broth mixture. Add the chile or pepper flakes. Reduce over medium-high heat for about 7 or 8 minutes, or until somewhat reduced.

Warm a serving bowl or platter in a low oven. If the oven is not practical, warm the bowl just before use with hot water, even a ladleful of the pasta cooking water.

Drain the pasta and transfer to the heated bowl. Sprinkle with the grated cheese, then toss well with the sauce and serve immediately.

 WINE SUGGESTION: any light red, such as Sangiovese

lardo

Aglio, olio e peperoncino

(Garlic, oil, and chile)

THIS IS THE quintessential Italian last-minute, nothing-in-the-house, what-will-I-ever-give-them-to-eat dish. It takes longer to boil the pasta than to make the sauce. For all its simplicity, everyone seems to have a theory of how it should be made. "All" it is is gently warmed extra virgin olive oil, garlic, and chile. As the ingredients suggest, its origins are southern, but its popularity drove it northward. Today all the Italian young people for whom it's a standard for spontaneous get-togethers would be very surprised to hear that it isn't native to wherever they live.

Some cooks insist on a sprinkling of minced flat-leaf parsley at the end, though if you've just got in from the airport dying for a bowl of spa-ghetti, you probably don't have any. Don't give it a thought. But the chile is a must, even if you use just a little.

Because the oil is never heated very hot and the garlic and chile never brown, the sauce maintains the bright, clean taste of extra virgin olive oil. The garlic comes across as a fragrance, not a smell. Be careful or you'll get oil splatters all over your shirt.

Just to give an idea of different approaches to so few ingredients, we give two versions here. The first was recounted to me some years ago by our friend Paola Di Mauro, doyenne of Castelli Romani winemakers and a renowned Roman home cook. The second is Oretta's.

 PASTA SHAPES The pasta shape used ninety-nine percent of the time is spaghetti, but *bucatini* and *tonnarelli* (page 334) are good too. For a short format, *penne rigate* would be most usual.

VERSION 1

For the *condimento*:

1 or 2 cloves garlic (depending on taste)
about ½ cup (100 milliliters) extra virgin olive oil
1 dried chile (or more or less, to taste), broken
    into pieces with its seeds

To make the dish:

1 pound (450 grams) spaghetti
1 heaping tablespoon finely chopped fresh
    flat-leaf parsley

Bring 5 quarts (5 liters) of water to a boil in an 8-quart (8-liter) pot over high heat. Add 3 tablespoons kosher salt, then add the pasta and cook, stirring occasionally, until *al dente*.

While the spaghetti is cooking, slice the garlic very, very thin. Put the oil in a small skillet, add the garlic and chile, and sauté over low heat very gently. The garlic should not color at all. It should just get soft.

Drain the spaghetti quickly and transfer to a warm serving bowl. Pour on the oil and garlic, sprinkle on the parsley, toss quickly, and serve immediately.

VERSION 2

For the *condimento*:

2 cloves garlic, crushed
½ cup (100 milliliters) extra virgin olive oil,
    preferably intensely fruity
1 piece dried chile, as large as you like

To make the dish:

1 pound (450 grams) spaghetti

Put 5 quarts (5 liters) of water on to boil in an 8-quart (8-liter) pot over high heat. Put the oil in a skillet large enough to hold the pasta later over medium heat. Add the garlic and chile and cook for 3 or 4 minutes or until the garlic just turns golden. Set aside and keep warm.

When the water boils, add 3 tablespoons kosher salt, then add the pasta and cook, stirring occasionally, until quite *al dente*. Scoop out and reserve about a half cup of its water.

Drain the pasta and add it directly to the skillet. Add 3 tablespoons of the pasta water and toss over medium heat for about 2 minutes or until the pasta has completely absorbed the water. Discard the garlic and chile and transfer the pasta to a warmed serving dish or else serve directly from the pan.

WINE SUGGESTION: an easy-drinking white from the Castelli Romani, near Rome, such as Marino DOC

Burro e salvia

(Melted butter and fresh sage)

THIS IS A classic of the northern regions of Italy, especially Piedmont and Lombardia, but even an olive oil culture appreciates the distinctive taste of butter once in a while, and this elegant but easy *condimento* is loved throughout the land when something subtle, sophisticated, and simple is needed. It is particularly well-suited to the more delicate ravioli and other stuffed pastas, as it allows the flavors of the filling to come through.

Only fresh sage will be fragrant yet gentle enough. If all you have is dried, skip the sage altogether. Nobody has ever objected to melted butter and freshly grated parmigiano-reggiano all by their lonesome.

The best butters in Italy come from the best cheese makers, such as Beppe Occelli, in Piedmont, or the producers of the parmigiano-reggiano consortium (page 391). Butter is the whole point of this sauce, so do make the effort to find a good one—always unsalted.

 PASTA SHAPES *Burro e salvia* is a classic with meat- or cheese-filled ravioli (page 302) or *cappellacci di zucca* (page 307), since the unwritten rule is that a stuffed pasta's sauce must be different from and must not overshadow the filling. It also works beautifully with *garganelli* (page 338), *gnocchi di patate* (page 364), *paglia e fieno* (page 331), and *agnolotti piemontesi* (page 295).

For the *condimento*:

4 tablespoons (60 grams) unsalted butter, diced
4 or 5 whole fresh sage leaves

To make the dish:

1 pound (450 grams) pasta (see suggestions above)
8 rounded tablespoons (80 grams) freshly grated parmigiano-reggiano
freshly ground white pepper

Bring 5 quarts (5 liters) of water to a boil in an 8-quart (8-liter) pot over high heat.

While waiting for the water to boil, melt the butter in a small saucepan over low heat. Raise the heat to medium and add the sage leaves. When they just begin to change color, about 1 minute, remove the pan from the heat and keep warm. Remove and discard the leaves or leave them in for visual effect.

When the water boils, add 3 tablespoons kosher salt, then add the pasta and cook, stirring occasionally, until *al dente*.

Warm a serving bowl or platter in a low oven. If the oven is not practical, warm the bowl just before use with hot water, even a ladleful of the pasta cooking water.

Drain the pasta (use a slotted spoon or spider strainer and a gentle hand for ravioli and other stuffed pastas) and transfer to the warmed bowl. Sprinkle with the grated cheese and add a generous grinding of white pepper. Pour on the sage butter, mix gently, and serve piping hot.

 WINE SUGGESTION: Pinot Nero dell'Oltrepo Pavese DOC, from Lombardia

---

Sugo alla panna e limone
(Cream and lemon)

PUT ON YOUR Audrey Hepburn sunglasses and your Grace Kelly silk scarf and step into your convertible Alfa Romeo for a toot along the Amalfi Drive. This luxurious, very retro sauce is redolent of both the boom years of the 1960s, when it was invented, and the extremely fragrant lemons still grown on the Sorrento Peninsula, whence it spread to become popular throughout Italy. It's perfect for a summer special occasion. And, like Princess Grace, beneath its beautiful blond outward appearance it conceals a sophisticated, complex, sweet-tart *je ne sais quoi*—thanks to the use of both zest and juice of the lemon.

In the 1960s and '70s, restaurants used to put cream on absolutely everything, one reason these retro recipes can be a hard sell nowadays. But this one works. The butter and cream, already used sparingly, are absorbed into the pasta, so they never pool or feel heavy. In fact, at first glance, you'll have to look closely to see any sauce at all. But never fear. It's all the more interesting when you taste the lemon surprise with the first bite. And the advantage of the bland background is exactly that the citrus pops out against it.

The simple sauce is made while the water boils. Just make sure you use the best organic lemons you can find.

 PASTA SHAPES Its natural companion is elegant *tagliolini* (page 332), but it is also excellent with *tagliatelle* (page 328), *farfalle* (page 336), or *maltagliati* (page 336), all made with *pasta all'uovo* (page 286).

For the *condimento*:

1 organic lemon
4 tablespoons (60 grams) unsalted butter
½ cup (100 milliliters) heavy cream
6 rounded tablespoons (60 grams) grated parmigiano-reggiano
freshly ground white pepper

To make the dish:

1 pound (450 grams) pasta (see suggestions above)
more heavy cream (if needed)

Put 5 quarts (5 liters) of water on to boil in an 8-quart (8-liter) pot over high heat.

While you wait for the water to boil, grate the lemon zest and squeeze the juice. Put both in a serving bowl. Cut the butter into tiny pieces and add to the bowl. Add the cream and cheese and mix well. Add a few grinds of white pepper.

Rest the bowl over the pot where the water is heating and let the butter melt there, stirring. When the water boils, remove the bowl to a warm place. It won't have to wait long.

Add 3 tablespoons kosher salt to the water, then add the pasta and cook, stirring occasionally, until *al dente*.

Lift the pasta out of the water with two forks, a handheld colander, or a spider strainer directly into the warm bowl. You want it to bring some of its water with it. Mix for 3 or 4 minutes, until the pasta has absorbed the sauce. Add a little more cream if it looks dry. Serve immediately.

 WINE SUGGESTION: a dry rosé from southern Italy, such as Regaleali Rosé from Sicily

---

tagliatella

Sugo semplice di pomodori pelati

(Simple canned-tomato sauce)

PLAIN TOMATO SAUCE for pasta revolutionized the tables of the poor under the Kingdom of Naples in the 1800s. For five centuries before that, the local pecorino alone had been used, but eventually Grand Tourists could stop at Neapolitan street corners to gawk at the *maccheroni* vendor and the steaming cauldron from which he extracted spaghetti to be dressed, at last, with both cheese and the most delicious tomatoes on earth, those grown on the fertile slopes of Mount Vesuvius. They still have no rival for sweetness and depth of flavor.

All the simple tomato sauces given here—consumed almost daily in households throughout Italy—can be varied as you wish with different herbs, such as fresh basil (suggested in this recipe), fresh or dried oregano, fresh marjoram, chives, fresh dill, mint, bay leaves, and more. In summer, basil is the classic. Use fresh herbs whenever you can, and try to keep to one herb at a time. The fragrance of the herbs will add body and substance to the sweetness of the tomato. But don't overdo it. The sauce is supposed to taste like tomatoes. Ideally, you'll eat it and believe you have never before really tasted a tomato.

 PASTA SHAPES Use these sauces on absolutely any kind of factory-made or homemade pasta that is suitable for use as *pastasciutta*. That means anything but the extra-tiny or extra-thin formats reserved for broth, a category that includes angel hair. Spaghetti and *raviolini di magro* (page 305) could be singled out as particularly suitable, *casarecce* too.

For the *condimento*:

1 clove garlic, crushed
6 tablespoons extra virgin olive oil
1 1-pound (450-gram) can peeled tomatoes with
    their liquid
10–12 fresh basil leaves (optional)
1 small piece dried chile
salt

To make the dish:

1 pound (450 grams) pasta (see suggestions
    above)
6 rounded tablespoons (60 grams) grated
    pecorino romano, parmigiano-reggiano, or
    other hard grating cheese
extra virgin olive oil for finishing (optional)

Put the garlic and oil in a saucepan, and sauté gently over low heat. Discard the garlic when it has turned a nice gold color, about 3 minutes.

Add the tomatoes, the basil (if using), the chile, and at least ½ teaspoon salt. Lower the flame and simmer, covered, for about 20 minutes, or until the sauce is visibly reduced and shiny, with the oil coming to the surface.

 MAKE-AHEAD NOTE: The process can be interrupted at this point and the sauce kept in the refrigerator for a couple of days or frozen.

Bring 5 quarts (5 liters) of water to a boil in an 8-quart (8-liter) pot over high heat. Add 3 tablespoons kosher salt, then add the pasta and cook, stirring occasionally, until *al dente*.

Warm a serving bowl or platter in a low oven. If the oven is not practical, warm the bowl just before use with hot water, even a ladleful of the pasta cooking water.

Drain and transfer the pasta to the heated serving bowl. Toss first with the grated cheese and then with the sauce. If desired, stir in a tablespoon or two of extra virgin olive oil before serving.

 WINE SUGGESTION: Frascati DOC or Marino DOC from the Castelli Romani, near Rome

Sugo semplice di passata di pomodoro

(Simple smooth tomato sauce)

ONE OF THE main end-of-summer activities in Italian homes, at least those with gardens, is the putting up of tomatoes for the winter (pages 30–31). They can be either pureed or in pieces, which is how Oretta puts up the succulent San Marzano–type tomatoes she grows in the country. Even if you don't have the gene that loves to fill and store jars, you can still buy a couple of pounds of plum or other red, ripe tomatoes at your farmers' market and make just enough fresh puree for a batch or two of sauce. See page 31 for instructions. You'll never want to go back to store-bought once you experience the true tomato taste that comes through.

 PASTA SHAPES This sauce goes with any long or short pasta shape except *capelli d'angelo* and the *pastina* group, both intended for broth. *Cordelle sabine* (page 364) and *penne* are especially good.

For the *condimento*:

1 small white onion
1 clove garlic
1 small carrot
1 small celery rib
6 tablespoons extra virgin olive oil
2 cups (400 grams) tomato puree
1 bay leaf
at least ½ teaspoon salt
1 piece dried chile (optional)

To make the dish:

1 pound (450 grams) pasta (see suggestions above)
6 rounded tablespoons (60 grams) grated parmigiano-reggiano, pecorino romano, or other hard cheese
extra virgin olive oil for finishing (optional)

Chop finely together the onion, garlic, carrot, and celery (in the food processor if desired) and put in a saucepan with the oil. Sauté gently until the vegetables are tender.

Add the tomato puree, bay leaf, salt, and chile, if using. Cover and cook over low heat for about 20 minutes, or until the sauce is completely cooked and the shiny oil comes to the surface. Fish out and discard the bay leaf.

MAKE-AHEAD NOTE: The process can be interrupted at this point and the sauce kept in the refrigerator for a couple of days or frozen.

Bring 5 quarts (5 liters) of water to a boil in an 8-quart (8-liter) pot over high heat. Add 3 tablespoons kosher salt, then add the pasta and cook, stirring occasionally, until *al dente*.

Warm a serving bowl or platter in a low oven. If the oven is not practical, warm the bowl just before use with hot water, even a ladleful of the pasta cooking water.

Drain and transfer the pasta to the heated serving bowl. Toss first with the cheese, then with the sauce. If desired, stir in a swirl of extra virgin olive oil before serving.

WINE SUGGESTION: any young Sangiovese-based wine, such as Di Majo Norante or Pratesi Locorosso

Arrabbiata

(Tomatoes, garlic, and chile)

THIS SIMPLE MEATLESS pasta was the favorite dish of the Roman dialect poet Carlo Alberto Salustri, better known by his pseudonym, Trilussa, for whom a piazza in his beloved Trastevere is named. Still today every trattoria in Rome offers *penne all'arrabbiata*. And when you need a break from pork fat and cheese, this thick, bright red, tomatoey, oily, and (sometimes very) spicy sauce can really hit the spot—and no cholesterol either. At home, it's easy to make, and, with your own good ingredients, bears no resemblance to the flavorless, debased versions dished out in low-end eateries.

You'd never know it from all those relentlessly similar menus, but numerous variations have been devised over generations. One is to add a handful of coarsely chopped dried porcini mushrooms (soaked and squeezed of course) when the sauce is almost done. Another adds basil along with the parsley, and still another sautés pancetta along with the garlic. The fact is that it's no use trying to imprison these traditional dishes in overly restrictive recipes.

PASTA SHAPES One format of pasta is associated above all with this *condimento*, *penne*, and nothing else would taste right to a Roman. Give the Romans their *penne*, but for other guests feel free to use the sauce on any flour-and-water pasta, such as *sedani*, *bucatini*, *casarecce*, rigatoni, spaghetti, *fusilli* (page 354), *fregnacce* (page 337), *gnocchetti* (page 342), and *lagane* (page 334).

For the *condimento*:

6 tablespoons extra virgin olive oil, preferably intensely fruity

3 cloves garlic, crushed

2 very hot dried chiles, broken in pieces (not crumbled)

24 ounces (700 grams) Italian peeled tomatoes, drained and chopped coarsely

at least ½ teaspoon salt

To make the dish:

1 pound (450 grams) pasta (see suggestions above)

extra virgin olive oil for finishing

2 heaping tablespoons minced fresh flat-leaf parsley

Put the oil, garlic, and chiles in a skillet over medium heat until the garlic is golden, about 2 minutes, then discard the garlic and chiles. Add the tomatoes to the flavored oil and season with the salt.

Simmer, covered, over low heat for about 30 minutes, stirring every so often. Feel free to remove the lid and raise the heat a bit to hasten the process. The sauce should be thick and shiny, with the oil separated and on the surface.

 MAKE-AHEAD NOTE: This much can be made earlier in the day, but there is little need to.

Bring 5 quarts (5 liters) of water to a boil in an 8-quart (8-liter) pot over high heat. Add 3 tablespoons kosher salt, then add the pasta and cook, stirring occasionally, until *al dente*.

Warm a serving bowl or platter in a low oven. If the oven is not practical, warm the bowl just before use with hot water, even a ladleful of the pasta cooking water.

Transfer the sauce to the warm serving bowl, add the drained pasta and a swirl of oil, mix well, sprinkle with the parsley, and serve immediately.

 WINE SUGGESTION: fruity Valpolicella, from the distant Veneto

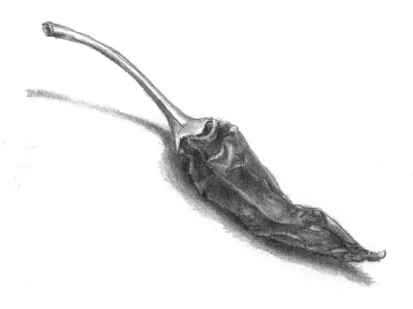

Sugo alla marinara

(Tomatoes, garlic, and oregano)

THE NAME OF this sauce belongs to the group we might call the gotcha group. *Sugo finto* (page 78) is one, *uccelli scappati* (veal birds) is another. Italian, and even other languages, are full of them. "*Alla marinara*" usually implies the presence of seafood, but here there is not a trace of the sea, except that the dish comes from Naples, where the sea is in every breath. This simple sauce is what the fishermen of Santa Lucia, on the Naples waterfront, used to make for themselves—their valuable catch was for sale, not their own lunch. They had the advantage of the famously delicious tomatoes grown in the volcanic soil of Mount Vesuvius. Since the sauce depends overwhelmingly on the quality of the tomatoes, don't bother with fresh unless they're straight from the garden in late summer. The garlic, oregano, and chile are strictly background players.

Incidentally, the same combination of ingredients is used on pizza, as *pizza alla marinara*, the standard pizzeria choice of anyone wishing to avoid cheese.

 PASTA SHAPES Traditionally the dish was made with *vermicelli*, but you can use spaghetti. To add something of the sea to the *marinara, ravioli con le sogliole* (page 304) are good.

For the *condimento*:

2 cloves garlic, finely chopped
6 tablespoons extra virgin olive oil
1 pound (450 grams) very high quality canned peeled tomatoes with their juice or red, ripe sauce tomatoes, preferably San Marzano, peeled and seeded (see page 30)

at least ½ teaspoon salt
a 1-inch piece dried chile
1 teaspoon dried oregano

To make the dish:

1 pound (450 grams) pasta (see suggestions above)

Sauté the garlic in the oil over low heat in a saucepan just until it begins to color, about 3 minutes.

Add the tomatoes and sprinkle with salt. Add the chile and half of the oregano. Simmer for 20 minutes on low heat, stirring often, or until the sauce is visibly reduced and shiny.

 MAKE-AHEAD NOTE: This much may be made ahead and kept covered overnight in the refrigerator.

Bring 5 quarts (5 liters) of water to a boil in an 8-quart (8-liter) pot over high heat. Add 3 tablespoons kosher salt, then add the pasta and cook, stirring occasionally, until *al dente*.

Warm a serving bowl or platter in a low oven. If the oven is not practical, warm the bowl just before use with hot water, even a ladleful of the pasta cooking water.

Drain and transfer the pasta to the heated serving bowl. Add the sauce, sprinkle with the remaining oregano, mix well, and serve.

 WINE SUGGESTION: any red with some acidity, such as a young Chianti, from Tuscany

MAINLY CHEESE

Gnocchi "alla bava"

(Potato gnocchi with cream and cheese)

ITALIAN METAPHORICAL FOOD names can be whimsical, descriptive, fanciful, irreverent, and even, as in this case, unappetizing. "*Alla bava*" literally means "with drool," but is used here as a synonym for *filante*, or forming strings, the way melted cheese does. You may well be able to find the recommended authentic cheeses at good cheese shops, but you can get away with parmigiano-reggiano and another cheese that melts smoothly, such as a Danish fontina, though its flavor will be pallid in comparison with the original Fontina from the Valle d'Aosta, in the Italian Alps, which is available from good cheese vendors outside Italy (page 391).

This dish is a great peacemaker. You can serve it to anybody willing to eat cheese. The finicky are seduced by the comforting creamy texture and apparent blandness of the sauce, while sophisticated diners are not deceived by its whiteness and perceive the wonderful nutty, mellow flavor of the cheeses.

Delicious without additional seasoning, this Piedmontese dish is also the perfect background for the white truffle of Alba. If you have only truffle salt or paste, or a very good white-truffle oil, we won't call the food police. Fresh white truffles are available, at great expense, between October and November.

While technically a *primo piatto*, this dish is so rich that in anything but very small portions it can be considered a *piatto unico*, or one-dish meal. It is soft and voluptuous and tastes of potatoes and cheese. Follow it with a crisp palate-cleansing salad.

 PASTA SHAPES While potato gnocchi are essential to the identity of this dish, the sauce would certainly be delicious on any short format of pasta.

For the *condimento*:

2 cups heavy cream

5 ounces (150 grams) grated *toma piemontese* cheese or parmigiano-reggiano

2½ ounces (70 grams) grated *fontina valdostana* or other melting cheese (see headnote)

To make the dish:

1 recipe *Gnocchi di patate* (page 364) or 1 pound (450 grams) store-bought potato gnocchi (kept on a floured tray while you make the sauce)

optional: 1 white truffle (*tartufo bianco di Alba*) weighing about 1½ ounces (40 grams) or less, brushed to remove surface dirt and wiped with a damp cloth. Alternatively (but still optional), some form of preserved truffle: a few sprinkles of truffle salt or ½ teaspoon truffle paste or 1 teaspoon truffle oil

Bring 5 quarts (5 liters) of water to a boil in an 8-quart (8-liter) pot over high heat.

While waiting for the water to boil, heat the cream to lukewarm in a saucepan and add the two grated cheeses. Stir the mixture carefully over very low heat until the cheeses melt. If using preserved truffles instead of fresh (see ingredients, above), stir in the chosen form. Keep the sauce warm while you boil the gnocchi.

When the water boils, add 3 tablespoons kosher salt, then drop the gnocchi gently in.

Warm a serving bowl or platter in a low oven. If the oven is not practical, warm the bowl just before use with hot water, even a ladleful of the gnocchi cooking water.

As soon as each *gnocco* bobs to the surface, use a slotted spoon or a spider strainer to fish it out and transfer it to the warm serving bowl. Layer the cheese sauce and gnocchi until both are used up. These are not neat layers, as for lasagne; alternating sauce and pasta in the serving bowl is one way to ensure even distribution.

If you're using a fresh truffle, use a truffle slicer or mandoline to shave very thin slices over the dish. Serve immediately.

 WINE SUGGESTION: a young Barbaresco DOCG, also from Piedmont

---

Gratin alla sorrentina

(Baked pasta with mozzarella and cheese)

NOT ALL SOUTHERN Italian pasta dishes contain tomatoes or even olive oil. This rich, delicious baked pasta dish from Sorrento (but also known as *gratin alla napoletana*) is sauced with butter and a combination of fresh and aged cheeses. You can substitute a good young pecorino, if it's not too salty, for the Calabrian *caciocavallo* called for, but the mozzarella must be the best buffalo-milk mozzarella you can lay hands on—nothing else has any taste. Put the mozzarella in the fridge for a couple of days to let it dry out; otherwise it will throw off too much liquid. (Do not do this with mozzarella you plan to eat on its own.)

Have all the ingredients prepped and ready when you put the pasta on to boil. The *condimento* is created quickly directly on the cooked pasta and finished in the oven. You will be tempted to add things to its white simplicity, but try it as written

the first time, with good cheese. The final product is the opposite of gloppy and creamy: the pasta, with its crisp breadcrumb and cheese topping, becomes one with the savory melted mozzarella, which provides the biggest hit of flavor.

The water buffalo was introduced into Italy in the sixth century and has been part of the daily life of the Italian South ever since. As a traction animal, it was essential for the farming of the Pontine Marshes, between Lazio and Campania, too wet for oxen. Today they enjoy a life of relative leisure and can be seen wallowing in what remains of its swampy past.

The reason the recipe calls for a Calabrian cheese lies in history: the Sila, a mountainous region of Calabria, used to belong to the Kingdom of Naples, and the capital was well supplied with cheeses from every corner of the kingdom.

 PASTA SHAPES Even though tradition dictates *fusilli* (either factory made or homemade, page 354) for this dish, you can get away with *farfalle* (page 336), *fregnacce* (page 337), *ruote*, or *scialatielli*.

For the *condimento*:

7 tablespoons (100 grams) unsalted butter, half at room temperature, half cold
7 rounded tablespoons (70 grams) grated *caciocavallo silano* cheese or pecorino romano
10½ ounces (300 grams) buffalo-milk mozzarella, diced

freshly ground white pepper
salt
1 heaping tablespoon plain fine dry breadcrumbs

To make the dish:

1 recipe *fusilli* (page 354) or 1 pound (450 grams) factory-made *fusilli*

Put 5 quarts (5 liters) of water on to boil in an 8-quart (8-liter) pot over high heat.

While the water is coming to a boil, get all the other ingredients prepped and ready to grab. Preheat the oven to 350°F (180°C). Butter a 3½-quart (at least) shallow baking dish.

When the water boils, add 3 tablespoons kosher salt, then add the pasta and boil, stirring occasionally, until quite *al dente*. Drain the pasta in a colander and put it back in the pot. Add the room-temperature half of the butter and 2 tablespoons of the grated cheese. Stir with a wooden spoon. Add the diced mozzarella and stir vigorously until it begins to melt and form strings. Grind on the white pepper generously and taste for salt.

Transfer the pasta to the baking dish and dot the cold butter on top.

 MAKE-AHEAD NOTE: This much can be done ahead of time, before the guests arrive.

Sprinkle with the remaining grated cheese and the breadcrumbs. Bake until a nice golden-brown crust forms, about 20 minutes. Let rest for a few minutes, then serve directly from the baking dish.

 WINE SUGGESTION: Furore Bianco, from the Amalfi Coast

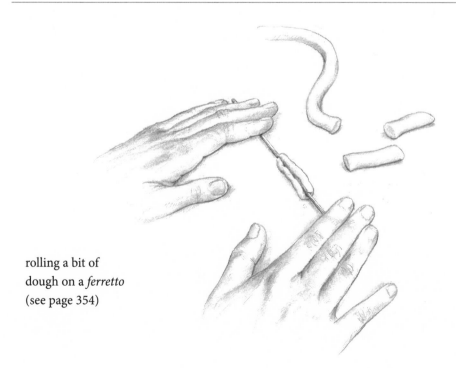

rolling a bit of
dough on a *ferretto*
(see page 354)

Sugo con la ricotta

(Ricotta)

IN ROME, WE are inordinately proud of our local sheep's milk ricotta, *ricotta romana*. It is rich and creamy with a delicate flavor that still manages to convey a pleasantly ovine note that reminds you of your favorite sweater, in a good way. And my guests are always happy with this embarrassingly easy dish, popular throughout central Italy, which I used mistakenly to think of as nursery food. Because of its apparent blandness and thick, creamy texture, it's a great choice for picky eaters like my fussy friend Francesca, whose joy when I serve her this sauce is heart-rending. Yet with good pasta and great ricotta, sophisticated diners will pick up the subtle but pronounced fragrances of the ricotta and the pasta itself, whose own flavor is too often neglected.

Only the very best Italian ricotta disdains a helping handful of parmigiano-reggiano. Go ahead and use even more than the amount suggested here if you want. Pepper adds interest, and we call for white pepper only for aesthetic reasons—to avoid specks of black in our nice white sauce. Should you have a white or black truffle around the house (it *does* happen), grate it on and mix it in just before serving. Be sure to use heated dishes. Since the sauce is uncooked, the pasta's own heat will dissipate quickly on cold plates.

 PASTA SHAPES Factory-made *penne rigate* are very traditional, but any *pasta corta* will do. Also good are *gnocchi di patate* (page 364), *gnocchetti* (page 342), and *fettuccine* (page 330), even though they are long.

NOTE: If you cannot find sheep's milk ricotta, you can assist decent cow's milk ricotta by mixing 1 tablespoon heavy cream for every 3½ ounces (100 grams). Most artisanal ricotta, cow or sheep, needs to drain in a basket or colander overnight in the refrigerator to lose its considerable water content.

For the *condimento*:

14 ounces (400 grams) very fresh whole sheep's milk ricotta, or the best you can find, drained in the refrigerator overnight in a colander

at least ½ teaspoon salt

freshly ground white pepper

1 heaping tablespoon or more grated parmigiano-reggiano (optional but recommended)

To make the dish:

1 pound (450 grams) pasta (see suggestions above)

Bring 5 quarts (5 liters) of water to a boil in an 8-quart (8-liter) pot over high heat.

Warm a serving bowl or platter in a low oven. If the oven is not practical, warm the bowl just before use with hot water, even a ladleful of the pasta cooking water.

When the water boils, add 3 tablespoons kosher salt, then add the pasta and cook, stirring occasionally, until *al dente*.

After about 5 minutes, approximately when the pasta has cooked halfway, take a ladleful of its cooking water and put it in the warmed serving bowl. Add the ricotta and sprinkle with salt and pepper to taste and the parmigiano, if using. Mash the ricotta with a fork until it is quite smooth. (A low-tech fork is all you need; just keep mashing while the pasta cooks. It will be enough.)

Drain the pasta, add it to the bowl, mix well, and serve immediately on warm dishes.

🥢 **WINE SUGGESTION:** a lush Pinot Bianco/Chardonnay blend from Friuli

---

fresh ricotta

Cacio e pepe

(Pecorino romano and black pepper)

THIS UTTERLY ROMAN and deceptively simple condiment for pasta is made with nothing but grated pecorino romano and cracked black peppercorns, though some cooks add a bit of olive oil as well. Some say—and Oretta approves—that a spoonful of oil in the pasta cooking water makes the cheese stick better, a handy trick if your cheese is on the old and dry side. Others add some oil to the pasta as soon as it is drained, before the cheese goes on, but only a little lest it introduce a strong, extraneous taste. If you choose to use oil, don't overdo it. For best results, the cheese should be only a few months old so that it stays grainy (rather than floury) when grated.

It's a traditional dish of Rome and Lazio that stayed in the background for generations until about the turn of the millennium, when it exploded onto restaurant menus all over the Eternal City and beyond. All of a sudden, foodie tourists were seeking out and comparing versions, and all of us Roman hostesses had to brush up our technique. It certainly deserved a little more attention than it had been getting, so I don't begrudge it its time in the spotlight. In fact, one result of the fashion years was that top chefs and gourmets began to experiment with rather grander cheeses than pecorino romano. Agata Parisella, chef of Agata e Romeo, in Rome, makes a knockout version with Szechuan peppercorns and *piacentino ragusano* cheese from Sicily—lest you be tempted to think of Roman tradition as static and boring.

As long as you don't call it *"cacio e pepe,"* feel free to try other cheeses that approximate the soapy, grainy consistency of a young pecorino romano. Oretta sometimes uses a mix of Sicilian pecorinos, including *tuma persa* and the Sicilian DOP pecorino. Whatever cheese you use, make sure it's freshly grated, on the young side, and the best you can find. In this dish, the cheese is right out there on its own with no meat or tomatoes to hide behind. Good pecorino romano is salty and sharp, though not too extreme, and stands up well to the piquancy of all that black pepper.

Although it's always a good idea to warm your plates as well as your serving bowl, it is crucial here. The sauce consists entirely of melted cheese, which will congeal unpleasantly on contact with chilly china.

This is not a dish to make for a crowd. The sauce forms as you mix grated cheese with wet, watery noodles. The smaller the quantity, the better the result. Of course, that makes it perfect to enjoy in glorious solitude with a nice glass of wine from the Castelli Romani, which is fortunate because you should make it several times for yourself before you try it for company. Once you've readied your three ingredients—pasta, fabulous cheese, and pepper—the success of the dish depends on technique, and every cook will just have to learn the feel of the sauce as it forms. Work quickly and confidently, practice, and you'll get the hang of it.

PASTA SHAPES *Tonnarelli* (page 334), spaghetti, and *bucatini* are the canonical pastas, but don't try to make too much at once. Although not accepted by purists, factory-made *fusilli* (page 354) and rigatoni are a good deal easier to handle, especially for more than a couple of portions.

4 heaping tablespoons (60 grams) black
    peppercorns
about 10 rounded tablespoons (100 grams)
    freshly grated young pecorino romano

1 pound (450 grams) pasta (see suggestions
    above)
1 tablespoon extra virgin olive oil (optional)

Bring 5 quarts (5 liters) of water to a boil in an 8-quart (8-liter) pot over high heat.

While the water is heating, fold the peppercorns into a sheet of waxed paper or an old cloth napkin and whack them repeatedly with a blunt instrument, such as a meat tenderizer, until very coarsely cracked. The pepper should be quite a bit coarser than what comes out of the peppermill.

Mix the cheese and pepper in a small bowl.

Warm a serving bowl or platter in a low oven. If the oven is not practical, warm the bowl just before use with hot water, even a ladleful of the pasta cooking water. Warm the individual plates too.

When the water boils, add 3 tablespoons kosher salt and, the oil (if using), then add the pasta and cook, stirring occasionally, until *al dente*.

When the pasta is almost done, add a large spoonful of its water to the serving bowl. Keep the bowl near the stove or on a food warmer.

When the pasta is *al dente*, transfer it, dripping wet, to the serving bowl. A spider strainer or two large forks (for long forms) are best for doing this because they transfer quite a bit of water along with the pasta. Reserve the cooking water. Sprinkle on the cheese and pepper and toss vigorously. The sauce will form right on the pasta as the residual water mixes with the cheese. Add some of the reserved cooking water to spread things around if need be.

Serve immediately if not sooner on warmed dishes.

WINE SUGGESTION: anything from the Castelli Romani, but if you want to buck tradition, try Dolcetto, from Piedmont, or other light fruity red, or a spicy Primitivo, from Puglia

Alfredo

(Parmigiano-reggiano and butter)

UNTIL THE 1980s, when the Michelin stars began piling up among the more modern, creative establishments, Alfredo alla Scrofa was probably Rome's most famous restaurant. As early as the 1920s, the members of what passed for the international jet set in an era before commercial aviation never missed a chance to dine there on the famous *fettuccine al triplo burro*—triple butter. The great and the infamous threw caution to the wind—nobody was thinking about cholesterol in those days. Both Churchill and Mussolini were patrons. Photographs of Clark Gable, Robert Mitchum, Ava Gardner, and even Greta Garbo look down from the wall in commemoration of past visits. While honeymooning in the Eternal City, Mary Pickford and Douglas Fairbanks famously awarded Alfredo a golden serving fork and spoon so that baser metals would not defile this ambrosia.

Nostalgic gastronomic pilgrims still order *fettuccine Alfredo*, as the dish came to be known, on Via della Scrofa, but elsewhere in the world "Alfredo sauce," made from recipes no Roman, much less Alfredo himself, would recognize, is glopped on everything from bruschetta to chicken and, yes, occasionally, even pasta. Such has been the price of Alfredo's success that most people today have no idea what the designation really means. But the restaurant hasn't given up. Mario Mozzetti, the current owner, has decided to organize classes.

The first important thing to know about *fet-tuccine Alfredo* is that there is no such thing as "Alfredo sauce." The *condimento* is created directly on the cooked pasta, not unlike the more humble *cacio e pepe* (page 102). We might think of it as a *cacio e pepe* suitable for royalty, Hollywood or otherwise. In order to create the sauce properly, you will need a round platter or rather flat, wide, shallow bowl, not a deep bowl.

There are only two ingredients besides the pasta, and they have to be perfect. There is no cream. That's right. None at all. Ever. Nope. Not a drop. Nor are there flavorings of *any* kind. According to the restaurant, there is unsalted butter, the freshest, best you can find (ideally from raw milk with not less than 82 percent fat), and parmigiano-reggiano, aged 24 months—not 18, not 36—and grated at the last possible moment. Younger cheese is too soft and will not grate properly, and older cheese will have begun to dry out. Only a two-year-old cheese has the right consistency. The restaurant recommends cheese from the area around Reggio Emilia—that is, from a subzone within the official parmigiano-reggiano production area—because, says Mr. Mozzetti, it has a thinner rind than the rest.

No other pasta shape than the thinnest *fettuccine* you can buy or make will do. They should be so thin that they are already cooked by the time the water returns to the boil. Nevertheless, says Oretta, to comfort us mere mortals, the fragrance of the butter and cheese melting on the warm noodles will still make us swoon, even if our *fettuccine* are a bit thicker and slower to cook.

There is nothing bland about this dish. Its characteristic flavor is that of the parmigiano. How could it not be when the weight of the cheese in the recipe is equal to that of the pasta? In fact, anyone who doubts what we say about going easy on the parmigiano when you want to taste anything else should try this dish to learn just how potent its flavor is. If you find the flavor too overpowering, next time use a *little* less or choose a cheese that is a *little* younger. Don't take too many liberties, however, or the consistency of the sauce won't be right.

Ladies and gentlemen, we give you the original recipe for *fettuccine Alfredo*, from the horse's mouth.

14 tablespoons (200 grams) unsalted butter, preferably from raw milk
1 pound (450 grams) parmigiano-reggiano aged 24 months, in one piece

1 pound (450 grams) freshly made *fettuccine* (page 330), as thin as possible, ideally not more than 0.02 inch (½ millimeter) thick (the thinnest setting on a home pasta machine)

Using a butter curler or small knife, curl or scrape all the butter and strew the pieces evenly over a plate so they can soften without overlapping. The pieces need to be quite thin; dice will not melt quickly enough when the time comes. Leave the butter at room temperature.

Put 5 quarts (5 liters) of water on to boil in an 8-quart (8-liter) pot over high heat. While the water is coming to a boil, grate the cheese. To grate the cheese, use a food processor or an old-fashioned grater with star-shaped holes, *not* one of the new type with rectangular openings (see page 38).

The serving plate must be *very* warm. Rinse it with boiling water or place it directly over the pasta pot while the water is coming to a boil instead of a lid. Transfer the butter curls or shavings to the serving plate, and again distribute evenly in a single layer.

When the water boils, remove the plate and keep it warm. Add 3 tablespoons kosher salt to the water, then add the pasta and stir. Paper-thin *fettuccine* made on the last setting of the machine will be done by the time the water boils again. Thicker *fettuccine* may need a couple of minutes more. In either case, don't take your eyes off the pot, as *fettuccine* cook quickly.

Lift the *fettuccine* out of the pot with two forks or a large kitchen fork and leave the water in the pot. If forks are too intimidating, use a handheld colander or spider strainer. Alternatively, reserve a cup of water and drain the pasta quickly in a colander. Whatever method you use, the pasta should carry quite a bit of water along with it. Plop it right on top of the butter in the serving plate and spread it out. Don't let plate or pasta get cold. You can put the plate back on top of the pot, if there is still hot water, or use an electric food warmer.

Sprinkle a couple of handfuls of the grated cheese over the *fettuccine* and, with slow, continuous movements, use a serving spoon and fork (which need not be gold) to mix the pasta and cheese, from top to bottom and scraping in from the edges. Add more handfuls of cheese and keep mixing. Some of the reserved pasta water can be mixed in a little at a time. This action of churning ingredients to make something creamy is called *mantecare* in Italian. It should take 2 or 3 minutes, certainly not more, for the butter, cheese, and water to combine to make a smooth sauce.

Serve immediately on very hot plates.

 WINE SUGGESTION: The restaurant prescribes Malvasia del Lazio, a lovely, floral white. A full-bodied, oaked Chardonnay would be a suitable alternative and easier to find in North America.

Fresh Vegetable, Herb, and Mushroom Sauces

The sauces in this section are intended to be seasonal. When your local farmers' market has fabulous broccoli rabe (late fall through early spring), that's when you make those sauces. Sauces with eggplant or peppers or fresh tomatoes are for summer. Don't be afraid of using good canned tomatoes all winter.

UNCOOKED SAUCES

Olio e prezzemolo

(Olive oil and parsley)

WHAT COULD BE easier than combining chopped parsley, olive oil, lemon, and pepper? But don't underestimate this simple Tuscan condiment of a beautiful transparent green. Each of the four flavors emerges in perfect balance.

My whole attitude toward parsley was turned upside down when I tasted the parsley Oretta grows in her garden. It tasted fresh and, well, like parsley, with the emphasis on taste. *That* is what you want for this sauce, *not* what has collected over the last two weeks in your vegetable drawer. You also want a nice fresh lemon worthy of this fabulous herb. It's a great summer sauce, especially if you've just cut the parsley from your own garden or even a flowerpot.

Although cold pasta dishes technically don't exist in Italy, or at least are not recognized by purists, this one offers a little wiggle room. It is never chilled, but can be left out on a buffet table.

PASTA SHAPES Any number of long pasta formats will do, egg or flour-and-water, such as *tagliatelle* (page 328), *fettuccine* (page 330), *maltagliati* (page 336), spaghetti, or *linguine/bavette/trenette*.

NOTE: Sometimes black pepper from a grinder is just too fine. To crush peppercorns so as to leave some large fragments that will explode in the mouth and remind us just how piquant and flavorful black pepper can be, fold the peppercorns into a sheet of waxed paper or an old cloth napkin and whack them repeatedly with a blunt instrument, such as a meat tenderizer, until very coarsely cracked. The pepper should be quite a bit coarser than what comes out of the peppermill.

For the *condimento*:

1 heaping cup finely chopped fresh flat-leaf parsley
the grated zest and juice of 1 organic lemon
2 tablespoons (20 grams) black peppercorns, coarsely crushed (see note above)

6 tablespoons medium fruity extra virgin olive oil
salt

To make the dish:

1 pound (450 grams) pasta (see suggestions above)

Put the parsley, lemon zest, crushed peppercorns, and oil in a serving bowl and add a pinch of salt. Let the flavors blend for 2 hours. No cover is needed, but to protect the sauce from assaults from the atmosphere, you can drape a kitchen towel over the bowl.

Bring 5 quarts (5 liters) of water to a boil in an 8-quart (8-liter) pot over high heat. Add 3 tablespoons kosher salt, then add the pasta and cook, stirring occasionally, until *al dente*.

Drain the pasta. Stir the lemon juice quickly into the parsley and lemon zest mixture, add the pasta, and toss until the pasta is completely coated. Even though the sauce is uncooked, the pasta is normally served hot. It can, however, be held at room temperature.

WINE SUGGESTION: an unoaked white, such as Collio Friulano, from Friuli–Venezia Giulia—the acidity in the wine would complement the lemon

---

Ruchetta e olive

(Arugula and olives)

THE ITALIAN WORD *ruchetta* covers the many varieties of bitter, peppery salad greens belonging to two different botanical genuses. *Diplotaxis tenuifolia* (also *D. muralis*) is what used to be called *rughetta selvatica* in Italian markets, and indeed it can still be found growing wild even in city parks and archaeological sites. It has a long, pointy leaf and quite a kick. Slightly milder are the varieties of *Eruca sativa*, or *rughetta coltivata* in the market vernacular. That is what corresponds most closely to the American arugula. Since the 1980s, it has pretty much all been cultivated and the terminology has adjusted. More varieties are available too, and the flavor is generally milder. Choose any variety of the greens known in English as arugula or rocket, but the more peppery the better.

The sauce, popular throughout Italy especially in summer, is uncooked. The bitterness of the arugula is set off by the saltiness of the olives and anchovies. Yes, it's a little like having salad on your pasta, but don't let that put you off. It's delicious.

 PASTA SHAPES Use spaghetti, *tagliolini* (page 332), *farfalle* (page 336), *maltagliati* (page 336), *pappardelle* (page 331), or *paglia e fieno* (page 331); also *ravioli con le sogliole* (page 304).

For the *condimento*:

1 small clove garlic
1 cup (150 grams) pitted black olives, preferably Gaeta or taggiasche
2 oil-packed anchovy fillets, drained and blotted dry
½ cup (100 milliliters) extra virgin olive oil, preferably intensely fruity
about 10 ounces (300 grams) arugula (gross weight including all the stems, which will be removed)
salt

To make the dish:

1 pound (450 grams) pasta (see suggestions above)
extra virgin olive oil for finishing
a piece of pecorino romano (optional)

Chop finely together the garlic, the olives, and the anchovies. Put the mixture in a serving bowl and stir in the oil.

Trim the arugula of all stems and tear the leaves into tiny pieces. You should have at least 3 cups tender pieces of leaves. If you have more, use it. Add it to the bowl. Taste for salt and mix well. Let rest for at least 30 minutes.

Bring 5 quarts (5 liters) of water to a boil in an 8-quart (8-liter) pot over high heat. Add 3 tablespoons kosher salt, then add the pasta and cook, stirring occasionally, until *al dente*.

Drain and transfer the pasta to the bowl with the arugula. Mix well, and add a swirl of oil. If desired, using a cheese slicer, shave the cheese over the top of the dish and mix in gently. Ideally you should serve immediately, but the dish can be held for up to about an hour and served at room temperature.

 WINE SUGGESTION: Livio Felluga Pinot Grigio, from Friuli

Erbe selvatiche e aromatiche

(Fresh herbs)

You won't find collections of dried herbs in many Italian kitchens. There's no need. Vendors at the markets freely distribute handfuls of basil and parsley and sell others, and most homes have at least a couple of pots of herbs growing on the balcony. It's well worth the effort to grow your own. Use any combination of herbs you like for this recipe, but don't even think of using dried. A spring freshness explodes in this lovely green sauce, made throughout Italy, with each of the herbs, the peppery arugula, the bite of the lemon, and the flavor of the oil coming forward in turn.

 PASTA SHAPES *Farfalle* (page 336), *maltagliati* (page 336), *trofie* (page 352), *tagliolini* (page 332), and *lagane* (page 334) all go beautifully with this quintessentially warm-weather *condimento,* but it's not at all fussy and almost any shape except those for soup will do nicely.

For the *condimento*:

about 1 cup coarsely chopped mixed fresh herbs, including some combination of fresh basil, flat-leaf parsley, thyme, marjoram, and spearmint
1 small bunch arugula, finely chopped (roughly 1 cup)
the grated zest of 1 organic lemon
freshly ground white pepper (but black will do)
6 tablespoons very high quality lightly fruity extra virgin olive oil

To make the dish:

1 pound (450 grams) pasta (see suggestions above)
the juice of the same organic lemon
at least 1 teaspoon salt
additional extra virgin olive oil for finishing, if needed
about 2 ounces (60 grams) parmigiano-reggiano in one piece

In a serving bowl, combine the chopped herbs, the arugula, and the lemon zest. Season with several grinds of pepper, add the oil, and mix well. Let sit at room temperature for at least 3 hours, stirring occasionally.

 MAKE-AHEAD NOTE: While the *condimento* must be made some hours in advance, don't get any ideas about making it the day before. Fresh is fresh.

Bring 5 quarts (5 liters) of water to a boil in an 8-quart (8-liter) pot over high heat. Add 3 tablespoons kosher salt, then add the pasta and cook, stirring occasionally.

While the pasta is cooking, add the lemon juice to the herb mixture. Add the salt gradually and taste. Mix well.

When the pasta is *al dente*, drain it and transfer to the serving bowl with the herb mixture. Mix very well. The pasta should be well coated with the flavored oil. Using a cheese slicer, shave the cheese directly on top of the pasta and mix again.

While the dish is best if served immediately, it will wait patiently for a while, such as on a buffet. Just remember that even if it cools to room temperature, it is not intended to be a cold pasta.

 WINE SUGGESTION: a herbaceous, bright white, such as Orvieto Classico, from Umbria, or Trebbiano d'Abruzzo DOC

Pasta alla checca

(Raw tomatoes and herbs)

PURISTS LIKE ORETTA do not acknowledge the legitimacy of cold pastas, but I am always looking for loopholes so I can make dishes ahead for summer terrace parties. This raw-tomato sauce, a popular summer favorite in much of Italy, is the perfect compromise. Though ideally served minutes after cooking, it will accept being parked on the buffet table and allowed to descend gently to room temperature. It should never be chilled. Remember that the tomatoes should be salad tomatoes according to the Italian standard—firm, acidic, and tending toward green—*not* bright red and very ripe. With the right tomatoes, the taste is as crisp and bright as the summer's best tomato salad.

The name tells us nothing about the taste. Checca is a diminutive of Francesca, and popular belief attributes the invention of the dish to an otherwise unidentified Roman woman.

 PASTA SHAPES *Conchiglie* do a particularly nice job of collecting the diced tomatoes, but *cavatelli* (page 345), *strascinati* (page 348), *lumachelle* (page 340), and *farfalle* (page 336) are also customary.

For the *condimento*:

1 pound (450 grams) firm salad tomatoes (with quite a bit of green), seeded and diced
½ cup (60 grams) green olives, pitted and sliced, coarsely chopped, or left whole
1 tablespoon minced fresh flat-leaf parsley
1 tablespoon chopped fresh basil
1 teaspoon fennel seeds or to taste

6 tablespoons medium-fruity extra virgin olive oil
at least ½ teaspoon salt
freshly ground black pepper

To make the dish:

1 pound (450 grams) pasta (see suggestions above)

Put the tomatoes, olives, parsley, basil, and fennel seeds in a serving bowl. Stir in the oil and season with salt and pepper. Let rest, covered, for about 30 minutes.

Bring 5 quarts (5 liters) of water to a boil in an 8-quart (8-liter) pot over high heat. Add 3 tablespoons kosher salt, then add the pasta and cook, stirring occasionally, until *al dente*.

Drain and transfer the pasta to the bowl with the tomato mixture. Toss well until the sauce warms up a bit and the pasta cools to about room temperature. Although best if served immediately, the dish will wait patiently for a couple of hours.

 WINE SUGGESTION: a fruity rosé from southern Italy, such as Salento rosé from Puglia, or Cerasuolo d'Abruzzo

Pomodorini e basilico

(Raw tomatoes and basil)

SUMMERTIME, WHEN THE basil is high and the tomatoes have flavor. . . . This sauce illustrates the extreme restraint of which Italian home cooks are capable, especially when the tomatoes come straight from the garden, sweet like the fruit they are. The garlic is merely a suggestion: it doesn't even touch the pasta. A single herb flavors the tomatoes and oil. You may be tempted to add more ingredients, but resist. You will think you have never tasted a tomato before in your life.

 PASTA SHAPES Short pasta is called for: *penne, maccheroni, casarecce, cavatelli* (page 345), *lumachelle* (page 340), *conchiglie, trofie* (page 352), or *maltagliati* (page 336).

For the *condimento*:

1 clove garlic, cut in half
1 pound (450 grams) cherry or grape tomatoes, quartered
1 cup minced fresh basil leaves
6 tablespoons extra virgin olive oil, preferably medium fruity
at least ½ teaspoon salt
freshly ground black pepper

To make the dish:

1 pound (450 grams) pasta (see suggestions above)
additional extra virgin olive oil for finishing

Rub the garlic around the rim of a serving bowl. Put the tomatoes in the bowl. Add the basil and the oil. Sprinkle with salt and grind on a little pepper (not too much or it will compete with the basil). Let stand for at least an hour, stirring often.

Bring 5 quarts (5 liters) of water to a boil in an 8-quart (8-liter) pot over high heat. Add 3 tablespoons kosher salt, then add the pasta and cook, stirring occasionally, until *al dente*.

Drain the pasta, add it to the bowl with the tomatoes, and toss gently until the pasta cools down slightly. Finish with a swirl of oil.

 WINE SUGGESTION: Lungarotti Torre di Giano, a fruity white from Umbria

Pesto alla genovese

(Basil, pine nuts, and pecorino)

THE FOOD PROCESSOR is inexorable and irresistible, but if you're willing to use a mortar and pestle to make your pesto the old-fashioned way, you'll probably never switch that motor on again.

The name *pesto* itself contains the method: a *pesto* is something *pestato*, pounded, with a pestle. For this reason, the word does not always mean a basil sauce for pasta: the qualifier "*alla genovese*" is not optional but essential to the definition of the dish. It is probably the most famous product of Liguria (the northwestern region of which Genoa is the capital), unless you count Christopher Columbus.

The Ligurians, says Oretta, are fixated on their famous *condimento*. The basil has to be the particular Ligurian variety with its pure fragrance and small leaves. The pine nuts have to come from the Lunigiana, the border area of Tuscany that is practically indistinguishable from southern Liguria. Walnuts are for a different sauce, not an alternative pesto. There is a local saying: "*Se il basilico è foresto, di sicuro non è pesto*" ("if the basil is from anywhere but here, whatever it is, it isn't pesto"). In other words,

nothing you do will satisfy an actual Genoese, so just use the freshest smallest-leafed basil you can lay hands on, and a very good, delicately fruity extra virgin olive oil, preferably Ligurian. And *pazienza*. Even with basil from a flowerpot thousands of miles from Genoa, your pesto can be fragrant, creamy, and an irresistible green.

Basil's fragrance evaporates quickly, so the pesto should be made and used the same day. If you use a food processor, you can, and should, make the pesto while the pasta is cooking. Although many people freeze pesto, preferably without the cheeses, Oretta dismisses the practice.

Nowadays *pesto alla genovese* is usually served alone on pasta, but the classic way—which is what we give here—includes potatoes and green beans (haricots). The amount of pesto the recipe makes is also correct for 1 pound (450 grams) of pasta should you decide to skip the potatoes and beans. The beans should be the thinnest, most flavorful you can find. Don't use great hulking specimens. And cook them until tender. You want the pasta to be *al dente*, but not the beans.

 PASTA SHAPES The canonical pastas to use with *pesto alla genovese* are *trenette* (as they are known in Liguria, and elsewhere as *linguine* or *bavette*), and *trofie* (page 352). But it also works just fine with *farfalle* (page 336), *gnocchetti* (page

342), and *fusilli* (page 354). In fact, in my never-ending search for buffet dishes for our Roman terrace parties, I've discovered that *fusilli al pesto* is always a hit, as well as very easy to eat from tiny plates with plastic forks.

For the *condimento*:

kosher salt

1 small piece of a garlic clove

about 3 cups packed leaves or 1 large bunch, about 7 ounces (200 grams), small-leafed fresh basil (don't use long-leafed basil)

½ cup (100 grams) pine nuts (not toasted)

6 tablespoons extra virgin olive oil, preferably lightly fruity

4 rounded tablespoons (40 grams) grated parmigiano-reggiano

3 rounded tablespoons (30 grams) grated *pecorino sardo* or pecorino romano

To make the dish:

8 ounces (225 grams) potatoes (any kind), peeled and diced

8 ounces (225 grams) (or a bit more) pasta (see suggestions above)

8 ounces (225 grams) thin green beans, the ends snapped off

Put a few grains of salt and the garlic in a mortar. Begin to pound (do not stir). Add the basil leaves and keep pounding. Add the pine nuts a few at a time. As you work, pour in the oil practically drop by drop. You will eventually have a beautiful green sauce. Add the cheeses and mix well. Your goal is to incorporate the cheeses completely into the sauce.

The food processor is not recommended, but if you must, put the garlic, basil, a pinch of kosher salt, and the pine nuts in the container and process at medium speed until finely chopped. Then, with the motor running, add the oil in a thin stream. Your goal is a smooth sauce. Transfer the mixture to a bowl and mix in the cheese by hand. Add a little more oil to liquefy the pesto a bit if it seems stiff.

 MAKE-AHEAD NOTE: Keep the pesto in the fridge in a glass jar with a layer of oil on top for not more than 24 hours.

Bring 5 quarts (5 liters) of water to a boil in an 8-quart (8-liter) pot over high heat. Add 3 tablespoons kosher salt, then add the potatoes and boil for a few minutes until tender. Scoop out with a slotted spoon and keep warm. Leave the water boiling.

In the same water, boil the green beans for about 12 minutes until tender (not *al dente*!). Scoop them out, keep warm, and add the pasta to the same water. Cook, stirring occasionally, until *al dente*.

Warm a serving bowl or platter in a low oven. If the oven is not practical, warm the bowl just before use with hot water, even a ladleful of the pasta cooking water.

When the pasta is nearly done, mix two generous tablespoons of the cooking water into the pesto. Drain and transfer the pasta to the heated serving bowl. Mix in the beans and potatoes. Pour the pesto over the pasta, mix well, and serve immediately.

 WINE SUGGESTION: fruity Vermentino from Sardinia or Liguria

Pesto alla trapanese

(Raw tomatoes, herbs, and almonds)

TRAPANI, A PROVINCIAL capital on Sicily's west coast, dominates a corner of the island that, though certainly influenced by the Greeks, was not actually colonized by them as the eastern part was. It remained a territory of indigenous people, the Elymians, and Phoenician and Carthaginian traders. There is still something exotic about its cuisine, which includes couscous. Today most people visit Trapani as a base for trips to Marsala, for its famous fortified wine, and to Erice, a beautiful medieval town above the sea, where I first tasted this delicious uncooked sauce, on *busiata* (see page 356). It exists in numerous variations, but, determined to get as close to the original as possible, Oretta consulted the Authority, Gaetano Basile (see page 130). Anyone who knows or cares about the popular history of Sicily regards Gaetano as perhaps the last repository of the true gastronomic traditions of the island. Only raw ingredients, he told her, must be used, which eliminates the fried eggplant some modern cooks add to make the sauce creamier.

If you want to do it really right, says Gaetano, you'll need the red garlic of Nubia. Not to be confused with the African toponym, the name designates an agricultural area near Trapani. The delicately flavored garlic grown there has been made a Slow Food presidium (that is, a protected traditional local food product). He also bans chile, calling it the *pepe*, black pepper, of the poor—anathema in the opulent cuisine of Sicily, with its herbs, spices, nuts, raisins, and generally luxurious approach. (Rome seems like Sparta in comparison.)

But fear not. *Pesto alla trapanese* can be good anywhere you can grow herbs and get flavorful tomatoes. It's the ideal way to use up some of those fifty kinds of herbs you planted and somehow never know what to do with. The ideal tomatoes would be the small pear-shaped *perini*, but San Marzano–type are great, and you have license to use other red, ripe flavorful tomatoes, with the emphasis on flavorful. This is a dish for late summer and is even good at room temperature. The taste and texture are complex. The crushed almonds, a nice Sicilian touch, play against the oily base of tomatoes and garlicky oil, while the extra-large quantity of fresh herbs make an assertive presence of green. Conversation at the table will revolve around guessing what combination of herbs you used. The *ricotta salata*, a dry, gratable ricotta typical of southern Italy, ties everything together nicely and adds texture.

Since practically nobody, even in Italy, will have Gaetano's precious garlic, we must at least choose the freshest, mildest we can. His recipe calls for twice as much as we give here—yes, eight crushed cloves. If you think yours is a poem of delicateness, like his, go ahead and add more, but do it carefully, one clove at a time and taste as you go.

The name "pesto" tells us that the sauce is made with a mortar and pestle. We do not expect most people to follow tradition in this. A food processor will be dandy.

PASTA SHAPES In addition to *busiata*, this sauce is perfect with spaghetti, *strozzapreti/pici* (page 344), or *strascinati* (page 348).

For the *condimento*:

4 cloves very fresh, mild garlic, crushed

¾ cup (180 milliliters) extra virgin olive oil, preferably intensely fruity

4 fresh, ripe tomatoes, San Marzano if possible, peeled, seeded, and diced

about 3 cups (70 grams) loosely packed mixed fresh herbs (such as fresh basil, flat-leaf parsley, rosemary, sage, and mint)

⅓ cup (60 grams) blanched almonds, lightly toasted

4 black peppercorns

1 teaspoon salt

To make the dish:

1 pound (450 grams) pasta (see suggestions above)

Macerate the garlic in half the oil for at least 4 hours.

Put the tomatoes, herbs, almonds, and peppercorns in a large mortar. Begin to pound and gradually add the garlic, two cloves at a time, and some of the oil. Incorporate the remaining oil and the salt. Keep pounding until the sauce is smooth and creamy.

Alternatively, put all the ingredients in a food processor and pulse until chopped fine, but not pulverized, then process for a few seconds on high speed until fairly smooth.

 MAKE-AHEAD NOTE: The sauce can be made up to this point earlier the same day, but do not refrigerate it or it will lose flavor.

Bring 5 quarts (5 liters) of water to a boil in an 8-quart (8-liter) pot over high heat. Add 3 tablespoons kosher salt, then add the pasta and cook, stirring occasionally, until *al dente*.

Warm a serving bowl or platter in a low oven. If the oven is not practical, warm the bowl just before use with hot water, even a ladleful of the pasta cooking water.

Drain the pasta and transfer to the warm serving bowl. Add the pesto and toss very well until the pasta is well coated with the sauce. This may take longer than usual. Although you should serve immediately, if it's a warm summer evening, the dish will afford a little leeway to have your antipasto first.

WINE SUGGESTION: Regaleali Tasca d'Almerita Chardonnay Sicilia IGT, from Sicily

---

Sugo con mandorle, capperi e origano

(Raw tomatoes, almonds, capers, and oregano)

SIMILAR TO *pesto alla trapanese* in the use of raw tomatoes and crushed almonds, this sauce differs in the assertive aroma of oregano and the salty bite of capers, typical, and famous, product of the island of Pantelleria, home of the recipe. Pantelleria belongs to the political region of Sicilia, but is actually nearer to Tunisia than to Sicily. For Carthage, near present-day Tunis, in the days when it was a commercial and military superpower, hated enemy of Rome, Pantelleria was a strategic stopping place on the way to Sicily.

 PASTA SHAPES The most traditional pasta to use would be *busiata* (page 356), but any long flour-and-water format is fine.

For the *condimento*:

1 pound (450 grams) fresh red, ripe tomatoes, San Marzano if possible, seeded and diced (about 2½ cups)
about ⅓ cup (60 grams) salt-packed capers, rinsed free of all salt (page 36)
¼ cup (50 grams) blanched almonds
1 heaping tablespoon minced flat-leaf parsley
1 level teaspoon dried oregano
1 small piece dried chile or ½ teaspoon red pepper flakes, or less, to taste

6 tablespoons extra virgin olive oil
1 clove garlic, crushed
salt

To make the dish:

1 pound (450 grams) pasta (see suggestions above)
extra virgin olive oil for finishing

Put everything but the garlic and salt in the container of a blender or food processor and process until smooth. Transfer to a convenient container or even a serving bowl and add the garlic clove.

Let rest for a couple of hours at room temperature. Taste for salt. The amount needed will depend on your capers. Fish out and discard the garlic.

MAKE-AHEAD NOTE: This much can be done earlier in the day, but don't leave the garlic in for more than 2 hours. It may become much too strong.

Bring 5 quarts (5 liters) of water to a boil in an 8-quart (8-liter) pot over high heat. Add 3 tablespoons kosher salt, then add the pasta and cook, stirring occasionally, until *al dente.*

Warm a serving bowl or platter in a low oven. If the oven is not practical, warm the bowl just before use with hot water, even a ladleful of the pasta cooking water.

Drain and transfer the pasta to the heated serving bowl and toss with the sauce. Add a swirl of oil and serve.

 WINE SUGGESTION: Tenuta di Terre Nere Rosso, from Mount Etna, Sicily

COOKED SAUCES WITH TOMATOES

Sugo con pomodorini gratinati alla calabrese

(Calabrian baked small tomatoes)

THERE'S SOMETHING ABOUT the oven that brings out the best in cherry tomatoes. Between the roasted tomatoes and the pecorino, this flavorful dish tastes much richer than it is. The garlic, hot pepper, and oregano make it Calabrian, but it lends itself to variation. Try fresh basil without the pepper flakes. Or—if your tomatoes are exceptional—roast them plain, with just enough oil to keep them from sticking, and use mellower parmigiano-reggiano in place of the pecorino. Fresh mint is good too as a change from basil. Just remember to exercise some restraint: let a single herb shine through.

 PASTA SHAPES Any *pasta corta* will do fine, but spaghetti works too.

For the *condimento*:

1 tablespoon medium fruity extra virgin olive oil
1 pound (450 grams) large cherry or grape
    tomatoes (about walnut-size), halved
2 cloves garlic, finely chopped
1 level teaspoon dried oregano (optional)
1 level teaspoon salt
1 level teaspoon red pepper flakes

To make the dish:

1 pound (450 grams) pasta (see suggestions
    above)
5 tablespoons medium fruity extra virgin olive
    oil
6 rounded tablespoons (60 grams) grated
    pecorino romano or *caciocavallo* from the
    Sila or Aspromonte in Calabria

Preheat the oven to 350°F (180°C). Brush an oven-to-table dish with the tablespoon of oil.

Place the tomatoes in the dish, cut side up and quite close together in a single layer. Sprinkle with the chopped garlic, oregano, salt, and red pepper flakes. Bake the tomatoes until quite soft, at least 30 minutes. They should be starting to color around the edges, but don't let them brown. Keep warm until the pasta is ready.

 MAKE-AHEAD NOTE: This much can be done earlier in the day. Reheat the tomatoes gently in a low oven while the pasta is cooking.

Bring 5 quarts (5 liters) of water to a boil in an 8-quart (8-liter) pot over high heat. Add 3 tablespoons kosher salt, then add the pasta and cook, stirring occasionally, until *al dente*.

Warm a serving bowl or platter in a low oven. If the oven is not practical, warm the bowl just before use with hot water, even a ladleful of the pasta cooking water.

Drain the pasta and transfer to the baking dish with the tomatoes just out of the oven. If the baking dish won't hold all the pasta, transfer the tomatoes to the warmed serving bowl, and then add the pasta and proceed as directed. Mix well, crushing the tomatoes gently as you toss the pasta. Mix in the remaining oil and the cheese and toss again.

Transfer the dressed pasta to the warmed serving bowl, if it's not there already, and serve immediately.

 WINE SUGGESTION: a bright, spicy Cirò Rosso from Calabria

Sugo semplice di pomodori da sugo ben maturi

(Ripe fresh tomatoes)

WITH THIS QUICK, simple, tasty, and extremely popular sauce, the pasta can be ready, from start to finish, in less than half an hour. Every Italian would recognize it as the mother lode of pasta sauces. The flavor is the flavor of tomatoes. Period.

Here and elsewhere, tomatoes are left unpeeled even when the seeds are removed. The peels are full of vitamins and minerals and also make the sauce more flavorful.

 PASTA SHAPES Use any pasta shape except *capelli d'angelo* and *pastina*. It's also delicious on *agnolotti con i carciofi* (page 300).

For the *condimento*:

1 small white onion
1 small carrot
1 small celery rib
6 tablespoons extra virgin olive oil
1 pound (450 grams) San Marzano tomatoes (or similar type, see page 30), seeded and cut in strips
1 bay leaf
1 small piece dried chile
salt

To make the dish:

1 pound (450 grams) pasta (see suggestions above)
6 rounded tablespoons (60 grams) grated parmigiano-reggiano or pecorino romano
1 heaping tablespoon minced fresh flat-leaf parsley
extra virgin olive oil for finishing (optional)

Chop finely together the onion, the carrot, and the celery (in the food processor if desired) and place in a saucepan with the oil. Sauté over medium-low heat until the vegetables are tender and just becoming golden, about 5–6 minutes.

Stir in the tomatoes, then add the bay leaf, chile, and salt to taste. Cover and cook over low heat for about 20 minutes, or until the tomatoes are falling apart and the oil has separated and come to the surface. Fish out and discard the bay leaf and chile.

 MAKE-AHEAD NOTE: If you don't want to use the sauce immediately, at this point it can be stored in the refrigerator for a couple of days or frozen.

Bring 5 quarts (5 liters) of water to a boil in an 8-quart (8-liter) pot over high heat. Add 3 tablespoons kosher salt, then add the pasta and cook, stirring occasionally, until *al dente*.

Warm a serving bowl or platter in a low oven. If the oven is not practical, warm the bowl just before use with hot water, even a ladleful of the pasta cooking water.

Drain and transfer the pasta to the heated serving bowl or platter. Toss first with the grated cheese, then add the sauce and mix well. Sprinkle with the parsley and add a swirl of oil if desired. Serve immediately.

WINE SUGGESTION: a light red, such as Dolcetto d'Alba or d'Asti, from Piedmont, or Sangiovese, from Emilia-Romagna

---

agnolotto

Boscaiola

(Canned tuna and mushrooms)

EVEN THOUGH TUNA and mushrooms are used everywhere in Italy, this dish, in which they are combined, is a pillar of the traditional central Italian kitchen. Its earthy, comforting, autumnal flavors and rather voluptuous texture belie the speed with which it can be prepared, but don't scrimp on the ingredients. Try to use good Italian (or Spanish) tuna and tomatoes, and do try to find something more interesting than ordinary button mushrooms, such as shiitake, hen of the woods, or chanterelles, or even just cremini or oyster mushrooms. Then the pronounced fragrance of the mushrooms will blend beautifully with the strong flavor of the tuna, everything softened by the sweetness of the tomato.

The ideal mushroom for this dish is the precious *ovolo* (*Amanita caesaris*). At one time it was so plentiful, and free, that it found its way into numerous homely dishes (see also, for example, page 262). In Italian markets today, the *ovolo* costs about three times as much as the already costly *porcino*, and is generally considered too valuable even to cook. It is, accordingly, usually sliced and served respectfully raw, garnished with shavings of parmigiano-reggiano and dressed with the finest extra virgin olive oil. How canned tuna fish ended up in such company is easily explained.

Boscaioli are woodsmen, and this was a favorite of the woodcutters working in the forests of Tuscany, Umbria, and Lazio. The woods of the Castelli Romani, the hill towns southeast of Rome, produce excellent mushrooms. Woodsmen could carry the tuna around with them easily, and at mealtime they could simply gather the mushrooms Mother Nature obligingly provided at no cost. That is also how we got *carbonara*, *cacio e pepe*, and other recipes favored by workers who needed to prepare meals out of doors far from a kitchen.

If you can find fresh porcini, use those, or a mix of chanterelles and button mushrooms. But even button mushrooms alone will make a tasty sauce, especially when, as in this recipe, you give them a booster of dried porcini.

As in most other recipes in this book, exact quantities are not important. If you're short on mushrooms or long on tuna, it won't make a bit of difference. What *will* matter, however, is not using good tuna packed in olive oil (see page 35).

 PASTA SHAPES Use this sauce with flour-and-water shapes, long and short: spaghetti, *linguine/bavette/trenette*, bucatini, *vermicelli*, *sedani*, *penne*, and *ruote*. Yes, these are all factory-made shapes, but that is what is customary with this sauce for the same reason as the canned tuna. Nevertheless, if you want to use homemade, you can choose *lagane* (page

334), *fregnacce* (page 337), *cavatelli* (page 345), *strascinati* (page 348), or *maltagliati* (page 336) made with flour and water. It's also delicious on *agnolotti con i carciofi* (page 300).

For the *condimento*:

6 tablespoons extra virgin olive oil
2 cloves garlic, crushed
¾ pound (340 grams) fresh mushrooms, any kind (see above), wiped clean and sliced not too thin, about ³⁄₁₆–¼ inch (5–7 millimeters) thick
¼ ounce (10 grams) or more dried porcini, soaked, squeezed, and coarsely chopped (page 37)
about 2¼ cups or 18 ounces (500 grams) Italian peeled tomatoes, cut into 3–4 pieces each, with their liquid

salt
freshly ground black pepper
1 7-ounce (200-gram) can oil-packed tuna, preferably Italian or Spanish, drained and flaked

To make the dish:

1 pound (450 grams) pasta (see suggestions above)
2 heaping tablespoons minced fresh flat-leaf parsley
extra virgin olive oil for finishing

Divide the oil between two skillets. Put the garlic cloves in one pan and both kinds of mushrooms in the other.

Cook the garlic over medium heat for 2 or 3 minutes and then discard. Add the tomatoes to the oil. Add ½ teaspoon salt, or more to taste, and a few grinds of pepper and continue cooking over low heat for about 15 minutes. The sauce should be visibly reduced and thickened, the tomatoes cooked, and the oil shining on the surface.

NOTE: There is no particular amount the sauce has to reduce. You will just notice that it looks thicker than it did a few minutes before and the oil has separated and risen to the top. This is an important stage in the making of a sauce and you will get used to watching for it. It takes more effort to imagine it from a written description than it does to recognize it on the stove.

Meanwhile, in the second pan, sauté the mushrooms over medium heat, stirring occasionally, for at least 3–4 minutes, or until they have given off their liquid and are cooked through. Stir in the crumbled tuna and turn off the heat.

Add the tomato sauce to the mushroom pan and let the flavors blend for a couple of minutes.

MAKE-AHEAD NOTE: The sauce can be made up to this point earlier in the day or the day before. Cover and refrigerate if you are planning to keep it for more than a couple of hours. Reheat gently when ready to use.

Bring 5 quarts (5 liters) of water to a boil in an 8-quart (8-liter) pot over high heat. Add 3 tablespoons kosher salt, then add the pasta and cook, stirring occasionally, until *al dente*. Warm a serving bowl or platter in a low oven. If the oven is not practical, warm the bowl just before use with hot water, even a ladleful of the pasta cooking water.

Drain and transfer the pasta to the heated serving bowl. Add the sauce and mix well. Finish with a sprinkling of chopped parsley and a generous swirl of oil. Serve immediately.

 WINE SUGGESTION: an earthy, lightly oaked Nebbiolo

canned tuna and fresh porcino

Sugo alla norma

(Sicilian eggplant sauce)

FLAGSHIP DISH OF Catania, main city of eastern Sicily, this voluptuous pasta sauce comes with a controversy about its name. Most people believe it is named for the opera *Norma*, by Vincenzo Bellini, a native son for whom the Catania opera house is named. That is why the dish's name is usually seen with a capital N, where normal Italian usage would use lowercase. But Oretta got the true story from her friend Gaetano Basile, greatest living historian of Sicilian cuisine.

One very hot July morning in the early 1900s, on a terrace in Civita, a historic quarter of Catania, two great Catanesi—Nino Martoglio, poet and playwright, and Angelo Musco, actor—were working on a new play. Eventually it got to be lunchtime. Enter Marietta Martoglio to say she had made a sauce of tomato and fried eggplant for lunch. Soon after she presented them with two plates of spaghetti topped with eggplant pieces, a snowfall of grated *ricotta salata*, and some basil leaves. The great thespian, overwhelmed, exclaimed, in Catanese dialect, "*Donna Marietta, ma chisti non è ca su' dui fila di pasta, chista è na norma. . . .*" ("*questi non sono due fili di pasta, questi sono la norma!*")—"this is not just a plate of spaghetti; this is a marvel!" The remark was widely quoted, and *norma*, the Catanese word for "marvel," became the name of the dish.

The dish is certainly not light—fried eggplant never is—but it is delicious and deeply satisfying, with the tomatoes, eggplant, cheese, and basil all coming forth.

❧ **PASTA SHAPES** Although there is no scientific reason, tradition demands spaghetti for this sauce.

For the *condimento*:

1 pound (450 grams) long dark-purple eggplants, sliced about ¼ inch (6 millimeters) thick, but not peeled

salt

2 medium white onions

3 cloves garlic

½ cup fresh basil leaves

1 cup (200 milliliters) extra virgin olive oil, preferably intensely fruity

2 pounds (900 grams) ripe sauce tomatoes, seeded and diced (not peeled), or canned peeled tomatoes

freshly ground black pepper

To make the dish:

1 pound (450 grams) pasta (see suggestions above)

7 ounces (200 grams) grated *ricotta salata* cheese

½ cup fresh basil leaves (for garnish)

If necessary (see headnote on page 154), sprinkle the eggplant slices lightly with salt and put them in a colander for about 1 hour.

Meanwhile make the sauce. Chop together coarsely (in the food processor if desired) the onion, the garlic, and the basil. Put the mixture in a saucepan, preferably terracotta, with 3 tablespoons of the oil and sauté over medium heat for about 4 minutes, or until the onion is becoming translucent.

Add the tomatoes, sprinkle generously with salt and pepper, and cook, covered, over low heat for 30 minutes, or until the sauce is visibly thickened and shiny.

Put the tomatoes through a food mill and stir 4 generous tablespoons of the oil into the resulting puree.

❧ **MAKE-AHEAD NOTE:** This fresh sauce should really be made the same day you serve it, but you can get a head start by preparing the tomatoes earlier in the day. Cover and refrigerate if holding for more than a couple of hours. The eggplant must, however, be fried as late as possible, preferably while you wait for the pasta water to boil.

If you have salted the eggplants, squeeze them and dry them well on paper towels or with a kitchen towel. The salt will come off with their water. Heat the remaining oil in a 16-inch (40-centimeter) skillet and fry the eggplant slices until golden brown on both sides. Drain on paper towels.

Bring 5 quarts (5 liters) of water to a boil in an 8-quart (8-liter) pot over high heat. Add 3 tablespoons kosher salt, then add the pasta and cook, stirring occasionally, until *al dente*.

Warm a serving bowl or platter in a low oven. If the oven is not practical, warm the bowl just before use with hot water, even a ladleful of the pasta cooking water.

Drain and transfer the pasta to the heated serving bowl. Toss the pasta first with half the cheese, then with the tomato sauce. Grind on plenty of pepper and mix well.

Garnish with the remaining basil leaves and a few slices of fried eggplant. Serve immediately, and pass the remaining eggplant slices and cheese for each diner to take according to taste.

 WINE SUGGESTION: a Sicilian red, of course—Nero d'Avola, and ideally Contessa Entellina DOC

Umido di cipolla

(Onions and tomato)

In Italy, every locality seems to have its own kind of onion. Today the sweet, red *cipolle di Tropea* (a seaside town in Calabria) are all the rage, but Piedmont and Romagna have their own onions too. This Bolognese recipe was a specialty of Oretta's grandmother, who used to comb the Bologna market for just the right onions, complaining all the while that you just couldn't find a decent onion anymore. Today, we can compromise and use plain white onions—the sweeter the better—to combine with the sweetness of the tomato puree. The parmigiano adds a gentle mellowness.

Don't try to rush the onions. They need to cook slowly and gently. If you have a terracotta pot or pan, now is the time to dig it out and use it. This light-red sauce, whose name means "onion stew," is comfort food, with just a couple of basic flavors and a soft, almost creamy texture; it can be made ahead and freezes beautifully to boot, so it's always there when you need it.

 PASTA SHAPES This sauce is versatile and works on both egg pasta, such as *garganelli* (page 338), and flour-and-water shapes, such as *gnocchetti* (page 342), spaghetti, *spaghettini*, and *linguine/bavette/trenette*. It also goes well with the blandness of *ravioli di ricotta* (page 302).

For the *condimento*:

2½ pounds (1.2 kilograms) white onions (any kind), very thinly sliced (about 8 cups)
3 tablespoons (40 grams) unsalted butter
4 tablespoons extra virgin olive oil, preferably lightly fruity
⅔ cup (150 grams) tomato puree
at least ½ teaspoon salt
freshly ground black pepper

To make the dish:

1 pound (450 grams) pasta (see suggestions above)
about ¾ cup (80 grams) grated parmigiano-reggiano

Put the onions in a large pan, preferably terracotta, with the butter and oil. Sauté over medium heat for about 20 minutes, stirring from time to time, until quite soft, being careful not to let them brown beyond a golden beige.

Add ½ cup (100 milliliters) water, let it evaporate somewhat, then add the tomato puree and cook over very low heat, stirring occasionally, until the onions have practically turned to mush, about 50–60 minutes. Add the salt and a few grindings of pepper.

MAKE-AHEAD NOTE: The process can be interrupted at this point and the sauce kept in the refrigerator for a couple of days or even frozen.

Bring 5 quarts (5 liters) of water to a boil in an 8-quart (8-liter) pot over high heat. Add 3 tablespoons kosher salt, then add the pasta and cook, stirring occasionally, until very *al dente*. Reserve a ladleful of the water.

Drain the pasta and add it to the onions. Stir in 2–3 tablespoons of the reserved pasta water and the cheese. Toss over low heat until the pasta has absorbed the liquid.

Warm a serving bowl or platter in a low oven. If the oven is not practical, warm the bowl just before use with hot water, even a ladleful of the pasta cooking water.

Transfer the pasta to the heated bowl and toss with the sauce. Serve immediately.

WINE SUGGESTION: Zerbina Sangiovese di Romagna

Sugo con i pinoli e tartufi
(Pine nuts and truffles)

THIS CLASSIC *condimento* comes from Piedmont, the large region on the French border known for its wines (Barolo above all), cheeses, and white Alba truffles. The two main ingredients, today luxury foods, once upon a time could be had free for anyone who could find them on the forest floor. They make a combination of flavors of the sort Italians like to call *raffinato*, "refined"—meaning the opposite of hearty, spicy, and red. But it's no less Italian for that. The distinctive aroma of the truffles blends beautifully with the creamy, sweet butter, which in turn contrasts with the crunchy pine nuts.

I'm embarrassed to say how long it took me to notice the connection between pine trees and pine nuts. It wasn't until I watched my husband, Franco, teach his young niece how to whack the fallen shells with a stone, extract the white kernel, and offer it to Uncle. I never again wondered why Italian pine nuts were so expensive. Incidentally, they are called *pinoli* in Italian, but the variant *pignolo* (in the singular) is a common adjective meaning meticulous to a fault, almost certainly related to the tedious job of getting the kernels out of the cones.

Any kind of truffle, black or white, will do in this recipe. This dish must be made at the last minute, but if everything is prepped and ready, it's a snap.

PASTA SHAPES The list of possible pastas is equally flexible: *tagliatelle* (page 328), *cappellacci di zucca* (page 307), *ravioli di ricotta* (page 302) and *agnolotti piemontesi* (page 295), *fettuccine* (page 330), *fusilli* (page 354), *strascinati* (page 348), *strozzapreti/pici* (page 344), and *gnocchi di patate* (page 364).

To toast pine nuts and almonds: Preheat the oven to 225°F (110°C). Spread the nuts out on a baking dish and put in the oven. Shake the pan every so often, until they turn ever so slightly gold. Their oils are delicate and will burn. Remove from the pan right away to prevent overcooking.

For the *condimento*:

7 tablespoons (100 grams) unsalted butter
2 heaping tablespoons (about 70 grams) grated
    fresh truffle, black or white
salt

To make the dish:

1 pound (450 grams) pasta (see suggestions
    above)
about 10 rounded tablespoons (100 grams)
    grated parmigiano-reggiano
½ cup (100 grams) pine nuts, lightly toasted

Bring 5 quarts (5 liters) of water to a boil in an 8-quart (8-liter) pot over high heat.

While waiting for the water to boil, melt the butter in a small pan. Add 1 heaping tablespoon of the grated truffle and 1 level teaspoon salt, let the flavors blend for a minute, remove from the heat, and keep the sauce warm.

When the water boils, add 3 tablespoons kosher salt, then add the pasta and cook, stirring occasionally, until *al dente*.

Warm a serving bowl or platter in a low oven. If the oven is not practical, warm the bowl just before use with hot water, even a ladleful of the pasta cooking water.

Drain the pasta and transfer to the warmed serving bowl. Toss first with the cheese, then with the remaining grated truffle, the pine nuts, and, last, the truffle butter. Serve immediately.

 WINE SUGGESTION: Barbera d'Alba, from Piedmont

Sugo con i broccoletti e prosciutto cotto

(Broccoli rabe and boiled ham)

BROCCOLI RABE, *BROCCOLETTI*, is one of the great joys of the winter months in Italy. Its flavor is peppery rather than bitter, but this is also thanks to careful yet aggressive trimming. Everything tough or otherwise imperfect has to come off. At markets in Italy, *broccoletti* are sold trimmed of close to half their weight. Little more than the leaves, florets, and thinnest stems remain. If you've always been put off by the bitterness of this nutritious vegetable, give it one more try and this time, trim it till you have practically only leaves and florets left, and only the most exiguous of the stems.

Although found throughout southern Italy, this dish originates in Puglia. The pasta is cooked in the water used first for the greens, which preserves nutrients. Also, since good-quality pastas absorb, a good deal of the vegetable's taste is transferred to the pasta through the cooking water. The dish is then finished in the skillet. The ingredients can be prepped ahead, but the cooking should be done all at the same time and the dish served immediately.

Ham, capers, and olives are unexpected but exciting, and very southern, additions to the already richly flavored broccoli rabe.

 PASTA SHAPES Use *penne rigate, maccheroni, fusilli* (page 354), *gnocchetti* (page 342), or any other short pasta.

For the *condimento*:

1 white onion
2 cloves garlic
6 tablespoons extra virgin olive oil
3½ ounces (100 grams) boiled ham, julienned
1 tablespoon (30 grams) vinegar-packed capers (see page 36)
10 olives, pitted and halved, preferably Gaeta or taggiasche
3 tablespoons kosher salt
1 pound (450 grams) broccoli rabe, trimmed aggressively of all tough stems and blemished leaves

To make the dish:

1 pound (450 grams) pasta (see suggestions above)
freshly ground black pepper
4 rounded tablespoons (40 grams) parmigiano-reggiano or any pecorino cheese
4 tablespoons top-quality or new extra virgin olive oil (see page 31)

Finely chop the onion and garlic together and put in a skillet (large enough to hold the pasta later) with the 6 tablespoons oil. Sauté over medium heat until transparent, about 4 minutes. Add the ham, capers, and olives. Lower the heat and cook for 3 or 4 more minutes.

Put 5 quarts (5 liters) of water on to boil in an 8-quart (8-liter) pot over high heat.

When the water boils, add the salt, then add the broccoli rabe and boil until tender, about 10 minutes.

Lift it out of the pot (you will cook the pasta in the same water), squeeze dry, chop coarsely, and add to the skillet. Cook for 4 or 5 minutes over low heat, until the flavors have blended. Taste for salt.

Meanwhile, bring the water back to a boil and cook the pasta, stirring occasionally, until quite *al dente*.

When the pasta is done, drain and transfer it to the skillet. Toss vigorously for 1 minute over a lively flame. Season generously with pepper. Mix in the cheese and the 4 tablespoons oil. Transfer to a warm serving bowl or platter or serve directly from the skillet. Serve immediately.

 WINE SUGGESTION: Salice Salentino, red from Puglia

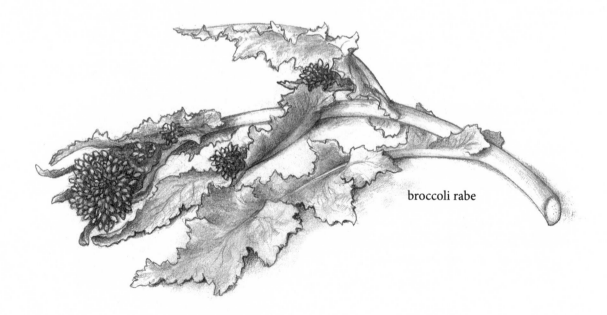

broccoli rabe

Sugo alla crema di peperoni

(Bell peppers)

IN TUSCAN COOKING, peppers are considered one of the products that go into the so-called *"sugo sull'uscetto dell'orto,"* literally, the sauce of the garden gate, traditional in the Maremma, the coastal area in the southern part of the region. To prepare the evening meal, women would just step into the garden and pick what they found. In summer, it was likely to be beautiful bell peppers, and this smooth sauce, boosted by just the tang of lemon juice and the fragrance of basil, conveys the true taste of sweet bell peppers. Yellow peppers are preferred for the golden color they impart to the sauce and because they are slightly sweeter than red, but if all you have is red, the sauce will still be good.

 PASTA SHAPES The sauce goes with any long or short shape, but *linguine/bavette/trenette* and *maltagliati* (page 336) are especially good.

For the *condimento*:

About 1 pound (450 grams) very firm bell
    peppers, preferably yellow
2 shallots, finely chopped
4 tablespoons extra virgin olive oil

To make the dish:

1 pound (450 grams) pasta (see suggestions
    above)
1 tablespoon freshly squeezed lemon juice
salt
freshly ground black pepper
a few fresh basil leaves for garnish

Preheat the oven to 400°F (200°C) or turn on the broiler.

Place the peppers on a grill rack over a drip pan and roast or broil, turning 2 or 3 times, for about 20 minutes, or until the skin is blistered and partly blackened. To facilitate peeling the peppers, put them in a plastic or paper bag or a covered saucepan until they are cool enough to handle. The steam will pop the skin from the flesh and make them easier to peel. When they are cool enough to handle, remove and discard the stem, skin, seeds, and membranes.

In a small skillet, sauté the shallots gently in the oil over low heat until transparent, about 4 minutes.

Cut each peeled pepper into 3 or 4 pieces and puree in a food processor or blender. Add the shallots and their oil to the peppers and process again at top speed until very smooth.

MAKE-AHEAD NOTE: This much can be done ahead of time or the day before or can even be frozen. The sauce can be reheated in the microwave, or else put it in a small saucepan over low heat and reheat very gently, covered.

If you are serving the dish right away, transfer to a warmed serving bowl and keep in a warm place while you cook the pasta.

Bring 5 quarts (5 liters) of water to a boil in an 8-quart (8-liter) pot over high heat. Add 3 tablespoons kosher salt, then add the pasta and cook, stirring occasionally, until *al dente*.

Stir the lemon juice into the pepper puree and season with salt and pepper. Drain and transfer the pasta to the serving bowl and toss with the sauce. Garnish with the basil leaves and serve.

 WINE SUGGESTION: Morellino di Scansano, a red from the Maremma area of southern Tuscany

Sugo con gli asparagi di bosco

(Asparagus or wild asparagus)

THE IDEAL ASPARAGUS for this sauce are the dark-green, pencil-thin wild asparagus, *asparagi di bosco*, both more flavorful and more delicate than cultivated. The dish is very popular in the Abruzzo region, where springtime finds aficionados taking long walks in the woods to find and gather the valuable spears. The "sauce" consists simply of oil and pieces of asparagus.

Grated cheese will overpower the delicate but distinctive flavor of the costly wild asparagus, but a sprinkling of freshly grated parmigiano-reggiano goes very well with ordinary asparagus if that's what you're using.

 PASTA SHAPES As for what pasta shape to use, there are two approaches. Delicate egg *tagliatelle* (page 328) or *tagliolini* (page 332), considered the noblest of pastas, are generally accepted as the most appropriate for such a costly vegetable. Top-quality spaghetti, *fettuccine* (page 330), or *linguine/ bavette/trenette* would also do. But an excellent case can be made for a concave shape that will trap the precious buds. That could be *conchiglie* or *mezze maniche*. Anything larger risks being too robust. Think delicate. If you choose to trap, be sure to cut the buds small enough to fit inside your chosen pasta. This sauce is also good with *agnolotti piemontesi* (page 295).

For the *condimento*:

About 4½ pounds (2 kilograms) asparagus, preferably wild
⅔ cup (150 milliliters) extra virgin olive oil
salt

To make the dish:

1 pound (450 grams) pasta (see suggestions above)
7 rounded tablespoons (70 grams) grated parmigiano-reggiano (only if using domestic asparagus)

Put 5 quarts (5 liters) of water on to boil in an 8-quart (8-liter) pot over high heat.

Break off the woody bottoms of the asparagus and discard. Cut off the asparagus tips, chop coarsely, and set aside. The next step involves the green stems.

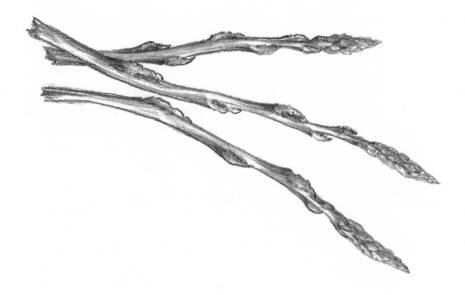

When the water boils, add 3 tablespoons kosher salt, then add the asparagus stems and boil for 20 minutes. Lift them out with tongs and discard, but reserve the water. You will cook the pasta in the same water.

Put the asparagus tips in a 10-inch (24-centimeter) skillet with the oil. Sprinkle with salt and sauté over medium heat for about 5 minutes, or until almost tender. Remove from the heat.

Bring the water back to a boil. Add the pasta and cook, stirring occasionally, until *al dente*. When the pasta is about half done, resume cooking the asparagus tips. Add a few tablespoons of the pasta water to them as they finish cooking. They should become rather tender. They shouldn't crunch.

Warm a serving bowl or platter in a low oven. If the oven is not practical, warm the bowl just before use with hot water, even a ladleful of the pasta cooking water.

Drain the pasta and transfer it to the skillet with the asparagus tips. Mix well, sprinkle with the cheese, if using, and transfer to the heated serving bowl or platter. Serve immediately.

This dish is so delicious that you probably won't have leftovers, but if you do, they will be perfect for a frittata (page 373).

 WINE SUGGESTION: a light-bodied Trebbiano d'Abruzzo

Sugo con i broccoli alla siciliana

(Broccoli, olives, and pistachios)

THE ITALIAN BROCCOLI and cauliflower terminology could drive you crazy—*broccoli, broccoletti, broccolo romano, broccolo siciliano, broccolo campano, cavoli, cavolfiore* all turn up in both singular and plural with a certain fluidity of meaning. This recipe is best with the delicate Sicilian broccoli, with their elegant flavor, few leaves, small florets, and fleshy ribs. As a substitute, use a normal white or green cauliflower or a green *broccolo romanesco* (popularly but erroneously dubbed simply "romanesco" outside Italy) or ordinary broccoli (which, just to keep things lively, is called *broccoli sicil-* *iani* in Roman markets). The true *broccoli siciliani* are more delicate and delicious than the substitutes, but such is life. A wonderfully warming dish in winter, when the broccoli are in season, this intensely flavored, richly textured sauce is sure to convert even the most unregenerate broccoli haters. The complex combination of capers, olives, and pistachios will help make the case, all the better if you can find the flavorful pistachios from Bronte, in eastern Sicily (see page 388, or bring them back from your next trip to Italy).

 PASTA SHAPES This sauce is most typically served with *busiata* (page 356), *fileja*, *penne*, *sedani* (all factory made), and *orecchiette* (page 349 or factory made). Other possibilities include rigatoni, *strascinati* (page 348), or *cecamariti* (page 361)—but always a *pasta corta*.

For the *condimento*:

2 cloves garlic
2 oil-packed anchovy fillets, drained and blotted dry
2 tablespoons salt-packed capers, rinsed free of all salt (see page 36)
3 ounces (80 grams) black olives, pitted, preferably Gaeta or taggiasche
1½ ounces (40 grams) shelled unsalted pistachios
6 tablespoons very fruity extra virgin olive oil
1 small piece dried chile, about an inch long

salt
about 2 pounds (1 kilogram) broccoli or cauliflower or one of their relatives, trimmed and cut into florets

To make the dish:

1 pound (450 grams) pasta (see suggestions above)
6 rounded tablespoons (60 grams) grated *pecorino ragusano* cheese (or a youngish pecorino romano)

Put 5 quarts (5 liters) of water on to boil in an 8-quart (8-liter) pot over high heat.

Chop coarsely together by hand the garlic, anchovy fillets, capers, olives, and pistachios.

Heat the oil gently in a skillet large enough to hold the pasta later. Add the chile and discard when it begins to color. Add the garlic mixture to the pan and sauté gently in the oil until the ingredients just begin to turn gold, about 2 minutes.

When the water boils, add 3 tablespoons kosher salt, then add the vegetable and boil until it can be pierced easily with a fork, about 5–7 minutes. The vegetable should be cooked, but *al dente*, not mushy.

Lift the cooked vegetable out of the pot with a slotted spoon or spider strainer right into the skillet, leaving the water in the pot (where you'll cook the pasta). Taste for salt (with the anchovies, olives, and capers you will probably not need any at all), and let the flavors blend for a couple of minutes over low heat.

Meanwhile, bring the water back to a boil. Add the pasta and cook, stirring occasionally, until *al dente*.

When the pasta is *al dente*, lift it out of the water with a handheld colander or spider strainer and transfer it, rather wet, to the skillet. Mix well over low heat for about 30 seconds, sprinkle with the cheese, and mix again. Transfer to a warm serving dish or serve directly from the skillet. Serve immediately.

 WINE SUGGESTION: a hearty Sicilian red, such as Nero d'Avola

Sicilian broccoli

Sugo alle cime di rapa

(Broccoli rabe)

WHAT CENTRAL ITALY calls *broccoletti* (broccoli rabe), Puglia calls *cime di rapa*, turnip greens. Another variation, the Neapolitan *friarielli*, grown on the slopes of Vesuvius, may well have the best flavor in the family. Once part of the daily diet, they are the reason that Neapolitans used to be known as *mangia foglie*—"leaf eaters." Vegetable vendors are always trying to explain the subtle differences, not always in the same way, but in all cases the turnip, usually vestigial, invisible, or nonexistent, is largely irrelevant, and whether there is more leaf or more floret (always small)

has no importance for the success of this recipe. The youngest, tenderest broccoli rabe, trimmed of everything tough or unsightly, will substitute for all of them.

Note the use of pancetta and white wine instead of the garlic and chile so often associated with strong vegetables. This way, the vegetable's flavor is exalted rather than overwhelmed, and over pasta it tastes rich and almost sweet. The sauce is a lovely green, and the vegetable practically melts into the pasta.

 PASTA SHAPES Use *orecchiette* (page 349), *cavatelli* (page 345), *casarecce*, or *strascinati* (page 348).

For the *condimento*:

About 2 pounds (about 1 kilogram) broccoli rabe, trimmed (see headnote page 137)
5 ounces (150 grams) pancetta or 3½ ounces (100 grams) *lardo*, diced
3 tablespoons dry white wine

To make the dish:

1 pound (450 grams) pasta (see suggestions above)
freshly ground black pepper
extra virgin olive oil for finishing

Bring 5 quarts (5 liters) of water to a boil in an 8-quart (8-liter) pot over high heat. Add 3 tablespoons kosher salt, then add the pasta and the vegetable together. Boil for about 10 minutes or until the pasta is *al dente*. By that time the vegetable will be tender too. In the unlikely event that there is a difference between pasta and vegetable timing, don't let the pasta overcook. The vegetable allows much more leeway.

While the pasta is cooking, put the diced pancetta or *lardo* in a skillet (large enough to hold the pasta later) over medium-low heat. As soon as the fat begins to melt, add the wine, raise the heat, and let the wine evaporate. Lower the heat and cook the pancetta until it begins to become crisp. (*Lardo* will become soft and melt.)

Drain the pasta and vegetable and transfer to the skillet. Mix well but gently so as not to break the florets. Taste for salt.

Grind on some pepper, add a swirl of oil, and serve immediately, right from the pan.

 WINE SUGGESTION: one of Puglia's many rosés, such as Salento rosé

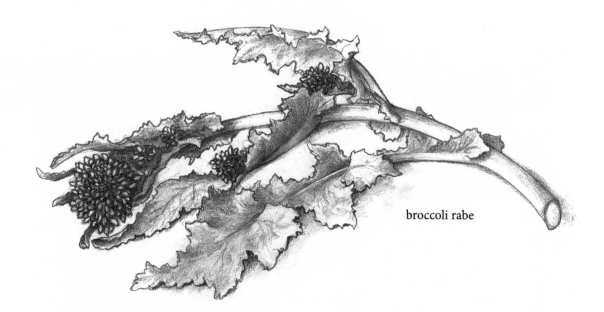

broccoli rabe

Sugo coi carciofi

(Artichokes)

FROM THE FIRST chilly weather of autumn to the first serious heat of late spring, Italian markets are artichoke heaven. In Italy, only the tomato and potato are cultivated in larger quantities. As you can imagine, many Italian regions contribute one or more varieties to the firmament. In Rome, while we wait patiently for the local globe *carciofi romaneschi* to arrive in early spring, we make do with excellent varieties from Sardinia (small, thorny, and delicious) and pear-shaped ones from Puglia, even better for braised *carciofi alla romana* than the Roman ones. This recipe, which is Tuscan, is meant to be made with Ligurian artichokes, small, thorny, and full of flavor, or else with the ovoid, purplish *violetti toscani*, but

don't be inhibited by that. Use what you can find. The principles are the same even if your artichokes come from California.

Unlike the Anglo-French method of boiling or steaming a whole artichoke, then requiring the diner to ritually dismember it with the hands, scraping the leaves through the teeth, and piling up the unsightly tooth-marked leaves on a porcelain plate, the Italian approach to artichokes leaves the mess in the kitchen and puts before the diner only what is edible. This technique of trimming artichokes, described in the recipe below, is at its best among the women of a certain age in the markets of Rome, and it is a useful technique to learn, as artichokes thus cleaned are ready for use on their own or in any number of dishes, including pasta sauces, as this one, or in a frittata or risotto. Once you've tasted the artichoke flavor preserved and enhanced by this method, you may never boil them whole again.

 PASTA SHAPES This sauce is nothing short of sumptuous. Eating tender, fiber-free artichokes and little else on pasta is a true luxury. It is a flexible sauce in that it goes well with almost every category of pasta—*strozzapreti/pici* (handmade flour-and-water; page 344), *tagliolini* (egg; page 332) and *paglia e fieno* (egg; page 331), or *linguine/bavette/trenette* (factory-made flour-and-water), as well as short formats, such as *penne*.

For the *condimento*:

1 organic lemon, halved
8 very fresh small to medium-sized artichokes (or correspondingly fewer if large)
1 clove garlic, crushed
6 tablespoons extra virgin olive oil, preferably lightly fruity
1 ounce (30 grams) lard or an additional 4–5 tablespoons extra virgin olive oil
at least ½ teaspoon salt
freshly ground black pepper

To make the dish:

1 pound (450 grams) pasta (see suggestions above)
1 heaping tablespoon chopped fresh flat-leaf parsley
8 rounded tablespoons (80 grams) grated pecorino romano

To trim artichokes: When people say that Roman cooking is "simple," I always want to hand them an artichoke and challenge them to trim it properly. And yet the technique can be learned, with practice. Squeeze the lemon into a large bowl of water and reserve the squeezed lemon halves. Snap off the tough outer leaves of an artichoke one layer at a time until you see a pronounced color change. With a small, sharp knife, ideally with a curved blade, cut away the tops of the remaining inner leaves. The most effective way to do this is to hold the knife in your right hand (if you are right-handed) and the artichoke in your left. Rest the blade at an oblique angle to the artichoke just where you see the green of the base modulating into the lighter green or yellow of the upper leaves. Press the artichoke gently against the knife, at an oblique angle, and spiral it up (sort of like peeling an orange). Keep the knife still and move only the artichoke. Don't strain or dig; just cut through only one layer at a time.

Cut artichokes turn black when exposed to air, so work as quickly as you can and rub the cut surfaces with one of the reserved lemon halves (an antioxidant). If your artichokes have stems, cut off the bottom third or so, then peel off the tough fibers that surround the tender core. As soon as you finish an artichoke, drop it in the acidulated water while you finish the rest. Then cut each artichoke in half and excise the choke with your little knife. Put the half, cut side down, on a cutting board and slice the artichokes very thin. Quickly drop the slices back into the acidulated water.

Do not turn your back on uncooked cut artichokes or they will turn black.

Put the crushed garlic in a skillet large enough to hold the pasta later with the oil and lard. After about 3 minutes over medium-low heat, or as soon as the garlic is golden, fish it out and discard it. Drain the artichoke slices in a colander and give them a shake. Add them to the pan and stir to coat the slices with the fat. Sauté for 5 minutes over medium heat. Add ½ cup (100 milliliters) of hot water and continue cooking, covered, until the artichokes are tender. This should take about 15 minutes, but every artichoke is different and more time may be needed. If the water evaporates completely, add a little more. Season with salt and pepper at the end.

 MAKE-AHEAD NOTE: Because all this business with trimming and slicing the artichokes is practically impossible to do while your guests are having their *aperitivi* or, worse, hovering in the kitchen, you can cook the artichokes a few hours in advance. Leave them in their pan, covered; do not refrigerate. Warm them up over low heat while you're cooking the pasta.

While the artichokes are cooking or reheating, as the case may be, bring 5 quarts (5 liters) of water to a boil in an 8-quart (8-liter) pot over high heat. Add 3 tablespoons kosher salt, then add the pasta and cook, stirring occasionally, until *al dente*.

Warm a serving bowl or platter in a low oven. If the oven is not practical, warm the bowl just before use with hot water, even a ladleful of the pasta cooking water.

Sprinkle the artichokes with the chopped parsley. Drain the pasta and add to the pan with the artichokes. Sprinkle with the grated cheese and mix well. Transfer to the heated bowl and serve immediately.

 WINE SUGGESTION: Artichokes murder all wines. Serve the wine with the *secondo*.

Sugo con le fave

(Fresh fava beans)

WHEN THE PEOPLE of the ancient Mediterranean talked about beans, they were talking about one or another variety of favas. Thanks to an unfortunate allusion to "fava beans" in a couple of successful films (*Silence of the Lambs* and its sequel) in the 1990s, there can be no more doubt how to translate *fava* (or its plural, *fave*) into English, although they are still also known as "broad beans," especially in the UK.

Another rather disquieting association with *fave* is much more ancient. The Pythagoreans, who believed in reincarnation, refused to eat them because they believed they contained human souls. Another theory why Pythagoras banned the beans was that he, or some of his followers, suffered from favism, a potentially fatal sensitivity to fava beans that occurs in some people of Mediterranean ancestry. It is the reason why in Italy today warning signs are posted where fresh favas are on sale.

Favas are my favorite harbinger of spring, and this sauce, made with fresh favas, not dried, is strictly a springtime dish. If you are dead-set against using pork fat, eat the favas raw with pecorino, another springtime ritual, and forget the pasta. The sauce, a beautiful light green, needs the extra flavor and creaminess that comes from *lardo*, pancetta, or *guanciale*. The fat will coat the pasta, and the beans stay pretty much whole, except for a small amount that are pureed as a vehicle for the rest.

 PASTA SHAPES *Farfalle* (page 336) go very well with this sauce. You can also do as they do around Urbino, in the Marche, and dilute the sauce with broth to make a soup. In that case, use *maltagliati* (page 336), *lagane* (page 334), or *pasta strappata* (page 335).

For the *condimento*:

1 small spring onion (white part and the beginning of the green part), finely chopped
2 heaping tablespoons minced fresh flat-leaf parsley
2½ ounces (70 grams) pancetta, diced fine
about 2 pounds (1 kilogram), about 2¼ cups, shelled fresh fava beans (do not peel the individual beans after they are removed from the pod)
salt
freshly ground black pepper

To make the dish:

1 pound (450 grams) pasta (see suggestions above)
7 rounded tablespoons (70 grams) grated pecorino romano

Put the onion, parsley, and pancetta in a large saucepan, preferably terracotta, and sauté gently for about 10 minutes, or until the fat melts and the onion is golden.

Add the fava beans and 2 cups (400 milliliters) hot water. Taste for salt (the amount will depend on the saltiness of your pancetta) and a few grinds of pepper. Bring to a boil, lower the heat, and simmer for about 20 minutes, or until the beans are quite soft and the liquid has reduced considerably.

Take a large spoonful of the favas and puree them in a food processor (or, better yet, food mill), then return them to the rest.

 MAKE-AHEAD NOTE: This much may be made ahead, even the day before. The sauce can also be frozen. Reheat gently while the pasta is cooking.

Bring 5 quarts (5 liters) of water to a boil in an 8-quart (8-liter) pot over high heat. Add 3 tablespoons kosher salt, then add the pasta and cook, stirring occasionally, until *al dente*.

Warm a serving bowl or platter in a low oven. If the oven is not practical, warm the bowl just before use with hot water, even a ladleful of the pasta cooking water.

Drain and transfer the pasta to the heated serving bowl. Toss first with the grated cheese, then add the sauce and mix well so that the liquid is absorbed into the pasta. Serve immediately.

 WINE SUGGESTION: a fruity white, such as Soave, from the Veneto

---

Sugo coi funghi

(Mixed mushrooms)

INDIAN SUMMER IS called St. Martin's Summer in Italy, and it's when the mushroomers—and there are many—go into the woods in force, armed with a special knife with a short, curved blade that leaves the mushroom spores in the ground to grow again. They will climb the most inhospitable slopes and tear clothing and skin on hostile bushes to get the best specimens of *ovoli*, porcini, chanterelles, and far less-well-known mushrooms.

This recipe will adapt itself easily to whatever interesting wild or cultivated mushrooms you are able to procure, such as shiitake, hen of the woods, or chanterelles, which could be used to supplement a base of portabella or cremini or oyster mushrooms (too pedestrian on their own). Nor could anyone object to a booster of dried porcini added to whatever fresh mushrooms you use. The mushrooms are practically the whole show and you want to taste the forest floor, or at least be reminded of it, so at least something wild is a must. If you think the amount of oil called for is rather a lot, which it is, it is because there is no other sauce, just mushrooms and oil, with a sniff of fresh herbs to assist the illusion of being lost in the woods.

 PASTA SHAPES *Pasta corta* is a must: *lumachelle* (page 340), *farfalle* (page 336), *conchiglie*, *maltagliati* (page 336), or *trofie* (page 352). The sauce is also good on *agnolotti con i carciofi* (page 300).

For the *condimento*:

1 clove garlic, crushed
1 cup (200 milliliters) extra virgin olive oil, preferably medium fruity
2 pounds (900 grams) mixed mushrooms, wiped clean and sliced not too thin
at least ½ teaspoon salt

freshly ground black pepper
1 tablespoon minced fresh flat-leaf parsley
leaves from 1 sprig fresh thyme

To make the dish:

1 pound (450 grams) pasta (see suggestions above)

Put the garlic and the oil in a skillet large enough to hold the pasta later and sauté over medium heat until the garlic is golden, about 3 minutes.

Discard the garlic and add the mushrooms to the pan. Sprinkle with salt and pepper and cook over lively (medium-high) heat, stirring occasionally, for 5 or 6 minutes, or until the mushrooms have released their water, the water has evaporated, and the mushrooms are cooked through, soft but not browned.

Scoop out a cup of the cooked mushrooms and puree it in a food processor. Stir in the chopped parsley and the thyme leaves. Return the puree to the pan with the rest of the mushrooms. Taste for salt. Keep warm.

 MAKE-AHEAD NOTE: This much can be done some hours ahead and the mushrooms reheated while the pasta is cooking.

Bring 5 quarts (5 liters) of water to a boil in an 8-quart (8-liter) pot over high heat. Add 3 tablespoons kosher salt, then add the pasta and cook, stirring occasionally, until *al dente*.

Warm a serving bowl or platter in a low oven. If the oven is not practical, warm the bowl just before use with hot water, even a ladleful of the pasta cooking water.

Drain and transfer the pasta to the skillet and toss briefly with the mushroom sauce over low heat. Transfer to the warm serving bowl and serve immediately.

 WINE SUGGESTION: Pinot Nero is a perfect pairing with mushrooms

Sugo con melanzane

(Eggplant)

IT IS VERY easy to think of eggplants as oil sponges whose primary role in a dish is to provide volume and an excuse to load on cheese, meat, tomatoes, or all three. But this delicate Southern sauce gets almost all its flavor and texture from the eggplant itself, deliciously enriched simply by extra virgin olive oil and pecorino romano. Make it at the height of summer with eggplants from a farmers' market. What does it taste like? It tastes like eggplant.

The thing that annoys most people about eggplant is the quantity of oil it absorbs. Although this recipe is scarcely oil-free, it does keep consumption under control thanks to a neat trick Oretta learned from the great Italian chef Gualtiero Marchesi. You precook the eggplants dry before adding any oil. (This works with mushrooms too.) They will absorb much less oil than otherwise.

The eggplants on the market today do not need to be salted and drained. They have been bred to resist harsh temperatures, and they are also sweeter, seedless, and, unfortunately, less flavorful. But some farmers still manage to grow old-fashioned eggplants, with all their faults and all their flavor. If you can get these, before use slice them thick, sprinkle with salt, and let them drain for a couple of hours. Lay the slices out on a cutting board and raise one end to incline the board. They need to lose their bitterness. Then rinse, pat dry, and proceed with the recipe. Hothouse eggplants don't need this step because they are not bitter.

 PASTA SHAPES Any short pasta will be fine.

For the *condimento*:

1½ pounds (700 grams) eggplants, diced small but not peeled

6 tablespoons extra virgin olive oil, preferably intensely fruity

1 clove garlic, crushed

1 small piece dried chile

1 tablespoon minced fresh flat-leaf parsley

To make the dish:

1 pound (450 grams) pasta (see suggestions above)

about 7 rounded tablespoons (70 grams) grated pecorino romano

If necessary (see headnote), sprinkle the eggplant slices lightly with salt and put them in a colander for about 1 hour.

Put the eggplant pieces in a 16-inch (40-centimeter) nonstick skillet with nothing else. Cook them over low heat, stirring every so often to keep them from sticking, 5 or 6 minutes, until they sort of wilt. Remove them from the pan. Add the oil, garlic, and chile to the pan and cook on medium for a minute or two. Return the eggplant to the pan, sprinkle with about ½ teaspoon salt, and cook, stirring often, for 8 or 10 minutes, or until cooked through.

Remove and discard the chile. In a food processor, puree a large spoonful of the eggplant and return it to the skillet. It will help make the sauce creamy.

 MAKE-AHEAD NOTE: The process can be interrupted at this point and the sauce kept in the refrigerator for a couple of days. Reheat gently while the pasta is cooking.

Stir in the parsley. Keep warm until the pasta is done, or reheat gently.

Bring 5 quarts (5 liters) of water to a boil in an 8-quart (8-liter) pot over high heat. Add 3 tablespoons kosher salt, then add the pasta and cook, stirring occasionally, until *al dente*. When the pasta is nearly done, scoop out about a cup of the water and reserve.

Warm a serving bowl or platter in a low oven. If the oven is not practical, warm the bowl just before use with hot water, even a ladleful of the pasta cooking water.

Drain and transfer the pasta to the heated serving bowl. Toss the pasta first with the cheese, then add the eggplant sauce and mix well. If the sauce seems dry, add a little of the reserved water, not more than a couple of tablespoons. Serve immediately.

 WINE SUGGESTION: a full-bodied red, such as Aglianico del Vulture, from Basilicata

Timballo di zite e peperoni

(Baked ziti and bell peppers)

THIS SUMPTUOUS *timballo*—baked pasta—always used to be included in wedding banquets in southern Italy, especially the Basilicata region. It was also shared with neighbors and the town's poor. Everyone had to celebrate the formation of the new family. In some southern towns, a similar *timballo* used to be made to take to the beach and eat with friends and families after swimming. In fact, it is excellent at room temperature and also freezes well.

The preparation sounds lengthy and laborious, but actually the only really tedious part is peeling the peppers, well worth the trouble for this crowd pleaser. The combination of capers and olives with the peppers is an intriguing contrast of sweet and salty, and their colors, layered with the pasta, have visual effect as well.

Since this is a party dish, it may be large. Double the quantities given here for the party version.

 PASTA SHAPES The pasta shape, *zite*, is included in the name. The name *zite* means brides; *ziti*, more common in America, means grooms, but the shape is the same, long and tubular. In America the name ziti is applied to a short tubular format, but in Italy they are as long as spaghetti. If you have long ones, often also called *candele*, break them into three or four pieces each. *Sedani*, small *penne*, and other slim tubes could be used.

For the *condimento*:

½ cup (100 grams) salt-packed capers, rinsed free of all salt (page 36)
½ cup (100 grams) pitted black olives, preferably Gaeta or taggiasche
about 3½ pounds (1.5 kilograms) red and yellow bell peppers, roasted and peeled as described on page 139
2 cloves garlic, crushed
1 cup plus 2 tablespoons (270 milliliters) extra virgin olive oil, preferably intensely fruity
1 cup (100 grams) fine dry breadcrumbs
freshly ground black pepper

1½ rounded teaspoons dried oregano
2 heaping tablespoons minced fresh flat-leaf parsley
salt

To make the dish:

1½ tablespoons (20 grams) unsalted butter (for the baking pan)
1 pound (450 grams) ziti, broken into 3 or 4 pieces if long

Preheat the oven to 350°F (180°C). Butter a 10-inch (24-centimeter) springform pan.

Chop the capers and olives together. Cut the peppers into thin strips.

Heat the garlic in a skillet, with the oil, until it is golden, then discard the garlic. Add the peppers, breadcrumbs, capers, and olives to the flavored oil.

Add a few grinds of black pepper and, stirring often, let the flavors blend over medium heat for about 5 minutes. Add the oregano and parsley. Taste for salt and cook for about 5 more minutes.

Bring 5 quarts (5 liters) of water to a boil in a 8-quart (8-liter) pot over high heat. Add 3 tablespoons kosher salt, then add the pasta and cook, stirring occasionally, until only half cooked.

Drain and transfer the pasta to a bowl or return it to the pot, and mix in a few tablespoons of the peppers (technically sauce, but not very saucy).

Arrange a layer of peppers on the bottom of the baking pan and a layer of ziti on top of that. Continue alternating layers until all the ingredients are used up. The last layer should be the peppers.

Bake at 350°F (180°C) for about 20 minutes, or until a nice brown crust has formed on top. Remove from the oven and let rest for 5 minutes before unmolding and slicing like a cake.

The *timballo* can be reheated successfully.

 WINE SUGGESTION: Aglianico del Vulture, from Basilicata

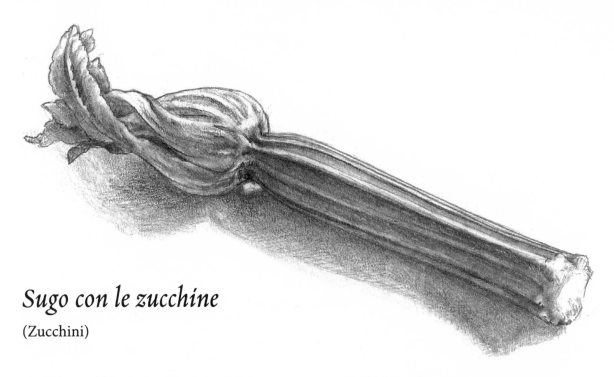

Sugo con le zucchine

(Zucchini)

IF YOU SAY you don't like zucchini to a Roman, he simply won't know what you're talking about. The Roman variety of zucchini, *zucchine romanesche*, is a variegated light green, striated, and fluted like a Greek column. It contains less water than other varieties, fewer seeds, even when allowed to grow unseemly large, and has a nice nutty flavor. This type of zucchini is beginning to turn up in North American farmers' markets, though the growers and vendors seem not to grasp its potential as the tastiest zucchini they've ever harvested. If you have a garden, it's well worth looking for the seeds to plant (page 388). But whatever kind of zucchini you're growing or buying, when mid-summer rolls around and you begin to cast about for new things to do with the surplus, give this recipe a try. Thanks to the herbs and extra virgin olive oil, it's a crowd pleaser with any kind of zucchini available anywhere. Just remember to choose slim, firm zucchini, lest they contain seeds and an excess of water.

It's a delicate pale-green sauce, subtle, but full of excitement as you taste the fresh herbs one by one. Scamorza is a semisoft cow's milk cheese, about the size and shape of a pear. It has a buttery flavor and, as a slightly aged relative of mozzarella, it melts beautifully. Its smokiness provides a nice contrast to the sweetness of the zucchini. The technique of processing a small part of the zucchini and returning it to the pan has the effect of creating a smooth sauce while leaving texture in the form of small zucchini pieces.

🌿 **PASTA SHAPES** Choose a short pasta, such as *gnocchetti* (page 342), *pasta strappata* (page 335), or *pizzicotti* (page 351), and, even better, a short pasta that can capture little pieces of zucchini, such as *orecchiette* (page 349), *strascinati* (page 348), *lumachelle* (page 340), or, for an egg pasta, *garganelli* (page 338).

For the *condimento*:

2 cloves garlic, crushed

2 tablespoons minced fresh mint leaves

2 tablespoons minced fresh chives

1 teaspoon dried oregano

6 tablespoons extra virgin olive oil, preferably medium fruity

1½ pounds (700 grams) small or medium firm zucchini, cut in ¼-inch (½-centimeter) slices

1 small piece dried chile

at least ½ teaspoon salt

To make the dish:

1 pound (450 grams) pasta (see suggestions above)

4 heaping tablespoons (60 grams) grated smoked scamorza cheese (or grated parmigiano-reggiano)

extra virgin olive oil for finishing

Chop finely together the garlic and all the herbs. Put in a 10-inch (25-centimeter) pan with the oil and sauté over medium heat for 2 or 3 minutes, or until the garlic is golden.

Add the zucchini and the chile, and sprinkle with ½ teaspoon salt. Cook over low heat, stirring often, until the zucchini are tender, about 15 minutes.

Remove and discard the chile. Remove 2 heaping tablespoons of zucchini and puree in a food processor. Return to the pan and stir in.

 MAKE-AHEAD NOTE: This much may be made earlier in the day.

Bring 5 quarts (5 liters) of water to a boil in an 8-quart (8-liter) pot over high heat. Add 3 tablespoons kosher salt, then add the pasta and cook, stirring occasionally, until *al dente*.

When the pasta is done, drain it and add it to the pan with the zucchini. Sprinkle on the cheese before tossing with the sauce. Add a couple of swirls of extra virgin olive oil, toss again quickly, and serve from the pan.

 WINE SUGGESTION: Marco Felluga Collio Bianco, from Friuli

Fish and Seafood Sauces

The heat generated by Atlantic/Pacific-fish fans and Mediterranean-fish fans when they debate which is better could sear a salmon. It didn't take me long living in Italy to abandon my North Atlantic roots for the Mediterranean faction. The warmer, saltier water makes for more flavorful fish, but this more pronounced taste is still quite delicate and subtle and *not* to be confused with tasting "fishy." Italian cooks aim to bring it out, not cover it with sauces aimed at compensating for a total absence of flavor. They believe that the less you do to a fish the better, and seafood recipes are usually quite simple.

These recipes are, necessarily, of Mediterranean origin, and many species of fish are simply unavailable from any other body of water. Although strong traditions often dictate that certain recipes are always made with certain creatures, to be perfectly honest most of the recipes will work well and be delicious with whatever similar species you can find locally. We've suggested some substitutions for hard-to-find Mediterranean species, but they are merely suggestions. The recipes will be delicious as long as you use good, fresh fish and seafood—even if it won't be the traditional Italian dish.

Remember to choose wild-caught fish in preference to farmed, and whole fish to store-bought fillets. Recipes using fish and seafood that can be stored (such as bottarga and canned tuna) are found in the "Last-Minute Sauces" section (page 50).

AMATRICIANA (page 70).
Tomatoes, *guanciale*, and pecorino romano over *bucatini*. *Lazio*.

CARBONARA (page 75).
Spaghetti with eggs, *guanciale*, and grated
pecorino romano and parmigiano-reggiano. *Lazio*.

GRATIN ALLA SORRENTINA (page 98).
Artisanal *fusilli* (page 354) baked with
mozzarella and pecorino. *Campania.*
Factory-made *fusilli* can be used as well.

Grated pecorino romano and crushed black peppercorns over *bucatini. Lazio.*

RUCHETTA E OLIVE (page 109).
Arugula, olives, and anchovies, with shaved pecorino romano, over *farfalle* (page 000).

PESTO ALLA GENOVESE (page 116).
Trofie (page 352), potatoes, and green beans tossed with crushed basil, pine nuts, garlic, and extra virgin olive oil. *Liguria*.

SUGO CON POMODORINI GRATINATI ALLA CALABRESE (page 123).
Small tomatoes baked until soft and tossed with short pasta, here *casarecci*.
Calabria.

TIMBALLO DI ZITE E PEPERONI (page 156).

Broken *candele* (long ziti) baked with bell peppers, olives, and capers.

Campania.

FINS

Sugo con le alici (o sarde) fresche

(Fresh anchovies or sardines)

Once when Oretta's husband, Carlo, took an early-morning walk while on vacation on the Gargano peninsula, in Puglia (the "spur" of the Italian boot), he met some fishermen returning with their catch. He offered to help them get the fish out of the nets and sort them, and afterward—thinking he'd needed work—they insisted on compensating him with a big bag of fresh anchovies. They also gave him this extraordinary recipe that, at its best, tastes of the sea.

Many people never think that the salty, savory anchovies you buy in jars or cans were once fresh fish and very good to eat. Even American guests who are phobic about "fish that tastes fishy" are pleasantly surprised when they taste my simple baked fresh anchovies.

This sauce uses the tasty and nutritious little fish to make a delicious one-dish meal. The quantity of tomatoes is deliberately small, so don't be tempted to add more. The recipe works well with fresh sardines, too. The sardines are larger and thicker, but the main difference will be the taste, much more pronounced (all right, fishier) with the sardines.

 PASTA SHAPES The sauce is very versatile: *farfalle* (page 336), *casarecce, busiata* (page 356), *fregnacce* (page 337), *fusilli* (page 354), *lagane* (page 334), *trofie* (page 352), *paccheri, penne, scialatielli,* or spaghetti.

How to clean fresh anchovies or sardines: Hold the fish in one hand and, with your thumbnail, slit it open from its tail to its head; then twist off the head. The spine and viscera should come out all at once. Separate into 2 fillets. Rinse to remove any extraneous bits and bones.

For the *condimento*:

1 pound (450 grams) fresh anchovies or sardines, cleaned and decapitated (see note above)
3 tablespoons lightly fruity extra virgin olive oil
1 clove garlic, finely chopped
2 heaping tablespoons minced fresh flat-leaf parsley
½ cup (100 milliliters) dry white wine

5 or 6 ripe cherry or grape tomatoes, quartered
1 teaspoon salt
freshly ground black pepper

To make the dish:

1 pound (450 grams) pasta (see suggestions above)
3 tablespoons lightly fruity extra virgin olive oil

If the fish have not been cleaned, clean them according to the directions above. If they are already clean, simply rinse again. Dry on paper towels.

Put the oil in a skillet and add the garlic. Sauté gently over low heat until the garlic barely begins to color, about 2 minutes. Make sure the chopped garlic does not brown at all, so don't take your eyes off it.

Add the fish. Raise the heat a bit and cook, stirring and poking with a wooden spoon to break them up somewhat, for about 2 minutes or until half done (they will begin to turn white). Add the parsley. Begin gradually to add the wine and continue cooking until the fish is just cooked through, about 5 minutes. The wine should evaporate completely.

Add the tomatoes, the salt, and a few grinds of pepper, then cook over low heat not more than 5 minutes, just enough to barely cook the tomatoes.

❧ **MAKE-AHEAD NOTE:** This much may be done some hours ahead and left at room temperature, covered loosely.

Bring 5 quarts (5 liters) of water to a boil in an 8-quart (8-liter) pot over high heat. Add 3 tablespoons kosher salt, then add the pasta and cook, stirring occasionally, until *al dente*.

Warm a serving bowl or platter in a low oven. If the oven is not practical, warm the bowl just before use with hot water, even a ladleful of the pasta cooking water.

Drain and transfer the pasta to the heated serving bowl or platter. Add the sauce and the remaining oil. Mix well and serve immediately.

❧ **WINE SUGGESTION:** a slightly smoky Greco di Tufo

Porri e acciughe

(Leeks and fresh anchovies)

I'LL GRANT YOU leeks and anchovies don't sound like much, and they *are* an unusual combination—a marvelous pairing of the sweet and the sea, typical of Piedmont, which has special varieties of each. The sauce, a classic of the *osterie* of Turin, is surprisingly delicious, subtle but interesting. As so often, the sauce consists almost entirely of its main ingredients in tiny pieces distributed over the pasta, thanks to the extra virgin olive oil.

If you can't find fresh anchovies, fresh sardines will work, but the flavor will change.

> ✱ PASTA SHAPES Use *fettuccine* (page 330), *tagliatelle* (page 328), *malloreddus* (page 346), *cavatelli* (page 345), *fregnacce* (page 337), *strozzapreti/pici* (page 344), *gnocchetti* (page 342), or *penne*.

For the *condimento*:

6 tablespoons extra virgin olive oil, preferably medium fruity
1 large leek, white and light green part only, washed and sliced thin
2 oil-packed anchovy fillets, drained and blotted dry
¾ pound (about 350 grams) fresh anchovies or sardines, cleaned and filleted (see page 161)
about ½ teaspoon salt, if needed

To make the dish:

1 pound (450 grams) pasta (see suggestions above)
1 heaping tablespoon minced fresh flat-leaf parsley

Put the oil, the leek, and the oil-packed anchovy fillets in a skillet, preferably terracotta. Sauté over medium heat for about 5 or 6 minutes, or until the leek is golden and the anchovies completely disintegrated.

Add the fresh fillets and cook over low heat for 2 or 3 minutes, breaking them up with a fork. Taste for salt and add only if needed; the oil-packed anchovies will probably provide enough salt.

MAKE-AHEAD NOTE: This much may be done a bit earlier in the day, but there is no real need to. If the ingredients are all prepped, the sauce is quite quick. No need to cover or refrigerate. You won't be keeping it that long.

Bring 5 quarts (5 liters) of water to a boil in an 8-quart (8-liter) pot over high heat. Add 3 tablespoons kosher salt, then add the pasta and cook, stirring occasionally, until *al dente*.

Warm a serving bowl or platter in a low oven. If the oven is not practical, warm the bowl just before use with hot water, even a ladleful of the pasta cooking water.

Drain and transfer the pasta to the heated serving bowl or platter. Add the sauce, mix well, and sprinkle with the parsley just before serving.

 WINE SUGGESTION: a Riesling from Piedmont

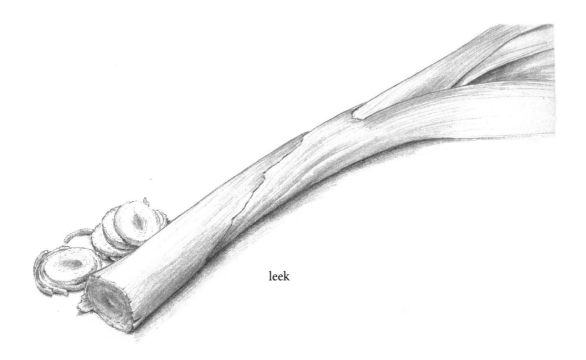

leek

Sugo con le sarde

(Fresh sardines with raisins)

PLUMP, SUCCULENT FRESH sardines belong to the category called *pesce azzurro*, literally blue fish, but not to be confused with the bluefish we love to eat in New England in the summer. *Pesce azzurro* is the group of humble but nutritious silvery-skinned, dark-fleshed fish that includes mackerel and anchovies. It was the poor who traditionally used them to make important, delicious dishes. This one is Sicilian, typical of Palermo, the Sicilian capital, with the taste of the sea blending with the sweetness of the raisins. It is found all over the island with small variations. In Palermo, they add a sprig of wild fennel. If you can't find it, you can approximate the taste with two or three fennel seeds instead.

The *condimento* consists essentially of the flavored fish broken up in little pieces, with the oil providing the background.

 PASTA SHAPES Use *zite spezzate* (broken in pieces), *penne*, *maccheroni*, spaghetti, *bucatini*, or *tagliatelle* (page 328)

To make the breadcrumbs: Start with good-quality, somewhat rustic bread a couple of days old, that is, neither fresh nor stale. Cut off the crusts and tear the bread into crumbs with your hands or pulse in a food processor until reduced into fairly uniform crumbs.

For the *condimento*:

1¼ pounds (550 grams) fresh sardines, cleaned, boned, and decapitated (see page 161)
6 tablespoons extra virgin olive oil, preferably intensely fruity
2 cloves garlic, crushed
¼ cup (60 grams) raisins (the best are currants, or Corinthian raisins), soaked for 15–20 minutes in warm water, drained, and squeezed

5 tablespoons (60 grams) untoasted breadcrumbs (see note above)
at least ½ teaspoon salt
freshly ground black pepper

To make the dish:

1 pound (450 grams) pasta (see suggestions above)

Rinse the sardines and pat dry on paper towels.

Put the oil in a skillet. Add the garlic, the raisins, and the breadcrumbs. Stir the mixture over medium heat for 2 or 3 minutes, or until the garlic is golden.

Add the sardines to the skillet and sauté over low heat, breaking them up with a fork until they are completely crumbled. Add the salt and a few grinds of pepper; discard the garlic.

 MAKE-AHEAD NOTE: This much can be done earlier in the day. Cover if holding for more than a couple of hours but do not refrigerate.

Bring 5 quarts (5 liters) of water to a boil in an 8-quart (8-liter) pot over high heat. Add 3 tablespoons kosher salt, then add the pasta and cook, stirring occasionally, until *al dente*.

Warm a serving bowl or platter in a low oven. If the oven is not practical, warm the bowl just before use with hot water, even a ladleful of the pasta cooking water.

Drain and transfer the pasta to the heated serving bowl. Add the sauce and mix well. Serve immediately.

 WINE SUGGESTION: Bianco IGT Sicilia

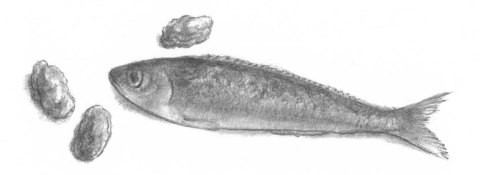

Sugo di baccalà

(Salt cod and dried mushrooms)

EVERY REGION OF Italy has recipes using *baccalà*, salt cod, and all over Italy people gather mushrooms in the autumn and put them to dry on the roofs of houses. This recipe comes from the Veneto, where there is a tradition of cooking salt cod in milk as well as an abundance of mushrooms, largely in the Dolomite mountains in the northern part of the region—mushroomers from all over Italy head there in summer and autumn.

On Thursdays and Fridays, many food shops in Italy still have tubs of *baccalà* that have been soaking since Wednesday for the convenience of customers, who buy it for their Friday fish dinners—still a tradition long after meatless Fridays ceased being obligatory for Catholics. If your salt cod has not been presoaked, you will have to desalt it yourself. Rinse off the salt you can see, then put the fish in a bowl in the refrigerator for about two days, changing the water every few hours. Before use, taste a bit of the fish to check that all the salt has washed away. Stockfish, air-dried and unsalted, requires soaking for only 24 hours or until it has softened completely.

The dominant flavor comes from the mushrooms, with a mild but distinct background taste from the fish, which, crumbled, also contributes to the velvety texture. The sauce is rustic but delicate, creamy, and thick with little bits of fish. Try to resist the temptation to use skim milk instead of whole.

PASTA SHAPES This substantial but delicately flavored sauce is good with *gnocchi di patate* (page 364) and a wide variety of pastas: *farfalle* (page 336), *fusilli* (page 354), *lagane* (page 334), *maltagliati* (page 336), *conchiglie*, *paccheri*, *penne*, *scialatielli*, and *sedani*.

For the *condimento*:

1 medium white onion

1 clove garlic

1 carrot

1 small rib celery

6 tablespoons extra virgin olive oil, preferably
   intensely fruity

2 whole cloves, crushed in a mortar, or 1 pinch
   ground cloves

1 pinch ground nutmeg, or a grating of whole
   nutmeg

the grated zest of 1 organic lemon (about 2
   teaspoons)

freshly ground black pepper

about 1 pound (450 grams) salt cod, soaked
   (see headnote), boned, skinned, and cut

crosswise into several strips about 1½ inches
   (3–4 centimeters) wide

½ cup (100 milliliters) dry white wine

1 cup (200 milliliters) whole milk

1 ounce (30 grams) dried porcini, soaked,
   squeezed, and finely chopped (see page 37)

2 heaping tablespoons minced fresh flat-leaf
   parsley

salt

3 tablespoons (40 grams) unsalted butter

To make the dish:

1 pound (450 grams) pasta (see suggestions
   above)

Chop finely together the onion, garlic, carrot, and celery (in the food processor if you wish). Put the oil in deep skillet and add the chopped vegetables. Then add the cloves, nutmeg, lemon zest, and a few grinds of black pepper. Sauté gently over medium-low heat until the vegetables just begin to color, about 5 minutes.

Add the cod and sauté, stirring with a wooden spoon. The strips can be added gradually if they don't all fit in a single layer to start. As you stir, they will break up, and there will be more room in the pan. After about 7 minutes the fish should be completely broken up into irregular pieces. Add the wine, raise the heat to high, and let it evaporate, about 2 or 3 minutes.

Stir in the milk. Add the chopped mushrooms and parsley. Taste for salt (the salt content of the fish will vary) and simmer over medium heat until the cod is completely cooked and flakes easily, about 20 minutes. Cut the butter into tiny pieces, add to the pan all at once, and let it melt.

While the sauce is cooking, bring 5 quarts (5 liters) of water to a boil in an 8-quart (8-liter) pot over high heat. Add 3 tablespoons kosher salt, then add the pasta and cook, stirring occasionally, until *al dente*.

Warm a serving bowl or platter in a low oven. If the oven is not practical, warm the bowl just before use with hot water, even a ladleful of the pasta cooking water.

Drain and transfer the pasta to the heated serving bowl. Add the sauce and mix well. Serve immediately.

WINE SUGGESTION: a fruity Valpolicella, from the Veneto, or a young Barbera, from Piedmont

Sugo con il pesce spada

(Swordfish)

EVEN BACK WHEN southern Italy was Magna Graecia, food lovers savored the swordfish caught in the Strait of Messina, between the toe of Italy and Sicily. Delicious also raw, its meat has a delicate but distinct flavor that works beautifully in this substantial sauce. This is a dish to consider a *piatto unico*, with substantial chunks of fish against a light tomato background. You can choose freely between black and red pepper, but discriminating Sicilians would choose black, if we are to believe Gaetano Basile (page 130), which we are.

With a starter of, say, caponata—that wonderful sweet-and-sour concoction of eggplant and an ever-varying array of other ingredients—and a salad to follow, your Sicilian dinner is complete.

🌾 PASTA SHAPES In keeping with southern traditions, handmade flour-and-water shapes are recommended, such as *busiata* (page 356), *fusilli* (page 354), *cavatelli* (page 345), *orecchiette* (page 349), *strozzapreti/pici* (page 344), or spaghetti.

For the *condimento*:

2 cloves garlic, crushed
6 tablespoons extra virgin olive oil, preferably intensely fruity
1 pound (450 grams) ripe red sauce tomatoes, peeled, seeded, and diced or 1 cup canned, peeled tomatoes (fresh is preferable)
1 pound (450 grams) swordfish, diced ¾ inch (1 centimeter) on a side
1 teaspoon salt

To make the dish:

1 pound (450 grams) pasta (see suggestions above)
freshly ground black pepper or dried red pepper flakes

Sauté the garlic in the oil over medium heat in a skillet large enough to hold the pasta later, and discard the garlic when it turns golden, about 2 minutes. Add the tomatoes and the fish together and sprinkle with the salt.

Cook, covered, over low heat for about 10 minutes or until the fish is cooked (test with a fork) and the sauce somewhat reduced and shiny.

MAKE-AHEAD NOTE: This much may be done earlier or even the day before. Cover and refrigerate if holding for more than a couple of hours.

Bring 5 quarts (5 liters) of water to a boil in an 8-quart (8-liter) pot over high heat. Add 3 tablespoons kosher salt, then add the pasta and cook, stirring occasionally, until quite *al dente*.

Warm a serving bowl or platter in a low oven. If the oven is not practical, warm the bowl just before use with hot water, even a ladleful of the pasta cooking water.

Drain and transfer the pasta to the skillet with the sauce. Mix well over low heat for 1 minute. Transfer to the heated bowl, and sprinkle generously with black pepper or red pepper flakes.

 WINE SUGGESTION: Planeta rosé, from Sicily

Sugo con la ricciola

(Fish steak and fresh tomatoes)

FRANCO AND I have a favorite restaurant, Il Giardino, on a favorite island, Ventotene, way out in the sea between Lazio and Campania—south of Rome, north of Naples, and not near anything but a few rocks. Mother Candida rules the kitchen, father Giovanni meets the fishermen every morning for the day's supply, and daughter Anna has launched their former trattoria into the world of fine dining. One evening, there we were in the middle of dinner when a fisherman walked in with a large and beautiful fish. Franco jumped to his feet in excitement and cried, "Tomorrow I want that head!" If you've ever wanted to know the secret of getting VIP treatment at fish restaurants, it is this: eat the head, all of it, not just the cheeks. The next day Signora Candida cooked an even fresher specimen with pasta for us as a *piatto unico*. The head went to Franco and the rest of the family got substantial chunks of fish. The dish is all about the fish, with the little tomatoes and pan juices providing the moisture and the capers a little zing. This recipe is adapted from Candida Sportiello's.

The fish that evening was a *ricciola*, a member of the *Seriola* genus whose name is translated as amberjack or yellowtail. The consistency of its meat, usually sliced into steaks, resembles a sort of cross between tuna and swordfish, either of which can be used in this recipe.

 PASTA SHAPES The southern flavors of this sauce go best with a flour-and-water pasta, and the chunks of fish pair well with large-bore tubes, such as *paccheri* or *mezze maniche*.

For the *condimento*:

6 tablespoons extra virgin olive oil
1 clove garlic, crushed
1 tablespoon salt-packed capers, rinsed free of all salt (page 36)
about 1 pound (450 grams) cherry or grape tomatoes, halved
about 8 ounces (225 grams) fresh tuna (see headnote), diced large, ¾ inch (1 centimeter) or a little more
at least ½ teaspoon salt
freshly ground black pepper

To make the dish:

1 pound (450 grams) pasta (see suggestions above)
1 tablespoon minced fresh basil

Put the oil in a skillet large enough to hold the pasta later, add the garlic, and sauté over medium-low heat until the garlic is just golden, about 2 minutes. Remove and discard the garlic.

Add the capers and tomatoes to the oil in the pan and cook over medium heat, stirring, for a couple of minutes, just to coat the tomatoes with the oil. Add the fish and sauté for another minute or so, again, just to coat the fish. Sprinkle with salt and a few grinds of pepper. Add ¼ cup (50 milliliters) water and cover the pan. Cook over medium-low heat until the fish can be flaked with a fork, about 10 minutes. Check frequently while the fish is cooking to make sure it has enough liquid. If the pan looks dry, add a little warm water. When the fish is done, remove the skillet from the heat.

 MAKE-AHEAD NOTE: If necessary, you could do everything up to this point a couple of hours or so in advance, but there is no need since the sauce will cook quickly while the water is coming to a boil.

While the fish is cooking, bring 5 quarts (5 liters) of water to a boil in an 8-quart (8-liter) pot over high heat. Add 3 tablespoons kosher salt, then add the pasta and cook, stirring occasionally, until *al dente*.

Warm a serving bowl or platter in a low oven. If the oven is not practical, warm the bowl just before use with hot water, even a ladleful of the pasta cooking water. You can also serve directly from the skillet.

Drain the pasta and add it to the skillet. Turn the heat to medium-high and toss the pasta and sauce together for about 30 seconds. Add the basil and toss once more. Transfer to the warm serving bowl and serve immediately.

 WINE SUGGESTION: Graci Etna Rosso or Etna Bianco from Mount Etna, in Sicily

SHELLS AND TENTACLES

Cozze, porcini e fiori di zucchina

(Mussels, fresh porcini, and zucchini flowers)

ONCE THE EXCLUSIVE province of Jewish cooks—who made an art form of cooking what other people tossed out—zucchini flowers (see also page 260) have, in the last couple of decades, become a favorite plaything of Italian chefs, who love their brilliant color and are always thinking up new places to put them. They're at their best from late spring to mid-summer. Their flavor is pleasantly mineral, and when cooked they have a wonderfully gossamer texture.

Zucchini flowers have gender. The busy, productive female flowers are attached to the zucchini, while the big, handsome fellows are attached simply to a stem. Both grow on the same, hermaphroditic plant. The ones you stuff and fry are the guys.

But the flowers are only one corner of this unusual Neapolitan triangle, in which land and sea compete in a light tomato base.

 PASTA SHAPES Use a short pasta, such as *pennette*, *strascinati* (page 348), or *fusilli* (page 354).

For the *condimento*:

1 pound (450 grams) mussels, scrubbed, rinsed thoroughly, and soaked in lightly salted water for 2 hours
6 tablespoons extra virgin olive oil
1 large leek, white and very light green part only, cut in half lengthwise, then crosswise in thin slices
¾ pound (350 grams) fresh mixed mushrooms, either wild or cultivated, or porcini (about 4 medium), wiped clean and sliced (suitable types: button, shiitake, hedgehog, chanterelle, portabella, or oyster mushrooms; these can be supplemented with 1 ounce/30 grams dried porcini, soaked, cleaned, drained, and chopped)

½ cup (100 milliliters) dry white wine
8 ounces (225 grams) ripe fresh plum tomatoes, San Marzano–type if possible, peeled, seeded, and cut in strips
salt
freshly ground black pepper
12 zucchini flowers

To make the dish:

1 pound (450 grams) pasta (see suggestions above)
2 rounded tablespoons (20 grams) grated pecorino romano
1 heaping tablespoon minced fresh flat-leaf parsley

Drain the mussels, put them in a skillet, cover, and place over medium heat until they open, about 5 minutes. Shell and reserve the mussels. Line a strainer with cheesecloth and strain the broth and reserve.

Put the oil in a separate pan, add the leek, and cook over low heat until transparent, about 6 minutes.

Add the mushrooms to the leeks and sauté over medium heat until the mushrooms have given up their liquid and are lightly browned and cooked through.

Stir in the wine, raise the heat to high, and let the alcohol evaporate, about 3 minutes. Then add the tomatoes and reserved mussel broth. Taste for salt and grind on some pepper. Lower the heat to medium and simmer, covered, for about 10 minutes, just enough to cook the tomatoes somewhat.

Meanwhile, bring 5 quarts (5 liters) of water to a boil in an 8-quart (8-liter) pot over high heat. Add 3 tablespoons kosher salt, then add the pasta and cook, stirring occasionally, until *al dente*.

While the pasta is cooking, mince the parsley if you have not already done so, and cut the flowers in half lengthwise and delicately remove the pistils with your fingers. Stir the flowers and steamed mussels into the sauce.

Warm a serving bowl or platter in a low oven. If the oven is not practical, warm the bowl just before use with hot water, even a ladleful of the pasta cooking water.

Drain and transfer the pasta to the heated serving bowl. Toss first with the sauce, then add the cheese, and finally the minced parsley. Serve immediately.

 WINE SUGGESTION: with button mushrooms, a light fruity white such as Friulano, but with shiitakes or porcini, a Pinot Nero

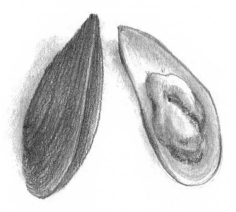

Sugo con le cozze

(Mussels)

Until only a few years ago, in central and southern Italy, so-called *cozzicari* sold mussels, *cozze*, at seaside stands for immediate raw consumption with plenty of fresh lemon juice, erroneously believed to take care of any bacteriological issues. Numerous cases of food-borne illness later, for which mussels, rightly or wrongly, were blamed, the *cozzicari* are no more, and Italian mussels are subject to strict controls.

Sometimes it doesn't matter whether you use fresh or canned tomatoes, but in this recipe, from the Salento peninsula (the heel of the Italian boot), you *have* to use fresh. The feeling it gives of being at the beach is heightened by cooking the pasta in a broth made with the mussel shells. That also means your guests do not have to shell their own mussels, which they will find succulent and vulnerable mixed with the pasta.

 PASTA SHAPES Pair this sauce with long formats, such as spaghetti, *tagliolini* (page 332), *scialatielli*, or *linguine/bavette/trenette*, but it also goes well with *lumachelle* (page 340).

NOTE: If your mussels are not farmed, they may contain a great deal of sand that no amount of soaking will remove. In that case, steam them open and shell them, as directed, but if they are farmed, they can be added directly to the sauce.

For the *condimento*:

about 3½ pounds (1.5 kilograms) mussels, scrubbed, rinsed thoroughly, and soaked in lightly salted water for 2 hours
2 cloves garlic
6 tablespoons extra virgin olive oil
about 1¼ pounds (600 grams) fresh, ripe sauce tomatoes, preferably San Marzano–type, peeled, seeded, and diced
½ teaspoon salt
1 heaping tablespoon minced fresh flat-leaf parsley

For the broth:

the mussel shells
an herb bouquet consisting of 6–8 sprigs fresh flat-leaf parsley, 3 sprigs fresh thyme, and 3 sprigs fresh marjoram
1 small spring onion (white part and beginning of the green part)
1 small carrot
½ cup (100 milliliters) dry white wine
freshly ground black pepper
salt

To make the dish:

1 pound (450 grams) pasta (see suggestions above)

Drain the mussels, put them in a skillet, cover, and place over medium heat until they open, about 5 minutes. Shell and reserve the mussels. Line a strainer with cheesecloth, strain the broth, and reserve. Put the shells in an 8-quart (8-liter) pot in which you will later cook the pasta and the shelled mussels in a small bowl.

Put the garlic, peeled but left whole, and the oil in a large saucepan or deep skillet over low heat and sauté until just golden. Discard the garlic and add the tomatoes and the salt to the pan. Bring to a boil and then lower the heat. Simmer the sauce for about 10 more minutes; it will thicken somewhat. Add the shelled mussels and strained broth to the sauce and let the flavors blend for 2 or 3 minutes. Remove from the heat. Stir in the parsley.

Now turn your attention to the pot containing the shells. Add the herbs, spring onion, and carrot. Add water just to cover, bring to a boil, and simmer, partially covered, for about 30 minutes. Strain this broth through cheesecloth and put it back in the pot. Add 2 more quarts (2 liters) of water and the wine. Taste for salt and add a few grindings of pepper.

Bring the broth to a boil, add 1 tablespoon kosher salt, and cook the pasta in this broth until *al dente*. While the pasta is cooking, reheat the sauce gently over low heat.

Warm a serving bowl or platter in a low oven. If the oven is not practical, warm the bowl just before use with hot water, even a ladleful of the pasta cooking water.

Drain and transfer the pasta to the heated serving bowl. Toss with the sauce. Serve immediately.

 WINE SUGGESTION: Prosecco or other young, white bubbly

Sugo con le vongole

(Clams)

SOMETIMES I THINK *spaghetti alle vongole* is the perfect food, all pleasure. The pasta needs to be unfailingly *al dente*, the clams succulent—size isn't so important—and cooked just to doneness and not a nanosecond beyond. Fragrant oil is the vehicle, but ideally a mysterious creaminess is produced from the combination of oil, clam broth, and starchy pasta water. A sauce forms right on the pasta redolent of garlic, chile, white wine, and the sea. In Italy, the clams are usually left in their shells, to tease. You have to work, not gobble. A virtuous sprinkling of fresher-than-fresh parsley provides the finishing touch.

All around Italy's coasts, at high-end restaurants and seaside joints, people love this dish without further embellishment—though I must say I enjoyed it with a sprinkling of bottarga in Sardinia. In the Campania region, and the south in general, some like it red. Cooks with a light hand speak of *macchiato*, like the coffee, meaning "with a spot," in this case of fresh small tomatoes. If you want a spot of red, add the optional tomatoes listed in this recipe.

Manila clams or button clams would be first choice as the next-best thing to Mediterranean small, delicate *vongole veraci*. Small littlenecks are fine, but any shells larger than a couple of inches (10 centimeters) should be removed once the clams are steamed open.

 PASTA SHAPES Spaghetti, *spaghettini*, or *linguine/bavette/trenette* are the only traditional options.

For the *condimento*:

about 2½ pounds (1.2 kilograms) Manila or other small clams, soaked for several hours in lightly salted water
4 tablespoons extra virgin olive oil, preferably medium fruity
2 cloves garlic, crushed
½ cup (100 milliliters) dry white wine
1 1-inch (2-centimeter) piece dried chile
½ pound (225 grams) cherry or grape tomatoes, quartered (optional)

To make the dish:

1 pound (450 grams) spaghetti
2–3 heaping tablespoons minced fresh flat-leaf parsley

Drain and rinse the clams. Put 1 tablespoon of the oil in a skillet large enough to hold the pasta later and add the clams, 1 garlic clove, and the wine. Cover the pan and turn on the heat to low. After 2 minutes, lift the lid and turn the heat to the absolute minimum. Using tongs, remove the opened clams one by one. The other clams will continue to open. When you have removed all the open clams, put the lid back on for several seconds and let the last clams open. Discard any clams that still don't open.

Strain the broth through a sieve lined with cheesecloth and reserve. If the clams are larger than about an inch and a half across (3 centimeters), remove them from their shells and discard the shells. If they have small, light shells, you may choose to leave them in the shell. Manila clams may be left unshelled.

 MAKE-AHEAD NOTE: While you can't make this sauce ahead of time, you can at least cook the clams up to this point before dinner. You can also do it while waiting for the pasta water to boil.

Put 5 quarts (5 liters) of water on to boil in an 8-quart (8-liter) pot over high heat.

While the water is coming to a boil, put the remaining oil in a large pan and add the remaining garlic and the chile. When the garlic and chile have colored nicely, add the strained broth.

Simmer over very low heat for not more than a couple of minutes. Remove the pan from the heat, discard the garlic and chile, and add the clams. Stir.

If using the optional tomatoes, add them now and sauté over medium heat for about 2 minutes, just until they are coated with oil and begin to wilt.

When the water boils, add 3 tablespoons kosher salt, then add the pasta and cook, stirring occasionally, until quite *al dente*, that is, a tad chewier than you would normally enjoy eating.

Warm a serving bowl or platter in a low oven. If the oven is not practical, warm the bowl just before use with hot water, even a ladleful of the pasta cooking water. You can also serve directly from the skillet.

Drain the pasta, not too dry, reserving 1 cup (200 milliliters) of the cooking water. Add the pasta to the clams. Add a splash of the pasta water. Toss and mix over low heat for not more than 1 minute.

Remove from the heat, transfer to the heated bowl, sprinkle with the chopped parsley, and serve immediately.

 WINE SUGGESTION: Est! Est!! Est!!!, a white from Lazio

Sugo con gamberi di fiume

(Crayfish)

TWENTY-FIVE THOUSAND YEARS ago, Cro-Magnon man sieved the beds of the rivers and streams of Italy for the delicacy that Italians call *gamberi di fiume,* "river shrimp," and that we call crayfish. Even a few decades ago the numerous watercourses that run through the countryside all over Italy were rich with the little creatures, which turn a beautiful fiery red when cooked. Today they are nearly extinct in the wild, but are successfully farmed and have a delicate taste for an elegant dish in which the red sweetness of the tomato competes with the red sweetness of the crayfish.

This sauce is also excellent for risotto. Use the broth in which the *gamberi di fiume* were cooked.

PASTA SHAPES Use *sedani, penne, conchiglie,* or *fusilli* (page 354).

For the *condimento*:

1 white onion, halved
6–8 sprigs fresh flat-leaf parsley, tied
1 small rib celery
1 carrot
2 cloves garlic, 1 whole, 1 crushed
salt
about 2 pounds (900 grams) crayfish

6 tablespoons extra virgin olive oil, preferably
  lightly fruity
1½ cups (300 grams) tomato puree

To make the dish:

1 pound (450 grams) pasta (see suggestions
  above)
extra virgin olive oil for finishing

Put a large pot of water on to boil. Add the onion, the bunch of parsley, the celery, the carrot, and the whole garlic clove.

When the water boils, add salt and cook for 5 minutes. Add the crayfish and let boil for another 10 minutes, or until they have turned bright red, indicating they are cooked.

Remove the crayfish with a slotted spoon or spider strainer. Strain about a cup (about 200 milliliters) of the broth and reserve.

Shell the crayfish. When you snap off the tail, the black intestine should come along with it. Reserve the tail meat. Discard the (yellowish) brain and intestine.

Process the shells in a food processor with the cup of reserved broth until the shells are broken into tiny pieces. Pour the contents of the container through a strainer and discard the bits of shell. Reserve the liquid.

Put the crushed garlic clove and the oil in a skillet, and sauté over low heat. Discard the garlic when golden. Add the tomato puree and the strained liquid from the processed shells. Mix well.

Cook the sauce over medium heat for 20 minutes, or until it is thick. Then and only then add the reserved tail meat. Let the flavors blend for a few minutes. Remove from the heat but keep warm.

Bring 5 quarts (5 liters) of water to a boil in an 8-quart (8-liter) pot over high heat. Add 3 tablespoons kosher salt, then add the pasta and cook, stirring occasionally, until *al dente*.

Warm a serving bowl or platter in a low oven. If the oven is not practical, warm the bowl just before use with hot water, even a ladleful of the pasta cooking water.

Drain and transfer the pasta to the heated serving bowl. Add the sauce and mix well. Finish with a swirl of extra virgin olive oil.

WINE SUGGESTION: a lively Vermentino di Sardegna DOC, from Sardinia

---

Sugo di gamberi

(Shrimp and tomatoes)

IT LOOKS SIMPLE. Tomatoes and shrimp, a flavorful sauce popular in all the coastal areas of southern Italy, embellished merely with a little garlic, chile, and parsley. But look again. The Italian way would be to leave the shrimp in their shells and present them on top of the pasta. Italians can peel shrimp and fruit, fillet fish on their plates, gnaw lamb chops on the bone and never make a mess or, seemingly, even sully their fingers. But for non-Italians, it is one thing to twirl spaghetti or *linguine* demurely on a fork without splattering and quite another to do it while shelling full-dress shrimp that have been cooked in oily sauce. In this recipe, we apologize to tradition and shell the shrimp in the kitchen. But lest we lose flavor, we put all the shells in a cheesecloth bag and add it to the pasta water. The pasta will absorb flavor from the water and nothing will be wasted.

Clearly the goodness of this dish depends on fresh, flavorful shrimp. For example, one summer, when Oretta was staying with her friend Teresa on the island of Stromboli—which is nothing more than an active volcano in the middle of the sea some distance from Sicily—she complained to the fishmonger that she never saw shrimp. Oh, you have to order those, he replied. They're too delicate to keep around. Come back in a couple of hours. So Oretta and Teresa went for a walk on the beach (with its black volcanic sand) where they saw the fishmonger on his boat catching shrimp. When Oretta calls for fresh shrimp, *that* is her criterion.

 PASTA SHAPES Spaghetti and *spaghettini* are most typical, but the sauce goes well with *tagliatelle* (page 328) and *tagliolini* (page 332), or *maltagliati* (page 336) and *farfalle* (page 336).

For the *condimento*:

1½ pounds (700 grams) large shrimp in their shells, preferably with their heads too
1 clove garlic, crushed
1 small piece dried chile
½ cup (100 milliliters) extra virgin olive oil, preferably medium fruity
1 pound (450 grams) fresh small sauce tomatoes, diced
at least ½ teaspoon salt

To make the dish:

1 pound (450 grams) pasta (see suggestions above)
1 heaping tablespoon minced fresh flat-leaf parsley

Wash, shell, and devein the shrimps. Place the shells and heads in a cheesecloth bag. Put 5 quarts (5 liters) of water in an 8-quart (8-liter) pot over high heat, and add the bag of shrimp shells. Let it simmer while you make the sauce.

Put the garlic, chile, and oil in a skillet large enough to hold the pasta and shrimp later and sauté over a lively flame until the garlic is golden, about 3 minutes. Stir in the shrimp and sauté for 3–5 minutes, or just until nicely pink; they do not need to cook completely at this point. Remove and set aside. Add the tomatoes. Sprinkle with the salt and cook over medium-high heat for 5 or 6 minutes, or until the tomatoes no longer look raw and begin to ooze juices that blend with the oil into something resembling a sauce. Discard the garlic and chile.

Return the shrimp to the pan. Mix to coat with the sauce, and cook, covered, over medium low heat until just cooked through, not more than 3 minutes.

 MAKE-AHEAD NOTE: You don't want to make this sauce very far in advance, but this much can be done at least before the guests arrive. Just leave the broth on low heat and the sauce in its pan, covered but not refrigerated.

Bring the pot of water to a boil, if it isn't already boiling. Discard the cheesecloth bag of shrimp debris. Add 3 tablespoons kosher salt, then add the pasta and cook, stirring occasionally, until quite *al dente*.

Warm a serving bowl or platter in a low oven. If the oven is not practical, warm the bowl just before use with hot water, even a ladleful of the pasta cooking water.

Drain the pasta and add to the skillet. Toss with the sauce and sprinkle with the parsley. Transfer to the heated serving bowl or platter and serve immediately. Or serve directly from the skillet.

 WINE SUGGESTION: a fresh Pinot grigio from Alto Adige

Zucchine e gamberetti

(Zucchini and small shrimp)

At Il Giardino, on Ventotene, every so often we get to eat something considered too old-fashioned or modest to put on the menu, such as Candida Sportiello's pasta with small shrimp and locally grown zucchini, which she ordinarily serves to family and ferry crew. In this recipe, adapted from Candida's, we remove the shells and heads to make the dish easier to eat, but use them to give flavor directly to the pasta as it cooks. (She leaves the shrimp fully armored.) Adding a grated zucchini is her trick for making the sauce creamy. Both the shrimp and the zucchini, which do not brown, have distinct but delicate tastes, and the overall impression is something like . . . Who knew delicate could have so much flavor?

 PASTA SHAPES *Linguine/bavette/trenette* or spaghetti would be the first choice of pasta shape, but tubular *mezze maniche* or *paccheri* would capture the bits of zucchini. A delicate egg pasta, such as *tagliolini* (page 332) or *maltagliati* (page 336), would blend well too.

For the *condimento*:

6 tablespoons extra virgin olive oil
1 clove garlic, crushed
2 medium zucchini, sliced ¼-inch
     (½-centimeter) thick
about 30 small shrimp, shelled and deveined;
     reserve the shells and heads, if you have
     them

2 tablespoons dry white wine
1 small zucchini, grated on the large holes of a
     box grater

To make the dish:

1 pound (450 grams) pasta (see suggestions
     above)
extra virgin olive oil for finishing (optional)

NOTE: If you shell your own shrimp, reserve the shells and heads, if you have them, and put them in a cheesecloth bag. When you put the pasta water on to boil, add the bag. When the water comes to a boil, cover, lower the heat, and simmer while you make the sauce. Bring the water back to a boil, discard the bag, salt the water, and cook the pasta normally. You can also leave a few shrimp unshelled for decorative effect.

Put the oil and garlic in a skillet large enough to hold the pasta later and sauté over low heat until the garlic is golden, about 3 minutes. Remove and discard the garlic and add the sliced zucchini and the shrimp to the pan. Sauté in the oil over medium-high heat for a couple of minutes or until the shrimp are just cooked through and a nice pink color. Remove the shrimp and set aside. Add the wine and let the alcohol evaporate, 1 minute.

Lower the heat to medium low, add the grated zucchini, and cook, stirring occasionally, until quite tender, about 10 minutes. The zucchini may throw off quite a bit of water, but if not, you can add a few tablespoons of warm water or broth from the shrimp shells while they cook. The zucchini should stay green and not brown. The pan juices and grated zucchini will form a light but creamy sauce.

Warm a serving bowl or platter in a low oven. If the oven is not practical, warm the bowl just before use with hot water, even a ladleful of the pasta cooking water.

Bring 5 quarts (5 liters) of water to a boil in an 8-quart (8-liter) pot over high heat. Add 3 tablespoons kosher salt, then add the pasta and cook, stirring occasionally, until quite *al dente*. Drain the pasta and add it immediately to the skillet. Toss gently over medium-high heat for half a minute or so, then add a swirl of oil, if you like.

Transfer to the heated serving bowl and serve immediately.

 WINE SUGGESTION: Ribolla Gialla, from Friuli–Venezia Giulia

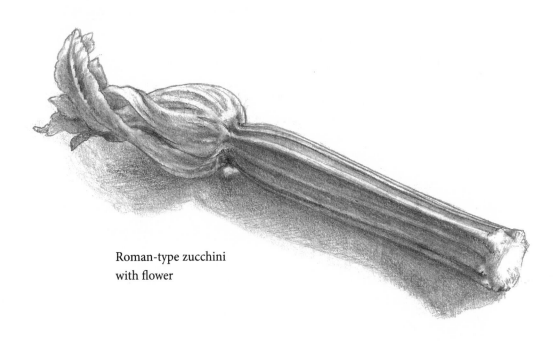

Roman-type zucchini
with flower

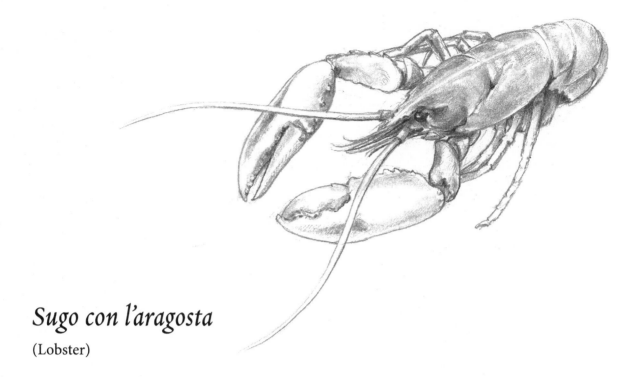

Sugo con l'aragosta

(Lobster)

THE *ARAGOSTA* IS the European spiny lobster (*Palinurus elephas*), and the best are reputed to come from the sea west of Sardinia, specifically from the shoals just west of the Isola del Mal di Ventre (which translates inauspiciously as "bellyache island"), not far off the wild coast near Oristano. Fishermen of the area recommend small lobsters for this typically Sardinian sauce. I can confirm that I ate the tastiest lobster of my life near Oristano, and I say that as a frequent visitor to Maine. Nevertheless, be confident that a two-pounder from the North Atlantic will

make a delicious dish. Its claw meat will be a plus that's lacking with the *aragosta*, and its sweetness will play beautifully against the sweetness of the tomato.

You do want to use a whole live lobster because you'll use its broth in the sauce. For the most tender and flavorful meat, drop the lobster into a couple of inches of boiling water. If you buy shelled lobster meat, ask the vendor if he has any shells to give you or else use fish broth (recipe, page 242) instead.

 PASTA SHAPES Use *tagliatelle* (page 328), *maltagliati* (page 336), *tagliolini* (page 332), *farfalle* (page 336), or *paglia e fieno* (page 331), all of which emphasize the delicate flavors of the simple sauce.

For the *condimento*:

1 2-pound (1.8-kilogram) live lobster
6 tablespoons extra virgin olive oil, preferably
    lightly fruity
1 medium white onion, finely chopped
1 rounded tablespoon minced fresh flat-leaf
    parsley

1 cup (250 grams) tomato puree
at least ½ teaspoon salt

To make the dish:

1 pound (450 grams) pasta (see suggestions
    above)

Bring 2–3 inches (5–8 centimeters) of water to boil in a pot large enough to hold the lobster. When the water boils, drop in the lobster, which will expire quickly, but clap the lid on as he will try to escape first. When the lobster is bright red, indicating that it is cooked, about 10–12 minutes, remove it from the pot and reserve the water. You can test for doneness by tugging sharply on the antennae. They will pull easily away when the lobster is done.

When cool enough to handle, dismember the lobster by twisting off the head, claws, and legs. Using nutcracker, pliers, a small fork, a pick, and even tweezers, extract every bit of the meat, including from the legs. Chop coarsely and set aside.

Put the oil in a saucepan with the onion and parsley, and sauté gently until the onion is transparent, about 3 minutes. Add the tomato puree, a ladle of the reserved lobster water (or fish broth), and the salt.

Cook over low heat for about 20 minutes, or until the tomato has visibly reduced and the oil come to the surface. Stir in the lobster meat and let the flavors blend over low heat for 3–5 more minutes, just enough to warm the lobster pieces through.

 MAKE-AHEAD NOTE: This much can be done earlier in the day.

Bring 5 quarts (5 liters) of water to a boil in an 8-quart (8-liter) pot over high heat. Add 3 tablespoons kosher salt, then add the pasta and cook, stirring occasionally, until *al dente*.

Warm a serving bowl or platter in a low oven. If the oven is not practical, warm the bowl just before use with hot water, even a ladleful of the pasta cooking water.

Drain very well and transfer the pasta to the heated serving bowl or platter. Toss with the sauce, and serve immediately.

 WINE SUGGESTION: Vermentino di Gallura, from Sardegna, or an unoaked Chardonnay

---

Sugo con i calamaretti

(Small calamari)

THIS SAUCE, WITH its intensely marine yet delicate flavor, is a favorite of fishermen on the Adriatic Riviera, the stretch of sandy coast, and very popular beaches, that extends from Abruzzo north to the Veneto. Once upon a time, small fish and even small squid were considered second-class catch and went to the fishermen's families, not for sale. Today we know better. What they lack in volume, they make up for in tenderness and lovely mild, sweet taste. There is rather a lot going on in this dish, with the little calamari and the diced pepper providing solids in an otherwise smooth tomato sauce. It could certainly be a *piatto unico*.

 PASTA SHAPES Use *tagliolini* (page 332), *paglia e fieno* (page 331), *linguine/bavette/trenette*, *fregula*, *gnocchetti* (page 342), *malloreddus* (page 346), or *pizzicotti* (page 351).

For the *condimento*:

6 tablespoons extra virgin olive oil, preferably medium fruity
2 cloves garlic, crushed
2 salt-packed anchovies, prepared as described on page 34 and coarsely chopped
1 large red or yellow bell pepper, seeded and diced
1½ pounds (700 grams) small calamari, cleaned and cut into rings or small pieces
1¼ cups (300 grams) tomato puree
salt, if needed

To make the dish:

1 pound (450 grams) pasta (see suggestions above)
1 tablespoon minced fresh flat-leaf parsley

Put the oil and garlic cloves in a skillet over medium heat. As soon as the garlic turns golden, add the anchovies. Stir them around in the oil for a minute or so until they begin to disintegrate.

Add the bell pepper. Sauté over medium-low heat until tender, about 8 minutes.

Remove the garlic cloves from the pan and stir in the calamari. Simmer over medium-low heat for a couple of minutes (they don't need to color), then add the tomato puree. Bring to a boil, then lower the heat to low and simmer, covered, until the calamari are cooked through and tender. Check them after 10 minutes. Taste for salt (you may not need any, thanks to the anchovies).

MAKE-AHEAD NOTE: This much may be made earlier or even a day ahead. Refrigerate, covered, if holding more than a few hours; otherwise, room temperature is fine.

Bring 5 quarts (5 liters) of water to a boil in an 8-quart (8-liter) pot over high heat. Add 3 tablespoons kosher salt, then add the pasta and cook, stirring occasionally, until *al dente*.

Warm a serving bowl or platter in a low oven. If the oven is not practical, warm the bowl just before use with hot water, even a ladleful of the pasta cooking water.

Drain and transfer the pasta to the heated serving bowl or platter. Add the sauce, sprinkle on the parsley, and mix well. Serve immediately.

WINE SUGGESTION: a lively Falanghina, from Campania

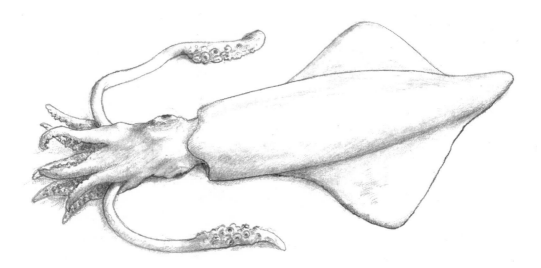

Sugo con il nero di seppia

(Cuttlefish ink)

IF YOU ARE lucky enough to have a fishmonger, ask him to clean the cuttlefish but to leave the ink sac intact or to save you some ink sacs. You will probably have to order them ahead. If you buy the cuttlefish already cleaned—which would be more usual—you can simply buy "squid ink" in a little bottle or packet, widely sold in fish and specialty stores. Its sharp, salty taste is modulated delicately by the sweetness of the tomato. A piece of cuttlefish in every bite provides texture.

A word to the wise: this dish can turn the teeth a disconcerting (but temporary) gray. You may not want to serve it for a romantic tête-à-tête.

 PASTA SHAPES Custom dictates spaghetti for this striking black sauce, whose recipe originates on the Salento peninsula (the heel of the boot), in Puglia.

For the *condimento*:

6 tablespoons extra virgin olive oil, preferably medium fruity
2 cloves garlic, crushed
1 teaspoon dried oregano
1 small piece dried chile
2 pounds (about 1 kilogram) small cuttlefish or calamari, cut in strips
3 or 4 tablespoons squid ink
½ cup (100 milliliters) dry white wine

1½ pounds (700 grams) small red, ripe sauce tomatoes (page 29), peeled, seeded, and diced, or canned small whole tomatoes with their juice
salt, if needed

To make the dish:

1 pound (450 grams) pasta (see suggestions above)

Put the oil, garlic, oregano, and chile in a skillet large enough to hold the pasta later. Sauté over medium heat for a couple of minutes.

Before the garlic begins to color, add the cuttlefish and the squid ink. Cook over lively heat 2 or 3 more minutes, then add the wine and tomatoes and cook over medium heat for another 15 minutes or until thick. Taste for salt. The squid ink may be salty enough by itself.

Bring 5 quarts (5 liters) of water to a boil in an 8-quart (8-liter) pot over high heat. Add 3 tablespoons kosher salt, then add the spaghetti and cook, stirring occasionally, until quite *al dente*.

Warm a serving bowl or platter in a low oven. If the oven is not practical, warm the bowl just before use with hot water, even a ladleful of the pasta cooking water.

Drain the pasta on the early side—it should be slightly undercooked—and transfer to the skillet with the sauce. Mix well over low heat for 1 minute before serving. The pasta will finish cooking to just the right degree of doneness. Transfer to the warmed serving bowl or serve directly from the pan. Serve immediately.

🌿 **WINE SUGGESTION:** an aromatic Pigato from Liguria

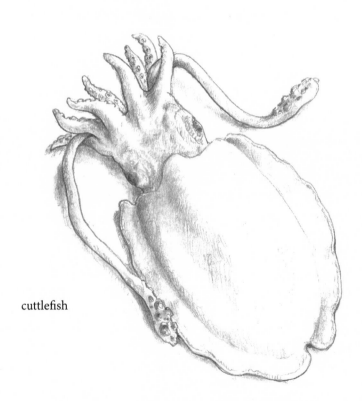

cuttlefish

scorpion fish

Ragù con lo scorfano

(Tomatoes, fish fillets, and calamari)

THE RED-TONED SCORFANO, scorpion fish, has quite delicious mild, large-flake, white flesh and deserves more respect. He's often relegated to soups, second-class status for a tasty fish of problematic appearance. The trouble is probably what looks like a rather aggressive facial expression and the spiky protuberances around his perimeter. But he's a gorgeous red color and is usually cooked with tomatoes, in varying quantities, that bring it out. Sometimes a nice, large specimen is served with pasta as a one-dish meal. In the classic version of this recipe, small *scorfani* are treated as soup fish and can be replaced with other small, tasty white-fleshed fish, such as red gurnard (*gallinella* in Italian) or porgy, whiting, or rouget (red mullet)—but you'll have to change the name of the recipe to *ragù con gallinella* (or whatever fish you use). Red snapper would also work.

Even though the recipe uses fillets, we suggest purchasing whole fish (and cleaning or having them cleaned) because they are much more flavorful than fillets you buy. Be sure to save the heads, bones, and odd bits for fish broth (page 242). If you are lucky enough to have a fishmonger, be sure he gives you all these extras.

This sauce comes from Sardinia. It's a red sauce in which the tender texture of the fish fillets contrasts in every bite with the more substantial cuttlefish or calamari.

 PASTA SHAPES Use this sauce with *lagane* (page 334), *maltagliati* (page 336), *pappardelle* (page 331), *farfalle* (page 336), *tagliatelle* (page 328), spaghetti, *linguine/bavette/trenette*, and *paglia e fieno* (page 331).

For the *condimento*:

1 large white onion
2 cloves garlic
6–8 sprigs fresh flat-leaf parsley
6 tablespoons extra virgin olive oil, preferably lightly fruity
about 10 ounces (300 grams) cuttlefish or calamari (about 3), cut in rings
1 cup (200 milliliters) dry white wine
1¼ pounds (550 grams) canned peeled tomatoes with their juice

at least ½ teaspoon salt
freshly ground black pepper
about 2 pounds (about 900 grams) fillets of porgy, whiting, or rouget, cut into 2-inch (5-centimeter) pieces

To make the dish:

1 pound (450 grams) pasta (see suggestions above)
extra virgin olive oil for finishing

Chop finely together the onion, garlic, and parsley (in the food processor if desired) and put them with the oil in a large skillet. Sauté until the onion is transparent.

Add the cuttlefish or calamari and sauté over medium heat for a couple of minutes. Add the wine and let it bubble until the smell of alcohol has dissipated, about 2 minutes.

Add the tomatoes, sprinkle with the salt and pepper, and simmer for about 20 minutes, or until the sauce is visibly reduced and shiny.

MAKE-AHEAD NOTE: This much may be done earlier. Reheat the sauce gently before proceeding.

Add the cut fillets to the finished sauce. Cover the pan and remove from the heat. Let the fish cook with only the heat of the sauce, which will take no more than a couple of minutes.

Bring 5 quarts (5 liters) of water to a boil in an 8-quart (8-liter) pot over high heat. Add 3 tablespoons kosher salt, then add the pasta and cook, stirring occasionally, until *al dente*.

Warm a serving bowl or platter in a low oven. If the oven is not practical, warm the bowl just before use with hot water, even a ladleful of the pasta cooking water.

Drain well and transfer the pasta to the heated serving bowl. Add the sauce and mix well. Add a swirl of oil and serve immediately.

 WINE SUGGESTION: Planeta Chardonnay, from Sicily

Sugo alla pescatora

(Mixed seafood)

Anzio, Roman Antium, on the Tyrrhenian Sea, south of Rome, has been known for many things over the ages. The emperor Nero had a villa there and was attending a musical competition when the great fire of Rome occurred: hence the story of his fiddling while Rome burned. The memory of the 1944 Battle of Anzio is kept alive there by moving ceremonies and a small World War II museum.

The rest of the time it was a fishing port. Today it's a bustling modern town with lots of restaurants an hour's train ride away from the capital. But it used to be a warren of straw huts, a tough five-hour trip away through the *macchia mediterranea* (maquis), the characteristic brush of Mediterranean coastal areas, along the Pontine Marshes, inhabited by boars, buffalo, and brigands. But its crabs and large shrimp have been renowned since antiquity, and the fishmongers of Rome are proud to label their freshest fish as coming from Anzio.

This fragrant, red *piatto unico* is perfect if you like assertive flavors and aren't put off by a few shells and tentacles.

You will need an extra-large skillet, 16 inches (40 centimeters) in diameter, with a lid.

 PASTA SHAPES Egg noodles are a must with this sauce, either *tagliatelle* (page 328) or the thinner *tagliolini* (page 332).

For the *condimento*:

About 2 pounds (1 kilogram) mixed seafood (small octopus, clams, small shrimp, langoustines, etc.), washed and cleaned as necessary but not shelled; thawed frozen octopus will do
2 salt-packed anchovies, rinsed and cleaned (page 34)
2 cloves garlic
6 tablespoons extra virgin olive oil, preferably lightly fruity

3 cups (800 grams) canned peeled tomatoes (1 28-ounce can), with their juice
salt, if needed

To make the dish:

1 pound (450 grams) pasta (see suggestions above)
2 heaping tablespoons minced fresh flat-leaf parsley

Prep the seafood. Soak the clams in salted water for 2 hours, then drain. Cut the octopus into bite-sized pieces.

Chop the anchovies with the garlic and sauté in the oil in a 16-inch (40-centimeter) skillet for about 2 minutes over medium-low heat, or until the anchovies have completely disintegrated.

Stir in the tomatoes. Cook, covered, over low heat for about 20 minutes. Add the octopus, which needs more time than the other seafood. After 15 minutes, add the remaining ingredients. Cook a bit more, not more than 5 minutes or until the clam shells have opened and the shrimp are a bright pink. Taste for salt.

Bring 5 quarts (5 liters) of water to a boil in an 8-quart (8-liter) pot over high heat. Add 3 tablespoons kosher salt, then add the pasta and cook, stirring occasionally, until quite *al dente*.

Warm a large serving bowl or platter in a low oven. If the oven is not practical, warm the bowl just before use with hot water, even a ladleful of the pasta cooking water.

Drain the pasta and add it to the skillet with the sauce. Mix quickly, sprinkle on the parsley, and mix again. Transfer to the heated bowl and serve immediately.

 WINE SUGGESTION: Vermentino di Gallura, a Sardinian white

clams and small octopus

Sugo di cernia e gamberetti

(Grouper and small shrimp)

THOSE OF US who knew Carlo De Vita, Oretta's late husband, loved the humor that he let show in his eyes while the rest of his face pretended to be deadly serious. And we never think of groupers without thinking of Carlo. Oretta tells the story of his frustration, summer after summer in Sardinia, where Carlo was determined to crown his vacation by landing a grouper. But year after year he watched other anglers walk away with their trophies, large and small, while he returned empty-handed. Then finally one day he came running triumphantly home from the beach holding aloft a fine grouper. Naturally Oretta cooked it whole for lunch. Carlo, characteristically, expressed his pride with just a look, a look that said, "You have simply never eaten a grouper like this one."

But you don't have to catch your own fish to enjoy this tasty sauce. Grouper fillets are easy to find, or you can use plaice, turbot, flounder, or sole.

Some may consider using a prized fish like grouper in a sauce wasteful. Don't listen. Its subtle flavor blends perfectly with pasta, and in any case, the dish should be treated as a *piatto unico*, that is, first and main course together. Just pink, from the small amount of fresh tomatoes, and combining two costly main ingredients, the grouper and shrimp, it is clearly a product of affluence, probably invented in the boom years of the 1960s by a seaside restaurant.

 PASTA SHAPES This sauce is typically served with *sedani* or *penne*, both factory made, but can also be used on homemade *maltagliati* (page 336), *tagliatelle* (page 328), or *busiata* (page 356).

For the *condimento*:

4 tablespoons extra virgin olive oil, preferably lightly fruity
1 shallot, finely chopped
8 ounces (225 grams) cherry or grape tomatoes, diced
1 small piece of dried chile
1 very fresh grouper fillet weighing about ¾ pound (300 grams), very finely diced
½ cup (100 milliliters) dry white wine

8 ounces (225 grams) raw shelled small shrimp
1 teaspoon salt

To make the dish:

1 pound (450 grams) pasta (see suggestions above)
1 heaping tablespoon minced fresh flat-leaf parsley
extra virgin olive oil for finishing (optional)

Warm the oil in a skillet over low heat. Add the chopped shallot and let it wilt, about 3 minutes. Add the diced tomatoes and the chile. Cook for about 5 minutes, then stir in the fish and cook for 2 more minutes.

Now add the white wine and let it evaporate quickly over medium-high heat, about 3 minutes. Add the shrimp and the salt and cook another 3 minutes or so until cooked through. Remove and reserve a few shrimp.

Bring 5 quarts (5 liters) of water to a boil in an 8-quart (8-liter) pot over high heat. Add 3 tablespoons kosher salt, then add the pasta and cook, stirring occasionally, until *al dente*. While the pasta is cooking, mince the parsley if you have not already done so.

Warm a serving bowl or platter in a low oven. If the oven is not practical, warm the bowl just before use with hot water, even a ladleful of the pasta cooking water.

Drain and transfer the pasta to the heated serving bowl. Toss the cooked pasta with the sauce, then top with the reserved shrimp, a sprinkling of chopped parsley, and a swirl of extra virgin olive oil if desired. Serve immediately.

 WINE SUGGESTION: a fragrant Arneis, from Piedmont

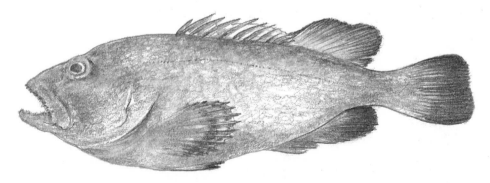

grouper

Meat Sauces

Anyone who has ever tried to translate cuts of meat from Italian to English, or vice versa, knows that it is practically impossible. It's not a problem of vocabulary, it's that the cuts don't correspond. The good news is that for pasta sauces, it really doesn't matter. For our purposes, boneless beef is boneless beef. The cuts called for in the recipes should be viewed as suggestions, not orders.

FOWL AND RABBIT

Ragù con le rigaglie di pollo
(Chicken giblets)

"RIGAGLIE," GIBLETS, IS a generic term in Italian to indicate the innards of chickens and other domestic birds. Under the heading come the liver, heart, gizzard, the rooster's comb and testicles (hard to find for sale even in Italy), and the hen's unlaid eggs (not used in the *ragù*). In Italy, giblets are sold ready to use. Otherwise, there is a painstaking preparatory phase. The liver has to be carefully cleaned of the greenish bits, which contain bile. The heart has to be cleared of blood clots and excess fat. Especially if the rooster had reached a certain age, his comb and wattles need to be blanched and peeled. The gizzard needs to be carefully cleaned, inside and out. The testicles, at least, can be used as is. Some people object to the bitter taste of giblets, but here it is tempered by the sweetness provided by the vegetables and the distraction of the ground meat, mushrooms, and other ingredients. The end result is a sumptuous red sauce, typical of central Italy, with a fragrance of mushrooms and spices that contrasts with the slight bitterness of the giblets.

PASTA SHAPES This elegant dish cries out for the rich delicacy of egg *tagliolini* (page 332) or *tagliatelle* (page 328) or *ravioli di ricotta* (page 302). *Bigoli*, made of whole wheat, work too.

For the *condimento*:

1 white onion
1 clove garlic
1 rib celery
1 carrot
3 tablespoons extra virgin olive oil
3 tablespoons (40 grams) unsalted butter
7 ounces (200 grams) ground veal
5 ounces (150 grams) ground pork
7 ounces (200 grams) chicken giblets (hearts, livers, gizzards; see headnote), cleaned, trimmed, and diced
1½ ounces (40 grams) dried porcini, soaked, squeezed, and chopped (page 37)

nutmeg
1 cup (200 milliliters) dry white wine
1½ pounds (650 grams) canned peeled tomatoes, drained
1 whole clove
at least ½ teaspoon salt
freshly ground black pepper
½ cup (100 milliliters) whole milk

To make the dish:

1 pound (450 grams) pasta (see suggestions above)
7 rounded tablespoons (70 grams) grated pecorino cheese (any kind)

Chop finely together onion, garlic, celery, and carrot, in the food processor if desired, and put in a large saucepan or deep skillet, preferably terracotta, with the oil and butter. Cook over medium heat until the vegetables are tender, about 8 minutes.

Add the ground meat and the giblets; mix well. Sauté gently, covered, over low heat, stirring occasionally, for about 10 minutes, or until the giblets are cooked through. If you have any doubt, cut a piece in half. There should be no pink.

Add the mushrooms and a pinch or grating of nutmeg. Let the flavors blend over low heat for a few minutes, then add the wine, raise the heat to high, and let it evaporate, stirring, about 5 minutes.

Lower the heat to medium. Add the tomatoes, the clove, salt, pepper, and another pinch or grating of nutmeg, and continue cooking. After about 30 minutes, stir in the milk. Cook for about 30 minutes more, at which point the sauce should be a concentrated deep red.

 MAKE-AHEAD NOTE: This much may be done earlier in the day.

Bring 5 quarts (5 liters) of water to a boil in an 8-quart (8-liter) pot over high heat. Add 3 tablespoons kosher salt, then add the pasta and cook, stirring occasionally, until *al dente*.

Lift out the meat with a slotted spoon and set aside. Pour the remaining sauce into a warm serving bowl and keep warm (the serving bowl can be placed over the pot where the water for the pasta is heating). Put the meat back into the saucepan, cover, and keep warm. We are essentially splitting what we have into two separate sauces, one liquid and one practically all solid, which is considered a very concentrated *ragù*. The two will be combined directly in the serving dish.

Drain the pasta and transfer to the serving bowl containing the sauce. Mix well until it has completely absorbed the liquid. Spoon the meat over it, and sprinkle with the cheese. Mix well and serve immediately and piping hot.

 WINE SUGGESTION: the Supertuscan Sassicaia or the more affordable San Guido Guidalberto

Ragù di coniglio

(Rabbit)

In Italy, the cuteness of bunnies is no reason not to make a fine rabbit *ragù*. A Boston friend still remembers the amusement of Oretta's other dinner guests years ago when she recounted that her large black pet rabbit had died of old age. Whether or not Blackie would, had he lived in Italy, have finished his days prematurely in a stew, rabbit meat is certainly much appreciated in Italy, but increasingly in North America as well.

In this hearty sauce, potentially a *piatto unico*, the rabbit is cooked in tomato puree enlivened by a surprising and refreshing scent of fennel. It comes from around Naples, specifically from the island of Ischia, best known for its hot springs and, in some circles, its excellent rabbits, introduced by the ancient Romans, who then watched helpless as the new arrivals munched their gardens.

 PASTA SHAPES Use *tagliatelle* (page 328), *lagane* (page 334), *penne, casarecce, tortiglioni, strozzapreti/pici* (page 344), or *ravioli di ricotta* (page 302).

For the *condimento*:

1 rabbit weighing about 4½ pounds (2 kilograms), cut into several pieces (frozen and thawed is fine)
2 ounces (60 grams) pancetta
1 white onion
1 carrot
1 rib celery
1 sprig fresh rosemary
2 tablespoons extra virgin olive oil, preferably lightly fruity

3 tablespoons (40 grams) unsalted butter
1 level teaspoon fennel seeds
⅓ cup (90 milliliters) dry white wine
2 cups (600 grams) tomato puree
1 teaspoon salt
freshly ground black pepper

To make the dish:

1 pound (450 grams) pasta (see suggestions above)
1 cup (150 grams) grated parmigiano-reggiano

Put the rabbit pieces in a deep 14-inch (35-centimeter) skillet without any fat. Heat over low heat until the meat throws off its water, about 5 or 6 minutes. Remove the meat and discard the liquid.

Meanwhile, chop finely together the pancetta, onion, carrot, celery, and rosemary (in the food processor if desired). When you have removed the rabbit pieces, put the oil and the butter in the same pan and add the pancetta mixture. Sauté over low heat for about 10 minutes, or until the fat melts and the vegetables are soft.

Return the rabbit to the pan and add the fennel seeds. Brown the meat, turning often and scraping up the brown bits from the bottom of the pan. Add the wine, turn up the heat, and let it bubble until the alcohol smell disappears, about 2 minutes. Add the tomato puree, sprinkle with salt and pepper, and simmer, covered, over medium heat for about 40 minutes, or until the rabbit is tender.

Remove the meat from the pan, then bone and chop it coarsely. Return it to the sauce. Let the flavors blend a few more minutes over low heat.

 MAKE-AHEAD NOTE: The process can be interrupted at this point and the sauce kept in the refrigerator for a couple of days or frozen. In any case, like other meat sauces, it will be tastier the second day than when freshly made.

Bring 5 quarts (5 liters) of water to a boil in an 8-quart (8-liter) pot over high heat. Add 3 tablespoons kosher salt, then add the pasta and cook, stirring occasionally, until *al dente*.

Warm a serving bowl or platter in a low oven. If the oven is not practical, warm the bowl just before use with hot water, even a ladleful of the pasta cooking water.

Drain the pasta and transfer it to the warmed serving bowl. Toss first with the cheese and then with the sauce. Serve immediately.

 WINE SUGGESTION: Pinot nero or another light, dry red

Ragù d'anatra

(Duck)

IN THE VENETO region, which extends from the Adriatic, and Venice, north into the mountains near Austria, *anara*, duck (*anatra* in standard Italian), both domestic and wild, is a traditional favorite in the kitchen. The duck of choice today in the Veneto, as well as in Lombardia, Emilia-Romagna, and the Marche, is the so-called *anatra muta* or *muschiata*, so called for its musky odor, Muscovy duck in English. In towns all over those regions, but especially in Friuli–Venezia Giulia, parades of ducks can be seen in the morning marching down the road from their families' homes to the nearest moat or ditch, where they will spend the day swimming until it's time to parade back in the evening for dinner, never failing to return to the right house.

This sauce, popular all over Italy but especially in the Marche region, begins with a whole duck, but in the best tradition of *cucina povera*, the actual meat from the duck is not used on the pasta but is served separately. The duck is used to make a delicious broth in which the pasta is cooked, and the giblets go into the sauce. Nevertheless one variant—the version we give here—does use a small amount of the boiled duck meat. The legs and breast are left intact for another use, but everything else is chopped and added to the sauce. The sauce is very light and delicate—it consists almost entirely of the pan juices—and contrasts pleasantly with any pieces of tender meat that are added. The sage, cloves, and pepper provide an interesting aftertaste.

It will be evident from many of the recipes in this book that what used to be *cucina povera* may today be available only to affluent sophisticates who can order online. The original recipe uses a Muscovy duck, which can be obtained online at a price (page 390), but don't miss this delicious sauce for want of an expensive duck. Use whatever kind you can find, including Pekin, and if you can't bring yourself to use a whole duck with its gorgeous breast meat, buy an equivalent weight of duck legs. If you can't get duck giblets, use chicken giblets.

 PASTA SHAPES This *ragù* is good with a variety of shapes, both egg and flour-and-water: *gnocchetti* (page 342), *pappardelle* (page 331), *tagliatelle* (page 328), *tagliolini* (page 332), *linguine/bavette/trenette*, *conchiglie*, *penne*, rigatoni, *bigoli*, or *sedani*. It's also good on *ravioli di ricotta* (page 302) and *gnocchi di patate* (page 364).

For the *condimento*:

1 carrot, cut in 1-inch (2.5-centimeter) lengths
1 small rib celery, cut in 1-inch (2.5-centimeter) lengths
1 white onion studded with 2 cloves
4 or 5 peppercorns
1 duck weighing about 3 pounds (1.5 kilograms), with its giblets (see headnote)
salt

3½ tablespoons (50 grams) unsalted butter
3 or 4 small sage leaves
½ cup (100 milliliters) dry white wine

To make the dish:

1 pound (450 grams) pasta (see suggestions above)
8 rounded tablespoons (80 grams) grated parmigiano-reggiano

Put the carrot, celery, clove-studded onion, and peppercorns in a pot with about 2 quarts (2 liters) of water. Bring to a boil, then simmer for 20 minutes.

Meanwhile, rinse the duck. Rinse, dry, and set aside the giblets. Add the duck to the vegetable broth with 1 level teaspoon salt. Simmer for about 1 hour, or until the duck is cooked through and tender.

Melt the butter in a small skillet, add the sage leaves, then the giblets, and sauté until golden brown.

Add the wine, raise the heat to high, and let it evaporate gently until the smell of alcohol has disappeared, about 2 minutes. Sprinkle with salt and continue cooking for about 15 minutes or until the giblets are tender. Remove the giblets, chop finely, and return them to the flavored butter in the same pan. Cook over very low heat for about 5 minutes, or until cooked through.

If the broth looks greasy, chill it and remove the fat that hardens on the surface. Remove the duck and strain the broth. Chop the breast meat coarsely. Add it to the giblets and keep warm. Alternatively, reserve the meat for another use and dress the pasta with just the giblets.

Return the broth to the heat and bring it to a boil. Add the pasta and cook, stirring occasionally, until *al dente*.

Warm a serving bowl or platter in a low oven. If the oven is not practical, warm the bowl just before use with hot water, even a ladleful of the pasta cooking water.

Drain and transfer the pasta to the heated serving bowl. Toss first with the cheese, then with the sauce. Serve immediately.

WINE SUGGESTION: Rosso or Brunello di Montalcino, or some other rich red with a touch of oak

GROUND MEAT AND SMALL CUTS

Ragù con carne macinata e funghi secchi

(Ground meat and dried mushrooms)

ALTHOUGH MANY OF the recipes in this book can be cooked in the time it takes to boil the water for the pasta, others are slow-cooked and benefit from a day of rest before being used. This basic, somewhat retro, meat sauce belongs to the second group. Its rich, multilayered flavors—meat, mushrooms, and tomatoes—characterize a sauce that is both sophisticated and deeply satisfying.

 PASTA SHAPES It works on any kind of pasta except the thin or tiny formats that belong in broth (and that includes *capelli d'angelo*) and meat-filled ravioli.

For the *condimento*:

1 spring onion, white part and the beginning of the green part; use a small white onion if you can't find green
1 carrot
1 small rib celery
10–12 sprigs fresh flat-leaf parsley
6 tablespoons extra virgin olive oil
11 ounces (300 grams) ground meat (veal, beef, pork, or a combination of all three; the cuts are unimportant)
1 cup (200 milliliters) full-bodied red wine
3 cups (750 grams) tomato puree

2 ounces (60 grams) dried porcini, soaked (page 37), squeezed, and chopped
1 clove
salt
freshly ground black pepper
½ cup (100 milliliters) meat broth, preferably beef (page 240)

To make the dish:

1 pound (450 grams) pasta (see suggestions above)
6 rounded tablespoons (60 grams) grated parmigiano-reggiano

Chop the onion, carrot, celery, and parsley together (in the food processor if desired). Put in a large saucepan, preferably terracotta, with the oil and sauté gently until the vegetables are tender, about 5–8 minutes.

Add the ground meat and sauté for a few more minutes, or until the meat has browned, about 5 minutes. Use a wooden spoon to break up the meat as it cooks.

Raise the heat and, when the meat begins to sizzle, add the wine. Let it bubble until the smell of alcohol has disappeared, about 4 minutes.

Add the tomato puree, the mushrooms, and the clove. Add 1 rounded teaspoon salt and a few grinds of black pepper. Bring to a boil, then reduce the heat to the minimum.

Simmer the sauce, covered, over low heat, adding the broth a few tablespoons at a time. It will need at least an hour, or even 90 minutes in terracotta. When the sauce is visibly reduced and the surface shiny with the oil that has come to the surface, take it off the heat. Taste for salt.

 MAKE-AHEAD NOTE: At this point, the sauce is done and can be kept in the refrigerator for a couple of days or frozen. In any case, it will be even richer and more flavorful the next day.

Bring 5 quarts (5 liters) of water to a boil in an 8-quart (8-liter) pot over high heat. Add 3 tablespoons kosher salt, then add the pasta and cook, stirring occasionally, until *al dente*.

Warm a serving bowl or platter in a low oven. If the oven is not practical, warm the bowl just before use with hot water, even a ladleful of the pasta cooking water.

Drain and transfer the pasta to the heated serving bowl or platter and toss with the sauce. Serve immediately and pass the cheese separately.

 WINE SUGGESTION: Montepulciano d'Abruzzo

Ragù di carne (bolognese)

(Bolognese meat sauce)

THE AUTHENTIC BOLOGNESE sauce has become a sort of Holy Grail for Italian-food lovers, who comb Internet boards and English-language cookbooks for the "authentic" version. But often what they find is something no self-respecting Bolognese would recognize. Tomatoes? Never! (A little tomato paste for color doesn't count.) Garlic? Never ever! "Bolognese" is not a synonym for "meat sauce" but a specific meat sauce from a particular place where garlic and tomatoes are not part of the tradition. Nor is spaghetti.

The Bolognesi, says Oretta, who is one herself, are very traditionalist in the kitchen and would appear to be no less fixated (her word) on the authenticity of their *ragù* than everybody else.

They have gone so far as to register with a notary the "true and authentic" recipe for *ragù*, which is the one we give here. They have also registered the filling of authentic *tortellini* (page 309) and the dimensions of *tagliatelle* (page 328), so "fixated" does seem to be accurate.

Few dishes on earth are as satisfying as a good *ragù*, meaning the real thing, like this one. It's virtually all crumbled meat, dark and meat-colored with reddish highlights. You'll be tempted to eat it with a fork right out of the pot before it ever catches a whiff of the pasta.

This recipe yields about 4 cups (700 grams), the correct amount for *Lasagne alla bolognese* on page 315.

🍃 PASTA SHAPES Need we mention that *ragù* is not served on spaghetti except to tourists? For that matter, in Bologna, traditionally spaghetti isn't served to anybody at all, much less with *ragù*. Rather, *ragù* is practically prescribed by law for Emilian egg *tagliatelle* (page 328) and *lasagne alla bolognese* (page 315). It is also excellent with other types of egg pasta, such as *pappardelle* (page 331), *fettuccine* (page 330), homemade *farfalle* (page 336), or wide *maltagliati* (page 336), and on *ravioli di ricotta e spinaci* (page 302).

For the *condimento*:

2 ounces (60 grams) pancetta
1 onion, white or yellow
1 carrot
1 rib celery
3 tablespoons (40 grams) unsalted butter
3 tablespoons extra virgin olive oil, preferably
    lightly fruity
5 ounces (150 grams) ground pork
5 ounces (150 grams) ground beef (any lean cut)
3½ ounces (100 grams) chicken livers, trimmed
    and coarsely chopped
2½ ounces (70 grams) unsliced *prosciutto di
    Parma*, diced

½ cup (100 milliliters) dry red wine
1 level tablespoon (10 grams) tomato paste
    dissolved in 1 cup (200 milliliters) warm
    water
salt
freshly ground black pepper
½ cup (100 milliliters) whole milk

To make the dish:

1 pound (450 grams) fresh egg pasta
10 rounded tablespoons (100 grams) grated
    parmigiano-reggiano

Mince the pancetta, onion, carrot, and celery together (in the food processor if desired). Put the butter, oil, and pancetta mixture in a large saucepan over medium heat and cook, stirring occasionally, until the pancetta just begins to brown, about 5 or 6 minutes.

Add the ground meats, chicken livers, and prosciutto. Cook gently, stirring occasionally with a wooden spoon, to brown everything evenly. Add the wine, turn up the heat, and let it evaporate, about 2 minutes. Add the dissolved tomato paste.

Simmer, covered, over low heat for about an hour and a half. At that point, the sauce should have a nice red color and have almost no liquid.

Add a level teaspoon of salt and a few grindings of pepper and cook slowly, covered, for another hour or so. Every so often, lift the lid and add a little of the milk until it is used up. Taste if you dare. You may want a second little spoonful, and then a third.

 MAKE-AHEAD NOTE: The process can be interrupted at this point and the sauce kept in the refrigerator for two or three days, tightly covered, or frozen. The sauce will certainly be tastier the second day.

Bring 5 quarts (5 liters) of water to a boil in an 8-quart (8-liter) pot over high heat. Add 3 tablespoons kosher salt, then add the pasta and cook, stirring occasionally, until *al dente*. Fresh *tagliatelle* (page 328) will cook in only a couple of minutes.

Warm a serving bowl or platter in a low oven. If the oven is not practical, warm the bowl just before use with hot water, even a ladleful of the pasta cooking water.

Drain and transfer the pasta to the heated serving bowl or platter. Sprinkle first with the grated cheese, then add the sauce and mix well. Serve immediately.

 WINE SUGGESTION: Sangiovese di Romagna from Fattoria Zerbina

---

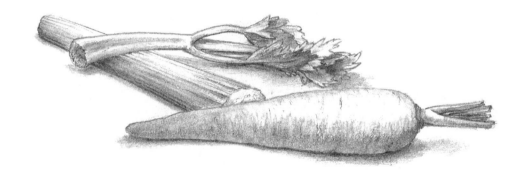

Ragù di agnello

(Lamb)

ONE WHIFF OF this hearty, fragrant sauce bubbling on your stove and you'll think you've just parachuted into the Apennines right in front of a trattoria, in sheep country. The mountains of central Italy—notably in the Abruzzo and Molise regions—have always been populated by shepherds. Consequently, lamb is the basic meat, and the cheeses are made from sheep's milk.

Shoulder would be our cut of choice, but really any lamb stew meat will do. Even though the recipe calls for boneless meat, if you have some lamb on the bone, throw it in. The bones will add flavor and will be easy to remove once the sauce is cooked. Lamb is fatty, so the sauce will benefit from overnight chilling and subsequent degreasing. But if you can't bear to throw away that yummy lamb fat, roast some potatoes Italian style—cut up in small pieces with lots of rosemary—and use the lamb fat instead of olive oil.

 PASTA SHAPES This sauce goes with both flour-and-water and egg pasta: *tagliatelle* (page 328), *conchiglie*, rigatoni, *sedani*, *tortiglioni*, *fregnacce* (page 337), *fettuccine* (page 330), *lagane* (page 334), *pappardelle* (page 331), or *paglia e fieno* (page 331). It's also perfect with *gnocchi di patate* (page 364).

For the *condimento*:

1 white onion
1 small carrot
1 small rib celery
a few sprigs fresh marjoram
3 fresh sage leaves
1 small sprig fresh rosemary
6 tablespoons extra virgin olive oil, preferably medium fruity
1 pound (450 grams) boneless lamb stew meat, cut into ¾-inch (2-centimeter) cubes
½ cup (100 milliliters) dry white wine
1 1-pound (450 grams) can peeled tomatoes, drained
1 small piece dried chile
salt

To make the dish:

1 pound (450 grams) pasta (see suggestions above)
6 rounded tablespoons (60 grams) grated *pecorino abruzzese* cheese or pecorino romano
1 heaping tablespoon minced fresh flat-leaf parsley

Mince finely together the onion, carrot, celery, marjoram, sage, and rosemary needles (in the food processor if desired) and put in a medium saucepan with the oil. Cook over low heat until the vegetables just turn pale gold, about 8 minutes.

Add the meat and brown gently, stirring.

Raise the heat and add the wine. Let it bubble until you can no longer smell any alcohol, about 2 minutes.

Add the drained tomatoes, the chile, and 1 level teaspoon salt. Lower the heat and cook, covered, for about an hour, stirring occasionally. You'll know the sauce is done when it has visibly thickened and the fat has separated and bubbles on the surface.

 MAKE-AHEAD NOTE: The sauce may be made ahead up to this point and refrigerated until the next day. After some hours of chilling, the fat will come to the surface and can be removed very easily.

Bring 5 quarts (5 liters) of water to a boil in an 8-quart (8-liter) pot over high heat. Add 3 tablespoons kosher salt, then add the pasta and cook, stirring occasionally, until *al dente*.

Warm a serving bowl or platter in a low oven. If the oven is not practical, warm the bowl just before use with hot water, even a ladleful of the pasta cooking water.

Drain and transfer the pasta to the heated serving bowl. Toss the pasta first with the cheese and then with the sauce. Finish with a sprinkling of parsley and serve immediately.

 WINE SUGGESTION: Montepulciano d'Abruzzo

Sugo con cavoli o broccoletti e salsicce

(Cauliflower or broccoli rabe and sausage)

YES, *CAVOLI* MEANS "cabbages," but yes, the sauce uses cauliflower. In Italian the *Brassica* family terminology tends to be loose, and in Naples, home of this recipe, *cavolo* is also a synonym of *cavolfiore*, cauliflower.

Those with absolutely no fear of pork fat can follow tradition and use finely diced *lardo* in place of the extra virgin olive oil. The hot pepper is optional, but if you do use it, don't spare it: if it's hot, it should be really hot.

In Campania, where this dish is very popular, the cauliflower tends to be green, giving the sauce a lovely green color and a slightly milder, more broccoli-like flavor. Green cauliflowers (not to be confused with the *broccolo romanesco*, which is similar but not the same) are increasingly available in American farmers' markets, but white will work just as well. Cauliflower and crisp crumbled sausage make for a rustic combination that evokes the Apennines in winter. And in fact the dish is also found in Abruzzo, Lazio, Umbria, and Tuscany. Broccoli and broccoli rabe are also perfect for this sauce.

PASTA SHAPES This sauce is typical with *strascinati* (page 348) and *orecchiette* (page 349). Other suitable shapes are *pizzicotti* (page 351), *fusilli* (page 354), and *sedani* or *penne*. Whatever shape of pasta you use, be sure to cook it in the same water in which you boiled the vegetable.

For the *condimento*:

3 tablespoons kosher salt
1 cauliflower weighing about 3 pounds
    (1.5 kilograms), trimmed and cut into
    florets, or same amount of broccoli or
    broccoli rabe, aggressively trimmed of
    tough stems and imperfect leaves
6 tablespoons extra virgin olive oil or 2 ounces
    (60 grams) *lardo*, diced
2 cloves garlic, crushed
1 small piece very hot dried chile or 1 teaspoon
    red pepper flakes (optional)

about 7 ounces (200 grams) finely ground
    unseasoned (no fennel, no chile) bulk sausage
    meat, as lean as possible, or 4 unseasoned
    sausages (of which 1 may be hot), skinned
½ cup (100 milliliters) dry, full-bodied red wine

To make the dish:

1 pound (450 grams) pasta (see suggestions
    above)
7 rounded tablespoons (70 grams) grated
    pecorino napoletano cheese or pecorino
    romano

Bring 5 quarts (5 liters) of water to a boil in an 8-quart (8-liter) pot over high heat. Add 3 tablespoons kosher salt, then add the vegetable and boil until just tender. Remove with a slotted spoon and set aside. Reserve the cooking water in the pot for boiling the pasta later.

Put the oil, the garlic, and the piece of chile, if using (but not the red pepper flakes), in a large, deep skillet that will hold all the pasta later. Sauté for a few minutes just until the garlic is golden and the chile has darkened, then discard the garlic and chile. Crumble the sausage meat into the skillet. Brown evenly, stirring, for about 5 minutes.

Raise the heat and add the wine. Let it bubble until the smell of alcohol has disappeared, about 2 minutes. Stir often to keep the meat from sticking. Add the boiled vegetable and mix well. If you are using red pepper flakes instead of a single piece of chile, add them now.

 MAKE-AHEAD NOTE: This much can be done earlier in the day.

Bring the vegetable water back to a boil and cook the pasta until *al dente*.

While the pasta is cooking, reheat the vegetable and sausage over low heat. After the pasta is half done, add a little of its cooking water to the sauce and let it absorb.

When the pasta is *al dente*, transfer it, dripping wet, with a handheld colander or spider strainer (or the like) to the skillet. Mix well over low heat for just half a minute.

Mix in the cheese and serve immediately, either straight from the skillet or in a warmed serving bowl.

 WINE SUGGESTION: Salice Salentino, from Puglia

Sugo con cotiche e salsicce

(Sausages and pork rinds)

HERE'S ONE FOR deep winter from the mountainous interiors of Abruzzo and Molise, in central-south-southeast Italy, a frugal, rugged land of unambiguous flavors scented with fresh herbs. This dense and satisfying tomato sauce has enough crumbled sausages and strips of fresh pork rinds to fuel a climb of the Gran Sasso, sub-Alpine Italy's tallest mountain.

The pork rinds add body, and protein, to the sauce, but can be omitted. Italian sausages widely available in North America, preferably without fennel seeds, will do very well. Ground pork shoulder, seasoned to your liking, can also be used in place of sausage meat.

 PASTA SHAPES Use a short pasta: *ruote, sedani, corzetti* (page 347), *casarecce, fregnacce* (page 337), *farfalle* (page 336), or *maltagliati* (page 336). Throughout central Italy, it is also served with polenta.

For the *condimento*:

3 tablespoons extra virgin olive oil, preferably intensely fruity
1 white onion, finely chopped
1 heaping tablespoon minced fresh marjoram leaves
1 tablespoon minced fresh thyme leaves
1 tablespoon minced fresh rosemary needles
About 1 pound (500 grams) bulk sausage, preferably hot, crumbled
12 ounces (350 grams) fresh pork rinds, scraped clean and cut in narrow strips (see page 33)
½ cup (100 milliliters) dry red wine

about 3 cups (700 grams) canned peeled tomatoes, with their juice
1 teaspoon salt
1 small piece dried chile or 1 teaspoon red pepper flakes, or to taste

To make the dish:

1 pound (450 grams) pasta (see suggestions above)
8 rounded tablespoons (80 grams) grated *pecorino abruzzese* cheese or pecorino romano

Put the oil in a large saucepan or deep skillet, preferably terracotta, and add the onion and herbs. Sauté over medium heat until the onion is transparent, 5 or 6 minutes.

Add the sausage meat and pork rinds. Cook, stirring, for 5 or 6 minutes, or until the sausage meat is cooked through. Add the wine and let it bubble until there is no more smell of alcohol, about 2 minutes.

Add the tomatoes, the salt, and the chile or red pepper flakes. Simmer, stirring occasionally, for about 1 hour or until the sauce is visibly reduced and shiny.

 MAKE-AHEAD NOTE: The sauce can be held in the refrigerator for up to 2 days or frozen. Thaw at room temperature and bring gently up to a boil before using.

Bring 5 quarts (5 liters) of water to a boil in an 8-quart (8-liter) pot over high heat. Add 3 tablespoons kosher salt, then add the pasta and cook, stirring occasionally, until *al dente*.

Warm a serving bowl or platter in a low oven. If the oven is not practical, warm the bowl just before use with hot water, even a ladleful of the pasta cooking water.

Drain the pasta well and transfer to the warm serving bowl. Toss first with the cheese, then mix in the sauce. Serve immediately.

 WINE SUGGESTION: a full-bodied Montepulciano d'Abruzzo

pork rinds and rosemary

Ragù con la salsiccia

(Sausage)

THIS IS ANOTHER stick-to-the-ribs sauce based on crumbled sausage in a large amount of tomato puree, but this one is from Naples. The giveaway is the oregano, the fragrance of the South.

There's no denying this dish has a fair amount of fat. It's a traditional dish, and people used not to have to jog off their dinner. Living was quite enough exercise. Today, we can ask for lean sausages or let the sauce rest for several hours or overnight in a cool place until the fat rises to the surface, when it can be removed.

The presence of an Umbrian cheese, *pecorino di Norcia*, in a Campanian dish is easily explained. Norcia was part of the Kingdom of Naples, and the cheese was used throughout the realm.

 PASTA SHAPES Use spaghetti, *linguine/bavette/trenette*, *gnocchi di patate* (page 364), *gnocchetti* (page 342), *pizzicotti* (page 351), *strozzapreti/pici* (page 344), *strascinati* (page 348), or *maltagliati* (page 336).

For the *condimento*:

1 clove garlic
1 small rib celery
1 carrot
6 tablespoons extra virgin olive oil, preferably intensely fruity
1 pound (450 grams) unseasoned sausages (no fennel seeds!), as lean as possible, removed from their casings and crumbled
½ cup (100 milliliters) red wine
2 cups (500 grams) tomato puree

1 teaspoon dried oregano
1 small piece dried chile
at least ½ teaspoon salt

To make the dish:

1 pound (450 grams) pasta (see suggestions above)
8 rounded tablespoons (80 grams) grated *pecorino di Norcia* cheese or pecorino romano

Mince the garlic, the celery, and the carrot finely together (in the food processor if desired). Put the oil in a large saucepan or deep skillet, preferably terracotta, and add the vegetables. Sauté over medium heat until the vegetables are soft, about 10 minutes. Raise the heat, add the meat, and brown evenly, about 5 or 6 minutes. Add the wine and let it bubble until the smell of alcohol has disappeared, about 2 minutes.

Add the tomato puree, the oregano, the chile, and the salt. Cover and cook over low heat for about an hour, or until the sauce has visibly reduced and the meat is completely cooked. Taste for salt.

MAKE-AHEAD NOTE: The process can be interrupted at this point and the sauce kept in the refrigerator for a couple of days or frozen.

Bring 5 quarts (5 liters) of water to a boil in an 8-quart (8-liter) pot over high heat. Add 3 tablespoons kosher salt, then add the pasta and cook, stirring occasionally, until *al dente*.

Warm a serving bowl or platter in a low oven. If the oven is not practical, warm the bowl just before use with hot water, even a ladleful of the pasta cooking water.

Transfer the pasta to the warmed serving bowl and toss first with the cheese, then with the sauce. Mix well and serve immediately.

 WINE SUGGESTION: Aglianico del Vulture, from Basilicata, or Salice Salentino, from Puglia

Ragù con le spuntature

(Pork ribs)

EVERY REGION OF Italy makes a sauce with ribs. In the Veneto, it goes with polenta, in the South with pasta. This recipe comes from the deep South, the Val d'Agri area of Basilicata, the small, almost landlocked region between the much larger Calabria and Puglia. As it happens, a particular type of extremely piquant local horseradish (*rafano* in Italian) comes into season in February, just about the time the family hog is slaughtered. This dish is the result. It's delicious even without the horseradish. Just add extra pepper.

Spuntature, rib tips, are cut from the end of the spareribs that wrap around the hog's chest. Instead of rigid bone, they have flexible tubes of cartilage that are mostly collagen and help thicken the sauce. Spareribs are fine, but should be cut into manageable lengths. The ribs are served right in with the pasta, which is coated in the thick, piquant tomato sauce, but are eaten on their own with the fingers. This is clearly a *piatto unico*.

PASTA SHAPES The sauce works with a great variety of pastas: spaghetti, *linguine/bavette/trennette, fusilli* (page 354), *gnocchi di patate* (page 364), *gnocchetti* (page 342), *pizzicotti* (page 351), *strozzapreti/pici* (page 344), *strascinati* (page 348), *lumachelle* (page 340), and *maltagliati* (page 336).

For the *condimento*:

12 ounces (350 grams) pork rib tips, trimmed of
    excess fat
1 large white onion, finely chopped
3–4 tablespoons extra virgin olive oil
2 ounces (60 grams) fresh pork rinds, cleaned
    and cut in strips as described on page 33
2½ cups (700 grams) tomato puree
1 ounce (30 grams) grated fresh horseradish or
    1 heaping teaspoon from a jar
at least ½ teaspoon salt
freshly ground black pepper

To make the dish:

1 pound (450 grams) pasta (see suggestions
    above)
about 8 rounded tablespoons (80 grams) grated
    Sila cheese or other pecorino

Put the ribs, the onion, and the oil in a large saucepan or deep skillet, preferably terracotta. Brown the meat lightly on both sides over medium heat, about 20 minutes. Stir in the pork rinds, and let the flavors blend for 5 or 6 minutes.

Add the tomato puree and the horseradish. Add the salt and a few grindings of pepper. Cover and let simmer over low heat, stirring once in a while, for about 1 hour or until the sauce has visibly reduced and the meat is cooked through and quite tender.

 MAKE-AHEAD NOTE: The sauce may be made up to 2 days ahead and kept covered in the refrigerator.

Bring 5 quarts (5 liters) of water to a boil in an 8-quart (8-liter) pot over high heat. Add 3 tablespoons kosher salt, then add the pasta and cook, stirring occasionally, until *al dente*.

While the pasta is cooking, simmer the sauce, uncovered, over medium heat for another 10 minutes.

Warm a serving bowl or platter in a low oven. If the oven is not practical, warm the bowl just before use with hot water, even a ladleful of the pasta cooking water.

Drain and transfer the pasta to the heated serving bowl. Toss the pasta first with the cheese and then with the sauce. Serve immediately. The ribs go right in with the pasta, and guests can pick them up with their fingers.

 WINE SUGGESTION: Amarone della Valpolicella, from the Veneto

---

LARGE CUTS

Ragù di carne

(Meat sauce)

IF "MEAT SAUCE" makes you think of a hearty dish of pasta laden with little gobs of chopped or ground meat with very little liquid, make *ragù di carne (bolognese)* (page 207). This recipe, one of a great many found in Italian cookbooks, is a less luxurious, more typical meat sauce, in which the meat adds flavor to the sauce but doesn't stick around to accompany the pasta. Rather, it is removed and spirited away to its destiny in another course or even another meal, perhaps minced and formed into meatballs, though once upon a time it was sliced and served as a main course at the same meal.

Meat sauce can be made of beef, veal, or fowl. Sometimes pork is added too. Ground meat can be used instead of a single piece, of course. This recipe, which takes its intense red color from plenty of tomato puree, is from the southern end of the spectrum and reminds us of the *"raù"* described by the great Neapolitan actor, playwright, and poet Eduardo De Filippo, the sauce his mother used to make with a piece of meat drowning in an enormous quantity of onions and tomato. (If you can follow the Italian, you can listen to Eduardo describing his *ragù* on YouTube: youtube/-hf3nK9oWSA.)

 PASTA SHAPES This sauce, which freezes beautifully, goes with many kinds of pasta, egg and not: spaghetti, *fettuccine* (page 330), *mafalde, penne, tortiglioni, sedani, conchiglie, farfalle* (page 336), *fiorentini, garganelli* (page 338), *gnocchi di patate* (page 364), *gnocchetti* (page 342), or *paglia e fieno* (page 331).

For the *condimento*:

2 white onions
1 small rib celery
1 carrot
6–8 sprigs fresh flat-leaf parsley
2½ ounces (70 grams) *guanciale* or pancetta, finely diced (¼ inch, or ½-centimeter)
3 tablespoons extra virgin olive oil, preferably intensely fruity

1 pound (450 grams) boneless beef in a single piece, such as chuck roast or chuck steak, tied with kitchen twine
1 cup (200 milliliters) full-bodied red wine
2½ cups (700 grams) tomato puree
2 bay leaves
at least ½ teaspoon salt
freshly ground black pepper
1 cup (200 milliliters) meat broth (if needed)

To make the dish:

1 pound (450 grams) pasta (see suggestions above)

4 rounded tablespoons (40 grams) grated parmigiano-reggiano

Mince finely together the onions, celery, carrot, and parsley (in the food processor if desired). Put in a saucepan with the pancetta or *guanciale* and the oil over medium-low heat.

When the vegetables are wilted and the pancetta or *guanciale* nicely browned, about 10 minutes, add the beef and brown on all sides, turning with tongs or two spoons (don't puncture it with a fork and let the precious juices escape).

Raise the heat and add the wine. Let it bubble until the odor of alcohol has disappeared, about 5 minutes. Add the tomato puree and the bay leaves. Add the salt and a few grinds of pepper and continue cooking, covered, over very low heat, for about 2 hours, until the sauce has visibly reduced and the oil has come to the surface. Add a little broth from time to time as the liquid evaporates.

Finally, remove the meat and reserve it, with a little of the sauce, for another course or another meal. Fish out and discard the bay leaves. You will be left with a thick but liquid sauce.

 MAKE-AHEAD NOTE: The process can be interrupted at this point, and indeed the sauce is at its best if held a day in the refrigerator. It will keep for a few days, however, and can be frozen.

Bring 5 quarts (5 liters) of water to a boil in an 8-quart (8-liter) pot over high heat. Add 3 tablespoons kosher salt, then add the pasta and cook, stirring occasionally, until *al dente*.

Meanwhile, reheat the sauce.

Warm a serving bowl or platter in a low oven. If the oven is not practical, warm the bowl just before use with hot water, even a ladleful of the pasta cooking water.

Drain and transfer the pasta to the heated serving bowl. Toss first with the grated cheese, then add the sauce and mix well. Serve immediately.

 WINE SUGGESTION: Rosso di Montalcino, from Tuscany, or Rosso Piceno, from the Marche

Tocco di carne alla genovese

(Genoa-style meat sauce)

IN GENOA, THE word *tocco* means sauce, the equivalent of *sugo* in standard Italian, and this recipe is for the traditional Genoese meat sauce. It's rich and red, with a lovely tangy complexity from the wine and earth tones from the dried porcini. Though full-bodied, the sauce is smooth, with the meat removed and served separately at another course or another meal. And the meat is delicious. Even after giving up its flavorful essence to the sauce, it takes on enough flavor from the tomatoes, wine, and other ingredients to make a very decent pot roast. Be sure to save out some of the sauce to serve later with the meat.

See page 225 for the Neapolitan sauce confusingly named *la genovese*.

❧ **PASTA SHAPES** Freshly made *corzetti* (page 347) with this tasty sauce is typical of the old cuisine of Genoa, but any short pasta will do fine. *Ravioli di ricotta* (page 302) are also good.

boneless lean beef prepared
for roasting and fresh porcini

For the *condimento*:

4 tablespoons extra virgin olive oil
1 clove garlic
1 white onion
6–8 sprigs fresh flat-leaf parsley
1 rib celery
1 carrot
2 bay leaves
1½ ounces (40 grams) dried porcini, soaked,
    squeezed, and chopped (see page 37)
1 pound (450 grams) boneless lean beef in a
    single piece, e.g., chuck or rump roast, tied
    with kitchen twine

at least ½ teaspoon salt
freshly ground black pepper
1 cup (200 milliliters) Barbera or other
    full-bodied red wine
1½ pounds (700 grams) canned peeled tomatoes
    with their liquid

To make the dish:

1 pound (450 grams) pasta (see suggestions
    above)
6 rounded tablespoons (60 grams) grated
    parmigiano-reggiano

Put the oil in a saucepan large enough to hold the meat, preferably terracotta. Mince finely together the garlic, onion, parsley, celery, and carrot (in the food processor if desired), add to the oil, and sauté gently for 5 or 6 minutes. Add the bay leaves and cook gently over low heat for 10 minutes more, stirring occasionally.

Add the porcini and the meat, sprinkle with salt and pepper, and brown on all sides, about 10 minutes. Add the wine, bring to a boil, and let it bubble until the smell of alcohol has dissipated, about 5 minutes.

Add the tomatoes to the meat and continue cooking over low heat, partially covered, stirring every so often, for about 1 hour, until the meat is cooked through (like a pot roast) and the dark sauce quite thick. Add a little hot water just if needed to keep the sauce liquid.

Finally, remove the meat and reserve it, with a little sauce, for another course or another meal. Fish out and discard the bay leaves.

❧ **MAKE-AHEAD NOTE:** The process can be interrupted at this point and the sauce kept in the refrigerator for a couple of days or frozen. In fact, it will be even more delicious the next day. The meat also freezes well with a little sauce.

Bring 5 quarts (5 liters) of water to a boil in an 8-quart (8-liter) pot over high heat. Add 3 tablespoons kosher salt, then add the pasta and cook, stirring occasionally, until *al dente*. Meanwhile, reheat the sauce, if necessary.

Warm a serving bowl or platter in a low oven. If the oven is not practical, warm the bowl just before use with hot water, even a ladleful of the pasta cooking water.

Drain and transfer the pasta to the heated serving bowl or platter. Toss first with the grated cheese, then add the sauce and mix well. Serve immediately.

WINE SUGGESTION: a big red from neighboring Piedmont, such as Barbaresco or Nebbiolo

---

SUGO CON LE SARDE (page 165).

Fresh sardines, raisins, and breadcrumbs over *busiata* (page 356). *Sicily.*

ZUCCHINE E GAMBERETTI (page 183):
Zucchini and small shrimp over *paccheri. Campania.*

SUGO CON L'ARAGOSTA (page 185).
Lobster and tomato over *tagliatelle* (page 328).

SUGO CON I CALAMARETTI (page 187).
Small calamari, bell pepper, and tomato over *paglia e fieno* (page 331).

RAGÙ DI CONIGLIO (page 201).
Rabbit, tomato, and herbs over *ravioli di ricotta* (page 302), with parmigiano-reggiano. *Marche*

RAGÙ DI CARNE (BOLOGNESE) (page 207).
Bolognese meat sauce (ground beef and chicken livers) over
tagliatelle (page 328), with parmigiano-reggiano. *Emilia-Romagna*.

RAGÙ DI AGNELLO (page 210).
Lamb, tomatoes, and herbs over *pappardelle* (page 331), with pecorino. *Abruzzo*.

SUGO CON CAVOLI O BROCCOLETTI E SALSICCE (page 212).
Broccoli rabe and crumbled sausage over *orecchiette* (page 349). *Puglia.*
Broccoli or cauliflower would be good too.

La Genovese

(Neapolitan meat sauce with onions)

THIS QUINTESSENTIALLY NEAPOLITAN sauce—despite a name that would seem to attribute it to Genoa—has a curious history that begins at the end of the sixteenth century in Palermo, in Sicily, second city of the Kingdom of Naples. That was when the city walls were built. For security, visibility of one mile was required, and thus trees or bushes that blocked the view for that distance were banned. The Genoese, who had a large trading operation there, obtained permission to plant not trees but nice low onions. Since onions would keep for a long time at sea and helped prevent scurvy, the onion trade, especially with Naples, flourished. Eventually this sauce, in which the dominant ingredient is onions, came to be the quintessential Neapolitan sauce and one of the great sauces of the Italian kitchen, alongside *ragù di carne (bolognese)* (page 207).

The consequent flourishing trade in onions, which involved above all the capital, Naples, eventually led to this unusual sauce. The meat flavor and dark reddish-brown color is provided by a pot roast, which is removed and served separately with some of the sauce. The protagonist, however, is onions cooked down to a sweet puree redolent of wine, herbs, and four different kinds of meat.

The *pecorino campano* cheese is milder than pecorino romano, but that is what should replace it.

Be sure to save some sauce to serve later with the pot roast.

 PASTA SHAPES Use a short, factory-made pasta, such as *penne rigate*, *maccheroni*, ziti, or *paccheri*.

For the *condimento*:

8–10 sprigs fresh flat-leaf parsley
a few fresh basil leaves
1 heaping tablespoon fresh marjoram leaves
2 carrots
1 rib celery
2 ounces (60 grams) prosciutto
2 ounces (60 grams) any Italian salami,
    Neapolitan if possible
¾ cup (180 milliliters) extra virgin olive oil
2½ ounces (75 grams) *lardo*, sliced thin
1 2-pound (900-gram) rump roast of beef or
    veal, tied with kitchen twine

about 2 pounds (1 kilogram) white onions, sliced
1 cup (200 milliliters) dry white wine
1 tablespoon (40 grams) tomato paste, dissolved
    in 1 cup (200 milliliters) warm water
at least ½ teaspoon salt
freshly ground black pepper

To make the dish:

1 pound (450 grams) pasta (see suggestions
    above)
8 rounded tablespoons (80 grams) *pecorino
    campano* cheese or pecorino romano

Chop finely (in the food processor if desired) the parsley, basil, marjoram, carrots, celery, prosciutto, and salami and set aside. Put the oil and *lardo* in a large saucepan, preferably terracotta, cover, and melt the *lardo* over very low heat, about 2 to 3 minutes.

Place the meat in the pan and brown it on all sides over medium heat, 3 to 4 minutes, then add the parsley mixture and the sliced onions. Stir the vegetables constantly over medium heat for about 10 minutes, or until they begin to soften.

Add the wine, mix well, and let it evaporate, stirring frequently, about 5 minutes. Stir in the diluted tomato paste and continue cooking, covered, over an imperceptible flame, for 1 hour or more, until the sauce has become dark and creamy and the meat is very tender.

If the sauce seems a bit dry, add a few spoonfuls of hot water. Add the salt and several grindings of black pepper.

Although this is not traditional, the sauce will be even more dense and delicious if you remove the roast for a moment, run an immersion blender in the sauce, and return the meat to the pot.

 MAKE-AHEAD NOTE: The process can be interrupted at this point and the sauce kept in the refrigerator for a couple of days or frozen. You'll use about two thirds of the sauce for the pasta. Reserve one third to serve separately with the meat.

Bring 5 quarts (5 liters) of water to a boil in an 8-quart (8-liter) pot over high heat. Add 3 tablespoons kosher salt, then add the pasta and cook, stirring occasionally, until *al dente*.

Warm a serving bowl or platter in a low oven. If the oven is not practical, warm the bowl just before use with hot water, even a ladleful of the pasta cooking water.

Drain and transfer the pasta to the heated serving bowl. Toss with the cheese and then with two-thirds of the sauce. Mix well and serve.

 WINE SUGGESTION: a big, spicy red, such as Primitivo

GAME

fresh thyme and
juniper berries

Ragù con il capriolo
(Venison)

THE VALLE D'AOSTA is the bilingual landlocked region on the French border nestled between Italy and France and home of Italy's former royal family. Books often tack the region onto the Piedmont chapter, but it deserves recognition on its own merits. It's an alpine land of spectacular natural beauty with a hearty cuisine, redolent of mountain tradition, that favors polenta, game, and what in Italy is called "the true" Fontina cheese.

My only experience of the region was a couple of days of half-hearted hiking on the way home from France, with thick Fontina-laden soups each evening. The reward for the long uphill treks was a fleeting glimpse of a *capriolo*, roe deer. That's what would ideally end up in this dark meat sauce with overtones of gaminess tempered by spices and alpine *grappa*. But other venison (see page 390) will be fine, farmed or fallen in the hunt. Only the amount of time the meat must marinate will vary—the wilder the animal, the longer the marinating.

The sauce will be creamy with a beautiful burnished color and the meat falling apart.

PASTA SHAPES In its natural habitat, you're likely to find this sauce on polenta, but it works wonderfully on *pappardelle* (page 331), large *farfalle* (page 336), Spätzle, *canederli* (page 362), and *pizzocheri* (page 366).

For the *condimento*:

1 white onion
1 clove garlic
6–8 sprigs fresh flat-leaf parsley
1 rib celery
1 carrot
about 2 pounds (about 900 grams) boneless aged
    venison, cut into 6 or more pieces
1 bay leaf
1 sprig fresh thyme
1 pinch ground cinnamon
3 whole cloves
5 juniper berries
freshly ground black pepper
about 2 cups (500 milliliters) full-bodied
    red wine

6 tablespoons extra virgin olive oil, preferably
    lightly fruity
½ cup (100 milliliters) *grappa*
about 1 tablespoon (20 grams) all-purpose flour
1¾ cups (400 grams) tomato puree
salt
¾ cup (180 milliliters) meat broth (page 240)
6 tablespoons heavy cream

To make the dish:

1 pound (450 grams) pasta (see suggestions
    above)
about 6 rounded tablespoons (60 grams) grated
    parmigiano-reggiano

Prepare the marinade for the meat. Mince the onion, garlic, parsley, celery and carrot together (in the food processor if desired). Rinse the meat and dry with paper towels. Put the meat and vegetables in a nonreactive bowl just big enough to hold them. Add the bay leaf, thyme, cinnamon, cloves, and juniper berries. Grind some pepper on top and add the wine. Cover the bowl and refrigerate for 3 days to marinate if you shot the animal yourself, only 8 hours if using farmed venison.

When it is time to make the sauce, remove the meat with a slotted spoon and pat dry. Strain the marinade and reserve. Discard the solids.

Heat the oil in a large saucepan. Add the meat and brown evenly on all sides over low heat for about 10 minutes. Add the *grappa*, bring to a boil, and let the alcohol evaporate, about 1 minute.

Sift the flour into the pan. Add the strained marinade and the tomato puree, sprinkle with salt, and simmer, covered, over low heat for about 2 hours, or until the meat is tender.

Heat the broth and stir it into the sauce a little at a time.

Remove the meat with a slotted spoon. Cut it into ¾-inch (2-centimeter) dice and keep warm.

Put the sauce through a food mill into a small saucepan. Add the cream and simmer for 5 more minutes. Taste for salt and add a few grinds of pepper.

 MAKE-AHEAD NOTE: The sauce can be kept refrigerated for up to 2 days.

Bring 5 quarts (5 liters) of water to a boil in an 8-quart (8-liter) pot over high heat. Add 3 tablespoons kosher salt, then add the pasta and cook, stirring occasionally, until *al dente*.

Warm a serving bowl or platter in a low oven. If the oven is not practical, warm the bowl just before use with hot water, even a ladleful of the pasta cooking water.

Drain and transfer the pasta to the heated serving bowl. Add the sauce and the diced meat and mix well. Pass the cheese at the table.

 WINE SUGGESTION: big, red, and intense, such as Barolo, from over the border in Piedmont

---

Ragù di lepre

(Hare)

ANYONE WHO HAS spent any time in the Tuscan countryside has encountered *pappardelle con la lepre*, broad egg noodles with a flavorful sauce that seems to be made entirely of shredded dark meat tasting not nearly as gamy as one fears.

When all the meat of the hare is used in the sauce, as in this recipe, the dish becomes a *piatto unico*. To make two courses, do as Oretta does and bone the hare but serve it separately as a main course, dressing the pasta with the pan juices alone.

Hare and rabbit may look alike, but, while rabbit famously tastes like chicken (an injustice with a kernel of truth), hare is dark meat and can be quite ripe unless marinated. In this recipe, the gaminess is tempered by the fragrance of the herbs and the bouquet of the aged Chianti. Don't scrimp on the wine. The rule that you shouldn't cook with a wine you wouldn't drink really applies here. The sauce is a lovely brownish red with shreds of flavorful meat and lots else going on thanks to the wine and fresh herbs.

Imported European hare can be purchased in the United States and online (page 390), but we have our own hares too: they're called jackrabbits, which are none other than North American hares. Yes, you have to shoot your own, but hunters and foragers take note.

PASTA SHAPES In addition to the canonical *pappardelle* (page 331), *tagliatelle* (page 328) and *maltagliati* (page 336) go very well with this sauce.

For the *condimento*:

1 whole hare weighing about 5½ pounds (2.5 kilograms)

1 cup (200 milliliters) red wine vinegar or cider vinegar

6 tablespoons extra virgin olive oil, preferably intensely fruity

1 yellow onion

2 cloves garlic

1 small rib celery

1 carrot

6–8 sprigs fresh flat-leaf parsley

5 fresh sage leaves

1 sprig fresh rosemary

1 bay leaf

2 sprigs fresh thyme

16 ounces (500 grams) canned peeled tomatoes, with their juice

at least ½ teaspoon salt

freshly ground black pepper

1 cup (200 milliliters) aged Chianti (or other full-bodied red wine)

To make the dish:

1 pound (450 grams) pasta (see suggestions above)

about 7 rounded tablespoons (70 grams) grated parmigiano-reggiano

Place the hare in a nonreactive container just big enough to hold it. Add the vinegar and just enough water to cover. Cover the container and leave in a cool place to marinate (preferably not in the refrigerator) for 24 hours to eliminate the gamy odor.

When you are ready to make the sauce, remove the hare from the marinade and rinse it well under running water. Separate and reserve the heart and liver, which butchers usually include with the rest of the hare. Remove and discard any blood and membranes. Cut the hare in 6–8 pieces and dry on paper towels. Dice the heart and liver.

Put the oil in a large saucepan or deep skillet, preferably terracotta. Chop finely together the onion, garlic, celery, carrot, parsley, sage, and rosemary needles (in the food processor if desired), and add to the oil. Add the bay leaf and thyme leaves and sauté over low heat for about 10 minutes, or until the onion is transparent and the other vegetables cooked through.

Add the pieces of hare, and the diced heart and liver, and brown evenly over medium-high heat, turning often, for 6 or 7 minutes more, or until the meat is nicely browned.

Scrape up the brown bits from the bottom of the pan and add the tomatoes, the salt, and a few grinds of pepper. Lower the heat to the minimum, cover, and simmer for about 2 hours. As it cooks, add the red wine a few tablespoons at a time, stirring often so the sauce does not stick to the pan. When the meat is completely tender and falling apart, remove from the heat. Fish out and discard the bay leaf.

Remove the meat from the sauce. When it has cooled somewhat, bone the meat with your hands and chop coarsely. Stir it back into the sauce.

MAKE-AHEAD NOTE: The process can be interrupted at this point and the sauce kept in the refrigerator for a couple of days or frozen.

Bring 5 quarts (5 liters) of water to a boil in an 8-quart (8-liter) pot over high heat. Add 3 tablespoons kosher salt, then add the pasta and cook, stirring occasionally, until *al dente*.

Warm a serving bowl or platter in a low oven. If the oven is not practical, warm the bowl just before use with hot water, even a ladleful of the pasta cooking water.

Transfer the pasta to the warmed serving bowl and toss with the sauce. Serve the cheese on the side.

 WINE SUGGESTION: Barbera d'Asti or Barolo, from Piedmont

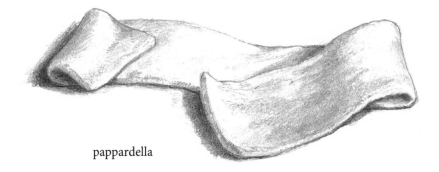

pappardella

Ragù di piccione

(Squab)

THE LAST TIME Oretta went to the butcher to buy squab for this meaty, savory sauce, he protested that his succulent little birds were too precious for a mere pasta sauce. They deserved to be stuffed, he exclaimed, and all but added "and served under glass." Thus have times changed. Back when your protein was free for the shooting or trapping, nobody thought it was too good to make a *ragù* from for a special occasion. And this sauce is truly special. Like other rich sauces with pieces of meat, it is usually considered a *piatto unico*, followed not with more meat but with a crisp green salad. It has a deep, ever-so-faintly gamy flavor and lovely burnt-orange color and is best if made a day ahead.

 PASTA SHAPES In Oretta's family, any remembrance of her grandmother Giulia in Bologna includes mention of the *ragù di piccione* she used to make for *garganelli* (page 338), a typical short pasta of Emilia–Romagna. *Tagliatelle* (page 328), a natural with meaty *ragù*, are also perfect.

For the *condimento*:

1 white onion, finely chopped
4 tablespoons extra virgin olive oil, preferably lightly fruity
3½ ounces (100 grams) pancetta, diced
3½ ounces (100 grams) *prosciutto di Parma* (or other sweet prosciutto), diced
2 squabs, ready to cook, with their hearts and livers, about 1¾ pounds (800 grams) total weight

1 cup (200 milliliters) dry white wine
7 ounces (200 grams) canned peeled tomatoes
1 teaspoon salt
freshly ground black pepper

To make the dish:

1 pound (450 grams) pasta (see suggestions above)
about 5 rounded tablespoons (50 grams) grated parmigiano-reggiano

Put the onion and the oil in a large saucepan, and add the pancetta and prosciutto. Sauté gently over medium-low heat for 5 or 6 minutes, or until some of the fat has melted and the onion is transparent.

Add the squab (but not the livers and hearts) and continue cooking gently until the pieces have browned nicely on all sides, taking care not to let the onion color too much. Raise the heat and add the wine. While it bubbles, scrape up the brown bits on the bottom of the pan. Boil until you can no longer smell the alcohol, about 10 minutes, but check the smell, not the clock. You want to smell the meat, not the wine.

Add the livers and hearts and the tomatoes. Add the salt and several grinds of pepper and continue cooking, partially covered, over low heat for at least 45 minutes, or until the meat is tender and the *ragù* considerably reduced. This sauce emphasizes the solids rather than the liquid, and you may need to raise the heat to concentrate the sauce. Remove from the heat and let cool.

With your hands, tear the meat and skin from the bones. Chop coarsely and return them to the sauce. Discard the bones.

 MAKE-AHEAD NOTE: Since now you have to let the sauce cool anyway, you can even refrigerate overnight. Like all meat sauces, it is even better the second day. Once you have boned the meat, you can also freeze the sauce.

Bring 5 quarts (5 liters) of water to a boil in an 8-quart (8-liter) pot over high heat. Add 3 tablespoons kosher salt, then add the pasta and cook, stirring occasionally, until *al dente*.

While the water is coming to a boil, reheat the sauce gently over low heat.

Warm a serving bowl or platter in a low oven. If the oven is not practical, warm the bowl just before use with hot water, even a ladleful of the pasta cooking water.

Drain and transfer the pasta to the heated serving bowl. Toss first with the grated cheese, then add the sauce and mix well. Serve immediately.

 WINE SUGGESTION: Franciacorta or dry Lambrusco or a Sagrantino di Montefalco, from Umbria

---

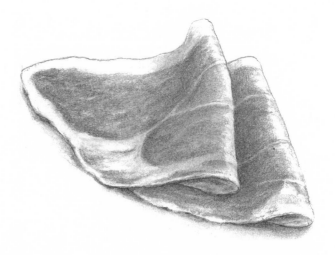

Ragù di cinghiale

(Wild boar)

THE TUSCANS LOVE to hunt, and this is one of the most famous recipes of the *cucina toscana*. Still today wild boars are plentiful in Italy (a limited number of animals may be killed each year). Boar meat can be found in every form—sausages, salami, prosciutto, as well as large cuts for stewing or grilling.

Farmers and vegetable gardeners are among those who consider the stewpot just revenge, protected status or not. Oretta's neighbor in the Sabine hills, an hour northeast of Rome, sits all night long on a large stone just daring the tusked marauders to mess with the tempting young plants in his garden.

Everything about this sauce says "winter." It's brown and intensely fragrant and all tender meat. Oretta won't make this *ragù* with just any brute her local hunters bring home. She requires a young, tender beast, not more than 22–33 pounds (10–15 kilograms), but will allow non-hunters to use wild boar stew meat they purchase online (page 390), especially since such young boars are hard to find. In North America, wild pig and heritage pork will also be very tasty cooked according to this recipe.

 PASTA SHAPES The classic pasta format is *pappardelle* (page 331), but *ravioli di ricotta* (page 302) would work too.

For the *condimento*:

1 onion
1 carrot
1 rib celery
1½ pounds (700 grams) wild-boar stew meat, cut in ¾-inch (2-centimeter) dice or smaller, gristle and larger bones removed
about 5 ounces (150 grams) unseasoned Italian sausages, removed from casing and crumbled
2 tablespoons (30 grams) lard
1 tablespoon extra virgin olive oil
2 whole cloves

2 bay leaves
at least ½ teaspoon salt
freshly ground black pepper
1 cup (200 milliliters) red wine
1 cup (200 milliliters) meat broth (page 240) or vegetable broth (page 243)

To make the dish:

1 pound (450 grams) pasta (see suggestions above)
6 rounded tablespoons (60 grams) grated parmigiano-reggiano

Chop coarsely together the onion with the carrot and celery (in the food processor if desired). Put the vegetables, boar meat, and sausage meat in a large skillet with the lard and oil and sauté over medium heat until the meat is browned on all sides, about 10 minutes. Add the cloves and bay leaves, and sprinkle with salt and pepper.

Cook over medium heat for about an hour, gradually adding the wine and broth. Have some hot water handy to add, a few tablespoons at a time as needed, if the sauce begins to stick.

The sauce is done when the meat has taken on a nice, dark color and is falling apart. Fish out and discard the bay leaves and cloves.

 MAKE-AHEAD NOTE: At this point, the process may be interrupted and the sauce kept in the refrigerator for a couple of days or frozen. In any case, like most meat sauces, it will have more flavor the next day.

Bring 5 quarts (5 liters) of water to a boil in an 8-quart (8-liter) pot over high heat. Add 3 tablespoons kosher salt, then add the pasta and cook, stirring occasionally, until *al dente*.

While the water is coming to a boil, reheat the sauce gently over low heat.

Warm a serving bowl or platter in a low oven. If the oven is not practical, warm the bowl just before use with hot water, even a ladleful of the pasta cooking water.

Drain and transfer the pasta to the heated serving bowl. Add the sauce and mix well. Serve immediately. Pass the cheese separately at the table.

 WINE SUGGESTION: Carignano del Sulcis DOC, from Sardinia

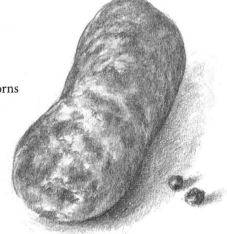

sausage and black peppercorns

SOUPS

The line between *pastasciutta*, pasta dressed with a sauce, and *zuppa* or *minestra*, soup, is not straight. Sometimes a cup or two of water, added or boiled away, is all it takes to turn one into the other. Legume soups often need a spoon when freshly made, but when it comes time for leftovers, they have absorbed all the water and can be eaten with a fork.

While all the sauce recipes in this book are calculated to dress 1 pound (450 grams) of *pastasciutta*, calculating amounts of soup is not so straightforward. The quantities of ingredients called for in these recipes are intended to make approximately the same number of servings as a pound of pasta, which is to say 4 to 6. Most soups will usually contain half the quantity of pasta—that is 8 ounces (225 grams)—but that may vary depending on what else is in the soup.

Also, you can always vary the amount of pasta you use in a soup according to your own preference. If you're trying to cut down on carbohydrates but can't bear to give up pasta altogether, by all means use less. The proportion of pasta to legumes can also favor one or the other ingredient, though a roughly even split would be normal.

We've grouped the soups into legumes, meatless, and containing meat or seafood, but sometimes the meat in question is just a bit of pork fat and can be replaced with olive oil for the lipophobic or vegetarian, though the soup will lose flavor and authenticity. But first come the three basic broths of Italian cooking.

If you need to make the soup in advance, don't add the pasta till you're close to serving. Once you have cooked the pasta, serve the soup as quickly as possible. This is true of all soups with pasta. The pasta will continue to soften (most Italians would consider it inedible mush the next day, but not everybody is quite that fussy) and may begin to go sour within a couple of days.

Although we throw in our lot with traditional values and call for transferring the soups to a warm tureen, we have no illusions that most people won't just serve from the pot. That's another reason we like terracotta cookware—it looks great on the table.

BASIC BROTHS

Brodo di carne

(Meat broth)

WHEREVER YOU GO in Italy, you'll find a different recipe for *brodo*, broth. Some cooks use chicken (ideally, hen, sometimes capon) or veal along with the basic beef, but sometimes also pork. My mother-in-law used a combination of beef and capon. Lamb and kid turn up as well, especially for holy days and other feast days. As a rule, different kinds of meat are used together in about equal quantities, but most often it's a single piece of beef tied to hold it together.

The boiled meat that remains after the *brodo* is made is not discarded. It can be used as the basis for numerous frugal dishes (two examples are on page 243) from the days when nothing was thrown away, and mothers could always invent new ways to recycle foods that had already given their best.

Italian *brodo* is more like consommé than stock, which is called *fondo di cucina* or *fumetto* in Italian.

Many people in Italy, including Oretta and me, like to pour a few tablespoons of red wine into their broth bowl, though others consider this a desecration of good *brodo*, which should look clear and taste simply like meat with elusive spicy overtones provided by the clove and pepper. If you decide to have the wine, Oretta recommends a generous spoonful of Lambrusco, the effervescent dry red wine always served in Bologna with *bollito misto*.

Not only a delicious end in itself, *brodo*, which can be frozen, is used as an ingredient in many soups and sauces or for making risotto.

Plenty of freshly grated parmigiano-reggiano is always served with *brodo*.

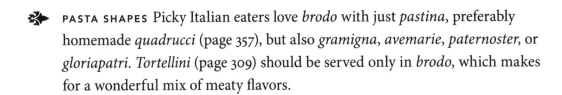 PASTA SHAPES Picky Italian eaters love *brodo* with just *pastina*, preferably homemade *quadrucci* (page 357), but also *gramigna, avemarie, paternoster,* or *gloriapatri. Tortellini* (page 309) should be served only in *brodo*, which makes for a wonderful mix of meaty flavors.

For 6–7 cups (1.4–1.5 liters) broth:

about 2 pounds (1 kilogram) beef for soup (any cut)
1 marrow bone
1 medium yellow or white onion
1 clove

1 carrot
1 rib celery, with its leaves
6–8 sprigs fresh flat-leaf parsley
1 bay leaf
6 black peppercorns
at least 1 level teaspoon salt

Put 3 quarts (3 liters) of cold water in a large soup pot and add the meat and the marrow bone. Bring to a boil and skim off the scum that comes to the surface.

Stick the onion with the clove and add to the pot. Then add the carrot, the celery, the parsley, including the stems (which contain the most flavor), the bay leaf, and the peppercorns. Simmer, covered, over low heat for 1½ hours, or until the meat is very tender. Add the salt at the end and taste. Add more if need be, but be careful, if you are going to reduce the broth further, it may get too salty. It's better to add salt gradually as needed.

Lift out the meat and reserve for another use. Strain the broth and discard the solids. Let the broth cool completely, uncovered, and place in the refrigerator overnight. After about 8 hours, any fat will rise to the surface and thicken or harden. Remove the surface fat and strain the broth through a fine strainer.

If you plan to serve the broth as the basis for *tortellini in brodo* or *pastina in brodo*, simply bring it to a boil and cook the pasta in the broth instead of in water. It can also be frozen.

 WINE SUGGESTION: when the broth is served alone, a dry Lambrusco

---

Brodo di pesce

(Fish broth)

You NEEDN'T—shouldn't—spend much money to make a good fish broth. Ask the fishmonger to give you some fresh but cheap (or relatively cheap) fish for soup. He may also throw in some heads of more prized specimens. Italian fish markets are always well stocked with small *merluzzi* (cod family) and other small fish collectively labeled "*zuppa*"—for soup. These may include dogfish as well as small mullet and bream that would fetch high prices in larger sizes. Ask the fishmonger for some heads and bones of flounder, sole, striped bass, and any other white fish left over from filleting the fish for his clients. The faint of heart may balk at the pound of fish heads called for in the recipe, but that's where the flavor is. This makes a dense but delicate broth that tastes of the sea. Don't use salmon, mackerel, or other strong-flavored fish. Try to get wild fish, as the flavor is vastly superior to farmed.

You can add a more valuable fish, a branzino or snapper, for example (Oretta would use a *scorfano*, scorpion fish), to the broth in the last ten minutes. The fish will be perfectly cooked and can be served as a main course, and the broth will have had a nice extra shot of flavor.

 PASTA SHAPES Fish broth is often used as an ingredient, but on its own it is delicious with *raviolini di magro* (page 305) and *capelli d'angelo* (page 332).

For about 5½ cups (about 1.2 liters) broth:

about 1½ pounds (750 grams) soup fish, about 6 pieces, cleaned
1 pound (450 grams) fish heads and bones
2 white onions, sliced
1 small leek (white and light green parts only), sliced and washed well

1 small rib celery, cut into pieces, about 1 ounce (30 grams)
1 sprig fresh thyme
1 bay leaf
1 cup (200 milliliters) dry white wine
1 tablespoon kosher salt

Cut up the larger pieces of fish and the bones. Put the vegetables and herbs in a large pot, and on top of them put the fish, heads, and bones. Cover with 6 cups (1.5 liters) water and the wine. Add the salt. Simmer gently, covered, for about 45 minutes. Strain the broth, taste for salt, and it's ready to use.

 WINE SUGGESTION: when the broth is alone, Est! Est!! Est!!!, a white from Lazio

Brodo vegetale (brodo di magro)

(Vegetable broth)

THIS RICH AND golden meatless broth (*magro* means both "meatless" and "lean") is easy to make and suitable for a variety of uses, including risotto. Because it is delicate, it is considered excellent for children. Just boil some tiny-format pasta (*pastina*) in it and add a handful of grated cheese. The fresh flavor is exactly that of the vegetables used to make it. The long, slow cooking extracts every bit of goodness from the vegetables so that you can feel no qualms about discarding them at the end.

If meat or fish broth is not specified in a recipe that uses broth, this vegetable broth will do nicely and certainly a good deal better than a bouillon cube.

NOTE: If the broth is to be held for more than a day, omit the potatoes, which can turn sour.

For about 8 cups (about 2 liters) broth:

½ pound (225 grams) potatoes (any kind), peeled and diced
2 white onions, diced
3 or 4 celery ribs (no leaves), diced
4 small carrots, preferably very fresh, diced

5 cherry tomatoes (left whole)
1 clove
4 whole black peppercorns
at least 1 teaspoon salt

Put all the ingredients except the salt in a heavy-bottomed pot. Cover with 2 quarts (2 liters) cold water and bring to a boil.

Turn the heat to very low, cover the pot, and simmer without stirring for an hour and a half. Add 1 teaspoon salt and taste. If desired, add more. Strain the broth.

 WINE SUGGESTION: when the broth is alone, or just with *pastina*, a light red, such as a young Montepulciano d'Abruzzo

---

MAINLY LEGUMES

Lagane e ceci

(Flour-and-water pasta and chickpeas)

Pasta e ceci, pasta with chickpeas, is a favorite dish in many parts of Italy. Here we give a version from Basilicata, the region that occupies the rugged terrain over the arch of the Italian boot, between Calabria (the toe) and Puglia (the heel). As it happens, that is where the ancient Roman poet Horace came from. Now, Horace wrote poems of exquisite refinement for his lofty patrons in Rome, but he was a son of a former slave and came from the sticks. He never forgot his origins (not that anyone would let him) and cast himself in his work in the role of the simple country mouse who couldn't wait to get out of the city back to his little farm. There, he wrote, he would

be greeted by a nice bowl of chickpeas, leeks, and *lagana*, a sort of proto-pasta, a name clearly related to the modern pasta name *lagane*.

It is entirely legitimate to channel Horace while eating this dish. Except for the chile, which came from the New World, the tastes are those of that land since time immemorial. Of course, as with so many once-humble foods, we have to do some creative sourcing to have anything like those anything-but-humble old tastes. Dried chickpeas, also known as garbanzos, are easy to find, but look for the smallest ones and, if you can, check the date, too. They should have been harvested within the past year.

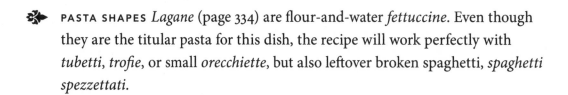 **PASTA SHAPES** *Lagane* (page 334) are flour-and-water *fettuccine*. Even though they are the titular pasta for this dish, the recipe will work perfectly with *tubetti*, *trofie*, or small *orecchiette*, but also leftover broken spaghetti, *spaghetti spezzettati.*

NOTE: To soak the chickpeas, pick over and rinse them, then place them in a bowl that leaves plenty of room for them to expand. Fill the bowl with water and let the chickpeas soak for 24 hours. They will at least double in volume so they should start to soak in about 3 quarts (3 liters) of water.

For the soup:

¾ pound (300 grams) dried chickpeas, soaked
and ready to cook
salt
2 bay leaves

Before serving:

8 ounces (225 grams) *lagane* (page 334) or
factory-made flour-and-water *fettuccine*
6 tablespoons extra virgin olive oil
1 small piece dried chile
1 medium leek, white and beginning of green
part, coarsely chopped and washed well

Drain the chickpeas and put them in a pot, preferably terracotta, with 6 cups (1.5 liters) of water,
1 teaspoon salt, and the bay leaves. Cook, covered, until the chickpeas are cooked through but not mushy.
Cooking time will vary quite a bit depending on your chickpeas, so check after 20 minutes and every 10
minutes or so after that. When the chickpeas are tender, turn off the heat and set the pot aside.

 MAKE-AHEAD NOTE: The chickpeas can be prepared a day ahead.

When ready to continue, bring the chickpeas to a boil, add a teaspoon of salt, stir in the *lagane* and
cover the pot. Turn off the heat and let the pot sit for about 10–15 minutes; discard the bay leaves. Taste for
salt. This method will work only with fresh pasta. For dry pasta, boil until *al dente*.

While the pasta is cooking, put the oil and chile in a small pan and add the chopped leek. Sauté over
medium heat until the leek wilts, 4–5 minutes. Discard the chile and stir the oil and leek into the soup.

Transfer the soup to a warm tureen and serve immediately.

 WINE SUGGESTION: a slightly floral red, such as Teroldego or Lagrein, from Trentino–Alto Adige, or
Monreale DOC, from Sicily

Ceci e baccalà

(Chickpeas and salt cod)

THE COMBINATION OF cod, chickpeas, and tomatoes with pasta seems to want to be eaten with a spoon, but up the proportion of pasta to liquid, give your guests forks, and you've got *pastasciutta*. This is comfort food with a twist of complexity. The thick, creamy texture comes from the chickpeas, which give a wonderful nutty flavor to play against the mild but substantial shreds of fish (more texture!) and the sweet-tart flavor of the tomatoes.

On the Gargano peninsula, the spur of the Italian boot, which is in the Puglia region, where this dish is traditional, the older women use a large terracotta pot with two handles on the same side to facilitate moving it around in front of the heat of the fireplace.

In olden times, the salt cod and chickpeas were soaked together and the soaking water used for cooking as well. This was to conserve precious salt, an expensive commodity that as late as the nineteenth century in many of the poorest parts of the South could not be bartered for at the markets, like other products, but had to be paid for in cash.

Today, we want to save time and limit our salt intake for other reasons, so soak them separately or buy them ready to cook. Throughout central Italy we can find both chickpeas and *baccalà* presoaked on Thursdays and Fridays, when many shops still observe the tradition of preparing them ahead of time for the convenience of customers planning a meatless Friday meal.

❧ PASTA SHAPES Flour-and-water pastas are used, e.g., *orecchiette* (page 349), *fusilli* (page 354), *cavatelli* (page 345), and *lagane* (page 334) for homemade shapes, *tubetti* for factory-made.

For the soup:

14 ounces (400 grams) salt cod, soaked and ready to cook (see headnote page 167), cut into 2-inch (5-centimeter) pieces, with all the bones removed

22 ounces (600 grams) fresh sauce tomatoes (see page 30) or 1 1-pound (450-gram) can Italian tomatoes with their juice

11 ounces (300 grams) dried chickpeas, soaked, drained, and ready to cook (see note, page 244)

2 cloves garlic, crushed

2 heaping tablespoons minced fresh flat-leaf parsley

3 tablespoons extra virgin olive oil, preferably intensely fruity

Before serving:

8 ounces (225 grams) pasta (see suggestions above)

3 tablespoons extra virgin olive oil, preferably intensely fruity

Rinse the cod and pat dry. If using fresh tomatoes, puree them in a food mill (see page 31). If using canned tomatoes, mash them with a fork or your hands.

Put the chickpeas in a 4-quart (4-liter) pot, preferably terracotta. Add 2 quarts (2 liters) of water.

Bring the chickpeas to a boil and lower the heat. Simmer over low heat. Check them after 20 minutes and frequently thereafter. They should be soft and done after about 40 minutes, but cooking time can vary quite a bit, depending on their age, drying method, and quality. Keep warm. Do not drain.

Put the garlic, parsley, and 3 tablespoons of the oil in another pot over low heat. When the garlic is golden, discard it, then add the tomatoes and the cod. Taste for salt and add a small amount if needed.

Simmer for about 40 minutes over medium heat, or until the cod is in flakes and the sauce visibly reduced. Add the chickpeas with their cooking water and let the flavors blend for a few minutes.

 MAKE-AHEAD NOTE: This much may be done earlier in the day.

If the soup is not already boiling, bring it to a boil, add the pasta, and cook until *al dente.* Just before serving, stir in the remaining oil.

 WINE SUGGESTION: for a red, Teroldego or Lagrein, from Trentino–Alto Adige; for a white Soave Classico, from the Veneto

---

Minestra di ceci, castagne e baccalà

(Chickpeas, chestnuts, and salt cod)

THREE INGREDIENTS OF the rural economy join forces in this winter soup typical of the Abruzzo region. All three contribute to the thick, creamy texture with little solid bits, and each contributes something different to the flavor. The chestnuts give a sweetness, the cod, salt, and the chickpeas something beany-nutty. Might we say *umami*? I know it's a strange combination, but it works. The texture is wonderfully rich, and with three main ingredients each used to being the star, plus the pasta, there's never a dull moment.

 PASTA SHAPES Use *volarelle* (page 338), *quadrucci* (page 357), *frascarelli*, *tubettini*, or *fregula*.

For the soup:

1 pound (450 grams) salt cod, soaked (see headnote page 167), skinned, and cut into pieces about 1¼ inch (3 centimeters) wide
1 pound (450 grams) dried chickpeas, soaked and ready to cook (see note, page 244)
1 pound (450 grams) shelled chestnuts (for sources, see page 387)

2 cloves garlic, crushed
6 tablespoons extra virgin olive oil
salt

Before serving:

8 ounces (225 grams) pasta (see suggestions above)
extra virgin olive oil for finishing

Put the cod and the chickpeas in a 4-quart (4-liter) pot, preferably terracotta, add about 2 quarts (2 liters) water, and cook, covered, over very low heat for about 40 minutes to 1 hour, or until the chickpeas are tender, which may be much sooner. The fish will have practically disintegrated.

Add the chestnuts and continue cooking until tender, about 20 minutes. How long this takes will depend on your chestnuts.

Put the garlic and oil in a small pan over low heat. Discard the garlic when it turns golden. Add this oil to the soup. Taste for salt.

Bring the soup to a boil and add the pasta. Continue cooking until the pasta is *al dente*, about 10 minutes, then transfer the soup to a warm tureen, add a swirl of oil, and serve hot.

 WINE SUGGESTION: a young, earthy red, such as Dolcetto, from Piedmont, or Montello dei Colli Ascolani, from the Marche

Sagne e lenticchie

(Lentils and noodles)

THIS WINTER RECIPE comes from the Sabine country an hour or two northeast of Rome, where *sagne*, as the locally made *fettuccine* are known, are practically a cult object. Every household makes them almost every day. They are almost as thin as *capelli d'angelo* and are cooked very *al dente*.

Lentils have been with us at least since Esau sold his birthright to his brother Jacob for a mess of potage, presumably a reasonable price. In Italy, even today, lentils cooked with *zampone* or *cotechino* sausage are essential for bringing in the new year. The more lentils you eat, the more money you can expect in the coming year.

Italy boasts numerous varieties of truly superb lentils—the smaller they are, the more highly prized, and some are very small indeed. The list of most respected lentils of Italy would include those from: Santo Stefano di Sessanio, on the slopes of the Gran Sasso, in Abruzzo; the island of Ventotene, which belongs to Lazio; the famous tiny ones from Castelluccio di Norcia and those of Colfiorito, both in Umbria, and from the Sicilian island of Ustica; and the green lentils of Altamura, in Puglia. They make great souvenirs from any trip to Italy, but are not a necessary condition of a good lentil soup. Any lentils will be good in this recipe, and domestic brown lentils, the smaller the better, will give the closest approximation of the original dish.

You'll make the soup in two pots, one for the lentils and one for the tomato condiment, which adds red highlights and sweet notes when blended with the brown lentils. Although this is technically a soup, it is quite dense, and you should certainly set forks at the table as well as spoons.

 PASTA SHAPES Use noodle shapes in this soup—*fettuccine* (page 330) or *lagane* (page 334), but also *maltagliati* (page 336) or *sagnette*.

For the soup:

1 pound (450 grams) lentils, washed and picked over
1 bay leaf
at least 1½ level teaspoons salt
3 tablespoons extra virgin olive oil
1 white onion, finely chopped
2 cloves garlic, chopped
2 cups (550 grams) tomato puree
1 small piece dried chile

Before serving:

8 ounces (225 grams) or less pasta
2 tablespoons, or more, best-quality extra virgin olive oil for finishing

Put the lentils in a 4-quart (4-liter) pot, preferably terracotta, with 6 cups (1.5 liters) water and the bay leaf. Add 1 level teaspoon salt, bring to a boil, then cook, covered, over low heat until tender. The cooking time can range from 20 minutes (for the best-quality tiny Italian lentils) to about 45 minutes, so keep an eye on them and check often. They should be tender but not mushy.

Keep a supply of boiling hot lightly salted water available on the stove and add it by the ladleful in the unlikely event your lentils begin to look dry. You can also use the water to make the soup more liquid.

Put the oil in a saucepan and add the onion and garlic. Sauté gently over low heat until transparent, about 10 minutes. Add the tomato puree, the chile, and ½ teaspoon salt. Cook for 20 minutes, or until the sauce is visibly reduced and the oil comes to the surface. Add this sauce to the lentils. You should have about 8 cups total. Taste for salt.

 MAKE-AHEAD NOTE: At this point, the process can be interrupted and the lentils kept until you are ready to complete the dish. The lentils freeze very well, too. They are best reheated in a double boiler.

When you are ready to continue, heat the lentils gently (if they are not already hot), add 2 cups (400 milliliters) lightly salted hot water, stir in the pasta, cover the pot, and cook over low heat until the pasta is *al dente*, which may be very quick.

Discard the bay leaf, stir in the oil, and let the soup rest for a few minutes before serving. It is also excellent served at room temperature.

NOTE: Lentils continue to absorb water like sponges long after they've finished cooking. In this case, you can certainly add water before reheating, but you will need to taste for salt. You can also just let them absorb as much as they want and eat the dish with a fork.

 WINE SUGGESTION: a young Sangiovese, such as Morellino di Scansano, from Tuscany

---

Minestra di fagioli alla padovana

(Paduan bean soup)

ORETTA REMEMBERS THIS hearty soup from the Veneto region from her early childhood in Padua during World War II. As with other bean soups, it can be made ahead without the pasta, which should always be added shortly before serving.

Borlotti beans stand out in markets with their pink marbled pods. The beans themselves are sort of piebald, shades of brown and white, but turn a monochromatic purple-tinged brown when cooked. Their closest equivalent outside Italy is the pinto or cranberry bean. The taste is stronger, more assertive than the gentler white beans, and, assisted by prosciutto fat and pork rinds, they are perfect for thick, robust winter soups like this one. (But see page 253 for how well they adapt to summer.)

Because not everyone cares for cheese with beans, the cheese is always served on the side, not added in the kitchen. The best cheese to use is an aged Asiago, also from the Veneto region, but be sure to get the sharper, older Asiago. The younger cheese, widely available, is much milder.

 PASTA SHAPES This soup is the perfect vehicle for either small factory-made shapes, such as *cannolicchi*, *tubetti*, or *farfalline*, or small handmade pastas, such as *quadrucci* (page 357) or *maltagliati* (page 336).

For the soup:

2 pounds (900 grams) dried borlotti (cranberry) beans, soaked for 12 hours or according to the directions on the package and ready to cook

salt

1 medium white or yellow onion

1 rib celery

1 small bunch fresh flat-leaf parsley

6 tablespoons extra virgin olive oil, preferably lightly fruity

2 ounces (50 grams) prosciutto fat, or pancetta, diced

5 ounces (150 grams) fresh pork rinds, blanched and cut into strips (see page 33)

Before serving:

8 ounces (225 grams) pasta (see suggestions above)

freshly ground black pepper

extra virgin olive oil for finishing

7 rounded tablespoons (70 grams) grated aged Asiago cheese (optional)

Put the beans in a 6-quart (6-liter) pot with at least 2 quarts (2 liters) of salted water, bring to a boil, and simmer until they are about half done—that is, when you can bite through a bean but wouldn't want to eat it. The older the beans, the longer they will take to cook. Check after 20 minutes and frequently thereafter. At the halfway point, you should be able to bite easily through a test bean.

While the beans are cooking, chop finely together the onion, celery, and parsley (in the food processor if desired). Heat the oil and prosciutto fat or pancetta in a second pot, preferably terracotta and large enough to hold the soup later. Add the onion mixture. Sauté gently over low heat until the onion is transparent but does not brown.

When the beans are half done, transfer them with the pork rinds to the pot with the onions along with about 6 cups (about 1.5 liters) of the bean cooking water. If there isn't enough bean water, add boiling water to bring the total to 6 cups. Taste for salt and bring the soup to a boil. Lower the heat immediately to a simmer and cook until the beans are quite soft, about 20 more minutes. The beans should make a quick transition from one pot to the other so that they never really stop cooking.

When the beans are quite tender, purée about ½ cup in a blender or food processor, then return it to the pot.

 MAKE-AHEAD NOTE: The process can be interrupted at this point. The soup will be even better the next day.

Bring the soup back to a boil, add the pasta, and cook until *al dente*. The soup should be quite dense. Finish with a few grindings of black pepper. Taste for salt. Ladle the soup into warm bowls and let each diner add a swirl of extra virgin olive oil and some grated cheese if desired.

 WINE SUGGESTION: a fruity Valpolicella or Recioto di Gambellara DOCG, from the Veneto

Pasta e fagioli

(Pasta and borlotti beans)

I HAVE NEVER seen beans taken so seriously as in Franco's family. I call his mother the Bean Queen, and it follows that it took me years to find the nerve to attempt this relatively humble dish. But now my beans too can make Franco purr.

You can use dried (and soaked) beans instead of fresh, but it's such a perfect summer dish, when shelling beans fill the markets—in Rome that means mainly borlotti (cranberry) beans—and tomatoes are full of flavor, that it never occurs to me to make it in winter. That's when I prefer chickpeas (page 244) or lentils (page 249). In summer, you can serve it at room temperature. You can always make it more or less soupy, and remember the beans and pasta will absorb a great deal of liquid, so even if it seems soupy when you take it off the heat, it will dry into a sort of potage (also good) unless you add more water. And if you add water, don't forget to taste and adjust the salt.

Don't get hung up on the tomatoes. If you have wonderful fresh ones, use those. If you don't like tomato pieces, use puree. Whatever the format, choose the most flavorful you can find. Nor should you worry about the amount. The dish can be more or less tomatoey according to taste and what you have on hand. The quantity given here is about medium. Add more or less, but adjust the water and bean liquid accordingly.

The soup should be thick with a creaminess that comes both from the starch in the pasta and from a small quantity of pureed beans. The basic flavor is that of the beans themselves, but there should be enough zing from the chile to make you sit up and take notice. Many people like to add red pepper flakes directly to their plate. A generous addition of the fruitiest, most assertive extra virgin olive oil you can find is essential at the end.

❧ PASTA SHAPES *Linguine/bavette/trenette* broken into pieces or fresh *quadrucci* (page 357), not too small, or *maltagliati* (page 336) are customary. Roman trattorias tend to favor *ditalini* or *cannolicchi*, the tiny tubes. But ever since Oretta told me that the ideal pasta for beans is a short tube just large enough to trap the bean, I've used Cavalieri brand (increasingly available in the United States) *tubetti*, larger than the usual *ditalini* and exactly the diameter of the average borlotti bean. As for all the soups, the quantity of pasta may be varied according to taste.

To make the soup:

1 pound (450 grams) shelled fresh borlotti beans,
    rinsed and picked over
salt
1 white onion, coarsely chopped
2 tablespoons extra virgin olive oil
about 1 pound (450 grams) red, ripe tomatoes,
    put through a food mill, or 2 cups canned
    Italian peeled tomatoes, broken into pieces,
    or 1½ cups tomato puree, preferably
    homemade
1 piece dried chile
1 bay leaf (optional)

Before serving:

8 ounces (225 grams) pasta (see suggestions
    above)
extra virgin olive oil, preferably intensely fruity
red pepper flakes

Place the beans in a 6-quart (6-liter) saucepan and cover with about 2½ inches (about 6 centimeters) of cold water. (This is more water than needed to cook the beans, but we will want it later for the pasta.) Cover the pot and bring the beans to a boil. Skim off the scummy foam that forms on the surface.

Cover the pot again, turn the heat to low, and simmer gently for about 30 minutes. At that point, check for doneness. When the beans are no longer crunchy but are still firm, add a good teaspoon of salt.

Continue cooking over low heat until the beans reach that stage of tenderness between resistant to the tooth and total mush. Remove from the heat but don't remove the lid for several minutes.

MAKE-AHEAD NOTE 1: Once they have cooled, the beans can be frozen with all or some of their liquid and used later in this recipe or others.

Meanwhile, in a larger pot, sauté the onion gently in the oil until transparent. Add the tomatoes or tomato puree. Add ½ teaspoon salt, the chile, and the bay leaf, if using. Let the tomatoes simmer for about 15 minutes, or until cooked through and slightly reduced. Fish out and discard the chile and bay leaf.

Remove a ladleful of beans with some liquid, puree in a food processor (or put through a food mill), and set aside. With a slotted spoon or handheld colander, transfer the rest of the beans to the tomatoes, then add about 1 cup (200 milliliters) of their liquid. Reserve the rest of the liquid.

MAKE-AHEAD NOTE 2: If you're not going to serve the dish within the next couple of hours, stop here until an hour or so before the guests arrive. You can also freeze the beans in the sauce.

Add additional water or bean liquid to the beans to come up to a minimum level needed to cook pasta. Start by adding 1 cup (200 milliliters), but keep a pot of boiling salted water or the bean liquid on the stove to top up the bean pot if you need more liquid to cook the pasta (never add cold water). Taste the liquid for salt (it should be pleasantly salty) and add some if needed. Bring to a boil, toss in the pasta, and cook until *al dente*. When the pasta is ready, stir in the reserved bean puree.

Alternatively, cook the pasta separately and add to the beans, but use the reserved bean liquid as part of the water.

Transfer to a tureen and stir in a couple of generous swirls of very flavorful extra virgin olive oil. Serve either piping hot or at room temperature. Offer a little dish of pepper flakes and more oil for guests to add individually as they wish.

 WINE SUGGESTION: for a red, Morellino di Scansano, from Tuscany, and for a white, a fragrant Pecorino from Abruzzo

Minestra di fagioli e cardoncelli

(Beans and oyster mushrooms)

IN THE BASILICATA region of the South, in a green valley that resembles a Swiss landscape (around the town of Sarconi), farmers are cultivating some twenty ecotypes of different beans that antedate the voyages of Columbus. Since the valley's woods are, in season, rich in mushrooms, tradition, in its wisdom, combined these two exceptional local ingredients.

The ideal bean to use would be the *fagiolo Maruchedda*, from Sarconi. Failing that, use borlotti (pinto or cranberry beans). The mushroom situation is better. *Cardoncelli* are *Pleurotes eryngji*, oyster or abalone mushrooms, not at all hard to find in North America. Thus on the one hand substance is provided by beans and pork rinds with, on the other, a contrasting but distinct delicate flavor of mushrooms.

 PASTA SHAPES This soup calls for a short pasta, such as *farfalline* or *maltagliati* (page 336).

For the soup:

2 pounds (900 grams) dried beans, preferably borlotti (cranberry), soaked and ready to cook

4 ounces (120 grams) fresh pork rinds, prepared as described on page 33 and cut in strips

at least 1 teaspoon salt

1 white or yellow onion, sliced thin

2 cloves garlic, crushed

3 tablespoons extra virgin olive oil

1 pound (450 grams) fresh oyster mushrooms, wiped clean with a damp cloth and coarsely chopped

Before serving:

8 ounces (225 grams) pasta (see suggestions above)

3 tablespoons extra virgin olive oil

about 8 rounded tablespoons (80 grams) grated *pecorino lucano* cheese or, failing that, *caciocavallo lucano* or pecorino romano

Drain the beans of their soaking water and put them in a pot with 6 cups (1.5 liters) of fresh water. Add the pork rinds, a teaspoon of salt, and simmer, covered, until the beans are tender. The timing will depend on the age of the beans. Check after 20 minutes and frequently thereafter. You want them cooked through, not at all crunchy.

Meanwhile sauté the onion and garlic in a skillet over medium heat with 3 tablespoons of the oil. As soon as they are golden, about 5 minutes, add the mushrooms, stir, and cook over medium heat, for about 15 minutes, or until the mushrooms have thrown off their liquid, the liquid has evaporated, and the mushrooms are cooked through. Discard the garlic.

Add the contents of the mushroom pan to the beans and taste for salt.

If the soup is not already boiling, raise the heat and bring to a boil. Stir in the pasta and cook until *al dente*.

Ladle the soup into individual bowls, drizzle with the remaining oil, and sprinkle with the cheese. Serve piping hot.

 WINE SUGGESTION: Aglianico del Vulture, from Basilicata, or Taurasi, from Campania

Minestra di fave

(Dried favas)

DRIED FAVA BEANS are very much a part of the local culture, food and otherwise, in southern Italy, especially Puglia. The ancient Romans used black and white favas to vote, and in later centuries the practice survived in the ballots of associations and organizations. They are also associated with superstitions and rituals. For example, if you open a pod and find seven beans, you will have good luck. The rest of us think that any time we can eat this creamy green(ish) soup, it's very good luck indeed.

Fava beans come out in the spring. If you are using dried favas in late winter, they are nearly a year old, assuming they are from the most recent harvest. They may need to soak for two full days and nights. If they are younger, 24 hours should do. Change the water every so often while they soak. When you are ready to make the soup, drain them and remove the skins. You can take a shortcut and use the dried kind without skins, but there will be a loss of flavor. The saving of time and trouble will, however, be considerable.

In keeping with local tradition, the pasta is cooked separately, then added to the soup. That final swirl of oil at the end is not optional; it's essential both to tradition and to waking up the favas to their full potential.

 PASTA SHAPES Use a small pasta, such as *cannolicchi*, *maltagliati* (page 336), or *volarelle* (page 338).

For the soup:

1 pound 10 ounces (750 grams) dried fava beans, soaked for 24–48 hours, depending on age
1 large white onion, finely chopped
4 tablespoons extra virgin olive oil
salt

Before serving:

8 ounces (225 grams) pasta (see suggestions above)
4 tablespoons extra virgin olive oil
6 rounded tablespoons (60 grams) grated pecorino romano or other pecorino

Remove the skins from the soaked favas (invite a friend to help).

Sauté the onion in the oil in a 6-quart (6-liter) soup pot, preferably terracotta. When the onion is transparent, add the favas and just cover with hot water, about 6 cups (about 1.5 liters). Add salt and bring to a boil. Lower the heat to the minimum and continue cooking, covered, until the favas have completely fallen apart, about 40 minutes to 1 hour, depending on the age of the beans. Stir occasionally, adding a ladle of hot water if needed. Ideally the soup will have the consistency of a smooth porridge, but if some broken pieces of fava are left, that is absolutely fine.

 MAKE-AHEAD NOTE: The soup can be held at this point just until the next day.

Bring 5 quarts (5 liters) of water to a boil in an 8-quart (8-liter) pot over high heat. Add 3 tablespoons kosher salt, then add the pasta and cook, stirring occasionally, until *al dente*.

Drain the pasta and add it to the favas. Let the flavors blend over low heat for a couple of minutes, stirring.

Transfer to a warm tureen, stir in the remaining oil and the pecorino, and serve.

 WINE SUGGESTION: a honeyed white, such as Fiano di Avellino, from Campania, or else a Brindisi rosso DOC

MEATLESS SOUPS

Minestra di zucchine, fiorilli e patate

(Zucchini, zucchini flowers, and potatoes)

THE TERM FIORILLI, for Italian *fiori*, tells us we are in Naples, whose particular climate and sea air bring the zucchini flowers (see also page 173) to market in spring, earlier than elsewhere. Then too the zucchini grown in the lava-rich soil of Vesuvius have a special sweetness (they are delicious raw, thinly sliced in a salad). In Naples, this is a typical springtime soup whose fragrance can be found among the ancient alleys of the city. Everyone else will probably make it in mid-summer.

The ease and simplicity of this soup are almost embarrassing—zucchini and potatoes? What could be humbler? Certainly the flowers add visual oomph, as well as a touch of luxury and their particular not-quite-zucchini flavor. But even without them, this recipe is an object lesson in the importance of raw materials. Go to the farmers' market, come home, start the soup. Better yet, pick the zucchini from your garden and start the soup.

 PASTA SHAPES Most small pasta formats will do, such as large *quadrucci* (page 357), *cannolicchi*, *volarelle* (page 338), or other medium-small pasta, but avoid tiny *pastina*.

For the soup:

1 large white onion, finely chopped
about ½ cup (135 milliliters) extra virgin olive oil
1 pound (450 grams) potatoes (any kind), peeled and diced
1 pound (450 grams) zucchini, sliced about ¼–⅜ inch (½–1 centimeter) thick
at least 1 teaspoon salt
1 level teaspoon freshly ground black pepper

Before serving:

8 ounces (225 grams) pasta (see suggestions above)
20 zucchini flowers
1 heaping tablespoon minced fresh basil
extra virgin olive oil for finishing

Sauté the onion gently in a 6-quart (6-liter) soup pot with the oil over medium-low heat until transparent, about 5 minutes. Add the potatoes and 1 cup (200 milliliters) hot water. Simmer, covered, over medium heat for about 15 minutes or until the potatoes are almost cooked through.

Add the zucchini to the potatoes. Add 6 cups (1.5 liters) hot water, or just enough to cover the vegetables. Season with 1 teaspoon salt and the pepper and simmer, covered, for 20 more minutes.

Add the pasta and cook, partially covered, until *al dente*. If more liquid is needed, add a few tablespoons of boiling water.

While the pasta is cooking, rinse the flowers carefully and pat dry. Tear the petals off the flowers. When the pasta is done, transfer the soup to a warm tureen and gently stir in the flower petals and the basil. Admire the colors. Add a swirl or two of extra virgin olive oil, and let the soup rest for 5 minutes before serving.

 WINE SUGGESTION: a white with rich tones and low acid, such as Chardonnay or Soave, from the Veneto, or Ischia bianco DOC from Campania

---

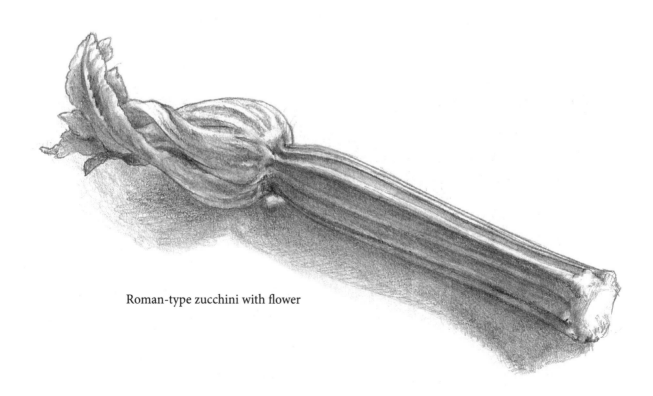

Roman-type zucchini with flower

Minestra di ovoli e patate

(Wild mushrooms and potatoes)

IN THE NARROW, boomerang-shaped strip of land that is the Liguria region, on the French border, sea and mountain are practically on top of one another and often meet in the region's recipes. Mushrooms are plentiful there in the autumn. The beautiful and noble *ovoli* (*Amanita caesaris*), accompanied by the discreet but distinct flavor of porcini, creates a particular fragrant soup that owes its all to the unique undergrowth of the region. The prized *ovoli* of this soup come from beneath chestnut trees, though some are found beneath beeches and oaks.

If you can't find *ovoli* (they can sometimes be purchased online; see page 388), use a mix of whatever wild mushrooms grow in your locality—that is certainly in the spirit of the original, even though the taste will necessarily differ. Still, you will get good results from some combination of shiitake, chanterelles, and hen of the woods. Their fragrance will combine beautifully with that of the potatoes and herbs. The creamy, pale-colored soup with bits of mushroom has the sort of delicate taste Italians call "refined."

 PASTA SHAPES Tradition dictates *pasta strappata* (page 335). You could also use *quadrucci* (page 357), *farfalline*, *tubettini*, or small *maltagliati* (page 336).

For the soup:

1 pound (450 grams) potatoes (any kind)
2 cups (about 500 milliliters) milk
salt
1 large white onion, finely chopped
3½ tablespoons (50 grams) unsalted butter, diced small
1 pound (450 grams) fresh *ovoli* or other wild mushrooms (see headnote), wiped clean with a damp cloth and sliced very thin

Before serving:

2 cups (about 500 milliliters) vegetable broth (such as that on page 243)
5 ounces (150 grams) pasta (see suggestions above)
1 sprig fresh thyme or marjoram
1 teaspoon salt
freshly ground black pepper
2 tablespoons minced fresh flat-leaf parsley

Boil the potatoes whole, in their skins, in plenty of unsalted water. When they are tender, drain and peel.

While the potatoes are still hot, put them through a ricer into a soup pot. Add the milk, 3 cups water (600 milliliters), and the salt, and mix well with a wooden spoon to blend all the ingredients. The result should be a thick puree. Leave it in the pot.

Put the onion in a large skillet with the butter and the mushrooms, and cook for about 20 minutes, or until the mushrooms have thrown off their liquid, the liquid has evaporated, and the mushrooms begun to color. Taste for salt.

In another pot, bring the broth to a boil. Bring the potato puree to a boil, and immediately stir in first the boiling broth, then the mushrooms and the pasta. Mix well.

Add the herbs and taste for salt and pepper. Cook for about 8–10 minutes more, or until the pasta is *al dente*. Sprinkle in the parsley and transfer the soup to a warm tureen. Serve immediately.

 WINE SUGGESTION: dry Lambrusco or Sangiovese from Romagna

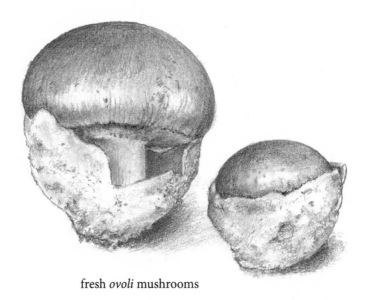

fresh *ovoli* mushrooms

Pasta e patate

(Pasta and potatoes)

IT TOOK ME a while to accept the double starch concept of pasta and potatoes. But I did notice that most people would assume a look of happy nostalgia at the very mention of *pasta e patate*. For good reason. And even those of us in whose childhood memories it does not figure can still grasp its attraction on a cold winter's night. It's thick and comforting, and the flavor subtle, but never bland and boring.

Probably every family has its favorite variations. For example, you can add a little cooked chard, spinach, or cabbage while the broth is heating.

To make a denser soup, reduce the amount of broth to 5 cups (1.2 liters). Make this soup the same day you plan to serve it.

 PASTA SHAPES *Quadrucci* (page 357) or *cannolicchi* are particularly appropriate, but *pasta grattata* (page 358) is also excellent, as are *spaghetti spezzati* (broken spaghetti). In Naples they used to use the broken spaghetti that collected on the bottom of the *madia*, the wooden chest where the pasta was stored. Sister Attilia, Oretta's childhood mentor in Bologna, used to put aside the odd cuttings from making *tagliatelle* to use in her exquisite potato soup.

For the soup:

1 small white onion
1 clove garlic
1 carrot
1 small rib celery
10–12 sprigs fresh flat-leaf parsley, with their
  stems
6 tablespoons extra virgin olive oil
6 cups (1.4 liters) meat or vegetable broth (page
  240 or 243)

22 ounces (600 grams) potatoes (any kind),
  peeled and diced quite small
salt

Before serving:

7 ounces (200 grams) pasta (see suggestions
  above)
8 rounded tablespoons (80 grams) grated
  parmigiano-reggiano
freshly ground black pepper

Chop finely (in the food processor if desired) the onion, garlic, carrot, celery, and parsley and put in a small skillet with the oil. Sauté over low heat until the vegetables are tender, about 6 minutes.

Bring the broth to a boil in a 6-quart (6-liter) pot and add the onion mixture and potatoes. Lower the heat and simmer for about 15 minutes, or until the potatoes are completely falling apart. Taste for salt; the amount will depend on how salty your broth is.

Add the pasta and cook *al dente*. Transfer to a heated tureen, stir in the cheese, grind on some pepper, and serve piping hot.

 WINE SUGGESTION: Don't overthink this one. Only you know what you like best with comfort food, and it will be fine. For an idea: Costa d'Amalfi bianco, from Campania.

Minestra con le castagne

(Chestnuts and wild fennel)

As LATE AS the 1950s, the majority of Italians lived in severe poverty. In times of famine, chestnuts, free for the taking, could be used to make flour for bread and pasta and also to make soups.

This soup, traditional for Christmas Eve, is rarely found nowadays, but it is native to the mountains behind Palermo, in western Sicily, where the wild fennel has an unmistakable fragrance. Wild fennel can be found in many places besides Italy (page 388), but if you can't find it, you can approximate the taste with two or three fennel seeds instead. Without the fresh fennel, however, you will lose the substantial green element it brings to the thick, almost sweet chestnut puree. For an unofficial workaround, use some fronds from ordinary fennel bulbs for the greens, getting the flavor from fennel seeds.

 PASTA SHAPES Use *ditalini, fregula, quadrucci* (page 357), *volarelle* (page 338), or *tubettini.*

For the soup:

salt
1 pound (450 grams) ready-to-use roasted and
    peeled chestnuts (see page 387)
2 bunches wild fennel, trimmed and chopped
    coarsely (about 1½ cups) or 2–3 fennel seeds
1 small piece dried chile

Before serving:

8 ounces (225 grams) pasta (see suggestions
    above)
4 tablespoons extra virgin olive oil

Bring about 6 cups (1.5 liters) of water to a boil in a 6-quart (6-liter) pot. Add 1½ teaspoons salt and the chestnuts, then the fennel and the chile. Simmer over medium heat until the chestnuts have disintegrated, about 40 minutes. Timing with canned chestnuts might vary.

Add the pasta and cook until *al dente*. If the water seems insufficient, add 2–3 tablespoons of boiling water. The final consistency should be that of a very thick potage, not at all watery. Transfer to a warm tureen, top with the oil, and serve hot.

 WINE SUGGESTION: a low-acid white blend from the Pomino region of Tuscany

Minestra di fagiolini e patate

(Green beans and potatoes)

THE FIRST TIME I had the nerve to invite Oretta and Carlo to dinner, I waited until summer so we could dine on the terrace. I sat them right opposite the Colosseum, hoping the view would distract them from the inevitable defects of the meal. We had pesto, made with our homegrown basil, followed by a truly wonderful *orata*, gilt-head bream, grilled as only my husband can. The *contorno* was green beans, and dessert was strawberries. As I had feared, after dinner Oretta critiqued the meal. The pesto passed! Franco's fish was a marvel! (Well, it was.) But the green beans, she said, were a little *al dente*, a little *all'americana*. I howled. Expecting something like that, I'd left the beans to boil until what I thought was the last possible moment, but they were still too resistant for her. This was particularly annoying because I can't abide the raw-tasting crunchy green beans my fellow Americans have been serving since the discovery, in the 1970s, that you don't need to boil your vegetables till they're dead.

 PASTA SHAPES This soup, a Calabrian springtime classic, is delicious even without any pasta at all, but better, of course, with egg *quadrucci* (page 357).

For the soup:

1 pound (450 grams) green beans (*haricots verts*), ends trimmed off and cut into 2–3 pieces each

8 ounces (225 grams) sauce tomatoes, seeded and diced, with their juice

1 pound (450 grams) potatoes (any kind), peeled and diced

1 onion, sliced thin

3 tablespoons extra virgin olive oil

2–3 cups fresh basil leaves, minced

1 teaspoon dried oregano

at least 1 teaspoon salt

freshly ground black pepper

Before serving:

4 ounces (115 grams) egg *quadrucci* (page 357) or other small soup pasta

3 tablespoons extra virgin olive oil

a few whole basil leaves for garnish

Put the beans, tomatoes, potatoes, and onion in a 6-quart (6-liter) pot, preferably terracotta, with 3 tablespoons oil. Let the vegetables soften slightly over very low heat, stirring, about 10 minutes.

Cover with 5 cups (1.2 liters) hot water, add the basil, oregano, 1 teaspoon salt, and a few grinds of pepper, and cook over low heat, covered, for about 20 minutes, or until the beans and potatoes are cooked through. Taste for salt.

Bring the soup to a boil (if it's not already there) and add the pasta. Cook over low heat until *al dente*, stirring often to keep the potatoes from sticking.

Transfer the soup to a warm tureen. Stir in the remaining 3 tablespoons oil and reserved basil leaves and serve.

 WINE SUGGESTION: a fruity rosé from southern Italy, such as Cantina del Taburno, from Campania

Minestra di fagiolini, pomodori e farfalline

(Green beans, tomatoes, and mini-bowties)

THIS FRAGRANT, COLORFUL soup, from southern Campania and Calabria, is traditionally made in springtime with the first, most tender green beans of the season. The delicate but distinct flavors of the beans and tomatoes are tied together by the richness of the cheese.

For the soup:

2 pounds (900 grams) green beans, ends
    removed, cut into 2–3 pieces each
2 cloves garlic, chopped
6 tablespoons extra virgin olive oil
12 ounces (350 grams) very ripe cherry or grape
    tomatoes, seeded and diced
¾ cup fresh basil leaves, minced
at least 1 teaspoon salt

Before serving:

8 ounces (225 grams) factory-made egg *farfalline*
6 rounded tablespoons (60 grams) grated
    pecorino napoletano or pecorino romano

Drop the beans in lightly salted boiling water for about 12 minutes, or until slightly *al dente* (not crunchy!): the cooking time will depend on their size and freshness. Drain.

Sauté the garlic in a large saucepan with the oil. Add the tomatoes, basil, and 1 teaspoon salt, and cook, covered, over low heat for about 20 minutes.

Add the beans and 1 quart (1 liter) warm water. Taste for salt and continue cooking for about 15 more minutes or until the flavor has developed irresistibly.

Add the pasta and cook until *al dente*. Transfer the soup to a warm tureen and serve. Pass the cheese separately at the table.

This soup is also excellent cold.

 WINE SUGGESTION: the Neapolitan classic, Lacryma Christi del Vesuvio, red or white

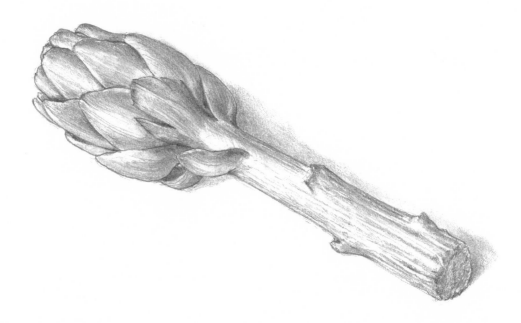

Minestrone bianco

(White vegetable soup)

IN OLDEN TIMES, the peasants of the mountainous part of Piedmont that borders on Liguria used to add a piece of *lardo* or pork rind or a hambone to this minestrone. Here we (reluctantly) offer the option of using extra virgin olive oil to what, without the pork fat, would be anybody's idea of healthful eating. *Bianco* means white, and indeed you may find the lack of warm Mediterranean colors disconcerting, but soldier on. The soup is absolutely delicious, with a different one of the many vegetable components coming to the forefront with each spoonful. Make it in winter, when

the ingredients are in season, and imagine you're in the Maritime Alps.

Minestrone is a generic term, literally "big soup," and does not indicate any particular formula, just one that contains a mix of many vegetables. The flavors and smooth, thick consistency of this soup are unlike the diced vegetables in broth that characterize most *minestroni*.

Because the peasants used to make this soup for special occasions, such as family reunions, the traditional recipe, given here, yields rather more than the others.

 PASTA SHAPES *Maltagliati* (page 336) or *tubettini* or any other middling-small format will do. The soup is quite dense, so tiny *pastina* shapes would not be first choice. You can even skip the pasta altogether and put a slice of stale or toasted bread in each bowl before you pour in the soup.

For the soup:

1 onion
1 rib celery from the heart
1 shallot
3 fresh medium sage leaves
1¾ ounce (50 grams) *lardo* or 6 tablespoons
    extra virgin olive oil
1 clove garlic
4 medium potatoes, peeled and diced
2 small, white turnips, peeled and diced
3 Jerusalem artichokes (also called sunchokes),
    peeled and diced (in season in North
    America from October to April but available
    year round)
1 fresh fennel bulb, peeled and diced
2 large leeks, white and light green part only,
    sliced thin and washed well

4 fresh artichoke hearts, sliced thin and held in a
    bowl of water acidulated with the juice of 1
    lemon (see page 148)
1 small head cabbage, trimmed, cored, and sliced
    thin, approximately 12 ounces (350 grams)
1 piece of parmigiano-reggiano rind, any size
salt
freshly ground black pepper
8 ounces (225 grams) dried white Spanish beans
    or gigantes beans, soaked and ready to cook

Before serving:

8 ounces (225 grams) pasta (see suggestions
    above)
7 rounded tablespoons (70 grams) grated
    parmigiano-reggiano

In a food processor, chop together the onion, celery, shallot, and sage with the *lardo*, if using. Put them in a 6-quart (6-liter) pot, preferably terracotta, over low heat and sauté until the fat has completely melted, about 5 minutes. If using extra virgin olive oil, chop the vegetables alone. Put the oil in the pot and add the vegetables.

Raise the heat to medium and continue to sauté until the vegetables just begin to turn golden, about 5 more minutes.

Add the garlic, potatoes, turnips, Jerusalem artichokes, fennel, leeks, artichoke hearts, and cabbage. Cover with 2 quarts (2 liters) hot water. Add the cheese rind, 2 teaspoons salt, and a few grinds of pepper. Simmer for about 30 minutes.

Add the beans and simmer the soup for about 1 hour more, or until the beans are quite tender (the cooking time of beans is very variable).

By that time, the vegetables should be falling apart, but if there are still any solid pieces, mash them with a fork or run an immersion blender right in the soup pot for a few seconds.

 MAKE-AHEAD NOTE: The process can be interrupted at this point and the soup kept in the refrigerator for a day or two but not frozen. In any case, after you have come this far, you'll definitely enjoy it more the next day.

Bring the soup to a boil, add the pasta, and cook until *al dente*. Transfer the soup to a warmed tureen and pass the grated cheese separately.

 WINE SUGGESTION: a Gavi, Arneis, or Erbaluce, or, for a red, Gattinara, all from Piedmont, like the soup

lardo

SEAFOOD AND MEAT

Minestra di fregula con le arselle

(*Fregula* and clams)

THIS UTTERLY DELICIOUS soup is a Sardinian classic and a favorite of the fishermen of Cagliari, the island region's capital, on its south coast. *Arselle*, also known as *telline*, are wedge-shell clams—tiny triangular morsels of delicate flavor. Wonderful ones used to be fished in abundance, even enough to export, from the beautiful Santa Gilla lagoon nearby, better known for the pink flamingos that inhabit it.

Fregula is a durum-wheat *pastina* typical of Sardinia. Once unknown elsewhere, *fregula* has been enjoying a moment of national and international celebrity with consequent debasement of quality. It is properly made by a technique much like that used for couscous, and, like couscous, the individual pieces should be irregularly shaped but roughly spherical, in sizes ranging from teensy to about as big as a small pea. Beware that most

of the *fregula* sold commercially, even in Italy, is simply spaghetti cut into very short lengths—easy to spot once you know to look. For this recipe, use any size, but try to find genuine artisanal *fregula* from Sardinia (page 388).

The final consistency of the dish should be liquid enough to justify the use of a spoon, but not much soupier than that. It should resemble a *risotto all'onda*, a very soft risotto. Any kind of broth will do to add depth and complexity of flavor.

Traditional recipes call for the *arselle* to be served in the soup on the half-shell. This is tedious for the cook and annoying for the diner, so we suggest shelling the clams entirely. But if you want to leave some on the half-shell to give a nice maritime feel to your dish, go right ahead. If the clams are quite small, you can also leave both shells.

For the soup:

About 2¼ pounds (1 kilogram) wedge-shell clams, or littlenecks, Manila clams, razor clams, or cockles, soaked for 2 hours in lightly salted water
6 tablespoons extra virgin olive oil, preferably medium fruity
2 cloves garlic, crushed
4 or 5 sun-dried tomatoes, finely chopped
1 heaping teaspoon minced fresh flat-leaf parsley

3 cups (700 grams) tomato puree
1¼ cups (300 milliliters) meat, fish, or vegetable broth (pages 240, 242, 243)

To finish the dish:

2 quarts (2 liters) meat, fish, or vegetable broth
8 ounces (225 grams) *fregula*
salt

Drain and rinse the clams. Put them in a 12-inch skillet over very low heat, covered. After 2 minutes, lift the lid and, turn the heat to the absolute minimum. If the heat is too high, all the broth might evaporate. Using tongs or a slotted spoon, remove the opened clams. The other clams will continue to open. When you have removed all the open clams, put the lid back on for a minute and let the last clams open. Discard any clams that still don't open. Strain the liquid that remains in the pan through a cheesecloth-lined strainer and reserve.

Shell the clams and chop coarsely if they are larger than about an inch (2.5 centimeters) across the shell. Discard the shells and set the clams aside in a bowl. Optionally, leave a few on the half-shell for decorative effect. If shelling all those clams is just too tedious, just leave them in the shells and let your guests do the work at the table.

Put the oil, garlic, and sun-dried tomatoes in a saucepan, preferably terracotta, and sauté over medium-low heat for 2–3 minutes, then discard the garlic. Add the parsley, the tomato puree, and the 1¼ cups broth. Cook over low heat for about 20 minutes, or until the sauce is reduced and shiny with the oil coming to the surface.

 MAKE-AHEAD NOTE: This much can be done earlier in the day.

Combine the 2 quarts broth, the reserved clam liquid, and the tomato sauce, bring to a boil, and add the *fregula*. Taste for salt, but what with the fish broth and the clam broth, you will probably not need it.

Simmer, stirring occasionally, for 8 or 10 minutes, or until the *fregula* is *al dente* (the time will vary with the size of the *fregula*; the large sizes may need 15 minutes). If your pot looks dry at any point, add a few tablespoons of hot water.

Remove from the heat and stir in the reserved clams. Mix well. If you have used a terracotta pot, you can take it directly to the table. Otherwise transfer to a warmed tureen. Serve immediately.

 WINE SUGGESTION: a Sardinian red, such as Monica di Sardegna DOC, Carignano del Sulcis DOC, or, easiest to find, Cannonau

---

Zuppa di broccoli e cappucci

(Broccoli rabe and cabbage)

THIS WINTER SOUP comes from Campania, the large southern region whose capital is Naples. Its basis is a beef broth with coarsely chopped greens and pasta. Pancetta cooked along with the beef rounds out the broth's texture. The result is a soup of intense flavor in which both vegetables and meat come forward and the general impression is of eating something that people have been eating in view of Mount Vesuvius from the beginning of time, or at least of agriculture.

Broccoli rabe is found all over Italy with very slight variations and many names. Ideally it's peppery rather than bitter, and for that reason needs to be used very fresh and trimmed of all that is not beautiful—the stringy stems, the large or imperfect leaves.

The meat surrenders its essence for the broth, but can still make a contribution in another recipe, such as the meatballs on page 377.

 PASTA SHAPES Use *ditalini*, *tubettini*, or other short pasta, such as *maltagliati* (page 336). In Campania, this soup is sometimes served with slices of stale bread at the bottom of each bowl instead of pasta.

For the broth:

1 1-pound (450-gram) piece of beef brisket
2½ ounces (70 grams) pancetta, in one piece
1 yellow onion
1 carrot
1 rib celery
several sprigs of fresh flat-leaf parsley or ¾ cup
    loosely packed flat-leaf parsley leaves
¾ cup (180 milliliters) dry white wine
½ teaspoon salt
5 whole black peppercorns

To continue the soup:

1 ounce (40 grams) prosciutto fat or *lardo*, diced
about 3 pounds (1.5 kilograms) cabbage,
    trimmed and chopped coarsely
about 3 pounds (1.5 kilograms) broccoli rabe,
    trimmed aggressively of all tough stems and
    blemished leaves and chopped coarsely
¾ cup (180 milliliters) dry white wine

Before serving:

8 ounces (225 grams) pasta (see suggestions
    above)
extra virgin olive oil for finishing

Put the beef and pancetta in a pot. Add the onion, carrot, celery, parsley, and ¾ cup of the wine. Cover with 2 quarts (2 liters) water, add the salt and peppercorns, and simmer for about 2 hours, or until the meat is tender.

Remove the meat and set aside; strain the broth. You should have about 6 cups (1.5 liters). Let cool completely, then refrigerate. Remove the layer of fat that forms on the surface after several hours or overnight.

 MAKE-AHEAD NOTE: This broth can and even should be made a day before the rest of the soup to give time for the fat to rise to the surface.

Melt the prosciutto fat or *lardo* over low heat in a large, deep skillet. Add the remaining ¾ cup wine and the cabbage and broccoli rabe, cover, and cook over low heat, stirring occasionally, until quite soft, at least 15 minutes.

Pour the 6 cups of broth over the vegetables. Let the flavors blend for a few minutes over low heat, then bring to a boil, stir in the pasta, and cook until *al dente*.

Transfer the soup to a warm tureen, add a swirl of extra virgin olive oil, and let rest for a few minutes before serving.

 WINE SUGGESTION: a full-bodied red, such as Taurasi DOCG, from Campania

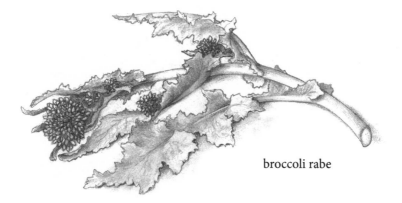

broccoli rabe

Zuppa di indivia

(Curly endive)

CURLY ENDIVE IS a winter vegetable, with a pleasantly bitter taste, that makes an excellent salad and an even better soup. It goes very well with the full flavors of the meat and final dose of uncooked extra virgin oil. This endive soup is typical of old Rome, where it was served in the most traditional trattorias of Trastevere. For variety, sometimes a sausage would replace the beef.

 PASTA SHAPES Use small *maltagliati* (page 336) or *quadrucci* (page 357).

For the soup:

1 large head curly endive (about 1 pound), cored and outer leaves removed

1 white onion, finely chopped

3 tablespoons extra virgin olive oil

about 1 pound (450 grams) boneless beef such as chuck roast, or half beef and half pork (such as butt), cut in cubes ¾ inch (2 centimeters) on a side

1 quart (1 liter) meat broth (page 240)

Before serving:

salt

8 ounces (225 grams) pasta (see suggestions above)

extra virgin olive oil for finishing

7 rounded tablespoons (70 grams) grated pecorino romano

Drop the endive leaves briefly into boiling salted water. Drain, squeeze, chop coarsely, and set aside.

Put the onion in a soup pot with the oil and sauté over medium heat until transparent, about 5 minutes. Add the diced meat and brown evenly, stirring. Add half the broth gradually, a few tablespoons at a time, and simmer until the meat is tender, about 15–20 minutes (but test with a fork).

 MAKE-AHEAD NOTE: If not serving the soup immediately, combine the endive and the meat and refrigerate, covered. It will keep for a day or two in the fridge, but doesn't freeze well.

When you are ready to make the soup, bring 3 quarts (3 liters) of water to a boil in a 5-quart (5-liter) pot over high heat. Add 1 tablespoon kosher salt, then add the pasta and cook, stirring occasionally, until *al dente*.

While the pasta is cooking, heat the remaining broth with the endive and meat; taste for salt. Stir in the pasta, and transfer the soup to a warmed tureen. Add a swirl of extra virgin olive oil, and let the soup rest for 5 minutes before serving. Pass the grated pecorino at the table.

 WINE SUGGESTION: Cesanese di Olevano DOC, a full-bodied red from Lazio

Minestra di trippa e verza

(Tripe and cabbage)

THE BEST CABBAGES are the ones picked in winter, when the cold makes them close up tight. Thus this nourishing soup is typical of winter and always used to be bubbling in large pots on small boats in the port of Genoa on frigid mornings to provide sustenance and warmth to sailors and longshoremen alike, while its fragrance spread throughout the waterfront. It was the cabbage that they smelled first, of course, but the creaminess comes from the potatoes. The tenderness of the tripe comes as a pleasant surprise.

Tripe is part of the popular culture of many parts of Italy, including Rome and Florence. But it has acquired an undeserved reputation as fatty, when in fact it contains only 4 percent fat and has nearly the same protein content as veal. Not only that, but it undergoes a process of pre-boiling and whitening, in which it loses what little fat it had. Its bad reputation is due more to the sauces with which it's served, but a bad reputation is hard to shake off.

 PASTA SHAPES Tiny *pasta grattata* (page 358) amalgamates beautifully with the soup and thickens it. *Maltagliati* (page 336) or *quadrucci* (page 357), both fresh, flat, and floppy, have a similar effect. For a factory-made shape, *pennette*, small and tubular, are customary.

For the soup:

3½ ounces (100 grams) pancetta
2 large white or yellow onions
1 carrot
1 rib celery
about 1 cup loosely packed fresh flat-leaf
    parsley leaves
4 tablespoons extra virgin olive oil
3 quarts (3 liters) meat broth (page 240)
2 pounds (900 grams) tripe, trimmed, washed,
    and cut in small pieces roughly 1 inch
    (2.5 centimeters) on a side

salt
freshly ground black pepper
about 3 pounds (1.5 kilograms) Savoy cabbage,
    trimmed, cored, and cut in thin strips
2 potatoes, peeled and diced

Before serving:

8 ounces (225 grams) pasta (see suggestions
    above)
6 rounded tablespoons (60 grams) grated
    parmigiano-reggiano

Chop finely together the pancetta, onion, carrot, celery, and parsley (in a food processor if desired). Put in a large saucepan with the oil and sauté gently for about 5 minutes, just to get them started cooking.

Heat 3 cups (700 milliliters) of the broth in a soup pot. Add the tripe. Taste for salt (the broth may already be salty), grind on some pepper, and simmer for about an hour or until the tripe is tender.

Meanwhile, put the remaining broth in a soup pot. Add the cabbage and potatoes and simmer for about 30 minutes, until both are cooked through.

Add the contents of the tripe pot to the cabbage and potatoes in their pot, and stir. Let the flavors blend over low heat for a few minutes.

🌿 **MAKE-AHEAD NOTE:** The soup will taste even better if this much is done the day before.

Bring to a boil, add the pasta, and cook until *al dente*. Stir again, and transfer the soup to a warm tureen. Serve hot, and pass the cheese separately.

🌿 **WINE SUGGESTION:** Colli di Luni Rosso DOC or Rossese di Dolceacqua DOC, both from Liguria

---

PASTA

The pasta recipes are organized by technique or shape type, but first come the basic doughs, *pasta all'uovo*, with egg, and *pasta acqua e farina*, with water, and the essentials of kneading and rolling. The ravioli family, small stuffed shapes, follows, each with its filling and some with a particular *condimento*. Where no *condimento* is given, look the shape up in the general index to see what sauces are suggested. Baked pastas come next, largely self-contained, with their own sauces and cheeses. Shapes cut from *la sfoglia*, the rolled sheet of pasta, are divided into noodles of different widths, most with egg, some without, and other kinds of shapes. Then we address unrolled dough. Some of the shapes are descendants of the *gnocchetto*, deriving in turn from a hand-rolled rope of dough; others are pinched directly off the loaf of dough. There are also some shapes made with different doughs and/or techniques, such as potato gnocchi, which couldn't be shoehorned into the other groups, and *pastina*, small formats for soup. Check the index to see where these shapes fit in the spectrum of sauces and soups.

Traditionally pasta is made in the morning for use in the evening. The recipes yield about 1 pound (450 grams) of usable dough, calculated with a few hours' drying in mind. Small variations in your final yield will make little or no difference to the success of the recipes. And if you just want to go out and buy ready-made *sfoglia*, assuming you have a good local source, buy a pound (450 grams).

BASIC DOUGHS

Most Italian pastas are formed from one of two basic doughs—flour and water (*acqua e farina*) and flour and egg (*pasta all'uovo*). Both are made with one essential technique: the wet and the dry ingredients are combined into a smooth mass and allowed to rest. The purpose of the rest period is to allow the gluten to develop. After about 30 minutes' rest, the dough can be (a) rolled and cut, by hand or machine, or (b) shaped with hands or traditional utensils, or (c) extruded through a fancy machine with interchangeable dies.

The goal in making the dough is to incorporate just enough liquid, be it water or egg or some of each, to make a silky dough that is not the least bit sticky. This can be done entirely by hand—with 30 minutes or more of kneading—or by food processor plus some hand kneading. A number of pasta shapes can be fashioned with hands directly from the basic dough. Others are rolled and cut, with the aid of either a rolling pin or a very hands-on machine. Occasionally other, very traditional, utensils are used. The basics are given in detail once at the beginning of the section. Variations of ingredients or shaping technique are given in the individual recipes.

It is very important not to overthink or overanalyze this dough making. You need to develop your own moves and learn to feel when the dough is smooth and the moisture content is correct. It should become instinctive and even fun. Making fresh pasta is all about feel and experience. It would be wise not to invite guests the first time you make ravioli, though for *gnoc-chetti*, which are pretty easy, you could invite your best friend. But the wisest approach is to make and roll the dough first, all alone. Feel with your hands and observe with your eyes the metamorphosis from pile of flour to smooth, silky loaf of dough. You'll know when it's done because it will be perfectly round and smooth and further manhandling would seem gratuitously violent. Touch and remember its moistness and elasticity.

The Italian way is to weigh the flour, not measure its volume, and so that is what we do here. We also weigh our eggs. Accept it. You will thank us later. The short pastas and stuffed pastas given here can be frozen. Put the pasta in a single layer on a tray in the freezer, making sure the pieces are not touching. When they are firm, transfer them to a plastic bag or any container you like. To cook, drop them in boiling, salted water without thawing.

Unless you're making pasta to freeze, don't make these fresh pastas very far ahead. Make them the same day they'll be eaten, and then keep until mealtime covered with a cloth or in the refrigerator.

Cooking time is very variable. Thin noodles made with soft wheat will cook in just a few minutes. Thicker handmade shapes made of durum wheat that have been sitting all day on a tray may well take 20 minutes or more. There is no way anybody else can tell you how long your pasta will take to cook. You will just have to taste and check. Make a note how long your pasta takes to cook, and you'll have an order of magnitude for next time.

Pasta all'uovo

(Egg dough)

As IMPORTANT AS it is to develop feel and instinct when making dough, there is a metric formula for making *pasta all'uovo*. The Bolognesi love them. For every 100 grams of flour, use 1 50–55 gram egg (net weight, i.e., without the shell), which corresponds to 1 USDA medium egg. Your kitchen scale is almost certainly bilingual, and it is much easier to use the metric system for this than fractions of ounces, but it works out to 1¾ to 2 ounces of egg for every 3½ ounces of flour.

Whole-wheat flour may be used if desired.

1 pound (450 grams) sifted all-purpose flour (*farina 00*)
5 medium or large eggs, or 4 extra-large or jumbo

extra flour for dusting and adjusting

Pasta acqua e farina

(Flour-and-water dough)

WHOLE-WHEAT FLOUR MAY be used if desired.

1 pound (450 grams) sifted durum wheat flour or semolina (*semolino di grano duro*)

1 cup (200 milliliters) water in a measuring cup, plus some extra if needed
extra flour for dusting and adjusting

The method for both doughs is much the same.

Hand method: Sift the flour onto a large wooden board (see page 40). Form the flour into a mound with the approximate profile of Mount Fuji. Form your hand into a loose fist, and, with the back of the fingers, gently ream out the center of the mound until you have something that resembles a low, broad volcano with a very deep crater. Italian cooks call this a fountain, *fontana*, for the pool of liquid in the center, but it's definitely a cone.

If making egg dough, break all the eggs into the crater one by one. Pierce the yolks with a fork and begin gingerly to use the fork to incorporate them into the flour with a movement something like scrambling eggs. If using water, pour about half the water into the crater and proceed as for eggs; add more water gradually as needed. Incorporate the liquid from the center outward. The walls of the crater will keep the liquid from running out.

When the liquid has absorbed enough flour that you now have a messy, wet dough surrounded by flour, knock what's left of the volcano in toward the center and begin to knead with your hands to incorporate the rest of the flour into the dough. Scrape up all the remaining flour and the dough bits and squeeze them into the dough.

Food processor method: Put all the ingredients in the container of a food processor fitted with the steel blade (not pastry hooks or the like). Let rip at high speed until you see crumbs forming. Keep going until the dough forms a ball. You may become convinced that your dough will never form a single ball, only many little ones. In that case, give up because you risk overheating the dough. Pour what you have out on the wooden board; use your hands to form the pieces into a single loaf of dough.

Kneading: The biggest mistake people make, says Oretta, is not using enough force. Skip the gym the day you make pasta and make kneading your workout. The women of Scandriglia, where Oretta has her country house, recommend making *fettuccine* as a remedy for backache in preference to those boring exercises. On the other hand, my friend Antonietta, who learned to make pasta as a child in Basilicata, tells me southern men enjoy watching the undulating hips of southern women as they knead the pasta dough. If it helps to put on some music and do the *maccheroni mambo* as you knead, go right ahead.

Plant your feet firmly on the floor and the heels of your hands firmly on the dough in front of you. A dining table will usually be a more comfortable height than a kitchen counter, which may be too high. With all your strength, and leaning in with your whole body, push the dough forward hard with the heel of one hand, then with the heel of the other hand. Then fold it over and continue the movement, alternating hands—or whatever works for you. You're pushing the whole piece of dough forward, so it moves on the board.

After each completed movement, give the dough a quarter turn and repeat. Keep this up for 30 minutes, or as long as you can stand. If you've used the food processor, 15 or 20 minutes will do. You can quit early, too, if you plan to use a rolling machine: send the dough through one extra pass for each minute of kneading saved.

As you work, the dough may seem dry, but you don't want it to be wet and sticky. It needs just enough moisture to hold it together, not a drop more. If your dough is so dry that you are quite sure it will never hold together, you can add a teensy bit of water, even for egg dough. (It used to be quite normal to use water to save eggs, which could be sold for cash.) Your goal is a single smooth loaf of dough that is not sticky to the touch. If the flour is either very freshly ground (hence moister) or very old (drier), you'll have to adjust by feel. When it feels just right—moist but not tacky, considerably drier than the average dog's nose—set it aside for a moment.

You'll probably need to clean the board about halfway through the process. Use a plastic scraper or the blunt side of a large knife to scrape up any bits that have stuck to the board. (Sharp knives may damage your nice wooden board, and their edges are dulled by scraping.) Likewise wash your hands, which are doubtless also encrusted with bits of dried dough by this time.

Resting: Once you have a beautifully silky loaf of dough (by whichever method), let it rest for 30 minutes to let the gluten develop. Wrap it in foil, or just place it on the board and invert a bowl over it until you're ready. By this time, you probably need to put your feet up too.

When the dough and you have rested, you can proceed to the next stage. Depending on what kind of pasta you want to make, this may involve rolling and cutting to make a pasta sheet (*sfoglia*) or pulling pieces directly from the loaf of dough and shaping them by hand.

La sfoglia

LA SFOGLIA IS the perfect, translucent sheet of egg dough and the basis of most noodle shapes (cut long and flat) and stuffed pastas. The instructions that follow are the basics. You'll need to practice, practice, and practice some more to make a smooth, elastic sheet with just the right degree of moisture. The specific thickness of the sheet may vary from recipe to recipe. If you don't have a large wooden board and extra-long rolling pin (page 40), your pasta will never come out right. You're better off using a machine. Both methods are given here. Don't forget to keep up a lively pace. The dough gets drier with every second that passes.

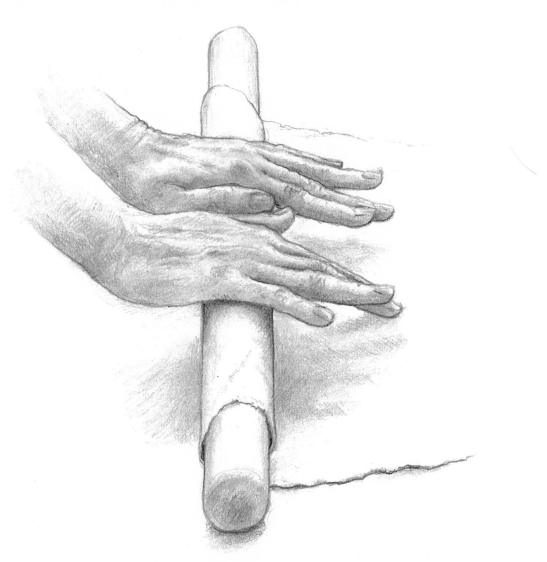

Hand-rolling method: Dust the board with flour and plop your lovely, silky dough in the middle. Begin to flatten it by pushing it out from the center with the heel of your hand all around. You want to maintain its circular shape. With a long rolling pin, roll the dough out from the center to near the edge. Don't roll over the edge. You want to keep a little border. Keep going, turning the disk of dough a quarter turn after each stroke of the rolling pin to help maintain the circular shape. Work quickly so that the dough does not dry out. Oretta says that the perfect circle is a Bolognese obsession. Nobody else is bothered if the dough tends toward the elliptical.

When you have a smooth, round, manageable floppy disk of yellow pasta, the fun really begins. Lay the rolling pin across the top of the disk, connecting 11 and 1 on an imaginary clock. Grip the disk with your hands at 12 o'clock, pull it toward you around the rolling pin (most of the disk is still on the table; you are working only about one fourth of the pasta), wrap it around the pin and jiggle it back and forth with your two hands while you simultaneously stretch it along the rolling pin as though your hands were repelling each other by an anti-magnetic force. The diameter will increase, eventually to the length of the rolling pin. Unroll the disk, give it a quarter turn, and repeat until you have been around the circle. Work fast because the clock is ticking on your dwindling moisture content.

You should end up with a perfectly smooth, translucent circle (or ellipse) of dough not more than ¹⁄₁₆ inch (2 millimeters) thick. Leave it on the board and sharpen your knife.

Machine-rolling method: Visually divide the loaf of dough into 6 pieces (or more), but cut off just one sixth. Keep the rest of the dough covered with a cloth or inverted bowl. Set the rollers of your pasta machine to the largest opening and sprinkle them with flour. Send the dough through the rollers, catching it with your other hand. Fold it over and send it through again. Set the opening one notch smaller and send the dough through. Fold and repeat. Keep going until you reach the next-to-last setting, unless a particular recipe tells you to stop at a different number. Send the dough through the first setting five or six times, then twice for each of the subsequent settings.

You will wind up with six narrow sheets of pasta in the neighborhood of 24 inches (60 centimeters) long. Lay them out on a clean cloth until you are ready to cut.

Ravioli and Company

Ravioli, agnolotti, cappellacci, cappelletti, tortellini, and still more names, all have in common that they are little packages with pasta encasing something tasty. Some are served as *pastasciutta,* with a sauce, others in broth. Most can be frozen, but otherwise should be consumed the day they are made. Exceptions are noted in the individual recipes.

The shapes can differ, and even where the recipe says to form a rectangle, if you're feeling it's a triangle sort of day, make a triangle. All measurements and sizes are to be considered approximate. The busy women who first cooked these recipes did not measure with a ruler. Some of the measurements will seem impossibly small; in that case, just increase the size (within reason) to something you can handle.

ALL THE RECIPES in this section begin with *la sfoglia* (page 291) made with *pasta all'uovo.* Try to roll the dough on the narrowest setting of the machine, since you will have a double thickness around the edges. If you can't, you can't. You will make fewer ravioli, but your guests will get about the same total amount of pasta to eat. We can't predict how many ravioli you will make from each recipe, but you will have about six portions.

When it comes to stuffing, the idea is to fill the *raviolo* or *agnolotto* to within an inch of its life. It should be hard to close, but don't let it pop its little zipper or all the filling will seep into the cooking water. How much to force will have to be a judgment call. And be sure to press out all the air. To seal the *raviolo,* press your fingers very hard around the filling, so that the two sides of the dough fuse together. If you tear a hole, pinch it closed.

There are two basic methods for filling ravioli. One is: lay spaced heaps of filling on a sheet of pasta, fold the sheet over, gently press out any air, then press all around the filling, and cut the little mounds apart with a wheeled pastry cutter or cut them out with a cookie cutter. Discard excess *sfoglia,* or save it for *maltagliati.* This is the easiest and fastest way to make ravioli, and is advisable if you are working alone. The other method is to cut individual rounds or squares of dough from the pasta sheet and either fold each around a heap of filling or place a second piece of dough on top; in either case, you press around the edges. If one method appeals to you more than the other, feel free to use it, even when the recipe suggests something else. *Tortellini* and *cappelletti,* which have more complicated shapes and closures, have to be made individually.

Have your filling ready by the time you roll

out the sheet (by hand or machine). If the dough dries out, you will never be able to seal the ravioli closed. Sad to say, most industrially produced *sfoglia* sold for lasagne will not work for ravioli, because it has been treated in such a way that the edges will never stick together. If you are lucky enough to live near a truly artisanal pasta shop, you can buy *sfoglia* from them, but to be on the safe side, say it's for ravioli.

The isolation of many home cooks today, even in Italy, is the antithesis of the old ways, when all the women, and some of the children, of an extended family could join forces to make light work of these labor-intensive, time-sensitive jobs. This is the moment to enlist an extra pair or two of hands. That way, one person (or team) can roll out the pasta sheets, and the other can be filling the ravioli before the dough dries out.

As for choosing a sauce, there is a rule. The sauce for ravioli-type pastas should be different from the filling. If the filling has meat, don't use a meat sauce. If the filling has, say, mushrooms, no mushroom sauce. In some cases the recipes include a sauce; this is mainly in the case of traditional dishes that are always paired with a certain *condimento*. But for many stuffed pastas, you can choose (fairly) freely. We make suggestions for sauce pairings, but as long as you observe the basic principle of what goes inside doesn't go outside, feel free to choose other sauces as well. And if the whole process of rolling, cutting, and stuffing has you completely exhausted, melted good unsalted butter and freshly grated parmigiano-reggiano make an elegant *condimento* for practically any type of ravioli that doesn't compete with even the most delicate filling.

Tortellini, however, are to be served only in broth. That is not a suggestion; it's an order.

THE COOKING directions for the whole group are the same. Boil them in salted water as directed in all the sauce recipes, but drop them in the water very gently, not all at once, or they might break. You will have to test the edge for doneness. There is no way to know how long yours will take to cook, but the order of magnitude is 5–7 minutes, more if the pasta is on the thick side. In other words, don't leave them unattended. To drain, lift them carefully with a slotted spoon or spider strainer directly into a warm serving bowl, then add the cheese, if called for in the sauce recipe, and the sauce.

Agnolotti piemontesi
(Meat-filled)

THE NAME AGNOLOTTI is found throughout Italy. They are always stuffed, but their size, shape, and filling vary from place to place and even family to family. This classic version is found throughout the Piedmont region, in the northwest next to France. The usual filling is a mixture of meats, but it may also be made of combinations of meat and vegetables, or vegetables alone, or Fonduta cheese. The recipe given here, of mixed meats and Savoy cabbage, which give an assertive, round taste, is typical of the Langhe, the low, oddly shaped hills in the province of Cuneo, known best for Barolo wine and Alba white truffles.

If you ever get the chance to visit a Piedmontese garden when the snow is beginning to fall, don't miss it. That's when all the winter vegetables, especially the Savoy cabbages, are at their best—tightly closed and bursting with flavor. Oretta maintains that to make a good filling for these *agnolotti* you really need cabbages picked from underneath the snow, but the rest of us do the best we can with what we have.

The traditional cheese to serve for sprinkling on top would be Piedmontese, either *Bra duro*, an aged, medium-sharp cow's milk cheese, or aged *seirass*, a cow's milk ricotta from mountain pastures (pages 389–90 for sources). Today parmigiano-reggiano is commonly used.

For the filling:

1 spring onion, white part and the beginning of the green
1 small carrot
1 rib celery
2 tablespoons (30 grams) unsalted butter
1 ounce (30 grams) lard or 4 tablespoons extra virgin olive oil
8 ounces (225 grams) boneless veal, diced
6 ounces (170 grams) lean boneless pork, diced

about 8 ounces (225 grams) Savoy cabbage, cut in thin strips
freshly ground black pepper
6 tablespoons dry white wine
1 cup (200 milliliters) meat broth (page 240)
at least ½ teaspoon salt
3 rounded tablespoons (30 grams) grated parmigiano-reggiano

Chop finely together the spring onion, the carrot, and the celery (preferably by hand).

In a large skillet, preferably terracotta, melt the butter and the lard (or melt the butter and add the oil) and add the minced vegetables. Cook over medium heat until they are almost tender, about 5 minutes. Then add the meats and brown evenly.

Add the cabbage to the meat mixture and grind on a little pepper. Raise the heat and add the wine. Let it bubble until the smell of alcohol has dissipated, about 2 minutes. Then gradually add only enough broth as needed to keep the filling moist while it cooks.

Cook over medium heat, stirring occasionally, until all the ingredients are cooked through and tender and all the liquid has evaporated. Sprinkle with salt. The mixture should be very dry. Set aside and let cool.

Put the mixture in a food processor and pulse with the steel blade just until the ingredients are finely minced. Stop well before they turn into a paste. The consistency you want is that of two or three times through an old-fashioned meat grinder—and if you have one, by all means use it.

Transfer the mixture to a bowl and add the cheese. The filling, which should be dense, is now ready to use.

To make the *agnolotti*: Make *la sfoglia* (page 291) with *pasta all'uovo* (page 286).

Using a wheeled cutter, either toothed or smooth, cut the sheet into squares about 2 inches (5 centimeters) on a side.

Place a heaping teaspoon of filling in the center of each square, and fold the pasta over to form a rectangle.

Press the edges of each *agnolotto* closed.

POSSIBLE SAUCES: *Burro e salvia* (page 84), *Sugo con i pinoli e tartufi* (page 135), *Sugo con gli asparagi di bosco* (page 141)

 WINE SUGGESTION: Choose your wine on the basis of the sauce, not the *agnolotti*.

agnolotto folded into a rectangle

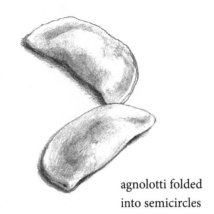

agnolotti folded
into semicircles

Agnolotti con i broccoletti

(Broccoli rabe and clams)

BROCCOLETTI ARE broccoli rabe, and typical of Puglia, and the best, of course, are gathered in the countryside there. They are usually eaten as a vegetable or over *orecchiette* (page 349), but they also find their way into more creative dishes, such as these *agnolotti*, which have an intense aroma and a pleasantly rustic taste.

Clams are certainly an unusual *condimento* for such a pasta. The sauce probably represents a successful attempt by an anonymous chef to join the flavors of the greens, cheese, and seafood, and, exceptionally, it worked. The dish is delicious and has been adopted into popular cooking. The real dialogue is between the greens and the cheese, with the clams a mere touch of fantasy. It should be filed under Don't try this at home. When chefs do that sort of thing it's called creative, but when mere mortals do it, it's considered inappropriate. When foreigners do it, well, hmph, they'll never understand Italian food.

For the filling:

2 cloves garlic, crushed
4 tablespoons extra virgin olive oil

about 11 ounces (300 grams) trimmed broccoli rabe (all stems and blemished leaves removed), boiled in salted water and squeezed very dry

Sauté the garlic with the oil in a small skillet over medium heat until golden. Add the broccoli rabe to the oil and let the flavors blend for 5 minutes over low heat. Discard the garlic.

Let cool and mince the broccoli rabe. If you use the food processor, stop before it turns into a puree.

To make the *agnolotti*: Make *la sfoglia* (page 291) with *pasta all'uovo* (page 286).

Spread the pasta sheet out on the board and, with a 1¼-inch (3-centimeter) cookie cutter or inverted liqueur glass, cut the sheet into little disks.

Place a heaping demitasse spoon (approximately) of filling on each disk. Fold the pasta over to make a semicircle. Press the edges well to create a seal.

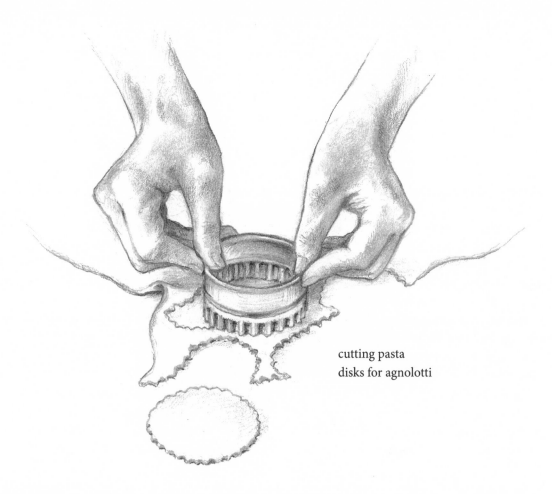

cutting pasta
disks for agnolotti

To finish the dish:

6 tablespoons extra virgin olive oil
1 white onion, finely chopped
about 2 pounds (1 kilogram) Manila clams or
**   other small clams (see headnote page 177)**
**   scrubbed, rinsed thoroughly, and soaked in**
**   lightly salted water for about 2 hours and**
**   drained**

2 ounces (60 grams) pecorino romano in one
**   piece**
freshly ground black pepper

Put the oil in a deep 12-inch (30-centimeter) skillet and sauté the onion, 3–4 minutes, until transparent.

Put the clams in another large skillet, cover the pan, and turn on the heat to low. (If the heat is too high, all the broth might evaporate.) After 2 minutes, lift the lid and turn the heat to the absolute minimum. Using tongs, remove the opened clams one by one. The other clams will continue to open. When you have removed all the open clams, put the lid back on for a minute to let the last clams open. Discard any clams that still don't open.

Strain the broth through a sieve lined with cheesecloth.

Add the clams, still in their shells, and their broth to the pan with the onion.

Bring 5 quarts (5 liters) of water to a boil in an 8-quart (8-liter) pot over high heat. Add 2 tablespoons kosher salt, then add the *agnolotti* and cook, stirring occasionally and very gently, only until quite *al dente*.

Warm a serving bowl or platter in a low oven. If the oven is not practical, warm the bowl just before use with hot water, even a ladleful of the pasta cooking water.

Lift the *agnolotti* out of the pot with a slotted spoon or spider strainer and deposit them directly in the skillet with the clams. Mix well but gently over low heat for 1–2 minutes. Transfer to the warm serving bowl, sprinkle with the cheese and a few grinds of pepper. Serve immediately.

OTHER POSSIBLE SAUCES: *Sugo semplice di pomodori pelati* (page 88), *Umido di cipolla* (page 133), *Erbe selvatiche* (page 111), *Olio e prezzemolo* (page 107). In Sicily, they would use eggplant, *Sugo con melanzane* (page 154).

 WINE SUGGESTION: For the clam sauce, Greco di Tufo or something with acidity yet richness. Otherwise, choose for the sauce.

Agnolotti con i carciofi

(Artichokes)

Its Barolo wines and Alba truffles are better known outside Italy, but cognoscenti go to Piedmont also for the cheeses, and not just the aged ones. The cow's milk ricotta known as *seirass* is redolent of the mountain pastures where the cows graze. Use the best, creamiest ricotta you can find and try to wish yourself into the Italian Alps. The taste is delicate but flavorful, the subtlety of the artichoke and ricotta interrupted by the hit of anchovy.

In Italy, ricotta, always quite creamy and fresh, needs to be drained in a colander overnight in the refrigerator. Elsewhere, the consistency of ricotta is very variable, and you will need to evaluate whether yours is already quite dry or oozing liquid.

For the filling:

2 tablespoons (30 grams) unsalted butter
1 spring onion, white and light greens parts only
2 cloves garlic
1¾ ounces (50 grams) prosciutto, sliced or whole
3 oil-packed anchovy fillets, drained and blotted dry
5 artichokes, trimmed as described on page 148, sliced thin, and held in a bowl of water acidulated with the juice of 1 lemon (if the artichokes are bigger than a tennis ball, use fewer)

1 bay leaf
4 fresh sage leaves
salt
freshly ground black pepper
8 ounces (225 grams) ricotta (*seirass* if humanly possible), drained overnight unless it's already quite dry
8 rounded tablespoons (80 grams) grated parmigiano-reggiano
1 egg

Melt the butter in a deep 12-inch skillet. Chop the spring onion finely with the garlic and the prosciutto and sauté in the butter over medium heat for 3 minutes. Lower the heat, add the anchovy fillets, and let them disintegrate, about 1 minute.

Drain the artichokes well and add them to the pan, along with the bay leaf, sage, and salt and pepper. Sauté over low heat for 6–8 minutes. Add a ladleful of hot water, cover, and continue cooking over low heat for about 20 minutes, or until the artichokes are tender and absolutely all the liquid is absorbed.

Let cool. Discard the bay leaf. Chop everything finely, preferably in the food processor. Transfer the mixture, which should be quite dry, to a bowl.

 MAKE-AHEAD NOTE: This much may be done the day before.

Add the ricotta, parmigiano, and egg. Blend until quite firm.

To make the *agnolotti*: Make *la sfoglia* (page 291) with *pasta all'uovo* (page 286).

Spread the pasta sheet out on a board and with a wheeled pastry cutter (see below) cut rectangles about 1½ by 3 inches (4 by 8 centimeters). Put a heaping teaspoon of filling in the middle of each and fold over the pasta to form a square. Seal the edges well with the pressure of your fingers.

SUGGESTED SAUCES: *Sugo semplice di passata di pomodoro* (page 90), *Boscaiola* (page 127), *Sugo coi funghi* (page 152)

🌿 **WINE SUGGESTION:** Artichokes are always a problem for wine. A dry sparkling wine, such as Franciacorta, is a possibility. Or do the right thing and serve the wine only with the next course.

Ravioli di ricotta o ricotta e spinaci

(Ricotta or spinach and ricotta)

GOOD RICOTTA PROVIDES the simplest and most delicate of fillings, enjoyed throughout Italy. It is the perfect neutral canvas for practically any kind of sauce except cheese. Be sure the ricotta is very dry (see note). The spinach variation is also very popular and can be dressed with the same sauces.

NOTE: If you cannot find sheep's milk ricotta, you can assist decent cow's milk ricotta by mixing 1 tablespoon heavy cream for every 3½ ounces (100 grams). Most artisanal ricotta, cow or sheep, needs to drain in a basket or colander overnight in the refrigerator to lose its considerable water content.

For the filling:

about 1¼ pounds (500 grams) well-drained best-quality ricotta

3 rounded tablespoons (30 grams) grated parmigiano-reggiano

1 heaping tablespoon minced fresh flat-leaf parsley (optional)

Put the ricotta, parmigiano, and parsley, if using, in a small bowl and beat with a wooden spoon until well blended.

To make the ravioli: Make *la sfoglia* (page 291) with *pasta all'uovo* (page 286).

Cut the pasta sheet into long strips about 4 inches (10 centimeters) wide.

Place a heaping teaspoon of ricotta at 1½-inch (3.5-centimeter) intervals along each strip, just to one side of the long axis.

Fold the sheet over and pat it down around the little heaps of filling, then press with your fingers between the piles to seal. Cut the ravioli apart with a wheeled cutter, either toothed or straight.

VARIATION: Ricotta and spinach filling

12 ounces (300 grams) well-drained best-quality ricotta

7 rounded tablespoons (70 grams) grated parmigiano-reggiano

3½ ounces (100 grams) fresh leaf spinach, trimmed, steamed, squeezed well, and finely minced

Proceed as above.

SUGGESTED SAUCES: Any *ragù* or mushroom sauce, *Ragù di coniglio* (page 201), *Ragù d'anatra* (page 203), *Ragù di cinghiale* (page 235), *Ragù con le rigaglie di pollo* (page 198), *Tocco di carne alla genovese* (page 222), *Sugo coi funghi* (page 152)

 WINE SUGGESTION: Choose for the sauce.

fresh ricotta and parsley

Ravioli con le sogliole

(Sole and ricotta)

ALTHOUGH THE MARCHE region has some of Italy's most rugged mountains, and a strong land-based gastronomic tradition (see, for example, page 306), most of Europe knows it for its a long, sandy Adriatic coastline. The fishermen there are particularly proud of the delicate but flavorful sole they catch. Here the fish, already mild, is further tempered by the ricotta, but jazzed up a bit by the zing of the lemon zest. Yes, it is unusual to combine fish and cheese, but there are always exceptions to every rule, including unwritten ones.

For the filling:

11 ounces (300 grams) sole fillets
11 ounces (300 grams) ricotta
1 heaping tablespoon minced fresh flat-leaf
    parsley

10 rounded tablespoons (100 grams) grated
    parmigiano-reggiano
the grated zest of 1 organic lemon
nutmeg
salt

Poach the fish for 5 minutes a small skillet filled with boiling salted water. Drain, pat dry, chop finely (if you use a food processor, stop before the fish turns to mush), and put in a bowl.

Add the ricotta, parsley, cheese, lemon zest, and a pinch each of nutmeg (grated or ground) and salt. Mix well.

To make the ravioli: Make *la sfoglia* (page 291) with *pasta all'uovo* (page 286).

Spread the whole pasta sheet out on the board and place hazelnut-sized bits of filling 1½ inches (3.5 centimeters) apart on half the sheet. Fold the other half of the sheet over to cover the filling and press down well with your fingers around the little heaps of filling. Use a toothed pastry cutter to cut the ravioli apart.

 MAKE-AHEAD NOTE: At this point, the ravioli can be frozen or held in the refrigerator for not more than 24 hours.

SUGGESTED SAUCES: *Ruchetta e olive* (page 109), *Sugo alla marinara* (page 94), *Sugo con le zucchine* (page 158)

 WINE SUGGESTION: Choose for the sauce.

Raviolini di magro

(Fish-filled)

THEORETICALLY, RAVIOLI FILLED with a paste of fish is a way to use up leftovers. It is, however, hard to imagine the modern American household regarding making ravioli from scratch as anything less than an end in itself. Therefore, if you don't happen to have any suitable leftovers, buy and poach fillets of white-fleshed fish, such as cod (and its relatives), the breams, or branzino. These *raviolini* from the Lazio region are served in fish broth, as a soup, the intense fragrance of the sea accentuated by the strong cheese.

For the filling:

About 8 ounces (300 grams) poached white-fleshed fish, patted dry and all bones removed
1 egg
at least ½ teaspoon salt

freshly ground black pepper
pinch of grated or ground nutmeg
5 rounded tablespoons (50 grams) grated parmigiano-reggiano

Mince the fish finely, preferably with a knife rather than food processor, and put in a bowl. Add the rest of the ingredients and mix well.

To make the *raviolini*: Make *la sfoglia* (page 291) with *pasta all'uovo* (page 286).

Cut the dough with a knife or wheeled cutter into one or more large rectangles.

Place the rectangles horizontally on the board and imagine a line running across the middle. Place pea-size bits of filling south of that line about 1¾ inches (4 centimeters) apart. Now fold over the top part of the rectangle and press hard all around the little piles of filling.

Now place a small cookie cutter or very small liqueur glass over each pile of dough and cut out the ravioli. Ideally it should be ¾ inch (2 centimeters) in diameter, but unless you are very dexterous or have tiny fingers, you will be happier with a 1-inch (2.5-centimeter) diameter.

To finish the dish:

6 cups (1.5 liters) fish broth (page 242)

5 rounded tablespoons (50 grams) grated parmigiano-reggiano

Bring the broth to a boil in a 6-quart (6-liter) pot and add the ravioli. Cook until *al dente*, about 5–6 minutes.

Transfer the soup to a warm tureen and serve immediately. Pass the cheese separately.

 WINE SUGGESTION: any light, fragrant white such as Pinot Grigio, Pinot Bianco or Friulano

Cappelletti marchigiani

(Meat-filled)

WITH TWO MEATS—pork and fowl—plus marrow, egg, cheese, lemon zest, and nutmeg, these "little hats" from the Marche have a complex, substan- tial flavor and feel. Serve them in capon or meat broth, such as that on page 240, never with sauce.

For the filling:

1¾ ounces (50 grams) beef bone marrow
7 ounces (200 grams) roast pork
3½ ounces (100 grams) boiled capon or turkey meat
1 large egg

10 rounded tablespoons (100 grams) freshly grated parmigiano-reggiano
the grated zest of 1 organic lemon
at least ½ teaspoon salt
freshly ground black pepper
nutmeg

Crumble the marrow into a small pan and melt it, stirring, over low heat.

Grind the roast pork and boiled capon or turkey twice in a meat grinder, or use a food processor to make a firm, smooth paste. Transfer to a bowl.

Add the egg, cheese, marrow, and lemon zest. Season with salt and pepper and a pinch or grating of nutmeg. Mix well and let rest for at least 1 hour; 24 hours would be even better.

To make the *cappelletti*: Make *la sfoglia* (page 291) with *pasta all'uovo* (page 286).

Cut disks from the sheet with a cookie cutter or inverted liqueur glass, about 1¼ inches (3 centimeters) in diameter.

Put a hazelnut-sized bit of filling in the center of each disk. Fold in half to make a half moon, and seal the edge well with the pressure of your fingers.

Wrap each filled half moon around the tip of your index finger and press the two ends together.

To finish the dish:

6 cups (1.5 liters) homemade meat (page 240) or capon broth

7 rounded tablespoons (70 grams) grated parmigiano-reggiano

Bring the broth to a boil in a 6-quart pot and add the *cappelletti*. Cook until *al dente*, about 10 minutes.

Transfer the soup to a warm tureen and serve immediately. Pass the cheese separately.

WINE SUGGESTION: Rosso Conero, from the Marche

Cappellacci di zucca

(Large ravioli with winter squash)

GREAT BIG RAVIOLI filled with a paste of the superb winter squash of northern Italy and plenty of parmigiano-reggiano used to be very good reason alone to get on a train and head for the Po Valley, especially Ferrara, Mantua, and Cremona. Today, they are found in restaurants and specialty shops in many parts of Italy, but if you ever get the chance to go to the area of origin, take it. You'll want to research the local variations. The filling may contain a spoonful of *savor* (a concentrated grape must), or sometimes finely chopped almonds or amaretti (yes, the cookies). Cremona,

famous for its sweet-and-spicy fruit relish known as *mostarda* (as well as for violins), adds a little to the mix. Whatever it contains, the squash paste should be slightly sweet, even with just the natural sweetness of the squash.

The Italian *zucca* is invariably translated "pumpkin," but that gives a wrong impression. The winter squashes of northern Italy are exceptionally sweet and flavorful, but this is one area where North America need apologize to no one. Use butternut squash in lieu of the original *zucca barucca*, and do it proudly.

For the filling:

About 3 pounds (1.5 kilograms) butternut squash, peeled, seeded, and cut into large dice, about 2 inches (5 centimeters) on a side
1 teaspoon sugar (if needed)
1 large egg

7 rounded tablespoons (70 grams) grated parmigiano-reggiano
nutmeg
salt
2 tablespoons (50–60 grams) very fine dry breadcrumbs (if needed)

Preheat the oven to 340°F (170°C). Bake the squash pieces in a nonstick pan for about 20 minutes or until quite tender. Force the squash through a sieve (or put through a food mill) into a bowl and taste. If it isn't sweet enough on its own, add the sugar.

Add the egg, the cheese, a grating or a pinch of nutmeg, and a pinch of salt. Mix well. The mixture should be quite firm. If it seems a little runny, dry it off by adding some breadcrumbs.

To make the *cappellacci*: Make *la sfoglia* (page 291) with *pasta all'uovo* (page 286).

Spread the pasta sheet out on the board and cut 3-inch (7-centimeter) squares. Place a heaping tablespoon of filling in the center of each square and fold the square over diagonally to make a large triangular *raviolo*. Continue until all the pasta is used up.

SUGGESTED SAUCES: *Ragù di carne (bolognese)* (page 220), *Burro e salvia* (page 84), with plenty of parmigiano (even without the sage)

 WINE SUGGESTION: Choose for the sauce.

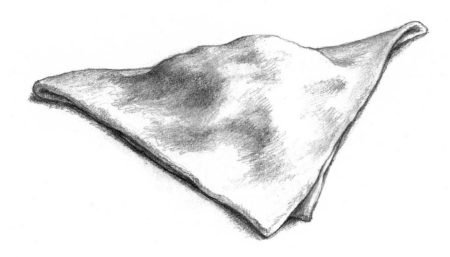

Tortellini

(Meat-filled)

ALONGSIDE *TAGLIATELLE* and lasagne, *tortellini* are the pride of Bologna's gastronomy. Five hundred years ago, the weekly market in front of the church of San Petronio sold *tortellini* by the single piece—so highly were they valued, and no bigger than a pea. The inspiration for this tiny and curiously shaped pasta was—the story goes—Lucrezia Borgia's navel, surreptitiously viewed through a keyhole by a Bolognese cook when the famous beauty passed through the city.

Bolognesi of a certain age know that the pasta must be practically transparent and that broth is the only way to serve them, but the barbarians are gaining. Some restaurants, even in Bologna, treat them as *pastasciutta* and dress them with butter and cream. This was once actually served to Oretta when she was attending a conference in Bologna. Indignant, she summoned the waiter and ordered him to take "this blasphemy" back to the kitchen.

Tortellini are funny. They are so delicate and intricately made, but a slight salami aftertaste keeps us off guard. Just don't serve them with *ragù* or cream.

For the filling:

1 tablespoon unsalted butter
3½ ounces (100 grams) pork or veal loin, diced
3½ ounces (100 grams) beef bone marrow
10 rounded tablespoons (100 grams) grated parmigiano-reggiano
3½ ounces (100 grams) *prosciutto di Parma*, diced

3½ ounces (100 grams) *mortadella di Bologna*, diced
2 large eggs
freshly ground black pepper
a pinch of grated or ground nutmeg

Melt the butter in a small skillet, add the pork or veal, and sauté over medium heat until evenly browned, about 5 minutes.

Transfer to a food processor and add the other ingredients. Pulse until smooth and completely blended.

To make the *tortellini*: Make *la sfoglia* (page 291) with *pasta all'uovo* (page 286).

Spread the pasta sheet out on the board and, with a knife or straight-edge wheeled pastry cutter, cut small squares, about ¾ inch (2 centimeters) on a side, though you should start with larger ones for practice.

Place a pea-sized bit of filling on each square and fold into a triangle. Press well to seal the edges. Pick up the triangle with both hands and hold it with one corner between the thumb and forefinger of each hand. With the third point of the triangle pointing skyward, your pinching fingers are parallel to the floor. Now pinch down, flattening the corners of the *tortellino* somewhat. This is the step many people forget. Wrap the two flattened corners of the triangle around your index finger and pinch them together.

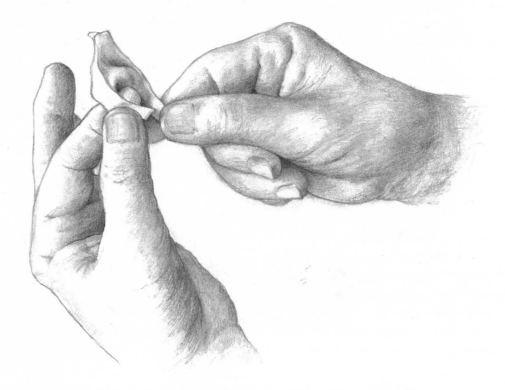

To finish the dish:

6 cups (1½ liters) homemade meat (page 240) or capon broth

7 rounded tablespoons (70 grams) grated parmigiano-reggiano

Bring the broth to a boil, add the *tortellini*, and boil until tender, about 5–6 minutes.

Transfer the broth and *tortellini* to a warm tureen and serve immediately. Pass the cheese separately.

 WINE SUGGESTION: a dry Lambrusco, from Emilia-Romagna

Culingionis

(Potato-filled large *tortelli*)

THE COMBINATION of pasta and potatoes is counterintuitive to non-Italians, but, really, what's not to like? In these voluptuous Sardinian stuffed pastas, the potato filling is rendered even more delicious with cheese, onion, and a hint of mint.

Franco and I even had them at our wedding lunch (in Orvieto, not Sardinia)—the menu chosen with Oretta's help of course—and they are the one dish whose taste I still remember years later.

For the filling:

1 cup (200 milliliters) whole milk
1½ pounds (600 grams) potatoes (any kind), peeled
5 rounded tablespoons (50 grams) grated *pecorino sardo* cheese or parmigiano-reggiano

3½ tablespoons (50 grams) unsalted butter
1 white onion
1 clove garlic
4 or 5 fresh spearmint leaves
½ cup (100 milliliters) extra virgin olive oil

Put 1 quart (1 liter) water and the milk in a large saucepan. Add the potatoes, whole, bring to a boil, and cook until quite tender, about 15–20 minutes (more or less, depending on size).

Drain the potatoes and put through a ricer into a bowl. Add the cheese, then the butter, in small pieces. Mix well until the butter is completely melted.

Chop finely together (in the food processor if desired) the onion, garlic, and spearmint. Put in a small skillet with the oil and sauté for about 5–6 minutes until quite soft. Add this to the potatoes and mix well.

To make the *culingionis*: Make *la sfoglia* (page 291) with *pasta all'uovo* (page 286).

Using a toothed wheeled cutter, cut the sheet into squares about 2–2½ inches (5–6 centimeters) on a side, or a bit larger if you prefer.

Place a tablespoon of filling in the center of each square, and fold over the pasta to form a triangle. Press the edges closed.

 MAKE-AHEAD NOTE: They cannot be frozen, but they can be made up to 2 days ahead and stored in the refrigerator.

SUGGESTED SAUCES: Any meat *ragù*, beef or lamb (page 205, 220, or 210), *Asparagi di bosco* (page 141), *Sugo semplice di pomodori pelati* (page 88), or *Sugo coi carciofi* (page 147)

 WINE SUGGESTION: Choose for the sauce.

Tortelli di melanzane e bietole

(Eggplant and chard)

THESE TRIANGULAR RAVIOLI are typical of Sardinia, where the eggplants of choice would be the small, flavorful locally grown ones. In Sardinia they dehydrate them for use in winter, but in summer they are used fresh in many fillings. The rest of us should use long, dark-purple eggplants, as small as possible. Spinach can be used instead of chard.

NOTE: If you cannot find sheep's milk ricotta, you can assist decent cow's milk ricotta by mixing 1 tablespoon heavy cream for every 3½ ounces (100 grams). Most artisanal ricotta, cow or sheep, needs to drain in a basket or colander overnight in the refrigerator to lose its considerable water content.

3½ ounces (100 grams) peeled (preferably) and diced eggplant
4 tablespoons extra virgin olive oil
7 ounces (200 grams) chard (about ½ cup cooked)
5 rounded tablespoons (50 grams) grated *pecorino sardo* cheese or pecorino romano
5 ounces (150 grams) ricotta

1 teaspoon minced fresh flat-leaf parsley
1 teaspoon minced fresh basil
1 teaspoon minced fresh sage
1 egg
1 ounce (30 grams) shelled walnuts, coarsely chopped (about 3 tablespoons)
salt

Put the eggplant in a nonstick skillet over medium heat for 3 or 4 minutes, stirring occasionally, or until it wilts. Add the oil and cook for another 2 or 3 minutes, or until the eggplant are quite soft. Transfer to a bowl.

Rinse the chard and steam it covered in the water that sticks to the leaves (just like spinach) until quite tender. Drain, then rinse quickly under cold water to stop the cooking. Squeeze out all the moisture you can. Chop and add to the eggplant.

Add the cheeses, the herbs, the egg, and the chopped walnuts. Mix well and taste for salt; depending on how salty the cheese is, you may need to add only a pinch.

To make the *tortelli*: Make *la sfoglia* (page 291) with *pasta all'uovo* (page 286).

Using a toothed wheeled cutter, cut the sheet into squares about 2–2½ inches (5–6 centimeters) on a side, or a bit larger if you prefer.

Place a tablespoon of filling in the center of each square, and fold over the pasta to form a triangle. Press the edges closed.

SUGGESTED SAUCES: *Sugo semplice di pomodori pelati* (page 88), *Ragù di carne* (page 220), or *Ragù di coniglio* (page 201)

WINE SUGGESTION: Choose for the sauce.

closing *ravioli*

Pasta al forno (Baked Pasta)

Baked and stuffed pastas were invented, and very widespread, in the 1800s as a way of using leftovers. In fact, the poet Olindo Guerrini (1845–1916), of Forlì, in Romagna, even wrote a little book called *L'arte di utilizzare gli avanzi della mensa* (The Art of Using Leftovers). Clearly the bourgeoisie of his day were very interested in household economy.

Lasagne alla bolognese

ORETTA HAS LIVED in Rome more decades than in her native Bologna, but Bolognese she is, complete with a Bolognese Aunt Vittoria, famous for two things. The first was the Latin and Greek exams she set at the *liceo* where she taught. The second was her lasagne.

Although her kitchen was equipped with a modern oven, when it was time to make her famous lasagne, she used to dig out of the cellar one of those aluminum prewar ovens that were used on top of the gas burners. On its great domed lid was a little indentation for the arms of the wood stove that heated the house. Their purpose was to radiate heat from the top down.

I remember the first time I made *lasagne alla bolognese*. It wasn't fun, but it was delicious. Marcella Hazan had not yet begun to publish. I used the recipe in *The Talisman Italian Cookbook*, the abridged English edition of *Il Talismano della Felicità*, by Ada Boni, the classic and perhaps greatest Italian cookbook. I was a newly married graduate student in Ann Arbor. I had no Bologna connection beyond a couple of dinners at Bolognese restaurants in Rome, but they had been enough: other lasagne seemed heavy and vulgar by comparison, with their dense pasta, gloppy tomato sauce, and thick layers of mozzarella and/or ricotta (thus I demonized them). In contrast, the Bolognese—yes, even mine—was ethereal, with its delicate spinach pasta, tasty *ragù* more solid than liquid, velvety béchamel (and not too much of it!), and freshly grated parmigiano-reggiano.

This recipe freezes beautifully and in any case, like other lasagne, benefits from a day's rest between assembling and baking.

For the pasta: Make *la sfoglia* (page 291) with spinach *pasta all'uovo* (page 330).

Spread the pasta sheet out on the board and, with a pastry wheel or sharp knife, cut it into squares about 4 inches (10 centimeters) on a side or strips about 6 by 4 inches (15 by 10 centimeters). Lay them out on a floured kitchen towel.

For the filling:

About 4 cups (700 grams) *Ragù di carne*
     ***(bolognese)* (page 207)**

2 cups béchamel (recipe below)

For the béchamel (make this when you are ready to assemble the lasagne):

3½ tablespoons (50 grams) unsalted butter
2 heaping tablespoons (50 grams) all-purpose
     flour
2 cups (500 milliliters) cold whole milk

1 teaspoon salt
1 pinch white pepper
1 pinch grated or ground nutmeg

Melt the butter in a saucepan over low heat, add the flour all at once, and stir with a wooden spoon until the butter has absorbed all the flour, about 2–3 minutes. Remove from the heat and stir in the cold milk. Add the salt, pepper, and nutmeg. Return the pan to the stove and cook, over very low heat, stirring constantly with a wooden spoon, until the sauce just comes to a boil. Cook for exactly 10 minutes more, stirring constantly. The resulting sauce will be quite thick, more spreadable than pourable.

To assemble the lasagne:

1 tablespoon extra virgin olive oil (for the baking
     pan)

8 heaping tablespoons (80 grams) grated
     parmigiano-reggiano

Bring 3 quarts (3 liters) of water to a boil. While waiting for the water to boil, warm the *ragù*.

Lay out several clean kitchen towels on which to place the boiled pasta. When the water boils, add 2 tablespoons kosher salt and a little oil. Drop a few pieces of the pasta into the water and remove them after a just a quick dip using a skimmer or padded tongs. Lay them out to dry on a kitchen towel, and continue this quick boiling in batches. As you lay out the pieces, make sure they are not folded or overlapping anywhere, which is trickier than it sounds. Continue like that until all the strips have been boiled.

Generously oil a rectangular baking pan, about 10 by 12 inches (25 by 30 centimeters). Since you can custom-trim your pasta, the exact size and shape of the pan doesn't really matter. The capacity should be about 2 quarts (2 liters). First place a smear of béchamel in the pan, then a layer of pasta, then a layer of *ragù*, a spoonful of béchamel spread thin, and a dusting of cheese. Continue making layers in this order until all the ingredients are used up. Finish with a generous dusting of cheese.

MAKE-AHEAD NOTE: The *ragù* has to be made ahead, but everything else should be done as close to when you assemble the lasagne as possible. But once it is assembled, the process can, preferably should, be interrupted and the lasagne held for a day, covered, or frozen for later use. If frozen, thaw and bring to room temperature before baking.

Preheat the oven to 350°F (180°C). Bake the lasagne for about 20–25 minutes, or until a nice brown crust has formed. Let rest 10 minutes, then cut into squares and serve.

 WINE SUGGESTION: as for *Ragù di carne (bolognese)* (page 207)

Lasagne di magro

(Fish)

FOR OBSERVANT CATHOLICS, the vigils of holy days used, like Fridays, to be meatless, which is what *magro* means (it also means thin). The letter, if not the spirit, of the law survives in today's lavish seafood dinners on Christmas Eve and New Year's Eve. Fast days or not, those evenings are still happy occasions to be celebrated, and with this rich but not ostentatious meatless lasagne from the Emilia-Romagna region, a *magro* dinner is still a party.

Like other lasagne, it should be made a day ahead and kept, covered, in the refrigerator until it's time to bake it and serve it (bring it to room temperature before baking). Nevertheless, in an emergency, live dangerously and have the lasagne the day you make it.

For the filling:

14 ounces (400 grams) John Dory or turbot fillets

2½ cups (600 milliliters) béchamel sauce (recipe on page 316 or use your own)

5 rounded tablespoons (50 grams) grated parmigiano-reggiano

1 tablespoon extra virgin olive oil

Cut the fish fillets horizontally to make thin slices. Dress with the oil and mix well. Warm the béchamel and stir in the grated cheese.

For the pasta: Make *la sfoglia* (page 291) with *pasta all'uovo* (page 286).

Spread the pasta sheet out on the board and cut rectangles about 2 by 5 inches (5 by 12 centimeters).

Bring 3 quarts (3 liters) of water to a boil. Add 2 tablespoons kosher salt, then add the pasta and cook a few at a time, stirring occasionally, for just a couple of minutes. Drain and lay out on a kitchen towel.

To assemble the lasagne:

14 ounces (400 grams) small fresh shrimp, shelled and chopped coarsely

salt

freshly ground black pepper

7 tablespoons (100 grams) unsalted butter

Spread a spoonful of béchamel on the bottom of a 7-by-12-by-2½-inch (18-by-30-by-6.5-centimeter) baking dish and a layer of pasta strips on top of that. Put some pieces of fish fillet and a few pieces of shrimp on top. Sprinkle lightly with salt and pepper.

Cover with a thick layer of béchamel and a few little flakes of butter. Repeat until all the ingredients are used up. Finish with a layer of béchamel and a few flakes of butter.

Cover the baking dish and put the lasagne in the refrigerator until the next day.

To bake and serve: Preheat the oven to 350°F (180°C).

Bake uncovered for about 30 minutes, or until a nice golden brown crust has formed. Let rest outside the oven for 5 minutes before slicing and serving.

 WINE SUGGESTION: Soave Classico, from the Veneto

Lasagne calabresi con la ricotta

(Ricotta and pecorino)

IN CALABRIA, THE milk of the sheep that graze in the mountain forests of the Sila and Aspromonte makes an extraordinary ricotta and an equally wonderful pecorino. Expatriate Calabrians replace the pecorino with pecorino romano, even though theirs is, they say, sweeter, more fragrant, and less salty. And makes you think of sheep. Replacing a mythical ricotta is not so simple, but sheep's milk ricotta can be ordered (page 392) and is well worth the trouble. The two cheeses contrast and harmonize to excellent effect—soft and creamy yet full of interest—and the whole dish puts the lie to the idea that Calabrian food is all about hot pepper and tomatoes. You will be tempted to add things, but don't give in.

The lasagne should be prepared a day ahead and kept, covered, in the refrigerator. Bring to room temperature before baking.

NOTE: If you cannot find sheep's milk ricotta, you can assist decent cow's milk ricotta by mixing 1 tablespoon heavy cream for every 3½ ounces (100 grams). Most artisanal ricotta, cow or sheep, needs to drain in a basket or colander overnight in the refrigerator to lose its considerable water content.

For the filling:

2 tablespoons (50 grams) unsalted butter
1 heaping tablespoon minced fresh flat-leaf
    parsley
1¾ cups (400 milliliters) whole milk
5¼ ounces (150 grams) grated *pecorino della Sila*
    cheese or pecorino romano

1 pound (450 grams) best-quality ricotta, sheep's
    milk if possible
freshly ground black pepper
salt

Melt the butter in a saucepan. Add the parsley and the milk and immediately remove from the heat. Add a third of the pecorino and stir with a wooden spoon. Add the ricotta and stir vigorously. Add a few grinds of pepper and taste for salt. The pecorino may be quite salty already.

For the pasta: Make *la sfoglia* (page 291) with *pasta all'uovo* (page 286).

Spread the pasta sheet out on the board and cut it into squares about 4 inches (10 centimeters) on a side. Lay them out on a floured kitchen towel.

To assemble the lasagne: Bring 3 quarts (3 liters) of water to a boil over high heat. Add 2 tablespoons kosher salt and 1 tablespoon extra virgin olive oil. Boil the pasta squares a few at a time for just a couple of minutes. Lift them out with a skimmer or spider strainer and lay them on a damp kitchen towel.

Oil a 7-by-12-by-2½-inch (18-by-30-by-6.5-centimeter) baking dish and line the bottom with a layer of pasta. Spread a layer of the ricotta mixture and sprinkle with some of the grated pecorino. Continue layering like this until all the ingredients have been used up. End with a sprinkling of cheese.

To bake the lasagne: Preheat the oven to 375°F (190°C).

Bake for about 30 minutes or until a nice golden brown crust has formed. Let rest a couple of minutes before slicing and serving.

 WINE SUGGESTION: a Calabrian white, such as Savuto Superiore DOC or Donnici DOC

fresh ricotta

Lasagne ripiene

(Meat and vegetables)

THIS MULTIFACETED BAKED pasta from Basilicata (the southern region over the arch of the Italian boot) has probably the most complex recipe in this book. Between the pasta sheets are layered artichokes, tiny meatballs, hard-boiled eggs, mozzarella, peas, and a porcini-scented tomato sauce.

Also called *pasta imbottita* (filled or stuffed), it used to be served only for holidays and was a traditional favorite of children. Families always made extra because it is so delicious reheated. Today béchamel is sometimes added.

For the filling:

2 white onions, one left whole, one sliced thin
1 carrot
1 rib celery
1¼ cup (300 milliliters) extra virgin olive oil
1 1-pound (450-gram) can Italian peeled
    tomatoes with their juice
2 ounces (55 grams) dried porcini, soaked,
    squeezed, and chopped (page 37)
salt
freshly ground black pepper
5 medium artichokes, trimmed as described on
    page 148, cut in 12–16 wedges, and kept in

water acidulated with the juice of 1 lemon
    (use correspondingly fewer artichokes if
    they are large)
7 ounces (200 grams) shelled English peas, fresh
    or frozen
10½ ounces (300 grams) lean ground beef
1 raw egg
3½ ounces (100 grams) grated pecorino romano
½ cup (80 grams) dry breadcrumbs
3½ ounces (100 grams) fresh mozzarella, sliced
    thin
5 hard-boiled eggs, sliced thin

Chop finely together the whole onion, the carrot, and the celery (in the food processor if desired) and put them in a saucepan with ⅓ cup (90 milliliters) of the oil. Sauté over medium-low heat until tender, about 7 minutes. Add the tomatoes and the porcini, season with salt and several grinds of pepper, and simmer, covered, for 30 minutes. Sieve this sauce and reserve.

In another pan, sauté the sliced onion until transparent in ¼ cup (50 milliliters) of the oil. Add the artichokes and, after 15 minutes, the peas if fresh. Season with salt and cook, covered, for about 15 more minutes or until the artichokes are quite tender. If using frozen peas, add when the artichokes are practically done. If the pan seems too dry, add 2–3 tablespoons hot water.

Put the ground meat in a bowl. Add the raw egg, 2 tablespoons of the pecorino romano, and a pinch each of salt and pepper. Mix well. Form the mixture into tiny meatballs the size of a hazelnut.

Spread the dry breadcrumbs out on a plate or on wax paper and roll the meatballs in them. Heat the remaining ⅔ cup oil and fry the meatballs until golden brown and cooked through, about 2–3 minutes. Blot on paper towels and set aside and try not to eat them.

To make the pasta: Make *la sfoglia* (page 291) with *pasta all'uovo* (page 286).

Cut the sheet into rectangles, about 4 by 8 inches (10 by 20 centimeters).

To assemble the dish: Bring 3 quarts (3 liters) of water to a boil. Add 2 tablespoons kosher salt and 1 teaspoon extra virgin olive oil. Boil the pasta strips, a few at a time, for just a couple of minutes. Remove them carefully from the water with tongs (the kind with protected tips) or a spider strainer and lay them out on a kitchen towel to dry.

Oil a square or rectangular baking pan 10 by 7 by 2½ inches (25 by 18 by 6 centimeters) and lay down a layer of pasta. The exact size of the baking pan is really not important. You'll just make more layers for a smaller one, fewer for a larger. Use a knife or wheeled cutter to trim the pasta pieces to fit. Next spread a layer of the tomato sauce, followed by meatballs, mozzarella, hard-boiled eggs, and the artichokes and peas. End with a sprinkling of pecorino romano. Begin again with a layer of pasta and the rest in the same order until all the ingredients are used up. Dust the surface with the remaining pecorino romano.

 MAKE-AHEAD NOTE: At this point, the lasagne can be refrigerated for a couple of days or frozen for later use.

To bake the lasagne: Preheat the oven to 375°F (200°C).

Bake for about 20 minutes, or until the cheese has melted and the top is nicely browned. Let rest for a few minutes, then slice and serve.

 WINE SUGGESTION: a dry yet rich red, such as Taurasi DOCG or Gravello, from Campania, Cirò rosso, from Calabria, or Basilicata's pride, Aglianico del Vulture

---

Cannelloni alla piemontese

(Pork-filled)

IF YOU BUY cannelloni dry to be filled, you immediately understand their name, which means big tubes. If, however, you make them at home, you'll roll your own from pasta squares. The latter are good deal easier to stuff and infinitely more delicate to eat. Cannelloni are eaten all over Italy, but these come from Piedmont. With spinach, meats, and cheese in the filling, and béchamel on the outside, this is a sumptuous dish for a special occasion, with strong flavors but an overall impression of delicacy and refinement.

Makes 2–3 per person. Exact number and size can vary with your pan.

For the filling:

10½ ounces (300 grams) fresh spinach, trimmed
    of all stems, steamed, drained, and squeezed
14 ounces (400 grams) roast pork
5¼ ounces (150 grams) baked ham
2 large eggs
9 rounded tablespoons (90 grams) grated
    parmigiano-reggiano

salt
freshly ground black pepper
nutmeg

To finish the dish:

2 cups (480 milliliters) béchamel (page 316)
2 tablespoons (50 grams) unsalted butter

Chop the spinach and put in a bowl. Chop the roast pork and the ham finely together in a food processor until smooth and completely blended, but stop the motor before the meat turns to a paste. Add the meat to the spinach. Add the eggs, half the grated cheese, a pinch of salt, a few grinds of pepper, and a grating of nutmeg (or a pinch of ground nutmeg). Mix very well by hand for a long time until the ingredients are thoroughly blended.

 MAKE-AHEAD NOTE: The filling may be prepared the day before and kept in the refrigerator.

To make the cannelloni: Make *pasta all'uovo* (page 286), but add a tablespoon of extra virgin olive oil along with the eggs. Then make *la sfoglia* (page 291).

Using a wheeled cutter, cut the sheet into 12–14 squares about 4 inches (10 centimeters) on a side. The exact number and size of the cannelloni can vary according to the size of your pan and the number of servings you need. Each diner should have 2–3 pieces, but they can be smaller or larger as you wish and depending on the rest of your menu.

Bring 3 quarts (3 liters) of water to a boil. Add 2 tablespoons kosher salt, then add the pasta squares, a few at a time and boil for just a couple of minutes. Remove them from the water with a spider strainer or padded tongs and lay to dry on a kitchen towel.

Place 1 heaping tablespoon of filling in the middle of each pasta square. Spread the filling out a bit to reach either side of the square and then roll the square into a tube.

To finish the dish: Preheat the oven to 425°F (220°C), and butter a baking dish.

Lay the filled cannelloni in layers. Dot each layer with butter, spread with béchamel, and sprinkle with cheese before laying the next. End with a layer of béchamel, butter, and cheese.

Bake for 10–12 minutes or until the top is a beautiful gold color. Let rest a couple of minutes and serve.

 WINE SUGGESTION: Nebbiolo d'Alba DOC, from Piedmont

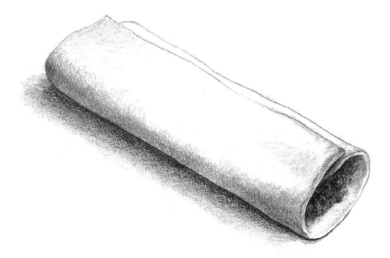

Gnocchi di semolino alla romana

(Semolina patties)

THIS FAMOUS ROMAN recipe used to be fashionable on bourgeois tables for special occasions. This version comes from the celebrated food writer Ada Boni (1881–1973). The Roman bourgeoisie of the early twentieth century used to look toward Belle Époque France for both fashion and cuisine, and this is why we find gruyère among the ingredients. After World War II, it lost its position to Italian parmigiano, and in the recipe may be replaced by the same amount of parmigiano-reggiano. Whichever cheese you use, the dish is full of flavor with a texture you just want to sink right into.

A modern variant, to help bind the dough, is to add two egg yolks to the semolina after removing it from the heat.

The traditional way to serve these is stacked up on a platter in a sort of pyramid, which causes great delight among the guests when brought to the table.

Semolino in Italian is semolina in English, which was very bad planning on somebody's part. It is durum-wheat flour ground a bit coarser than normal flour.

1 quart (1 liter) whole milk
1 teaspoon salt
10 ounces (300 grams) semolina
About 10 tablespoons (150 grams) unsalted
    butter

1½ cups (150 grams) grated
    parmigiano-reggiano
3 egg yolks
4 tablespoons or 1½ ounces (40 grams) grated
    gruyère (or parmigiano-reggiano)

Put the milk and salt in a large saucepan and bring to a boil. Add the semolina in a shower while you stir vigorously with the other hand to prevent the formation of lumps.

Cook the semolina over medium heat for about 10 minutes, stirring constantly with a wooden spoon. Remove the semolina from the heat and stir in 3½ tablespoons (50 grams) of the butter and 3 heaping tablespoons of the parmigiano. Add the egg yolks one at a time and mix well.

Turn out onto a wet marble surface. Spread into a single layer about ⅜ inch (1 centimeter) thick. Use the back of a wet spatula to smooth and level the surface. Let cool completely, about 30 minutes, then use a cookie cutter or inverted liqueur glass to cut out disks about 2 inches (5 centimeters) in diameter. You can also cut rhombuses about 2½ inches (6 centimeters) on a side. Save the odd cuttings.

To assemble the dish: Butter a baking dish 12 by 6 by 2½ inches (30 by 15 by 6 centimeters).

Place the odd cuttings on the bottom of the baking dish, sprinkle with parmigiano, and dot with butter. Cover this layer with a layer of the disks, which are the gnocchi, letting them overlap slightly. Sprinkle with parmigiano and dot with butter. Repeat this procedure until all the gnocchi are used up. Finish with butter, then sprinkle with the gruyère.

 MAKE-AHEAD NOTE: The dish can be assembled in advance and can be kept, covered, in the refrigerator overnight. Bring to room temperature before baking.

To cook and serve: Preheat the oven to 400°F (200°C).

Bake uncovered for about 15 minutes, or until a nice brown crust has formed. Let rest for 10 minutes before serving in the baking dish.

 WINE SUGGESTION: a light, fruity red, such as Dolcetto, from Piedmont, or a honeyed white, such as Fiano di Avellino, from Campania

---

Tagliatelle and Company

The pastas in this group are all long noodles cut from a pasta sheet, *la sfoglia* (page 291), which can be either *pasta all'uovo* or *pasta acqua e farina*. They differ from one another only in width and occasionally also slightly in thickness.

Tagliatelle
(Flat egg noodles)

THE BEST *TAGLIATELLE* made in Bologna, as by Oretta's mentor, the legendary Sister Attilia, are transparent. In southern Italy, the *sfoglia* is a bit thicker, but the pasta is just as good.

Make *pasta all'uovo* (page 286). When the dough has rested, roll it out with a wooden rolling pin into a thin sheet less than 1/16 inch (1 millimeter) thick. If you use a pasta machine to roll the dough, finish at the smallest setting. If this is too thin for you to handle, stop at the next-to-last setting instead. Nobody will care.

Spread the pasta sheet out on the board and roll it loosely like a jellyroll. With a large, sharp knife, cut the roll at less than 1/4-inch (5-millimeter) intervals. Set aside any odd bits for *maltagliati* (page 336).

You can also use a pasta machine to cut the noodles. In that case, trim the sheet into regular lengths up to 24 inches (60 centimeters). Feed the sheets through the cutting attachment.

Fluff the noodles gently with your fingers and set them down in little heaps on floured kitchen towels. Let them dry a bit—just enough so the pieces don't stick together.

Fettuccine

FETTUCCINE ARE the same as *tagliatelle* except that they are a hair's breadth thicker and wider.

Make *la sfoglia* (page 291) with *pasta all'uovo* (page 286) as directed in the basic recipe. Proceed as for *tagliatelle*, but cut the noodles at ¼-inch (6-millimeter) intervals, or even a tiny bit wider.

If you use a machine to roll the dough, stop at the second-to-last setting.

Tagliatelle verdi
(Spinach noodles)

ORETTA SAYS THAT if you ask whether you can use frozen spinach, she'll never speak to you again. Essentially all you do to make these lovely green noodles is add some well-drained finely chopped spinach along with the eggs when you make *pasta all'uovo*. As you knead, the dough will go from looking speckled to something like that beautiful green-striped marble called cipollino (for its rings-of-an-onion-like appearance). Then, if you finish rolling in a machine, the rollers will force the spinach into the dough until the sheets turn a uniform bright green.

For lasagne instead of *tagliatelle*, use a knife or wheeled cutter to cut the *sfoglia* into large squares or rectangles rather than noodles.

Make *pasta all'uovo* (page 286), adding 2 tablespoons of cooked spinach to the dough. This is how.

Rinse about 2½ ounces (70 grams) fresh leaf spinach and trim scrupulously, removing all stems. Steam the spinach in just the water that sticks to the leaves. When the leaves have wilted, remove from the heat, drain well, squeeze hard, and chop finely with a knife.

Hand method: Make the usual mound of flour on the wooden board, as for normal *pasta all'uovo*. Make a well in the mound and break the eggs into it. Beat the eggs with a fork for 2–3 minutes. Crumble the spinach on top of the eggs, then begin to work the dough. Using a fork, gather the flour from the edge of the well. At a certain point you will see that the fork has become useless. That is when you start to use your hands. Knead away until the flour has absorbed all the liquid and you are looking at a firm little loaf of dough.

Food processor method: Put all the ingredients in the container of a food processor. Run the machine at medium speed for a few minutes or until large crumbs form. Empty the container onto a wooden board and proceed by hand.

Make *la sfoglia* (page 291), and proceed as for normal *tagliatelle*.

Paglia e fieno

THE NAME MEANS "straw and hay"—thin egg noodles half of which contain spinach, for a bichrome effect (half white, or yellow, noodles, half green). In the 1970s, it seemed as though almost every restaurant in Italy had them on the menu with some sort of cream-based sauce. Today they are a bit retro, but they are amusing and versatile, as well as delicate and delicious. They deserve a revival.

Make half a recipe of *tagliatelle* (page 328) and half a recipe of *tagliatelle verdi* (page 330). Cook and sauce the two together.

Pappardelle

THESE BROAD EGG noodles are classic with Tuscan game-based sauces, such as hare (page 230) and wild boar (page 235).

Make *fettuccine* (page 330), but cut the noodles about 1 inch (3 centimeters) wide.

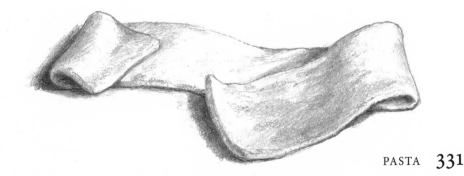

Tagliolini

WHEN EVEN *TAGLIATELLE* aren't delicate enough . . .

Make *tagliatelle* (page 328), but cut the noodles even narrower, not more than 1/16–1/8 inch (2–3 millimeters).

Capelli d'angelo

YES, EVEN "angel hair" pasta can be made at home. You need a very sharp knife, steady hand, and the patience of an angel to practice. Roll your failures out again and make something fun, like *maltagliati* or *farfalle*, as a consolation prize.

Make *la sfoglia* (page 291) with *pasta all'uovo* (page 286) and roll as for *tagliatelle*. Follow the instructions for cutting *tagliatelle* by hand (you can't do this with an ordinary home machine), but cut about twice as thin as you think is humanly possible. They aren't called *angel* hair for nothing.

Aside from the thinness, the only procedural difference with respect to *tagliatelle* is that your *sfoglia* needs to be a bit drier than for *tagliatelle*. You will just have to work on this, practicing cutting at different stages of dryness. Obviously, once you reach the optimum moisture content, the pasta isn't going to wait for you. It will keep getting drier, so you have to work fast.

Tajarín

IF YOU TAKE a trip through the Langhe, the low hills populated with medieval castles and villages that are the heart of gastronomic Piedmont, you will doubtless encounter two types of pasta. One is tiny meat-filled *agnolotti* (page 295) and the other is *tajarín*, local dialect for *tagliarini*. The trattorias of the area vie with one another to see who can make the thinnest—they have to be thinner than angel hair—and who can incorporate the most egg yolks into the dough. One restaurant in Bra claims to use 40 yolks to a kilo of flour.

The egg-rich pasta yields more like 6 to 8 portions, as opposed to the normal 4 to 6.

This is the recipe from the famous menu collection of the medieval archaeologist Edoardo Mosca (1928–1992), who was also a great scholar of the material culture of the Langhe.

Make *pasta all'uovo* (page 286), but instead of the 5 whole eggs, use 8 yolks and 2 tablespoons of white wine. Roll out the *sfoglia* (page 291) in the usual way and proceed exactly as for *capelli d'angelo*.

SUGGESTED SAUCES: *Ragù con le rigaglie di pollo* (page 198), melted unsalted butter and grated Alba truffle, *Ragù di carne* (page 220 or others), *Burro e salvia* (page 84), *Ragù di coniglio* (page 201)

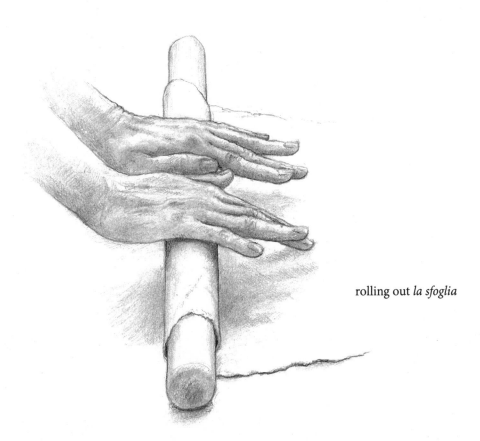

rolling out *la sfoglia*

Lagane

LAGANE (the accent is on the first syllable) are central and southern Italy's flour-and-water equivalent of egg *tagliatelle* and *fettuccine*.

Make *la sfoglia* (page 291) with *pasta acqua e farina* (page 287). Proceed exactly as for *fettuccine* (page 330).

Tonnarelli

TODAY THE PASTA shops and trattorias of Rome offer *tonnarelli* made of *pasta all'uovo*, but traditionally they are made from flour-and-water dough, and what's the point of making them at home if you don't use the traditional recipe? In Rome, they are a must with *cacio e pepe* (page 102).

The shape is the same as spaghetti *alla chitarra* or *maccheroni alla chitarra* (literally "guitar"), made in Abruzzo by pressing a sheet of flour-and-water dough down on a wooden frame strung with wires (the "guitar"). The wires cut the dough into strips, usually as wide as they are thick, so that the resulting strands are square in section. The best way to achieve the same result at home today is to use the narrowest cutting attachment on a pasta machine, but don't roll the sheet too thin. The thickness should be equal to the width. Just remember that they have to be square or they're *tagliolini* or something, not *tonnarelli*.

Make *la sfoglia* (page 291) with *pasta acqua e farina* (page 287), but roll the sheet thicker than usual, about ⅛ inch (2–3 millimeters). Cut the sheets by hand, as for *tagliatelle*, to the same width. Alternatively, put them through the narrowest cutting attachment of the machine.

If you don't have a narrow enough cutting attachment, forget *tonnarelli* and make *lagane* (above).

OTHER THINGS TO DO WITH *LA SFOGLIA*

Pasta strappata

THE NAME, LITERALLY "torn pasta," gives the technique. Have the water boiling when you finish making the *sfoglia*. The cooking method is an inherent part of this shape's identity.

Make *pasta acqua e farina* (page 287), using either durum wheat flour or all-purpose flour.

When the dough has rested for about 20 minutes, put 5 quarts (5 liters) of water on to boil in an 8-quart (8-liter) pot over high heat.

When the dough has finished its nap (at least 30 minutes), make *la sfoglia*, a bit thicker than usual, ⅛ inch (3 millimeters) thick. If you have rolled the dough by hand and have one big sheet, fold it into quarters. Long sheets from the machine can simply be cut into manageable lengths.

Have your pot of water ready and boiling. Add 3 tablespoons kosher salt. Rest the folded sheet directly on the edge of the pot and quickly tear off bits of dough. The size is not important. Toss them into the boiling water. This has to be done quickly so that the pasta will cook evenly. Boil the pasta, stirring occasionally, until *al dente*, about 7–10 minutes (but check, check, check).

Maltagliati

MOST *MALTAGLIATI* TODAY are short, stout noodles or lozenge shapes. But I love the original concept, expressed in their wonderful name. "*Maltagliati*" are literally "things that are badly cut." Anything that doesn't require neat cutting in a straight line gets my vote, but the real beauty of the name is in the language: in a single word, Italian can express subject, verb, and adverb and at the same time conjure an image of a happy kitchen where women are rolling *la sfoglia* and neatly cutting out regular shapes for ravioli or tortellini, tossing the odd bits of leftover dough—the *maltagliati*—aside to be used later in a fragrant soup already bubbling on the stove.

Today, commercially sold *maltagliati*—sometimes house-made in restaurants—are a misnomer: pert diamonds or strips of *pasta all'uovo* intended for use either in soup or as *pastasciutta*.

You can make *maltagliati* from scratch (this recipe) or just take odd cuttings of *sfoglia* left over from making other shapes, such as what's left after cutting out ravioli, and call them *maltagliati*. In that case, the only thing you have to do is not throw them away.

Make *la sfoglia* (page 291) with either *pasta all'uovo* (page 286) or *pasta acqua e farina* (page 287).

Using a sharp knife or wheeled pastry cutter, cut the pasta into short strips any size you like. After all, they are called *maltagliati*.

Farfalle

FIRST THERE WAS the butterfly, *farfalla* in Italian, then the bowtie, also *farfalla*, named for the insect, and then the pasta shape, named for the cravat. They sound fancy, but *farfalle* are among the easiest shapes to make at home. This is one of the shapes to get small children involved in. Flour-and-water *farfalle* are common on supermarket shelves, but you'll use egg dough at home. Commercial manufacturers also make mini-*farfalle*

for use in soups. People like to complain that the crimped middle of *farfalle* doesn't cook properly, but look at the silver lining: that is where the sauce collects and is trapped.

Make *la sfoglia* (page 291) with *pasta all'uovo* (page 286), although *pasta acqua e farina* (page 287) can be used if preferred.

Spread the pasta sheet out on the board and, using a scalloped pastry cutter, cut strips about ¾ inch by 1½ inches (2 by 4 centimeters). The size may vary somewhat according to preference or need.

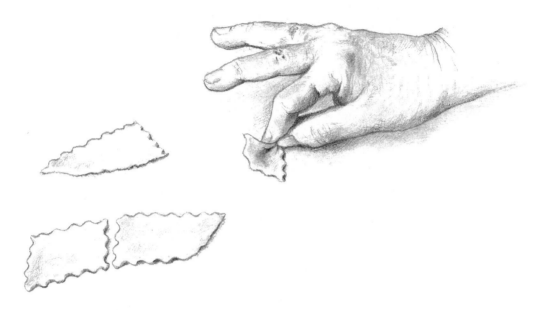

Pinch each little rectangle gently in the middle, sort of pleating the pasta. Pinch just hard enough so the dough stays crimped, but not hard enough so that it loses its shape and makes a lump in the middle.

To be sure they don't stick while cooking, add a tablespoon of oil to the cooking water.

Fregnacce

THIS FLOUR-AND-WATER SHAPE whose name means trifles, lies, and worse, is traditional in northern Lazio, Abruzzo, and the Marche. It can be made with either eggs or water.

Make *pasta all'uovo* (page 286) but use durum-wheat flour instead of all-purpose flour. Then make *la sfoglia* (page 291).

Using a straight or scalloped pastry cutter, cut diamonds 1½ by 2 inches (4 by 5 centimeters).

They should cook in about 5–7 minutes.

Volarelle

VOLARE MEANS TO fly, and these pasta diamonds are probably named for their lightness. *Pasta acqua e farina* is rolled thin, cut into diamond shapes, and added to soup, especially legume soups, though in the city of L'Aquila, capital of Abruzzo, they are used on Christmas in a broth made of cardoons. The difference is that half the recipe goes in as fresh pasta, while the other half is fried first in olive oil until crisp before being added to the soup.

Make *la sfoglia* (page 291) with *pasta all'uovo* (page 286).

Using a knife or wheeled pastry cutter, cut diamonds ⅝ inch (1.5 centimeters) on a side. Lay them out on a floured cloth as you work.

To finish the dish and serve: Put extra virgin olive oil in a pan to a depth of about 3 inches (7–8 centimeters) and heat. Fry half the *volarelle* on both sides in the oil until crisp.

Bring the soup to a boil, stir in the other half of the *volarelle*, cover the pot and turn off the heat.

Let the pot sit for about 5 minutes, then transfer the soup to a heated tureen or ladle into individual bowls. Pass the fried *volarelle* separately in a basket.

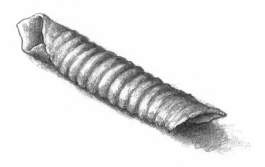

Garganelli

LEGEND HAS IT that *garganelli* were invented when a housewife was getting ready to make *tortellini*—all her little squares of *sfoglia* were ready and waiting—and the cat ate her filling. But it's unfortunate to think of the little *garganelli* tubes as a stuffed shape manqué. It's a lovely pasta that takes well to all kinds of sauces. Factory-made *garganelli* are also available. *Garganelli* are customarily made by rolling the pasta square around a little stick and over a ridged board. These are easy to find in low-end housewares shops all over Italy. The determined can improvise with a thick pencil and a butter paddle or something along those lines.

Make *pasta all'uovo* (page 286). For variety you can replace 3–4 ounces (about 100 grams) of flour with the same weight of grated parmigiano-reggiano.

Make *la sfoglia* (page 291) and cut squares 1¼ inches (3 centimeters) on a side.

Take a square of dough and place it at a 45-degree angle to the dowel (or pencil, or whatever). Roll it around the dowel and then against the ridged side of the little board, pressing just hard enough to make a tube with a ridged pattern. Slide the tube off the dowel and pick up the next square of dough. Lay the *garganelli* out on floured kitchen towels.

They should cook in about 6–7 minutes.

Lumachelle

THE NAME IS a diminutive of *lumaca*, snail, which the shape resembles, sort of. *Lumachelle* are made with the same little ridged wooden board and dowel as *garganelli*, but gain interest because of the addition of a flavoring to the dough.

Make *pasta all'uovo* (page 286), but along with the flour add 1 level teaspoon of ground cinnamon *or* the grated zest of an organic lemon.

Make *la sfoglia* (page 291), not more than ¹⁄₁₆ inch (1–2 millimeters) thick.

Using a sharp knife or straight-edged pastry cutter, cut strips about ⅜ inch (1 centimeter) wide and 1¼ inches (3 centimeters) long.

Wrap each strip around a small dowel (like the one for *garganelli*), about ½–¾ inch (1.2–2 centimeters, more or less the diameter of a candle) in diameter. Use a thick pencil or wrap a candle in aluminum foil or waxed paper. Press the pasta closed around the dowel to seal it in a ring, and then roll on the *garganelli* board or a substitute (see pages 338–39) to make a pattern. Slide the pasta ring off the dowel and lay it on a floured kitchen towel. Continue until all the dough is used up.

They should cook in about 6–7 minutes.

Gnocchetti-type

This group of pastas begins with *pasta acqua e farina* that is pinched off, rolled into ropes, and cut into short lengths. Although some require quite a bit of practice, others are great for beginners. In all cases, have ready some floured kitchen towels on trays or the table and lay the pasta pieces on them as you make them. Make sure the *gnocchetti* are well spaced and not touching or they will stick to one another and cook as a lump of dough. Cover with another kitchen towel to keep them from drying out too much, but don't leave them lying around too long. Two to three hours is the maximum; much less is much better.

Gnocchetti

IF YOU'VE ALWAYS wanted to make fresh pasta but were put off by all that virtuoso kneading and rolling and cutting, start with these simple flour-and-water dumplings. Even a child can make them. In fact, if you have any small children around the house, get them involved. Their tiny fingers are able to handle the smallest *gnocchetti* (also known as *gnocchi acqua e farina*), and they'll have so much fun, they won't even realize how cynically they've been exploited.

Fine dry breadcrumbs can be added to the dough. Or some of the flour can be replaced by an equal quantity of cornmeal. Or eggs can be used instead of water.

Make *pasta acqua e farina* (page 287), using half all-purpose flour and half durum wheat flour and a pinch of salt.

When the dough has rested, pinch off a piece of dough about the size of a small apple. Using both hands, roll it on a wooden board into a rope about ½ inch thick (about 1 centimeter).

The exact diameter doesn't really matter and will vary from region to region and family to family. Likewise the length doesn't matter since you will be cutting it anyway. For the recipes that follow, the size of the *gnocchetto* with which you start may vary.

Repeat, making more ropes until the dough is used up. Cut the ropes into ¾-inch (2-centimeter) lengths. Those are the *gnocchetti*.

--- VARIATIONS ---

- Replace part of one or both of the flours with an equal quantity of corn flour. Note that the cooking time will be somewhat longer.

- Replace 3–4 ounces (about 100 grams) of the flour with the same weight of boiled potato or ricotta or dry breadcrumbs.

- Use 5 eggs instead of water.

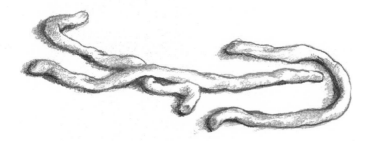

Strozzapreti and pici

ONCE THE DOUGH is made, these hand-shaped *spaghettoni* (thick spaghetti) require no special skills, and so are excellent for beginners—though patience helps. The name *pici* is associated with southern Tuscany, but the simple shape is known by many names, including "earthworms," *lombrichelli* and *ombrichelli*, in Umbria. It's a quick, simple pasta to make, and as a result can be found in varying lengths and thicknesses, as well as with different names. "Strozzapreti" is a popular favorite as names go because it means "priest stranglers," the origin of which is variously explained.

Most probably it comes from the underground humor in the former Papal States, in which gluttonous priests were seen as the unwelcome minions of an oppressive ecclesiastical regime. *Strozzapreti*, unlike names like "earthworms," which actually suggest a shape, contains no inherent information about what the pasta looks like, and indeed the name is used throughout central and southern Italy for a number of shapes. To simplify things, think of *strozzapreti* as essentially the same as *pici*, but shorter, any length you like.

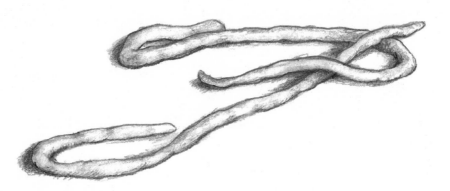

Make *pasta acqua e farina* (page 287) with all-purpose flour, adding a pinch of salt and a tablespoon of extra virgin olive oil to the dough. If desired, add an egg (and reduce the starting amount of water by 4 tablespoons). You can also replace half the all-purpose flour with an equal amount of durum wheat flour.

Make *gnocchetti* as directed but a bit on the large side. You'll need walnut-size pieces of dough. Using both hands, roll and stretch each *gnocchetto* on the board into long, thick, irregular spaghetti.

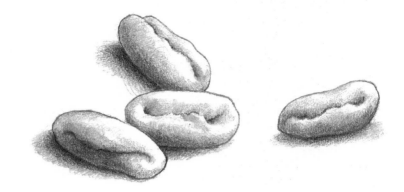

Cavatelli

IN SOUTHERN ITALY, where this is a common homemade shape, a special utensil—a blunt-tipped knife called *sferre*—is used, but with just a little practice your thumb will do a fine job.

Make *pasta acqua e farina* (page 287).

When the dough has rested, pinch off a small handful and, with your hands on a wooden board, roll out a rope of dough about 5⁄16 inch (8 millimeters), the approximate diameter of a thick pencil or a thin candle. The length doesn't matter. Cut the dough at 3⁄8-inch (1-centimeter) intervals.

Place your thumb on top of one of these little pieces of dough with the tip of your thumb touching the board beyond the pasta. (This keeps the border from being too thick.) Using more pressure than you think you need, but not so much that you completely squash the dough, pull your thumb toward you, allowing the dough to curl up around your fingernail. Your goal is to have a "concavity" in the middle of each piece of pasta (hence the name *cavatelli*). It takes practice.

Lay the *cavatelli* out on floured kitchen towels until ready to use, but not more than about 4 hours.

Malloreddus

ALSO KNOWN AS *gnocchi sardi*, Sardinian gnocchi, these hand-formed short shapes are something like a thick-walled shell. Traditionally, the surface pattern is made by pressing each piece of dough against the bottom of a wicker basket. Factory-made *malloreddus* are widely available for sale.

The decorative pattern is the only real difference between *malloreddus* and *cavatelli*.

Make *pasta acqua e farina* (page 287), but add a pinch each of salt and powdered saffron to the flour. Make *gnocchetti* as directed (page 342).

Press each *gnocchetto* with the pad of your thumb against something that will make a pattern on the outer surface. This might be a clean basket, a cheese grater, a fork, a butter paddle, or the little board used for *garganelli* (page 338). Feel free to think of something else.

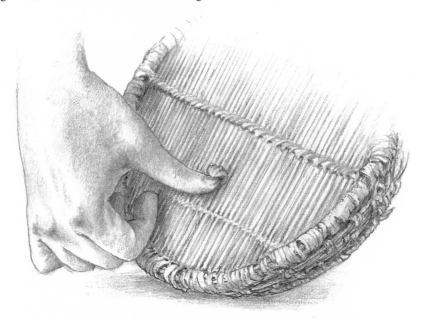

As you press, draw your thumb toward yourself so that the dough curls around the tip of the thumb. This is to make the characteristic concavity.

Cooking time will be about 10 minutes, longer if you've made them on the thick side.

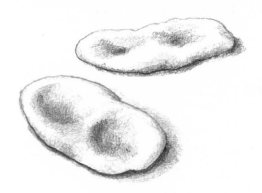

Corzetti

THERE ARE TWO basic kinds of *corzetti*, with the standard complement of variations. To make the traditional kind, *corzetti stampati*, you need two wooden molds, something like the dies used for striking coins. But most modern *corzetti* are the kind for which you simply need two index fingers.

Follow the instructions for *gnocchetti* (page 342).

Place a *gnocchetto* in front of you on the board. Position your two index fingers tip to tip on top of the *gnocchetto* and press gently into the dough to make two adjacent impressions. But you're not just poking holes.

Without lifting your fingers from the dough, pull them slightly apart, then push them gently back together. This will form a little ridge of dough between the two indentations made by the two index fingers.

Cooking time will be at least 6–7 minutes, longer if you've made them on the thick side.

Strascinati

THE NAME MEANS "dragged," and the technique is given in the name. The basic technique involves dragging a *gnocchetto* on the board with varying numbers of fingers. The technique is much like that for the single-finger *cavatelli*, but you can use two or three fingers or, using two hands, four or six fingers, to make multiple indentations for a bean-pod effect. Obviously the shape will be longer or shorter according to how many fingers you use.

Make *gnocchetti* (page 342). Vary their size according to how long you want to make the *strascinati* and the size of your fingers. It makes no difference to the finished dish as long as all the pieces are the same size.

The technique is the same as that for *cavatelli* (page 345), but using any number of other fingers instead of the thumb. For two-finger *strascinati*, place the pads of your two index fingers on top of the *gnocchetto* with the tip of your fingers touching the board beyond the pasta. (This keeps the border from being too thick.) Using more pressure than you think you need, but not so much that you completely squash the dough, pull your fingers toward you, allowing the dough to curl up around your fingernails. Your goal is to have two "concavities" in the middle of each piece of pasta.

For three-finger *strascinati*, you can use the index, middle, and ring finger of one hand. For four-finger *strascinati*, use a slightly larger *gnocchetto* and the index and middle fingers of each hand. And so on: up to four fingers on each hand.

Cooking time will be at least 7–8 minutes, longer if you've made them on the thick side.

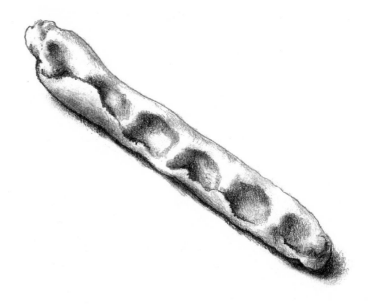

Orecchiette

ONCE YOU HAVE mastered *cavatelli*, you can try these. The name means "little ears," but I always think of them more as "little Chico Marx hats." The point is they are small and sort of bowl-shaped, all the better to grab little bits of broccoli rabe in the delicious, nutritious *condimenti* of their native Puglia. Do not attempt this if you have long fingernails.

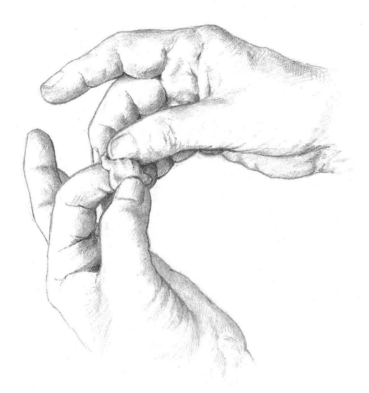

Make *gnocchetti* (page 342). Then, start to make *cavatelli* (page 345) with either thumb or index finger. Pick up each *cavatello*, put it on top of your index finger and turn it inside out. Place each one carefully on a floured towel while you make the rest.

The cooking time will be at least 10–12 minutes, but may be substantially longer. You'll just have to keep checking.

Pinch type

This is not an official category of pasta but one traditional, very simple, easy technique for making flour-and-water shapes. Instead of rolling sheets or ropes of dough, you simply pinch some dough off and do something quick with it with your hands. These are great for beginners, who can have the satisfaction of making something traditional and fresh with no concern for perfection.

Pizzicotti

ANYONE WHO HAS ever played a violin or other stringed instrument is familiar with the technique called *pizzicato*, whereby the bow is laid aside and the strings plucked, *pizzicato*, with the fingers. The word actually means pinched, and to make this shape, you lay aside your rolling pin and merely pinch the dough. The dough can be either raised pizza-type dough or ordinary *pasta acqua e farina*.

Make either *pasta acqua e farina* (page 287) or pizza dough as for *cecamariti* (page 361).

Pinch off hazelnut-sized pieces until the dough is used up. Cook and serve as normal *pastasciutta*.

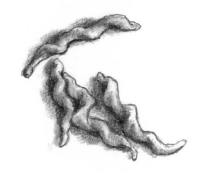

Trofie

THIS IS AN easy, fun shape of short pasta typical of Liguria, a classic with *pesto alla genovese* (page 116). Tiny bits of pasta are elongated into a twisted spindle shape with the friction of the palms.

Make *pasta acqua e farina* (page 287).

When the dough has rested, pinch off pea-sized pieces of dough and rub them vigorously between the palms into a spindle shape. They should be all about the same size.

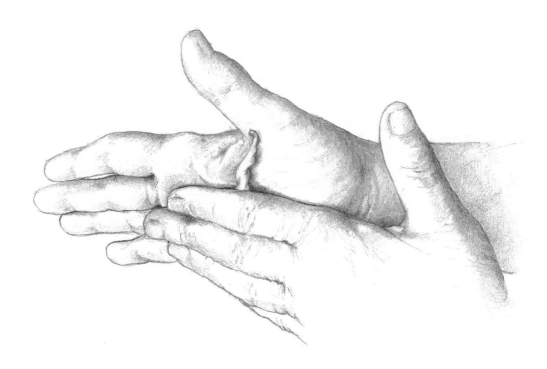

Depending on the size of your pea of dough, which should be pretty tiny, the *trofie* will need 8–10 minutes to cook.

RAGÙ CON LE SPUNTATURE (page 218).
Pork ribs, pork rinds, and tomato over *gnocchi di patate* (page 364),
with grated pecorino. *Basilicata*.

RAGÙ DI CARNE (page 220).
Meat and tomato sauce over *fiorentini*, sprinkled with parmigiano-reggiano. *Campania*.
The pot roast (*background*) used to make the sauce is served separately.

SAGNE E LENTICCHIE (page 249) (*above*). Lentils with *sagnette*.
PASTA E FAGIOLI (page 253) (*below*). Borlotti (cranberry) beans with *ditalini*. *Lazio*.

PASTA E PATATE (page 264).
Potatoes and *maltagliati* (page 336) in *brodo vegetale*, vegetable broth (page 243).

MINESTRA DI FREGULA CON LE ARSELLE (page 273).
Clams, tomato, and broth with *fregula*, a Sardinian *pastina*.

CAPPELLACCI DI ZUCCA (page 307) CON BURRO E SALVIA (page 84).
Squash-filled pasta with butter and sage. *Emilia-Romagna*.

LASAGNE RIPIENE (page 322).
Egg pasta sheets layered with meatballs, artichokes, peas, hard-boiled eggs,
tomato sauce, mozzarella, and grated pecorino romano. *Basilicata*.

CANEDERLI ALLO SPECK (page 362).
Bread dumplings with smoked pork shoulder in
brodo di carne, meat broth (page 240). *Lombardia.*

Made with the *Ferretto*

One of the problems with handmade pasta shapes is that they can be too thick to cook evenly. The risk is that the center will still be tough while the outside is fast getting mushy. The solution, devised by home cooks long ago, is to eliminate the middle altogether and make a tubular pasta, which will cook more evenly and more quickly. This is achieved with the help of a simple utensil called a *ferretto* ("ferro" means iron and by extension tool). In Southern Italy and the islands, many women still possess amazing dexterity with the *ferretto* (which they may call by many different names).

The *ferretto* is a thin metal rod, about the length of a knitting needle and, like a knitting needle for socks, headless. Unlike a smooth, round knitting needle, however, the *ferretto* is square. Some women in the south (it's always women) use a long piece of straw, which is even more difficult, but produces very delicate *fusilli*. My friend Antonietta, a native of Basilicata who lives in Rome, can do this with astonishing speed and ease and prefers the straw to the metal tool.

Oretta still uses the *ferretto* that belonged to her mother-in-law, to whom this book is dedicated. Mamma Viola was born in Basilicata and inherited an amazing ability to make *fusilli*—she could even manage to make three at a time on the same *ferretto*. Still today in Basilicata, every family makes its own *fusilli* by hand, and of course, every household has its *ferretto*.

Fusilli

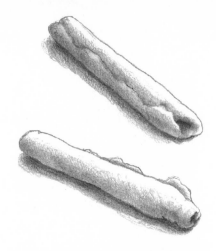

MOST PEOPLE KNOW the factory-made cork-screws, but those are rather different from the handmade version made by rolling and wrapping a knob of dough around a *ferretto*. The word *fusilli* actually comes from the word for spindle, and spindle-shaped means cylindrical with tapering ends. Think of the fuselage of an airplane.

Homemade *fusilli* may range in length from a couple of inches (5 centimeters) to as long as 6 inches (12 centimeters), still considered a short format.

Make flour-and-water dough (page 287), but add a pinch of salt to the dough.

When the dough has rested, pinch off a piece about as large as a hazelnut (or a walnut for extra-long). Place the piece of dough on a wooden board and flatten it slightly with your hand. Place a *ferretto* (see page 353) or your improvised substitute lengthwise on top of the flattened piece of dough and roll the dough quickly to wrap it around the rod. You want a tube of dough encasing the rod.

As you roll this assembly back and forth, let your hands pull apart as if by reverse magnetic force (don't lift them from the pasta), which will lengthen the nascent *fusillo* slightly along the *ferretto*.

Now comes the really tricky part. You have to withdraw the *ferretto* from the tube of pasta. Pick up the *ferretto* where there is no dough and give it a rap in the open palm of your other hand to loosen the pasta. To facilitate withdrawal, while holding the pasta very, very gently, twist the *ferretto* back and forth, like winding a watch. You should be left with a single perfect tube in your hand. This takes practice, to put it mildly.

Try to make the *fusilli* all the same length. Uniformity matters more than absolute size.
They will need about 10–12 minutes to cook.

Busiata

BUSIATA IS A Sicilian shape, much like *fusilli* except long like spaghetti. They are essentially the same shape as the original *bucatini*, whose factory-made present incarnation bears little resemblance, except in length and vestigial hole, to the original handmade shape.

Make flour-and-water dough (page 287), but add a pinch of salt along with the flour.

Pinch hazelnut-sized pieces from the dough and roll them into little ropes about 4–5 inches (10–13 centimeters) long and about 1/16 inch (2 millimeters) thick.

Lay your *ferretto*, or whatever you're using in its stead, on the board (preferably wooden) and lay a little rope of dough on top of it along its length. Now, with two hands, roll the dough and *ferretto* together until the rod is encased in dough. Keep rolling back and forth as your hands separate as by reverse magnetic force. As they separate, the pasta tube will lengthen along the *ferretto*.

Remove the *ferretto* from the pasta tube as for *fusilli*.

The *busiata* will need 10–12 minutes to cook.

Pastina

Pastina is a generic term that covers all the pasta formats so small as to be suitable only for use in soup because the only way to deliver them to the mouth is on a spoon. Here we give three classics of the homemade *pastina* repertoire, each made with a very different technique. In all cases, the *pastina* is cooked directly in the soup or broth, not in water.

Quadrucci

THE NAME MEANS "little squares," and that's all they are, egg noodles cut crosswise to make flat squares of pasta to toss in *brodo*, *pasta e fagioli*, or other soups. You can make a whole recipe or just save out some *fettuccine* when you make them, cut them as *quadrucci*, and dry on kitchen towels for when you need them. You can also start with *pappardelle* to make extra-large squares for extra-hearty soups, such as *pasta e fagioli* (page 253).

Make *pasta all'uovo* (page 286) with, if desired, a pinch of grated or ground nutmeg added to the flour.

Make *fettuccine* (page 330) or *pappardelle* (page 331). Lay the noodles out on a cutting board and, with a knife, cut crosswise at intervals equal to the width of the noodles to make little squares of pasta.

The *quadrucci* will cook in 3–5 minutes and, once they are dried thoroughly, will keep for 2 to 3 weeks in a jar or canister.

Pasta grattata

THE NAME MEANS "grated pasta," and that is what it is. You will need a grater. This very old pasta shape, found in many variations throughout Italy (with as many different names), represents an attempt to make couscous without specific knowledge of how to do so. For us today it offers a glimpse of the ingenuity and imagination of the home cooks of yesteryear. One might grate the stiff dough on a cheese grater. Another might mince the dough with a chopping knife.

Another would patiently crumble the dough with her fingers. Others invented heaven-knows-what kind of method or gadgetry to obtain the desired result.

Nowadays, we use an egg dough, which does not require excessive drying, but at one time, when spring water was used instead of eggs, the pasta had to be dried thoroughly or else it would dissolve and turn the broth or soup into a sort of polenta.

Make *pasta all'uovo* (page 286) using durum-wheat flour (though all-purpose flour will do) and a pinch of salt.

When the dough has rested and is quite firm, cut it into manageable pieces and grate it like cheese on a large-holed cheese grater or the grating blade of the food processor.

Spread the *pasta grattata* on a kitchen towel to dry. It needs about an hour for same-day use. You can also dry it to store for up to a week, in which case leave it out for 3 or 4 hours.

It will need about 5–7 minutes to cook.

If you keep it longer than a week, the cooking time will increase. The longer you keep it, the longer you have to cook it. Exactly how long is hard to regulate or predict, which is why we suggest not keeping it around more than a week.

Malfattini

THE NAME, ONE of several by which they are known, means "little badly made things," and indeed they are characterized by their irregularity of shape.

Make *pasta all'uovo* (page 286). When the dough has rested, pinch off small fistfuls. Roll these with the hands into small salami shapes. Slice each "salami" at intervals of about ³⁄₁₆ inch (4 millimeters). Then take a kitchen knife and chop each slice into several small irregular pieces.

OTHER DOUGHS

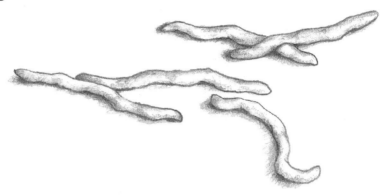

Cecamariti

THIS NATIVE OF northern Lazio belongs to the category of fresh pastas made from bread or pizza dough. In Italy it's still very easy to go to your neighborhood *forno*, bakery, and buy fresh dough by weight. If you don't have access to anything like that, you'll have to make the dough from scratch. We provide a recipe for convenience, but any pizza-dough recipe that works for you will be fine.

"Husband blinders" is what the name means, and we are to take that as a good thing, as in the dazzlement caused by something bright and won-drous. As with all these fanciful names (cf. *strozzapreti*), which have nothing inherently to do with the actual shape (the way spaghetti, for example, tells you the shape is string-like or *fusilli* spindle-shaped), don't be surprised if you see the name applied elsewhere to some other shape. These *cecamariti* are a short shape, but exactly how short can vary according to preference. Just try to make the whole batch the same length and thickness so they'll cook evenly.

1 ¼-ounce (7-gram) packet active dry yeast
1 cup (200 milliliters) warm water
12 ounces (350 grams) all-purpose flour

1 teaspoon salt
1 tablespoon extra virgin olive oil

Crumble the yeast in the warm water. Cover and let rest for about 20 minutes or until it foams. Meanwhile, sift the flour with the salt. Form the flour into a mound on a wooden board and make a well, as for pasta dough (page 287).

Pour the yeast and its water into the well and add the oil. Again, proceed as for pasta dough. Knead well until the dough comes cleanly away from your hands and the board.

Put the dough in a bowl, cover, and let rise until it doubles in volume, about 90 minutes (less in warm weather).

When the dough has risen, pinch off pieces about the size of a chickpea.

Roll each piece between the hands into a spindle shape, that is, thicker in the middle and almost pointed at the ends.

Canederli allo speck

FUNCTIONALLY PASTA, AND certainly a *primo piatto, canederli* are closer to dumplings. They come from the Lombardia region of northern Italy (its capital is Milan) and speak with an Austrian accent. Indeed, they may sometimes be called *Knödel*, German for dumplings. In that spirit, they can be served alongside stewed or braised meat. But the more usual way is in broth.

Typical of the border country between Italy and Austria, speck is lightly smoked pork shoulder. Its cured meat resembles prosciutto (though prosciutto is from the leg and usually not smoked). Partnered by the onion and chives (*erba cipollina* in Italian), the speck inclusions in these dumplings help create a tasty Bavarian or Tyrolean aura. The bread and butter create concern that you'll never get into that dirndl again.

11 ounces (300 grams) day-old country-style bread, diced
2 ounces (60 grams) speck, minced
1½ tablespoons (20 grams) unsalted butter
1 spring onion (white and light green parts only), minced
1 large egg (optional)
about 1 cup (240 milliliters) whole milk

1 heaping tablespoon minced fresh flat-leaf parsley
2 tablespoons (50 grams) all-purpose flour

To finish the dish:

6 cups (1.5 liters) meat broth (page 240)
1 tablespoon minced fresh chives

Put the bread and speck in a mixing bowl. Melt the butter in a small skillet and sauté the spring onion until transparent. Let cool.

Beat the egg, if using, with the milk and pour over the bread and speck. If not using the egg, just pour the milk. Mix in the parsley, and let rest for 30 minutes.

Add the sautéed onion when it has cooled.

Sift the flour into the bread mixture and mix well. The resulting dough should be quite firm. Portion it into 12 parts. With wet hands, form each part into a sphere, rolling it between the palms.

Boil the *canederli* in salted water for 15 minutes, then lift them out of the water with a slotted spoon or spider strainer directly into a warm tureen. Bring the broth to a boil, and pour it over the *canederli*. Sprinkle on the chives. Let rest for 5 minutes before serving.

 WINE SUGGESTION: an interesting red from Alto Adige, such as Lagrein or Collio rosso riserva

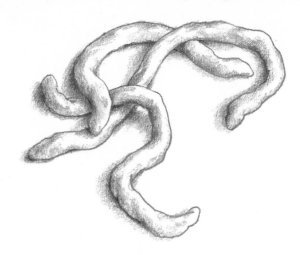

Cordelle sabine

A CORDA IS a string or cord (and so is a *spaghetto* for that matter); *-elle* is a diminutive suffix; and *sabine* refers to the Sabine country of northeastern Lazio, where Oretta does some of her best cook-ing. These little Sabine strings look like *strozza-preti* (page 344), but differ in being made of raised dough.

Proceed exactly as for *cecamariti*, but pinch walnut-sized pieces of dough to make a longer shape, much like *pici* or *strozzapreti*.

Gnocchi di patate

EVERY THURSDAY, all over Rome, people go to their local trattoria to have potato gnocchi because in Rome, Thursday is gnocchi day. Nobody asks existential questions like "If their main ingredient is potato, can we still call them pasta?"

I used to be terrified of making gnocchi, for fear of peeling all those potatoes only to wind up with something leaden and soggy. But if you take precautions so your potatoes aren't too wet—they shouldn't be too young, for one thing—and you use Oretta's tricks of drying the potatoes and adding an egg to the dough, you'll find they are really quite easy to make. Even though the original recipe does not call for the egg, Oretta says it helps hold the gnocchi together in case the potatoes absorbed too much water when they were boiled. Boiling the potatoes whole in their skins helps

keep the moisture down, too. Steaming instead of boiling is even better.

Extra flour may be needed if the potatoes, despite your best efforts, are still too moist. Rather than planning on extra flour, however, it's better to dry the potatoes carefully before mashing. Put them in a warm place, such as a warm oven that has just been turned off, or on top of the radiator, until all the moisture is absorbed.

Potato gnocchi freeze very nicely. Lay them on a cookie sheet and put them in the freezer. When they are firm, transfer them from the cookie sheet to a plastic bag. When it's time to cook them, toss them, still frozen, into boiling water. The ideal gnocchi taste like great potatoes and are light as a feather.

about 11 ounces (300 grams) mealy potatoes, such as russet

about 5 ounces (150 grams) sifted all-purpose flour

1 egg, slightly beaten

Put a steamer basket in a large pot over cold water. Put the potatoes in their skins in the basket, bring to a boil, lower the heat, and steam, covered, until tender. You can also boil the potatoes, in which case it is helpful to dry them a bit after draining. Put them back in the pot and put the pot over a very mild source of heat, such as a radiator or a food warmer.

Peel the potatoes while they are still hot and put them through a ricer right into a bowl. You can also use the fine-grating attachment of a food processor (*not* the steel blade). Break the egg into the potatoes and mix in well. Pour out onto a floured wooden board.

Sprinkle the heap of potatoes with some of the flour and work it in. Keep kneading quickly and adding flour until the mass holds together and no longer sticks to your hands. The amount of flour is very variable. Just have plenty on hand and pay attention to the consistency of your dough.

When you have a nice smooth dough, pinch off an egg-size piece and roll it with hands on a wooden board into a rope about ¾ inch (2 centimeters) in diameter. The length doesn't matter.

Cut the rope into pieces about as long as they are thick. To make the characteristic grooved decoration, roll each piece on a little grooved gnocchi board (see *garganelli*, page 338) or on the back of a cheese grater, or on the tines of a fork. To use the fork, place the *gnocco* on the board and run the convex side of the fork over it.

Place the gnocchi on a floured tray and cover with a kitchen towel until it is time to cook them, up to 2 to 3 hours.

To finish the dish: To cook the gnocchi, drop them into a pot of boiling salted water. Scoop them out as soon as they bob to the surface, a couple of minutes at most. A spider strainer is the perfect utensil for lifting them gently from the water, but a slotted spoon will do.

Make sure your serving bowl and sauce are nearby and warm when you drop the gnocchi into the boiling water. As you fish them out, put them right into the bowl and cover with some sauce.

Pizzoccheri valtellinesi

(Buckwheat noodles with cheese)

THE LOMBARDIA REGION is best known for its capital, Milan, in the Po valley, stifling in summer, bitter in winter, and flat. But go north toward Switzerland and you come to the Valtellina, an alpine zone surrounded and protected by mighty and terrible mountains. It remained isolated for centuries, developing its own culinary traditions based on its own special butters, cheeses, and buckwheat, *grano saraceno*, resistant to those temperatures and that altitude. Cows and goats graze in those mountain pastures, and strong-tasting cheeses, such as *bitto* and *casera*, are essential for this very old and traditional dish.

With potatoes, Savoy cabbage, and two cheeses as well as the buckwheat pasta, it's a hearty mountain dish, soft and creamy with wonderful rounded flavors.

Dried *pizzoccheri* can be found easily in specialty stores, but they are usually made fresh. The cheeses, which are not that easy to find even in other parts of Italy, can be purchased on the Internet (page 391). Otherwise, Oretta suggests an equal quantity of parmigiano-reggiano or else a combination of parmigiano and pecorino romano, which would be sharper than parmigiano alone, or even parmigiano-reggiano with some cubes of taleggio (without the rind), a wonderful washed-rind cheese from not too far away. Taleggio has become very popular in North America and is not hard to find. Claudio Volpetti, my go-to cheese man in Rome, suggests Fontina (the real stuff, from Valle d'Aosta) or raclette. Naturally, if you substitute cheeses, you'll still have a tasty dish of *pizzoccheri*, but you can no longer attribute it to the Valtellina.

For the pasta: Make *pasta acqua e farina* (page 287) but replace the durum flour with buckwheat flour.

Roll the sheet out to a thickness of about ⅛ inch (3 millimeters). With a sharp knife or straight-edged wheeled cutter, cut short noodles, ¾ inch (1.5 centimeter) wide and 3¼ inch (8 centimeters) long.

Lay them out on floured kitchen towels for at most 4 hours.

For the *condimento*:

10 ounces (300 grams) potatoes (any kind), peeled and diced ⅝ inch (1.5 centimeters) on a side

1 head Savoy cabbage weighing about 2 pounds (1 kilogram), trimmed of outer leaves, rinsed, drained, and sliced

1⅓ cups (300 grams) unsalted butter

3 cloves garlic, crushed

5 fresh sage leaves

3½ ounces (100 grams) grated Bitto cheese

3½ ounces (100 grams) grated Casera cheese

Put 2 quarts (2 liters) water in a pot, add 1 tablespoon kosher salt and the potatoes. Bring to a boil and continue cooking for 7 or 8 minutes or until the potatoes are soft. Scoop the potatoes out with a slotted spoon or spider strainer and set aside. Reserve the water in the pot.

Bring the water back to a boil and add the cabbage. Boil for about 10 minutes or until just tender.

Without removing the pot from the heat, add the *pizzoccheri* to the cabbage and continue cooking until the pasta is *al dente*.

Add the boiled potatoes. Remove the pot from the heat, cover, and let rest for 5 minutes. Meanwhile, melt the butter in a small skillet and add the garlic and sage. Sauté over medium-low heat for 2–3 minutes, until the garlic is just gold and the sage wilted. Discard the garlic and sage. Combine the cheeses.

Warm a serving bowl in a low oven. If the oven is not practical, warm the bowl just before use with hot water, even a ladleful of the cooking water.

Drain the combined potatoes, *pizzoccheri*, and cabbage. Layer the mixture in the serving bowl with some of the melted butter and a good dusting of cheese. Cover the bowl and let rest 5 minutes before serving.

 WINE SUGGESTION: Valtellina superior DOCG, from the same part of Lombardia

Tacconi

CONTRARY TO COMMON belief, polenta made from corn flour is not the exclusive property of northern Italy. These pasta "patches" (or such is one explanation of the name) are made from a mix of wheat and corn flour and are found in Abruzzo, Molise, Campania, and the Marche.

Once upon a time they were made by kneading polenta into wheat-flour dough, but today the usual method is simply to combine corn and wheat flours and to proceed as for normal pasta. They are good with hearty meat sauces.

6 ounces (150 grams) finely ground corn flour
5 ounces (150 grams) all-purpose flour

2 large eggs

Sift the two flours together and knead with the eggs as for *pasta all'uovo* (page 286). Let the dough rest for 30 minutes, then roll out a *sfoglia* (page 291) 4 millimeters thick, or less if desired.

Using a wheeled cutter or sharp knife, cut the sheet into strips about ¾ inch (2 centimeters) wide. Cut the strips crosswise to make squares or diamonds.

Lay the *tacconi* out to dry on a floured kitchen towel, covered with another towel, until it is time to cook them, preferably not more than 2 hours.

They will need to boil for about 20 minutes.

THE DAY AFTER

In the unlikely event that you have leftover pasta, there are a couple of standard next-day things to do with it besides heating it up in the microwave. Naturally, by "leftover pasta" we mean pasta with sauce. Any pasta that has been boiled and not immediately tossed with a *condimento* is not fit for human consumption.

PASTA

Pasta ripassata in padella

(Sautéed leftover pasta)

THIS TRADITIONAL TREATMENT of leftover pasta is so simple as scarcely to require a recipe, but so good that, like Oretta's grandmother Giulia, you will want to make extra just to have the leftovers.

Cover the bottom of a skillet comfortably with extra virgin olive oil. Add the pasta, and sauté over medium heat, stirring with a wooden spoon to coat with the oil. Put it on a plate (preferably warm) and eat immediately and without ceremony.

Frittata di spaghetti

(Leftover-pasta frittata)

THE FRITTATA is similar to an omelet but differs principally in being a full circle, cooked on both sides, not folded. Outside Italy, it tends sometimes to be confused with a dumping ground for a week's worth of odds and ends. In Italy, it usually contains one predominant ingredient, such as asparagus, artichokes, or zucchini—possibly leftover but usually not—with perhaps a bit of onion or cheese or herbs as embellishment. The pasta frittata is usually made with leftovers, but after observing the delight with which my party guests greet a spaghetti frittata, I've been making them from scratch as well.

It is certainly regarded as informal comfort food, as welcome as a midnight snack or easy picnic dish as at the lunch or supper table. A slice or two of pasta frittata is the perfect emergency food for a train or plane trip—easy to pack, no drips—and it's generally just a wonderful thing to have in your repertoire. Floppy spaghetti and other long formats mix best with the eggs. Tubular formats can be chopped coarsely before they are added.

If you add extra cheese, which you certainly may, be sure to serve the frittata warm, so the cheese is soft or even melted. Otherwise the frittata can be served at room temperature. In fact, this is a great way to use up all those pieces of mystery cheese that have been accumulating in your fridge.

NOTE: These quantities are for an average frittata, but even if you use just one egg and eat it all yourself, the technique is the same and the result just as good, if not better. Just make sure your proportion of egg to pasta will hold together.

4 eggs
parmigiano-reggiano or other grated cheese
    (optional)

up to 4 cups leftover pasta, sauce and all
3 tablespoons extra virgin olive oil
salt and freshly ground black pepper if needed

Beat the eggs in a mixing bowl with a wire whisk until well blended but not frothy. Add the grated cheese, if using.

Add the pasta. Mix well with the eggs so the pasta is completely coated.

Heat the oil gently in a 10-inch (24-centimeter) curve-sided skillet or omelet pan (or smaller, for fewer eggs). Pour the egg mixture into the skillet and distribute evenly.

Cook over medium-low heat until the eggs have just set. As the frittata cooks, use a flexible spatula to detach the edge of the frittata gradually from the pan. Eventually, you will be able to loosen the whole frittata from the pan so that it can slide around freely.

Now turn it over. Do not even consider sticking it under the broiler. Turning the frittata is easy. Using the spatula, slide the frittata onto a plate or the inside of a lid. Invert the skillet over the frittata and flip the assembly over 180 degrees so that the uncooked side is now facing the skillet.

Cook a few minutes more to brown side B, then slide the frittata out onto a plate. Let it rest for a couple of minutes, then slice into wedges and serve warm or at room temperature. It can also be cut into dice and speared with toothpicks as an hors d'oeuvre.

 WINE SUGGESTION: Prosecco, or anything that's open

Scammaro

(Leftover pasta "frittata")

THE WORD "frittata" derives from the verb "to fry" and has nothing inherently to do with eggs, although it is usually used for an egg dish. The Neapolitan "scammaro" is a large eggless frittata made by pressing leftover sauced spaghetti into an iron pan with oil. It used to be served on the meatless eves of holy days. *Scammaro* is Neapolitan for *mangiare di magro*, to eat meatless, the opposite of *cammaro* (*mangiare di grasso*), to eat fat, meaning meat. In fact, this treatment is not used for leftover seafood or meat pastas.

It is not recommended if you are in a hurry. In the sautéing, it is shaken; never stirred. The more pasta you put in the pan, or the thicker the frittata, the longer it will take to reach the desired crisp exterior and heat the softer middle.

Cover the bottom of an iron skillet comfortably with extra virgin olive oil. Add the pasta, and top with a few spoonfuls of grated or diced parmigiano or pecorino if desired. Cook, covered, over medium-low heat, without stirring, for about 5 minutes. Peek inside occasionally, and when you see a crust beginning to form, uncover the skillet and continue to cook until the frittata slides a bit in the pan when shaken, signaling it is ready to be turned over. With the help of the spatula, slide the frittata onto a plate or the inside of a lid. Invert the skillet over the frittata and flip the assembly over 180 degrees so that the uncooked side is now in contact with the skillet.

Cook a few minutes more to brown side B, over medium-low heat, until a crust has formed on the other side. Slide the frittata out onto a plate. Let it rest for a couple of minutes, then slice into wedges and serve warm.

 WINE SUGGESTION: Whatever you drank with the pasta the first time around will be fine.

MEAT

Lesso rifatto con le cipolle
(Leftover boiled beef with onions)

WHEN THE MEAT has given its all to a *brodo* or sauce, frugal cooks still find something to do with it. Here what it lost in meat flavor it gains back in onion, which some might consider a pretty good deal.

1½ pounds (700 grams) boneless boiled beef
1 pound (450 grams) white onions, sliced very thin
6 tablespoons extra virgin olive oil, preferably intensely fruity

½ cup (100 milliliters) dry white wine
4 tablespoons meat or vegetable broth (page 240 or 243)
freshly ground black pepper
salt if needed

Slice the meat. Put the onions in a skillet with the oil. Sauté over medium heat for about 5 minutes, or until the onions begin to become translucent.

Add the meat slices, then add the wine and let it evaporate over medium heat until the odor of the alcohol has disappeared, about 3 minutes. Add the broth and a few grinds of pepper. Taste for salt. The amount will depend on how salty the broth is. Let the flavors blend over low heat for 5 to 6 minutes. Transfer to a warmed platter and serve piping hot.

Polpette di lesso
(Boiled-beef meatballs)

THIS IS JUST one of many ways to get new life out of a piece of boiled meat. The cheeses sharpen the flavor of the minced cooked meat, while the cream-soaked bread helps soften the texture so it can be shaped into patties. Pick them up in your fingers and eat them as soon as they're fried, or cook them further in tomato sauce.

1¾ ounces (50 grams) crustless bread, preferably country style
½ cup (100 milliliters) heavy cream or milk
leaves from 6–8 sprigs fresh flat-leaf parsley
2 cloves garlic
1 pound (450 grams) boiled boneless beef, trimmed of all fat and membranes
1 heaping tablespoon grated parmigiano-reggiano
1 heaping tablespoon grated pecorino romano
3 large eggs
at least ½ teaspoon salt
freshly ground black pepper
4 ounces (100 grams) all-purpose flour
7 ounces (200 grams) dry breadcrumbs
1 cup (200 milliliters) medium-fruity extra virgin olive oil

Soak the bread in the cream, then squeeze it well, discarding the excess liquid. Chop together finely the parsley leaves and garlic. Mince the meat (in the food processor if desired) until quite fine but stop before it becomes a paste. Transfer to a bowl and add the parsley and garlic mixture, the soaked bread, the cheeses, and 1 egg. Season with salt and pepper and mix until well blended.

Break the remaining 2 eggs into another bowl and beat gently with a pinch of salt. Form the meat mixture into small patties. Dredge them first in the flour, then dip them in the eggs, and finally in the breadcrumbs. Heat the oil in a skillet over medium heat. Fry the patties in batches on both sides, just a few minutes or until nicely browned. Drain on paper towels; set aside and keep warm.

The patties can be eaten just like that as a snack or warmed in tomato sauce as a meat dish.

WINE SUGGESTION: Fontana Candida Rosso, from the Castelli Romani, or a dry Lambrusco, from Emilia-Romagna

GLOSSARY OF PASTA SHAPES AND OTHER TERMS

All pastas suggested for pairing with the sauce recipes are listed here.

Pronunciation is given only where we think a name will cause trouble. Accents are on the next-to-last syllable unless noted, and there are usually fewer syllables in Italian words than English-speakers tend to think.

agnolotti	Small stuffed pasta, largely synonymous with ravioli. Size, shape, and filling vary throughout Italy (recipes pages 295–301).
angel hair	See *capelli d'angelo*.
bavette	Synonym of *linguine*.
bigoli	Whole-wheat *spaghettoni* typical of Venice, they were originally hand-extruded through a machine called a *torchio*, but today are widely available factory made. Pronounced BEEgolee.
bucatini	Long flour-and-water factory-made pasta similar to thick spaghetti but with a narrow hole through its length, hence the name ("pierced with a hole").
busiata	Handmade flour-and-water long pasta made on a reed. Also available factory made.
candele	See *zite*.
canederli	Dumplings made with stale bread and speck, from northeastern Italy (recipe page 362). Pronounced caNAYderlee.
cannelloni	Large pasta tubes to be stuffed and baked (recipe page 324).
cannolicchi, cannolicchietti	Small, short pasta tubes usually used in soups. Pronounced cannoLEEKy, cannoleekYETtee.
capelli d'angelo	Literally "angel hair," factory made extra-thin long pasta meant to be eaten in broth; they can, with difficulty, also be made by hand (page 332).
cappellacci	Literally "old hats," a large (at least two bites) stuffed pasta often, but not always, filled with winter squash (recipe page 307).
casarecce	Short factory-made pasta format something like a short noodle rolled along its length into an S-shape.
cavatelli	Short handmade flour-and-water pasta with an indentation (think of "concave") (page 345).

cecamariti	Literally "husband blinders," the name is applied to various traditional flour-and-water formats of central Italy, but they are usually short and made from raised bread or pizza dough (page 361).
conchiglie	Literally "shells," a shell-shaped factory-made pasta of various sizes. Pronounced conKEELyay.
cordelle sabine	Thick spaghetti made with bread dough, which puffs up during cooking (page 364).
corzetti	Short flour-and-water handmade shape (page 347).
country bread	This seems the closest equivalent in English to the Italian style of bread known as *pane casereccio*, literally "home-style bread." At its best, it is baked in a wood-burning oven in long or large, round loaves and has a very coarse, chewy texture and plenty of flavor.
ditalini	Small factory-made pasta tubes (literally "little thimbles"), usually used in soups.
DOC, DOCG	Denominazione d'Origine Controllata, Denominazione d'Origine Controllata e Garantita, governmental designations for specific wines made in delimited areas according to specific criteria.
farfalle	Literally "bowties," may be made of either flour-and-water or egg dough may be factory made or handmade (page 336); *farfalline*, usually factory-made, are tiny ones for soup.
ferretto	A thin square rod around which dough is rolled to make handmade *fusilli* and other traditional shapes.
fettuccine	Flat noodles made from egg dough, practically synonymous with *tagliatelle*, but may be ever so slightly wider and thicker. Factory-made flour-and-water *fettuccine* are also sold; when homemade, these may be called *lagane*.
fileja	Rather thick *fusilli* of varying lengths. Pronounced feeLAYya.
fiorentini	A short, squiggly factory-made pasta.
fregnacce	Literally "trifles," diamond shapes cut from a *sfoglia* (sheet) of either egg dough or flour-and-water dough (page 337). Pronounced fraynYACHay.
fregula	Dried crumbs of pasta dough of irregular size and shape, typical of Sardinia. Pronounced FRAYgula.
fusilli	Originally spindle-shaped pasta tubes of varying length rolled on a *ferretto* (page 354), but today's factory-made *fusilli* are usually short corkscrews.
garganelli	Short tubular pasta made from rolling a square cut from an egg-dough sheet; best if homemade (page 338) but also available factory made.
gnocchetti	Simple flour-and-water short format cut from a rope of dough (recipe page 342), also the basis of more elaborate formats, such as those in the recipes on pages 344–49.

gnocchi	Generic term usually translated "dumpling," but used for so many different kinds of pasta, and more, as to be incomprehensible without some qualification. However, most people understand the word used alone to mean *gnocchi di patate*. Pronounced NYOKee.
gnocchi di patate	Small dumplings made by combining cooked potatoes with small amount of flour and dressed like pasta (recipe page 364).
lagane	Flat noodles (*fettuccine*) made from flour-and-water dough instead of egg (page 334). Pronounced LAganay.
lasagna, pl. lasagne	Very broad noodles or squares or rectangles cut from a sheet of egg dough, usually (but not always) layered with a wide variety of sauces and fillings, then baked (recipes pages 315–23).
linguine	Long factory-made pasta, approximately the same size and heft as spaghetti but lens-shaped, not round. Note that the correct Italian ending is –*e*, not –*i*, as is commonly found in America.
lumachelle	Literally "little snails," vaguely snail-shaped short pasta particularly suitable for sauces containing solid bits, which work their way inside the "shells."
maccheroni	A term with many meanings—it may even be used as a synonym for pasta—but today is generally understood as a short factory-made format.
mafalde	A long factory-made noodle shape with ruffled edges.
malfattini	An irregularly shaped *pastina* (page 360).
malloreddus	Also known as *gnocchi sardi*, Sardinian gnocchi. Short pasta shape similar to *gnocchetti* or *corzetti* but with an impressed pattern on one side.
maltagliati	Literally, "badly cut things," they were originally odd cuttings of *sfoglia*, but today may be sold as regular lozenge shapes (page 336). Pronounced maltalYATee.
mezze maniche	Literally "short sleeves," a factory made pasta very similar to rigatoni, but shorter. Pronounced MEDzay MAnikay.
orecchiette	Literally "little ears," a flour-and-water pasta originally from Puglia but today popular throughout Italy. Although factory-made versions are sold, they are best made by hand (page 349). Pronounced orekYETtay.
paccheri	Factory-made tubes of flour-and-water pasta, technically a short format for their proportions, but quite large. Pronounced PAKkeri.
paglia e fieno	Literally "straw and hay," white and green *tagliatelle* or *tagliolini* cooked and sauced together for a bichrome effect. Pronounced PAHLya ay FYAYno.
pappardelle	Extra-wide *tagliatelle*.
pasta corta	Generic term for all short pasta shapes, not including *pastina*. If you can spear it with a fork, it's *pasta corta*.

pasta grattata	Pasta dough grated on a grater (page 358), used in soups.
pasta lunga	Generic term for long strands of pasta, such as spaghetti, *linguine*, and *fettuccine*, meant to be twirled on a fork.
pasta ripiena	Generic term for stuffed or filled pasta formats, such as ravioli.
pasta strappata	Pasta literally "torn" from a sheet and tossed into boiling water (page 335).
pastina	Generic term for very small pastas meant to be cooked in broth and eaten with a spoon.
penne	Literally "quills," an extremely popular short tubular factory-made format. Can be *liscie* (smooth, pronounced LEESHay) or *rigate* (ridged); *pennette* are small *penne*.
pici	Long pasta made by rolling lumps of flour-and-water dough by hand until they resemble thick, somewhat irregular spaghetti (page 344).
pizzicotti	Short pasta "pinches" made by pinching off small quantities of dough and tossing directly in boiling water (page 351).
pizzoccheri	Short buckwheat noodles typical of Lombardia (recipe page 366). Pronounced peetzOCKeri.
quadrucci	Squares of fresh pasta meant to be used in soup and, though the size may vary, always small enough to be eaten with a spoon (page 357).
ravioli	General term covering a variety of shapes and fillings, but always denoting a stuffed pasta, usually large enough for one or two bites (recipes pages 293–305).
raviolini	Very small ravioli often used in soups.
rigatoni	Short, wide-diameter tubular factory-made pasta.
ruote	Factory-made wheel-shaped pasta.
sagne	The local name for *fettuccine* in parts of northern Lazio; *sagnette* are short, wide *sagne*, available factory made.
scialatielli	Thick flour-and-water *fettuccine* of varying lengths. Pronounced shalaTYELLee.
sedani	Literally "celeries," short pasta tubes, usually factory made, somewhat thinner than rigatoni. Pronounced SAYdanee.
sfoglia	The sheet of egg pasta rolled out and ready to cut into shapes. Note that the pasta sheet is called *la sfoglia*, while *pasta sfoglia* is a kind of pastry crust. Pronounced SFOLya.
spaghetti	Literally "strings," factory-made flour-and-water long pasta; *spaghettini* are thinner than spaghetti, but sufficiently thicker than angel hair to be used with sauce; *spaghettoni* are thicker than spaghetti.
Spätzle	Irregular pieces of varying kinds of dough, usually containing egg, made with a specific gadget and cooked fresh; characteristic of the parts of northeastern Italy that border Austria.

spezzato, spezzetato	Literally "broken up." You might break spaghetti to put it in soup, never for eating with a fork.
strascinati	Literally "dragged," small flour-and-water pasta shaped by dragging with the fingers on a wooden board.
strozzapreti	Literally "priest stranglers," a name that has much to do with social history and nothing in particular to do with shape, it is applied in different places to different formats, but most often closest to *pici*, but usually shorter (page 344).
tacconi	Short pasta shape cut from a sheet of mixed corn and wheat doughs (recipe page 368).
tagliatelle	Flat egg noodle cut from *la sfoglia* (page 328).
tagliolini	The same as *tagliatelle* but narrower (page 332).
tajarin	Exquisitely egg-rich *tagliolini* from Piedmont (recipe page 333). Pronounced tayaREEN.
tonnarelli	Fresh, square-cut pasta, originally flour-and-water but today usually made with eggs (page 334). Synonymous with *maccheroni alla chitarra* or *spaghetti alla chitarra*.
tortellini	Small stuffed pasta originally from Bologna, made with a tricky closure and a particular meat filling (recipe page 309).
tortiglioni	Short tubular factory-made pasta similar to rigatoni but slightly twisted (think of "torsion"). Pronounced torteelYOni.
trenette	Synonym of *linguine*, usually associated with Liguria.
trofie, trofiette	Ligurian short flour-and-water pasta shaped like a twisted spindle (page 352). Pronounced TROFyay, trofYETTay.
tubetti, tubettini	Very short tubular factory-made pasta, usually used with legumes.
verde, pl. *verdi*	Green. Pastas are made green by the addition of a cooked, chopped green vegetable to the dough, usually spinach.
vermicelli	Literally, "little worms" and properly speaking, a synonym of spaghetti; factory made vermicelli today are midway between spaghetti and *spaghettini*; the name means little worms.
volarelle	The name derives from the verb "to fly." They are thin diamonds of flour-and-water pasta usually used in soup. Sometimes a portion of the *volarelle* are held back and fried before being added to the soup (page 338).
zite, ziti	Factory-made short tubular shape, but the original *zite* are long tubes meant to be broken into three or four pieces.

SELECT BIBLIOGRAPHY

This list represents merely a selection of the most important published sources of traditional, authentic Italian recipes, nowhere near exhaustive. It does not include unfindable, privately published texts.

Agnoletti, Vincenzo. *La nuovissima cucina economica o sia la Cucina Economica a Maggior semplicità e chiarezza seguendo il gusto più moderno.* Roma: Vincenzo Poggiali, 1814.

Alberini, Massimo. *Storia della cucina italiana.* Casale Monferrato: Piemme, 1982.

Artusi, Pellegrino. *La Scienza in cucina e l'Arte di mangiar bene.* Milano: Benporad, 1913.

Basile, Gaetano, and Anna Maria Musco Dominici. *Mangiare di festa. Tradizioni e ricette della cucina siciliana.* Palermo: Kalòs, 2004.

Bevilacqua, Osvaldo, and Giuseppe Mantovano. *Laboratori del gusto. Storia dell'evoluzione gastronomica.* Milano: Sugar Edizioni, 1982.

Boni, Ada. *Il talismano della felicità.* Roma: Edizioni della rivista *Preziosa*, 1936.

Braccili, Luigi. *Abruzzo in cucina.* Pescara: Costantini Editori, 1980.

Callovini, Luigi, and Marco Romano, edd. *Ricettario della memoria. La cucina di una locanda alpina tra Impero asburgico e Regno d'Italia.* Trento: Nitida Immagine Editrice, 1999.

Capatti, Alberto, Alberto De Bernardi, and Angelo Varni, edd. *Storia d'Italia. L'Alimentazione.* Torino: Giulio Einaudi, 1998.

Capatti, Alberto, and Massimo Montanari. *La cucina italiana storia di una cultura.* Bari: Laterza, 1999.

Cavalcanti, Ippolito, duca di Buonvicino. *Cucina teorico-pratica divisa in quattro sezioni. La vera cucina casareccia.* Milano: Antonio Bietti 1904.

Cervio, Vincenzo. *Il trinciante.* Venezia: Tramezzino, 1581.

Coltro, Dino. *La cucina tradizionale veneta.* Roma: Newton Compton, 1983.

Coria, Giuseppe. *Profumi di Sicilia. Il libro della cucina siciliana.* Palermo: Vito Cavallotto 1981.

Corrado, Vincenzo. *Il cuoco galante.* Napoli: Stamperia Raimondina, 1773.

Corsi, Guglielma. *Un secolo di cucina umbra.* Assisi: La Porziuncola, 1974.

Dubois, Urbano, and Emilio Bernard. *La cucina classica. Studi pratici, ragionati e dimostrativi.* Milano: Società dei cuochi milanesi, 1887.

Goria, Giovanni. *La cucina piemontese. Il mangiare di ieri e di oggi.* Padova: Muzzio Editore, 1990.

Gosetti della Salda, Anna. *Le ricette regionali italiane*. Milano: Solares, 1967.

Guarnaschelli Gotti, Marco, ed. *Grande enciclopedia illustrata della gastronomia*. Milano: Selezione dal Reader's Digest, 1990.

Leonardi, Francesco. *L'Apicio moderno*. Roma: Mordacchini, 1807.

Lombardi, Anna Maria, and Rita Mastropaolo. *La cucina molisana*. Campobasso: Edizioni Cultura & Sport, 1990.

Mazzara Morresi, Nicla. *La cucina marchigiana tra storia e folklore*. Ancona: Aniballi, 1978.

Ministero per i beni culturali e ambientali. *Gli archivi per la storia dell'alimentazione*. Roma: Archivi di Stato, 1995.

————. *Le cucine della memoria*. Roma: De Luca, 1995.

Montanari, Massimo, and Françoise Sabban. *Atlante dell'alimentazione e della gastronomia*. Torino: Utet, 2004.

Perna Bozzi, Ottorina. *La Lombardia in cucina*. Milano: Giunti Martello, 1982.

Pilia, Fernando. *Sapori di Sardegna*. Cagliari: Unione Sarda, 1988.

Ratto, Gianbattista, and Giovanni Ratto. *La cuciniera genovese*. Genova: Frilli, 1863.

Restivo, Maurizio. *La cucina della memoria. Cibi e tradizioni alimentari dell'antica Lucania*. Potenza: Ermes, 1960.

Righi Parenti, Caròla. *La cucina toscana. I piatti tipici e le ricette tradizionali*. Roma: Newton Compton, 1995.

Sorbiatti, Giuseppe. *La gastronomia moderna*. Milano: Boniardi-Pogliani, 1855.

Stanziano, Angelina, and Laura Santoro. *Puglia la tradizione in cucina*. Fasano: Schena, 1998.

Stelvio, Maria. *La cucina triestina*. Trieste: Edizioni Italo Svevo, 1987.

Tanara, Vincenzo. *L'economia del cittadino in villa*. Napoli: Lombardi, 1878.

Teti, Vito. *Il colore del cibo*. Roma: Meltemi, 1999.

Touring Club Italiano. *Guida gastronomica d'Italia*. Milano: TCI, 1931.

Veronelli, Luigi, ed. *Il Carnacina*. Milano: Garzanti, 1961.

Vialardi, Giovanni. *Trattato di cucina pasticceria moderna e credenza*. Torino: Favale, 1854.

Zanini De Vita, Oretta. *Popes, Peasants, and Shepherds: Recipes and Lore from Rome and Lazio*. Translated by Maureen B. Fant. Berkeley: University of California Press, 2013.

Zannoni, Mario. *A Tavola con Maria Luigia*. Parma: Artegrafica Silva, 1991.

ONLINE SOURCES OF INGREDIENTS

With its insistence on high-quality, genuine Italian ingredients, this book would not have been possible twenty years ago. But today all the items we consider pantry essentials, and many fresh ingredients as well, are available in North America online and from specialty purveyors. The list is always changing, and new ingredients are appearing outside Italy all the time. Here are some links to get started, but bear in mind that links can and do become obsolete. For up-to-date opinions and sources, the Internet search engines, such as google.com, and the discussion boards on chowhound.com and egullet.com are invaluable. I have created an Amazon gourmet shop on my Web site (http://goo.gl/iJhmW) for relevant foods and cookware available through amazon.com and will continue to add items (and new links) as they become available. All the specialty purveyors cited here have large and interesting sites and are well worth clicking around and browsing for more products, and often good product information, than given here.

Legumes

BORLOTTI BEANS
Pasta Cheese: http://goo.gl/2vtS9
Culinary District: http://goo.gl/3iybS

LENTILS
Market Hall Foods: http://goo.gl/xDSRs
Alma Gourmet: http://goo.gl/gZQTM
Pasta Cheese: http://goo.gl/sDM1E
Pasta Cheese: http://goo.gl/GpTXT

CANNELLINI BEANS
Pasta Cheese: http://goo.gl/kCtDA

CHICKPEAS
Pasta Cheese: http://goo.gl/33Pmv

DRIED FAVA BEANS

Pasta Cheese: http://goo.gl/womQM

Canned San Marzano tomatoes

For information about this protected variety of tomato:

http://goo.gl/UHhJJ

GUARANTEED SAN MARZANO (DOP)

Gustiamo: http://goo.gl/16zNq

SAN MARZANO–TYPE AND *POMODORINI* IMPORTED FROM ITALY

http://goo.gl/16zNq

Salt-packed capers

Alma Gourmet: http://goo.gl/EbM4Y

Culinary District: http://goo.gl/bYXsH

Di Palo: http://goo.gl/qZ8os

Pasta Cheese: http://goo.gl/gQM9X

Gaeta and other olives

Alma Gourmet: http://goo.gl/EvGRV

Pasta Cheese: http://goo.gl/ts9Wg

Chestnuts

Amazon: http://amzn.to/114tD1K

http://amzn.to/15nWzaQ

http://amzn.to/15ojvaa

Pistachios

Gemmellaro's: shop.italianpistachioproducts.com

Wild fennel

If you don't forage for it yourself, the plant or its tiny flowers mixed with pollen can be found in farmers' markets in California from March to May and in the northeast in the summer.

For photographs of the plant, pollen, and flowers: http://www.gliaromi.it/linearistoratori.asp.

The Web is full of foraging tips but no sources to buy the whole plant except, of course, farmers' markets.

Fresh mushrooms

PORCINI, HEN OF THE WOODS, TRUMPET, CHANTERELLES, SHIITAKE, FRESH TRUFFLES

Earthy Delights: http://goo.gl/2vu2Q

Marx Foods: http://goo.gl/gJfFP

Oregon Mushrooms: http://goo.gl/Cnhgw

Plant your own garden from Italian seeds

ARUGULA, BASIL, BORAGE, CAPERS, WILD FENNEL, MARJORAM, OREGANO, PARSLEY

Grow Italian: http://www.growitalian.com

Pasta

SARDINIAN *FREGULA* AND BENEDETTO CAVALIERI PASTAS

Amazon: http://amzn.to/15ojJho

Au Marché: http://goo.gl/5hWNm

Di Palo Selects: http://goo.gl/jAuk7

Amazon: http://amzn.to/11ktUfZ

Seafood

BOTTARGA
Delitaliana: http://goo.gl/aSwBA
Buonitalia: http://goo.gl/nRh6L
Gustiamo: http://goo.gl/nRh6L

ANCHOVIES IN SALT OR OLIVE OIL
Buonitalia: http://goo.gl/nRh6L
Pennsylvania Macaroni: http://goo.gl/yffz9
Gustiamo: http://goo.gl/bfeuW
Far Away Foods: http://goo.gl/uDkom
Zingerman's: http://goo.gl/L58F9

CANNED TUNA IN OLIVE OIL
Di Palo Selects: http://goo.gl/9hHL4
Pasta Cheese: http://goo.gl/YK8nZ
Far Away Foods: http://goo.gl/OQA7B

SQUID INK
Amazon: http://amzn.to/11kkAtZ

SALT COD
Amazon: http://amzn.to/Z5yDFt
Corti Brothers: http://goo.gl/IGXZC
Delitaliana: http://goo.gl/h8EIh (sells desalted baccalà)

Meats

BRISKET
Aviglatt: http://goo.gl/Cqo08
Williams-Sonoma: http://goo.gl/rJfC7

GAME AND OTHER MEATS

Extremely informative article on substituting domestic meat for wild game; wild boar, venison, rabbit, duck, hare from Hank Shaw, Hunter Angler Gardener Cook:

http://honest-food.net/2009/03/23/on-cooking-wild-vs-domestic-meat

D'Artagnan: http://goo.gl/iHYOp (for farm-raised rabbit, free-range venison, wild boar, and wild Scottish hare)

Venison

Broken Arrow Ranch: http://goo.gl/VxkD0

Underhill Farms: http://goo.gl/GDwwY

Onkaparinga Valley Venison (Australia): http://fallowvenison.com.au (good information, but does not ship to the United States)

Local Harvest: http://goo.gl/qEhvq

Allen Brothers: http://goo.gl/xfx74

Wild boar

Broken Arrow Ranch: http://goo.gl/lnxuo

Scottish hare

D'Artagnan: http://goo.gl/wobzy

Rabbit

LocalHarvest: http://goo.gl/g3kgJ

Quail

Broken Arrow Ranch: http://goo.gl/AC0Az

Corti Brothers: http://goo.gl/RZSRh

PORK

Everything you ever wanted to know about pork:

http://amazingribs.com/recipes/porknography/pork_cuts.html

U.S. pork and pork products

Compart: http://goo.gl/ksbCI

Spring Lake Farm: http://goo.gl/SoXI9

Local Harvest: http://goo.gl/sKdZh

Heritage Foods: http://goo.gl/5ErSt

Lardo, guanciale, pancetta, prosciutto, sausage, salami

La Quercia: http://goo.gl/lK1YK

Salumeria Biellese: http://goo.gl/F8Cml

Amazon: http://amzn.to/ZBGw0R

Milano's: http://goo.gl/RIu3W

Imported from Italy

Delitaliana: http://goo.gl/4ADs6

Di Palo Selects: http://goo.gl/PQ1Q5

Buonitalia: http://goo.gl/g5rXD

Cheese and dairy

BITTO, CASERA, FONTINA, PECORINO ROMANO, PARMIGIANO-REGGIANO, RICOTTA SALATA

Alma Gourmet: http://goo.gl/LN8sk

Buonitalia: http://goo.gl/g5rXD

Di Palo Selects: http://goo.gl/3F43O

Formaggio Kitchen: http://goo.gl/IftQ0

Murray's: http://goo.gl/KrZNW

Zingerman's: http://goo.gl/y8iBK

BUTTER

Piazza Italian Market: http://goo.gl/gZe2M

igourmet: http://goo.gl/tXYi6

RICOTTA

Imported from Italy: ricotta salata, *sheep's milk and buffalo milk ricotta*

Pasta Cheese: http://goo.gl/95z4f

Alma Gourmet: http://goo.gl/Ei32W

U.S. sheep's milk ricotta

3-Corner Field Farm: http://goo.gl/cU34S

Renowned cow's milk ricotta, available only in stores in New York area

Salvatore Bklyn: http://goo.gl/CLfoJ

PECORINO SARDO

Artisanal Cheese: http://goo.gl/m4kXc

Cookware

TERRACOTTA AND CERAMIC COOKWARE

Emile Henry: http://www.emilehenryusa.com

http://goo.gl/GMv8k (Emile Henry braiser)

Europaeus: http://goo.gl/kZEw7

Bram: http://goo.gl/uTkxj

Terra Allegra: http://goo.gl/AQZcK

PASTA-MAKING EQUIPMENT

www.artisanpastatools.com

(Note that only maple and beech utensils are suitable for pasta. Other woods may impart their fragrance to the dough.)

INDEX

Recipe titles and page numbers are in bold. Pages on which pastas, sauces, or soups are suggested for pairing are in italics. Frequently used ingredients, usually background players or garnishes, such as broth, parmigiano-reggiano, pecorino romano, basil, and parsley, are listed only where they emerge from the ensemble to play a more important role, and when they are the star of the recipe, the full Italian recipe title is given (in bold).